ANTONIO ROSMINI

A
NEW ESSAY
CONCERNING THE
ORIGIN OF IDEAS

Volume 3

Translated by
DENIS CLEARY
and
TERENCE WATSON

ROSMINI HOUSE
DURHAM

Translated from
Nuovo Saggio sull'Origine delle Idee
Vol. 3, Intra, 1876

Typeset by Rosmini House, Durham
Printed by Bell & Bain Limited, Glasgow

ISBN 1 899093 65 6

Note

Square brackets [ ] indicate notes or additions by the translators.

References to this and other works of Rosmini are given by paragraph number unless otherwise stated.

Contents

PART TWO

Application of the Criterion to Demonstrate the Truth of Pure Knowledge

PART THREE

Application of the Criterion to Demonstrate the Truth of Non-pure, or Materiated Knowledge

PART FOUR
Errors to which
Human Knowledge is Subject

SECTION SEVEN
The Forces Present in *A Priori* Reasoning

SECTION EIGHT
The First Division
of the Branches of Knowledge

Part One: The criterion of certainty.

Part Two: Application of the criterion to show the truth of pure knowledge.

Part Three: Application of the criterion to show the truth of non-pure or materiated knowledge.

Part Four: Errors to which human knowledge is subject.

Part Five: Conclusion.

PART ONE

THE CRITERION OF CERTAINTY

CHAPTER 1
The nature of certainty, truth, and persuasion

1044. 'Certainty is a firm and reasonable persuasion that conforms to the truth.'

1045. *Truth* in the human being, therefore, is not the same as *certainty*. I can have a true opinion present to my spirit, yet doubt its truth. In this case I do not have certainty.

It is not sufficient for a thing to be true in itself in order for it to be true for us also. If it is to be true for us, we must have a motive producing a *firm persuasion* in us, and producing it *reasonably*, that is, according to a *reason* which must convince us that our opinion or belief is true and undoubted.[3]

Although logical truth certainly has no existence in itself outside all subsistence, it exists in itself outside the human intellect. This justifies the distinction between something true in itself, and true for me as a result of the *certainty* I have of this *truth*. All this is evident, and for the moment I need not investigate the nature of truth any further — I shall do this elsewhere.

1046. The definition I have given of *certainty* shows the difference between *certainty*, *persuasion* and *truth*.

Persuasion can be very firm (or declared so by the person who has it), but about something false. This is not certainty.

Persuasion can be very firm and even conform to the truth, but rest on a false and unreasonable motive.[4] In such a case we

---

[3] I call *opinion* or *belief* any proposition whatsoever conceived by a human being, to which he can give or deny assent.

[4] Sometimes the motive impelling human beings to a very firm persuasion is reasonable, although they themselves are unaware of its reasonableness and unable to express it. Nevertheless they are *certain*. We must be careful,

would be persuaded of the truth and partly possess it, but we would not, strictly speaking, be certain unless, of course, we wished to distinguish two kinds of certainty, one reasonable, the other unreasonable. But I am not happy with this distinction which only confuses rather than clarifies the present discussion.

1047. *Certainty*, therefore, results from three elements: 1. *truth* in the object, 2. firm *persuasion* in the subject, 3. a motive, or *reason*, producing the persuasion.

therefore, not to confuse belief lacking a reason (or based upon a false reason) with believing as a result of a true reason while being unable to explain the reason. Many people believe the Gospel. When asked, they may not be able to explain why they believe, but this does not mean that they believe without a reason. They believe on divine authority and on the strength of a truth that speaks to them internally. They are convinced by the best of reasons without being able to reflect on it, or note what takes place in them sufficiently well to communicate it clearly to others.

[1047]

CHAPTER 2
Certainty can never be blind

1048. Because certainty depends upon a *reason* which convinces us and compels us to assent to a proposition, it can never be *blind*, nor a pure *fact*, nor a purely *instinctive* submission.

Reid, the founder of the Scottish school, was the first in modern times to maintain such an absurdity, casting philosophical truth into an abyss from which it could never have extricated itself. Shocked by the universal scepticism caused by the philosophy of Locke, Reid was, I think, the discouraged victim of his own limited reason. Unable to accept his painful state of doubt, he sought help in others' opinions and clung like a shipwrecked sailor to the plank of common sense. According to him, common beliefs could not be proved or justified; they rested upon an irresistible necessity to assent, that is, upon a law of nature to which human beings were subject. *Nature* itself comes to the aid of powerless *reason* and instinctively compels humanity to give credence to first notions which reason is unable to justify. Humanity naturally flees annihilation, which would be its fate if human beings were able to deny faith in the first, essential principles.

In this way Reid believed he had completely eradicated scepticism. In fact he had more firmly strengthened and entrenched it.

Propositions cannot be true if, as he says, a necessity of nature makes me believe them. If I assent to them in order to preserve my existence, which would end without such assent, I am impelled solely by the very strong, irrefutable, but nevertheless *blind* principle of self-interest. But does it follow that what is useful and necessary for me is also true, or to put it more bluntly, have we not changed *truth* into *utility* and *necessity*? Truth no longer exists; only utility and necessity exert power over me. If this is the case, I am still in darkness, but in a necessary and essential darkness, greater than before.

Furthermore, I am not condemned only to *ignorance*. *Error* is prescribed and imposed on me as a condition of my existence, because it is an error to call truth that which is only utility and cruel necessity. We are commanded to commit a crime and forced to the vilest of actions: considering utility and non-utility as the sole norm of what is true and false is a crime which debases the nobility of my rational nature. How cruel nature is to dictate such a law! What a cruel benefit: to be saved from annihilation by the extinction of every spark of human excellence! How foolish and deceitful of nature to cancel the character she herself has impressed on my rational soul, to repent of intelligence, and to abandon the call to virtue she has given me by which I become master of the entia about me! A more ruinous tyranny could not be exercised over the essentially free element of our human spirit. The absurdity contained in such a system would usurp the throne of truth, eliminating truth forever from the universe and from the ranks of what is essential. Our understanding, deprived of the light that forms it, would act aimlessly and instinctively. A dull, pitiless fear would form the foundation of the human being, as he fled unceasingly and blindly the emptiness surrounding him. A strange deity incessantly pursues and torments the human being created by these philosophers. Unknown, fatal, inconceivable — such is the deity to whose care mankind is committed.

This apparently gentle, caring system already produced the evil poison we are speaking about, as it passed from England into Germany and became Kantianism, which is only the Scottish system engendered, enhanced and clothed in more regular and dignified forms.

Reid had said that as a whole we human beings believe in certain first notions by means of a direct movement of our spirit which necessarily gives assent to these notions. He posited this as an inexplicable fact. Kant accepted the fact, adding only that if we could not entirely explain it, we could at least analyse it accurately. According to him, the intimate power of our spirit, by means of some kind of suggestion, sends forth of itself the common principles of reason and our belief in them.[5] This

---

[5] The very *principles* of reason were confused with the faith or *assent* given them. One can understand that an internal suggestion moves us to assent to certain known principles. But it is impossible to understand a suggestion which produces the principles themselves. Reid and Kant both confused these two actions of the spirit, *intuition* and *assent*, and claimed to explain them by a single *hypothesis*.

power could be determined and discerned by its effects, which Kant attempted to distinguish.

The result of his work was that this kind of spiritual instinct manifests itself in a certain number of functions. The partial power by which the spirit performs each of these functions he called *form* of the spirit. This is the origin of the 'forms' proper to transcendental philosophy. Reid thought in good faith that he had defended the possession of objective truth for human beings, but Kant realised that Reid's system did the opposite: it removed objective truth entirely. He analysed the system and declared that theoretical reason had no objective value whatsoever; the truth of all human reasoning could only be subjective, that is, apparent to the subject. He was unaware, however, that speaking about 'subjective truth' was in the last analysis a misuse of words. *Subjective truth* is not truth; the expression contains a profound repugnance.

1049. In Italy, this strange teaching has always been resisted, and never taken root.

In France, the Scottish school appeared in 1811. Before this, Condillac reigned absolutely, while a countless number of his followers jealously vaunted their possession of freedom of thought [*App.*, no. 1].

Later, German philosophy found an opening in France, partly disguised as 'eclecticism'. The passage from 'critical philosophy' to 'eclecticism' was easy because a philosophy that questions all systems could easily pick and choose amongst them. But I am not going to object simply about a change of names.[6]

The real nature of this philosophy is not known by everyone in France, because it is still new, and its ultimate consequences have yet to come to light. It is only the past stages of a philosophy which allow final judgment on their progenitor's value, absolving or condemning her forever.

---

[6] The name *critical philosophy*, however, does contain something presumptuous and absurd. It implies that one human being passes judgment on everyone else's reasoning, as though he were something other than a human being. 'Eclecticism' is free of this defect. But 'eclecticism', because it means a *choice* of teachings, does not express the *unity* without which only a mass of unconnected opinions, not true philosophy, exists. *Eclectics*, if they were to be judged according to their self-imposed name, would be considered memorisers, not thinkers.

Some strive hard to make such a philosophy serve the interests of religion, but we must not be surprised if there are others who, without any regard for its religious consequences, show themselves ready to accept all its consequences whatever they may be. Such people hasten the development of the system, and its death sentence. Our only preoccupation as we await the execution of the sentence is that judgment is never passed on any defective, philosophical teaching before it has sacrificed many to error.

CHAPTER 3

The two principles of certainty

1050. We must distinguish two principles of certainty.

One is a proposition which expresses the constituents of *truth* and could be called *principium essendi* [principle of being].[7]

The other, a proposition which expresses a sure sign of the truth, could be called *principium cognoscendi* [principle of knowing].

1051. It is clear that the principle which expresses the essence of truth must also be the principle of certainty. Whenever I can see the truth in what is presented to my mind, I need no other motive for being certain of the thing thought. In the same way, whenever I have a *sure sign*, according to which I must believe that what I think is true, I can reasonably and firmly believe what is presented to my thought, although I see neither its reason nor its truth.

1052. Let us see how these two principles relate to the three elements of certainty, that is, to *truth* in the object, *firm persuasion* in the subject, and a *reason* which produces the persuasion.

But we must first decide how to present our argument so that the discussion may proceed more clearly.

Anything whatsoever to which we give or withhold our assent can be expressed as a proposition. A proposition present to our spirit can also be called knowledge, in so far as we understand and know the proposition. I will therefore use the word 'proposition' not to express any particular form of my mental conceptions but to express everything to which my

---

[7] This careful distinction of the two principles of certainty gives me the advantage of avoiding many ambiguities in the course of the argument, and the reader the advantage of avoiding many misunderstandings. At the same time it shortens the discussion, which is always prolonged when uncertain and confused. We must also bear in mind that while certainty has a cause outside us, the properties of this cause, which have no relationship with certainty, must be excluded by the very nature of the present discussion.

persuasion is referred, even in the case of a simple idea. As I have said, even an idea can be changed into and expressed as a proposition.[8]

Granted this, I say that the assent or dissent I give to a *proposition* forms or removes *persuasion* in me.

Assent must be motivated by a *reason*, if it is to produce a persuasion which gives *certainty*.

Thus, a *reason* is the general cause of certainty; and the third of the three elements from which certainty results is that which generates certainty in the individual, the only real subject of certainty.[9]

1053. In order to assent to a proposition and so generate certainty in myself, I must therefore be moved by a *reason*; I must not assent at random or blindly.

A *reason* is necessary for one purpose only: to produce in me persuasion of the *truth* of the proposition. But if *truth* is intuitively manifest to me, the *reason* moving me is truth itself; I recognise truth, which presents itself to my spirit, and I experience it as the force generating in me an unmovable, reasonable persuasion. This persuasion is reasonable precisely because produced by the truth to which alone I have surrendered myself. Thus, the elements of my certainty are reduced to two: *truth* in the object (which is also the reason for my persuasion), and *persuasion* itself, caused in me, the subject, by that truth.

But when I do not see the *truth* which is the *supreme reason* and *evidence* for the proposition, I must, in order to give a reasonable assent, have a motive, that is, some indication or

[8] Every acquired idea presupposes a judgment. The first idea thus becomes a proposition if it is applied to itself by saying, for example, ' Being is'.

[9] The *subject* of certainty is always an *individual* who alone can give or withhold assent to a proposition, because only individuals really exist on this earth: humanity is purely an abstract idea. It would therefore be absurd to say (by changing an abstract into a real person, as the Abbé de Lamennais does) that humanity, not individuals who compose humanity, assent and produce certainty. Moreover, to give assent is to pronounce a judgment. Hence, the proximate judge of certainty is without any doubt the individual, just as the *proximate judge* of moral actions is the conscience of each human being. This does not mean, however, that the individual need not follow a rule independent of himself in carrying out such a judgment.

sign by virtue of which I can reasonably believe that the truth is in the proposition[10] (even if I do not see it myself). This sure sign of the truth must be such that it cannot deceive me: it may be, for example, an infallible *authority*[11] in which I reasonably believe, although I may not understand what the authority is affirming. But again, generally speaking, any *sure sign* of the truth of a proposition can produce certainty in me, although the sign is extrinsic to the proposition and incapable of making me perceive and know[12] directly the truth contained in it.

These two principles of certainty, therefore, must be distinguished: we say one is 'intrinsic' and the other 'extrinsic' to the proposition. The first is directed not only to persuading and convincing us that truth must be present in the proposition, but is part of the proposition, showing us its truth clearly and making us intuit it with the eyes of our intellect. On the other hand, the second is not in the proposition, nor does it always relate to its contents. This principle, therefore, does not require us to understand clearly the proposition. Whatever the proposition contains and in whatever way we understand it (even if stated in a foreign language or written in unintelligible characters), we

[10] *Erret necesse est qui assentitur rebus incertis* [Anyone who assents to what is uncertain is bound to err] (St. Augustine, Lib. 2, *Contra Acad* ., c. 4).

[11] The *authority* is not the extrinsic *principle* of certainty considered in all its generality, but a particular principle subordinate to the general principle. Certain parts of arguments *ab absurdo* are subject to the same principle, that is, all those arguments in which the absurdity relates to the contents of the proposition materially understood. As a result, it would be absurd to suppose the proposition false, although its contents are either not known, or of no importance.

[12] St. Augustine thinks that the verb 'to know' indicates better the intuition of truth, and 'to believe' indicates better the assent given to a proposition on the faith of others or according to sense data: *Proprie quippe cum loquimur, id solum scire dicimur, quod mentis firma ratione comprehendimus. Cum vero loquimur verbis consuetudini aptioribus. — non dubitemus dicere scire nos et quod percepimus nostri corporis sensibus, et quod fide dignis credimus testibus DUM TAMEN INTER HAEC ET ILLUD QUID DISTET INTELLIGAMUS* [Strictly speaking, we are said to know only that which we understand by a firm reason of our mind. But in normal speech we have no hesitation in saying that we know both what we perceive with our bodily senses and what we believe from witnesses worthy of our trust, ALTHOUGH WE UNDERSTAND THE GAP BETWEEN THESE TWO PROPOSITIONS] (*Retract.*, bk. 1, c. 14).

prove to ourselves by means of the principle and become rationally convinced that the proposition MUST contain the truth. We must therefore give our full assent to its contents.

The order between the intrinsic and the extrinsic principle of certainty

1054. When I have a *sure sign* of the truth of a proposition (for example, an infallible authority affirming the proposition), I cannot doubt its certainty.

But the sign, in order to be effective, must first be *certain* itself. In this case, therefore, one *certainty* produces another *certainty*: I am certain of the proposition because I was first certain of the *sign* or reasoning that convinced me about the proposition. The certainty of the truth, therefore, produced for me by the extrinsic principle, is a certainty which presupposes a preceding certainty.

But where does this *sign* obtain its certainty? If from another *sure sign*, we must ask where the certainty of that sign comes from. We obviously cannot continue the succession of *signs* to infinity: if I verify the first by the second, the second by the third, and so on to infinity, I must hold in mind an infinite succession of signs, which is absurd. Moreover, we would never discover the first sign on which all the others depend, and from which they draw their value. We must therefore end at a sign whose truth is known through itself, not through another sign. Thus, the *extrinsic principle* of certainty must be reduced to the higher, *intrinsic principle* of certainty. In this way, the ultimate principle of certainty is reduced to one only, that is, to *truth*, seen directly by the mind through intuition. Truth is self-evident, devoid of sign and without intervening arguments.[13]

---

[13] We should note that the motive or reason impelling our assent must always be *truth*, because only *truth* could really persuade us that something is true. For example, if self-interest made me declare a proposition true, the proposition would not be certain; I would know that the reason moving my assent was *utility*, not *truth*. If a murderer threatens to stab me in the chest, unless I swear to some teaching, he is not persuading me; he is simply making me a perjurer. I know well enough that the threatened injury itself does not produce certainty because I know it not as *truth* but as *injury*, which has neither right nor power over my intellectual assent. Again, a person may be forced to assent to some teaching by suffering lengthy oppression or

CHAPTER 5
How we see truth

1055. We have seen that there are two principles of certainty, one *intrinsic*, the other *extrinsic*. The intrinsic principle is the *intuitive knowledge of truth*; the extrinsic, the *knowledge of a sure sign of truth*.

The extrinsic principle is never the ultimate principle; it is ordered to, and dependent on the *intrinsic principle* because a *sure sign* of truth cannot exist without a preceding *certainty*. And this certainty can only be given in the last analysis by the intuitive *knowledge of truth* (cf. 1054).

Hence, the supreme or ultimate principle of certainty is one only, the intuition or *vision of truth*.

1056. We must now explain how it is possible for us to see, that is, to know *intuitively*, the truth of a proposition.

We say we know the truth of a proposition when we know the *reason* for it.

But the reason for a proposition can be expressed by another proposition; for example, the reason for the proposition, 'The human being is the noblest of animals', can be expressed by the proposition, 'Because the intelligence with which the human being is endowed is more noble than sense alone'.

But if one proposition provides the reason for another, a third may provide the reason for the second: the reason for the reason, the explanation of the explanation. Thus, the reason for the proposition, 'Intelligence is a more noble faculty than sense alone', is given by the proposition, 'Because intelligence has being in all its universality as its object, while sense is confined to a body'.

If, in order to say we know the truth of the third proposition,

servitude, or by a continuous succession of sufferings accompanied by other means of persuasion (but never by the *truth*). Such treatment could produce a kind of persuasion, which however would not be certainty because it was produced by motives extraneous to the truth. A persuasion which had been initially caused by motives alien to the force of truth would become certainty only at the moment it was confirmed by truth coming into our spirit. The vision of truth, therefore, is the sole motive capable of producing certainty.

we need to know its reason, we will need a fourth proposition to express it.

The same argument, however, will require us to look for the reason for the fourth proposition, and then the reason for the fifth, and so on. Eventually we will come to a final proposition beyond which we cannot go because it contains and expresses the supreme reason. This supreme reason must satisfy us of itself (when it is well understood), and completely assuage our desire for reasons. It is the real reason for the whole series of propositions and therefore the reason even for the first proposition whose truth we cannot say we know intuitively until we have reached it in its ultimate reason where the intellect is fully satisfied.

1057. Our closest attention is necessary here. We wish to know 'when it is that we intuitively apprehend the truth of a proposition'. Observation of fact reveals that the human understanding is not completely satisfied and at rest, nor does it believe and say it sees the *truth* of a proposition, until it has seen the *ultimate reason* for the proposition. The *truth* therefore of any proposition which is not the ultimate proposition, is not the proposition itself but its *ultimate, supreme reason*. And this ultimate reason is called (according to the common meaning of the word) 'truth' of the proposition. To see the *truth* is simply to see this *reason*.

1058. The criterion of certainty, therefore, expressed in the words, 'the intuitive knowledge of truth', can equally be expressed as 'knowledge of the ultimate reason for the proposition'[14] under consideration.

---

[14] I say 'of the *proposition*' and not 'of the subject matter of the *proposition*' The *reason* for the proposition is a *logical reason*; the reason for the subject matter of the proposition is a *metaphysical reason* or final reason, etc. For example, in the proposition, 'The human race exists', the human race is the subject matter. To be certain about this proposition, I have no need at all to know the ultimate reason for the human race but simply the ultimate reason that *proves* its existence. The proposition concerns the existence, not the *origin* of or *reason* for the human race.

CHAPTER 6

The principle of knowledge must also be the principle of certainty

1059. When I want to know whether a proposition is true or false, I seek its *reason* (cf. 1055–1058).

This reason can be expressed by another proposition, whose reason I also want to know. In order to be completely satisfied,[15] I move from one proposition to another, from one reason to another, until I reach the self-evident *ultimate* reason. I then say I have grasped the truth of the first proposition intuitively, because I have the *supreme principle of its certainty*.

We must pay careful attention to this fact.[16] As long as we are investigating the truth or falsity of a proposition, we distinguish between *knowledge* and *certainty*. We may know and understand the sense of the proposition without knowing whether it is true; our *knowledge* of the proposition is not the same as the truth or *certainty* we are looking for. This distinction between the *knowledge* and *certainty* of a proposition is present in the whole series of propositions or reasons, until we reach the final reason. When we have reached the *ultimate reason, knowledge* necessarily becomes one with *certainty* without any real separation remaining between them.

In fact, I called *ultimate reason* any proposition which, when understood, draws our assent by its own intrinsic authority and power. If we are speaking seriously and do not wish to complicate what is clear, we can neither desire nor look for another

[15] In fact, human beings are not always reasonably satisfied with their investigations. Sometimes they are satisfied by frivolous reasons, as people *en masse* often are. These reasons are often more striking than solid, true reasons. We can therefore ask what is the law according to which human beings find satisfaction in their search for the reasons of things, and we can determine it as: 'In a series of subordinate propositions, human beings find satisfaction when they have reached a proposition they no longer doubt,' whatever the cause removing the doubt.

[16] Note that I have not yet answered the sceptics. I am simply presenting the *facts*, and analysing them. I am describing what happens to human beings, and what they think happens to them. In other words, I am talking about people in general, not sceptics, whose position I will discuss later.

reason because the reason we now have is seen as justified in itself, and satisfies us fully. As soon as we know the ultimate reason, we say we see the *truth* of the matter (cf. 1055–1058). *Knowledge* and *certainty* identify in such a way, therefore, that at the point where our investigation ends, *knowledge* is also *certainty* for us.

1060. Note, however, that we do not stop at the ultimate reason simply because we feel satisfied with it. We could be *satisfied* even with a non-ultimate reason, and go no further. We stop at the ultimate reason necessarily as well as willingly. 'Ultimate' means the reason beyond which we cannot truly find any other reason or give any assent or know anything further except by deceiving ourselves. The *ultimate reason* of a proposition, therefore, is the terminal point of our knowledge as well as of our assent and persuasion. It is the principle both of certainty and of knowledge, as I proposed to show.[17]

---

[17] When this point has been reached where *knowledge, truth* and *certainty* are one single thing, we see how absurd it is to try to produce knowledge from the senses, which cannot generate certainty. The Peripatetics saw that judgment about the truth of things could not be a property of the senses. This should have been sufficient (if people had carefully reflected on the matter) for them to be aware that knowledge could not derive from the senses as from its formal cause, because ultimately knowledge is the same as certainty. Cicero, referring to the opinion of the Peripatetics and Academicians, says, *Tertia philosophiae pars, quae erat in ratione et disserendo, sic tractabatur ab utrisque* (the Academicians and the Peripatetics). *Quamquam oriretur a sensibus, tamen non esse IUDICIUM VERITATIS in sensibus. Mentem volebant rerum esse iudicem: solam censebant idoneam cui crederetur, quia sola cerneret id quod semper esset simplex, et unius modi, et tale quale esset. Hanc illi IDEAM appellabant, iam a Platone ita appellatam: nos recte* speciem *possumus dicere* [Both (the Academicians and the Peripatetics) dealt with the third part of philosophy, which consisted of reasoning and discussion. The JUDGMENT OF TRUTH, although aroused by the senses, is not in the senses. These philosophers considered the mind as judge of things. Only the mind can be believed, because the mind alone discerns what is always simple and of one kind, and discerns it exactly as it is. This they called 'IDEA', as Plato had, although we can rightly call it 'species'] (*Acad.*, 1). Thus, the Peripatetics made *ideas* the principle of certainty. But if they had noticed how one idea is generated from another, they would have found the *first idea*, source of all other ideas, and hence the unity of the source of knowledge and certainty. Whatever the Peripatetics thought, it is certain that anyone realising that the *judgment* of certainty comes only from the mind, can discover (if he intends to be coherent with himself) that *knowledge* also must have the same origin.

[1060]

CHAPTER 7

There is a single principle of certainty for all possible propositions

1061. I have not yet moved to show against the sceptics that a valid principle of certainty exists for human beings. This present chapter aims only at demonstrating what such a principle, if it really exists, would have to be in order to merit its name.

If the principle of certainty exists, it can only be *one* for all possible propositions. This is a consequence of what has been said.

I showed that, if we wished to know the truth of a proposition, we needed to discover its *ultimate reason*.[18] Thus we had to know whether this *ultimate reason* must also be the final reason of all other propositions. I found that the nature of this *ultimate reason* was not only the principle of certainty but also the *principle of human knowledge* (cf. 1059–1060).

Throughout the whole of volume one, however, we have seen that there is only one principle of all human acts of knowledge, BEING IN ALL ITS UNIVERSALITY.[19] If, therefore, the principle of certainty exists, it can only be one for all possible propositions, and must in fact be this unique idea of *being*, inserted in us by nature to make us intelligent, that is, to make us capable of perceiving the truth.[20]

---

[18] St. Augustine recognises that 'ideas' can fittingly be called 'reasons'. In fact a *reason* can only be an *idea*. The great bishop of Hippo says: *Ideas latine possumus vel* formas *vel* species *dicere, ut verbum e verbo transferri videamur. Si autem* RATIONES *eas vocemus, ab interpretandi quidem proprietate discedimus: rationes enim graece* λόγοι *appellantur, non ideae, sed tamen quisquis hoc vocabulo uti voluerit, a re ipsa non errabit* [In our own language we can call ideas *forms* or *species*, using one word in place of another. But calling them REASONS is not strictly correct. In Greek 'reasons' are called λόγοι, not 'ideas'. However, if anyone prefers to use 'reasons', he would not be making a mistake] (*Lib. 83 Quaest.*, 2. 46).

[19] Ancient thinkers recognised that the principle of certainty had to be something most universal, as we can see in Sextus (*Hypotyposis*, bk. 2, c. 9).

[20] In this sense the statement by the author of *Saggio sull'Indifferenza* must be true: 'Certainty is the essential basis of reason' (5, 2).

CHAPTER 8

A very simple way of refuting scepticism

1062. The sole form of human reason is being in all its universality (cf. vol. 2, 385–1039), which is both the principle of knowledge and of certainty.[21]

Being in all its universality, considered as the *principle of knowledge*, is called IDEA, the first or mother-idea; considered as the *principle of certainty*, it is generally called 'final reason', and TRUTH of our intellections (cf. 1048–1049).

This is sufficient to justify what I wrote in *Saggio sui confini della ragione*: 'TRUTH is the sole form of human reason' (*Theodicy*, 151).

1063. We must note carefully that this correct way of speaking is sufficient of itself to offer an easy refutation of the sceptics. Common sense is indeed immune from the assaults of sophists who, although they think they are attacking it, do not even direct their blows against it. When we confront the sceptics with the whole of mankind, they can be shown to be fighting their own phantasies rather than common sense.

Any dialogue between common sense and scepticism will develop more or less as follows. Common sense says that the truth and falsity of some propositions can be known; scepticism maintains that no human being can know the truth.

Common sense asserts that we reason continually; we have ideas, join ideas to make judgments, and link judgments to form arguments; these different actions of our spirit allow us to know whether a proposition is reasonable or not, true or false. For scepticism this is a waste of time; the ideas obtained by reasoning are illusions and always devoid of truth.

Although common sense admits that it may not be as sophisticated or far-seeing as scepticism and cannot therefore desire to be on a level with it, it attains satisfaction before scepticism does. For its part, scepticism despises the entire cause of common sense's complete satisfaction and contentment. It despises

[21] Common sense accepts this as true also. The sceptics attack common sense, but I will defend it in the following chapters.

truth, and seeks something beyond it. In any case, it believes that common sense can never find *truth*.

Scepticism readily accepts that the human spirit reasons, but considers such actions valueless. Common sense, however, is not concerned about the value of reasoning, but that it is in fact carried out. By means of reasoning, common sense arrives at an *ultimate reason* for propositions whose truth or falsity it wishes to ascertain. Scepticism considers of no authority or value whatsoever the *ultimate reason* to which common sense reduces all its reasoning; reasoning is valueless precisely because its foundation is a gratuitous, unproven and unsupported *ultimate reason* to which assent must be given gratuitously.

At this point common sense, baffled by the subtlety of the sceptics' argument, asks if they know the correct name for the ultimate reason of reasoning. They reply that words have no importance; the problem concerns things, not words. Common sense points out that without agreement on the meaning of words the parties to a discussion cannot know what is being discussed, and insists that the 'ultimate reason' under discussion is properly called TRUTH.[22]

Common sense proclaims therefore that the difference between the common mass of people and sceptics lies precisely in the people's satisfaction with *truth* and the sceptics' desire to go beyond it in their endeavour to find something more worthy of them than truth. Ordinary people are content to state the fact. Without deciding who is right or wrong, they simply want to clarify their position so that sceptics will at least know what they are attacking.

Common sense is aware that at this point the mass of people

---

[22] We have shown that being constitutes what is generally called the 'light of reason', or, according to the Schoolmen, the 'light of the acting intellect'; it is the ultimate reason through which all other things are known. St. Augustine himself calls this light and reason *truth*: *Lux increata est ratio cognoscendi et lux sola increata EST VERITAS* [Uncreated light is the reason for knowledge, and only uncreated light IS TRUTH] (*De V. Relig.*, c. 34 and 36). He calls the *reason for knowledge* 'uncreated' because everything positive in it is uncreated and divine. The limits, however, with which it is manifested to human beings are *co-created* with human beings. Thus it can also be called 'created light', as St. Thomas calls it without disagreeing with St. Augustine.

are reproached by sceptics for their *misuse* of words in calling 'truth' the ultimate reason in which all human reasoning terminates. According to sceptics, this misuse is particularly foolish because the difficulty lies precisely in knowing whether the *ultimate reason* is true or illusory. According to sceptics, the rest of mankind considers the question settled before it is discussed.

Common sense insists once more that mankind has difficulty grappling with the subtleties of sceptics whatever the question under discussion. Moreover, it is the people in general, educated and uneducated, who name things authoritatively. Even the sceptics, before becoming philosophers, were educated in human society, where they learnt the very language they now use in order to argue with people. This language had been formed before they began to philosophise, think, or were even born; they used it in common with all other people in order to express their ideas. It is impossible therefore for the word *truth* to be used with a meaning different from that given by society, past and present.

Nor can the whole human race be accused of misusing words. It is society that makes and sanctions the law of language, which must be obeyed by educated and uneducated alike if they wish to understand each other. Sceptics are guilty of extraordinary presumption in imposing on the human race a law controlling the meaning of the very words they themselves have received from mankind!

Sceptics certainly have the right to subtle reasoning, but human society must be allowed its right over language, a right which cannot be taken away or violated with impunity. Human society, from the beginning of its existence until now, has always understood that, in affirming that it knows the truth of a proposition, it knows the final reason and element of the proposition. This is the only value human society has given to the word 'truth'. Sceptics therefore cannot deny *truth*; they do not even attack it if they agree that human beings, on analysing every argument, reduce it to its ultimate element or *reason* of reasoning.[23] To call this *reason* false is a misuse of words,

---

[23] Sceptics do not deny appearances. Hence, they do not deny *knowledge*; they simply declare it devoid of certainty. They attack the *truth* of knowledge at its base, that is, at the ultimate principle of certainty [*App.*, no. 2].

because what we call *truth* is this very reason. *Truth* therefore is immune from the sceptics' attacks, and the difference between the *sceptics* and *common sense* is simply this: common sense, once it has attained the truth, is satisfied, and acknowledges its satisfaction, whereas scepticism is unaware of the truth it has attained and continues its search for something more elevated, arbitrarily and misleadingly called 'truth'.[24]

1064. Anyone who appreciates the force of this confrontation will find that common sense has not only vindicated the existence of truth but put it beyond question.

He will also see that the origin of the sceptics' harrowing mistake lies ultimately in a misuse of abstraction.

Error is very easy in any argument that considers abstractly, and not in itself, the object which is its sole concern. An abstract concept is not the perfect concept of an object, and therefore does not possess everything contained in the object. It lacks that which, as proper to the object, determines it to the exclusion of every other object. The lack of this important element must result in error and false reasoning.

This is the error made by the sceptics when discussing truth. They consider it abstractly, as a quality predicated of different propositions whose truth or falsehood is sought. In using this general, abstract concept of truth we distinguish between a *proposition* and its *truth* with the result that the proposition can always seem separate from its truth. Hence, the sceptics claim that no proposition is true, and that the union of the two elements, proposition and truth, can never be realised.

But they certainly could not have claimed this if they had formed the proper concept of truth by considering truth in

---

[24] The example I have given indicates the necessity of the correct study of words before we impugn the opinions of common sense, which are found solely in the use of words. Reflection on this important point reveals the intimate union between ideas and words, and shows how the latter alone contain the tradition proper to human opinions. Ancient thinkers considered etymology, or better, the study of the value of words, an extremely necessary part of logic. Cicero gives us the teaching of the Academicians and Peripatetics on the matter: *Verborum etiam explicatio probabatur, qua de causa quaeque essent ita nominata: quam etymologiam appellabant* [Words were explained to discover why things had received their particular names. They called this explanation 'etymology'] (cf. *Acad.*, bk. 1).

itself, not abstractly. In this case, they would have seen that truth in all conclusion-propositions is indeed separate from the propositions themselves. Here the *truth of the proposition* is one thing and the *proposition* another. But truth is nothing other than a *first pro*position. With this in mind, they would have seen that there is a proposition which expresses truth itself, that is, a reason which everyone calls TRUTH. Having examined truth closely, not as some vague, abstract notion, but in itself, and discovered that it is an ultimate reason expressed in an ultimate proposition, they would have known clearly that it is absurd and contradictory to deny that *truth* is *truth*. Their error therefore consists in misusing words and neglecting to understand their value.

As a result, the problem posed by scepticism is entirely altered. We no longer ask, 'Can we know truth?' but 'Must we be satisfied with truth?', and assent to it? Is what the human race calls 'truth' so authoritative, so absolute that nothing more noble, satisfying or worthy can be found beyond it?

This new way of posing the question, which clearly indicates the correct solution vainly rejected by the sceptics, is the only one that can stand. We will see this better in the following chapters.

PART TWO

APPLICATION OF THE CRITERION TO DEMONSTRATE THE TRUTH OF PURE KNOWLEDGE

CHAPTER 1

The intuition of being, the source of all certainty, is shown to be justified *per se*

Article 1

Sceptical objections to the intuition of being

1065. Generally speaking[25] at least, sceptics do not deny appearances. Without denying that we feel, they affirm that our perception deceives us and cannot therefore promote and sustain truth.

Our first natural *intellection*, on which all others depend (cf. 1044–1064), is that of being. Sceptical doubts against the veracity and genuineness of being can be reduced to three:

I. How do we know that the understanding of being (the form of any knowledge whatsoever) is not a pure illusion, having only apparent truth as far as we are concerned?

II. How can human beings perceive anything outside themselves? How can they get outside themselves? What forms the passage between human beings and things different from or outside them?

---

[25] According to Sextus Empiricus (*Hypotyposis*, bk. 1, c. 8), even Pyrrho admitted sensible appearances; he simply denied that their reality could be proved.

III. Even if what the spirit saw were not an illusion and did in fact possess some reality, would this object not be changed and falsified by the way we see it? Would it not seem natural for the spirit, in seeing things, to clothe them with its own forms as a mirror reflects the images of things, diminishing or enlarging them according to its own convex or concave plane? The mirror never shows things as they are, but as images formed in itself according to the shape it has.

The sceptics' arguments can be reduced to these three, to which we must now reply. But first it will be helpful to penetrate the human mind and note the steps leading it to such extreme attitudes of doubt.

Article 2

The source of the objections

1066. From the moment we come into this world our attention is continually occupied with sensible perceptions. If as adults, we devote ourselves to study, all the powers of our spirit are taken up and exhausted by an interminable quantity of evermore subtle, arduous, abstract and prolonged arguments. However, such an immense mass of perceptions and arguments, capable of absorbing and conquering all possible intellectual vigour, attracts by the vivacity and splendour of its composition: our needs, inclinations and noblest thoughts seek and long for satisfaction in the ocean of things that can be thought and felt.

Withdrawing our minds from all these perceptions and from the entire sphere of arguments that we love so much must be extremely difficult. Retreating into a kind of intellectual solitude, where the object of our attention is no longer the knowledge we have acquired but the mere *possibility* of some kind of knowledge, must inevitably be distasteful and abhorrent to our nature. Nevertheless, if we want to give our attention simply to the idea of *being in all its universality*, we have to distance and separate ourselves through abstraction from every kind of acquired knowledge and retain only our capacity for directing our attention, which is the outcome of the development we have undergone. If we succeed in concentrating on this *idea*, nothing indeed remains except the simple *possibility* of knowledge. This kind of abstinence, if we can call it that, is burdensome even if practised a little; it seems to reduce our thought to nothing, or annihilate us in sterile contemplation; it appears neither necessary nor helpful. Abstract meditation of this kind is therefore uncommon, and only embarked upon when a person is motivated by the particular necessity and urgent need that springs from a desire to find a foundation for all endangered human cognitions.

1067. It is a fact, of course, that research into the veracity of human knowledge is everyone's concern, and that everyone has something to say about it.

But the arguments offered to throw doubt upon all that ordinary people take as certain are the result of acquired, deducted knowledge. As I said, the human mind is drawn more forcefully to studies in all their extension with their untold riches. This is the mind's constant preoccupation.

The investigator sees that some of his observations are incorrect, and some of his arguments fallacious; one argument unexpectedly finds a counterpoise in another of equal or greater weight; an opinion held at one time is later discredited; discussion becomes a subtle, ferocious industry. Finally, sophists make their appearance, openly professing and methodically teaching how to test the pros and cons of everything. Their aim is to divert and prolong argument, to avoid every conclusion and to forestall agreement. And certainly it is impossible to reach any conclusion with someone whose aim, whether he is right or wrong, is to eschew every conclusion and never give way in any argument.

Human experience of the fallibility of reason, the flexibility and continual corrections found in discussions, the constant possibility of causing mental confusion, and the senseless ambition of proving one's intellectual ability through falsehood finally give rise to a doctrine of absolute *scepticism* amongst superficial or bewildered people.

But we must insist that the sophist's research in these matters concerns only the normal part of knowledge, to which learned people are usually attracted. It never draws on the entire range of knowledge. The consequence of this research, however, is *not* restricted to that part of knowledge in which such difficulties have been found; their conclusion is not limited to the section of knowledge which enfolds their premises, but extended to universal knowledge which they declare to be invalid and false, or at least doubtful.

1068. The part is taken for the whole without any realisation that the research has been confined to only one section of deduced knowledge, and does not extend to knowledge as a whole. This reduced part, undoubtedly of splendid breadth, is the continual object of human understanding, but another part, which is never subject to attacks attempting to render it doubtful, is passed over unnoticed. Like a shadow or a tiny, disregarded seed, it is left abandoned in a corner of the mind, or rather treated as a servant of the lowest order, unworthy of notice. This little element is overlooked, as infinity is in mathematics, or set aside as the poor are by the rich. As a result, arguments against knowledge remain unanswered; the uncertainty of a part of knowledge is predicated and arbitrarily affirmed of knowledge as a whole. People never imagine that this humble scrap of knowledge, confused with the rest of knowledge in human intelligence and not deigned worthy of thought, should be exempt from the general law or that it alone could save from condemnation the great, inflated knowledge of which we are so proud and which we think forms the whole of our understanding.

But here too the lowly must be exalted; the foundation of all certainty is found in a tiny, unobtrusive point of knowledge which, despite its minuteness and almost imperceptibility, is firm and rock-solid, a suitable resting place for the lever of reason to move human thought to extremely effective operations. This point is the *idea of being* from which, as we have seen, all the ideas that human beings possess derive their source and their being as ideas.

We maintain, therefore, that the first element of knowledge (which exists, but is normally unobserved) cannot be included in a general argument intended to annihilate all knowledge. The idea of being can be attacked only directly, and then will be seen as unassailable.

The reader should not be content with general arguments such as those employed by sceptics, but ask himself if they are

[1068]

valid when applied to individual parts of knowledge. In this way he will, I am sure, see clearly that the sceptics' arguments, although they may accord with all other parts of knowledge, can never accord with the idea of being, against which they are not only invalid but totally vain and indeed meaningless.

The reader can only be convinced of this, however, if he pays attention to understanding fully the character and nature proper to the idea of being. When his reflection on this idea has enabled him to experience its intimate nature and form, there is no doubt that he will understand for himself the irrelevance of sceptics' arguments. I hope to show this by presenting the proper characteristics of the idea of being, replying at the same time to the three sceptical doubts previously set out.

Article 3

First doubt: 'Could not the thought of existence in all its universality itself be an illusion?'

§1. *Reply*

1069. As we have said (cf. 1066–1068), this doubt cannot arise if the intuition of existence in all its universality has been correctly understood according to its own particular nature, without being confused with other intellections.

An illusion or deceptive thought indicates something that is not. I deceive myself, for example, if I look and imagine that I see a human being at night in a wood under a new moon when I actually see a shadow, or a tree trunk, or a mass of rock. In taking an appearance for reality, however this may occur, I delude and deceive myself. The concept of illusion contains two elements, therefore: 1. appearance, and 2. reality. *Appearance* is that which appears to me, *reality* is what I judge to lie behind the appearance of what I see. I deceive and delude myself when I judge that something truly is, which only appears to me, and in fact is not.

No deception could arise within me, however, if something appeared to me, or I experienced a sensation, or saw something and I did not go beyond it, that is, did not judge that some reality corresponded to that appearance. The very possibility of deception necessarily presupposes a judgment on the part of the person who deceives himself. If there is no judgment, there is no illusion. Deception of this kind requires, therefore, two elements, an *appearance* and a *reality*, the second of which does not correspond to the first.

1070. These two conditions are lacking when we think of being in all its universality. This idea is perfectly *simple* (cf. vol. 2, 542–546). It is a pure intellective intuition, devoid of all judgment, and cannot therefore be the source of illusion. When I say 'existence in general' I neither affirm nor deny anything (*ibid.*). Thinking of being in all its universality does not even entail thinking that something subsists. If I think that something subsists, I can deceive myself; what I am thinking of can in fact not subsist; and what I consider not to subsist, could subsist. But to think of being in all its universality is not to think of one thing rather than another; it is to think of the possibility (cf. vol. 2, 408, 409) of anything whatsoever, that is, to think, but not to think of anything determined. In a word, *possibility* is simply *thinkability* (cf. vol. 2, 542–546). Possibility is simply an entity *sui generis* which serves as a light to the mind without bearing within itself any contradiction or conflict.

Contradiction or internal mental conflict is possible only if the elements of the conflict are received individually in my mind. The union of these contradictory elements cannot be thought of. Such a union would be sheer nothing; one element would destroy or remove the other; nothing would remain. But there can be no contradiction in something totally undetermined; it is something I can conceive mentally, something thinkable, something *possible*.

In the pure and simple intuition of being, therefore, deception and illusion are impossible.

§2. The sceptic continues to press his point

1071. It is a *fact*[26] that we have the concept of being. In other words, being is thinkable.

If the sceptic affirms that this concept of being is an illusion or deception, his words are meaningless, as I have shown. He applies deceit to what is incapable of deceiving. All he can do

[26] Antiquity was aware that the whole of philosophy began with the fact of the intuition of being in all its universality, that is, with the fact of the existence of intellective cognition. Antiquity was also aware that a fact cannot be known without the help of experience. It saw, too, that the *fundamental fact* of philosophy was a matter of *internal experience*, attested by consciousness. This experience was neglected by sensists who systematically abandoned it, as I have often noted. Evidence of antiquity's awareness of this primary source of philosophy can be found in a witness from the 13th century, the subtle philosopher and theologian from Duns. *EXPERIMUR in nobis quod cognoscimus actu UNIVERSALE* (he starts with experience of the universal): *EXPERIMUR enim quod cognoscimus ENS, vel qualitatem sub ratione aliqua communiori, quam sit ratio primi objecti sensibilis, etiam respectu supremae sensitivae. EXPERIMUR etiam, etc., quodlibet autem istorum cognoscere est impossibile alicui sensitivae potentis tribuere* (it is a fact that intellective knowledge is essentially different from sense knowledge). *Si quis autem* (denying the *first fact* destroys all possibility of argument) *proterve neget illos actus inesse homini, non est cum eo ulterius disputandum; sicut nec cum dicente, non video colorem; sed illi dicendum: tu indiges sensu, quia coecus es. Ita quia quodam sensu, id est perceptione interiori* (this is the interior experience of consciousness), *experimur istos actus in nobis, si istos neget, dicendum est eum non esse hominem, quia non habet illam visionem interiorem, quam alii experiuntur se habere* ['We EXPERIENCE in ourselves what we know by our UNIVERSAL act' (he starts with experience of the universal); 'for we EXPERIENCE that we know ENS, or quality, in a way more common than that in which we know the sensible object, relative to our supreme sensitive potency. We also EXPERIENCE, etc., the impossibility of attributing knowledge of anything of this kind to any sensitive potency' (it is a fact that intellective knowledge is essentially different from sense knowledge). 'But if anyone contumaciously denies that these acts are present in human beings, there is no question of further argument with him' (denying the *first fact* destroys all possibility of argument). 'We can only say what we would say to someone affirming that he is unable to see colour: "You are blind, you are sense-deficient." If anyone denies that we experience these acts in ourselves with a certain sense, that is, with interior perception' (this is the interior experience of consciousness), 'we have to declare that he is not human; he lacks that interior vision which others experience'] (John Duns Scotus, in bk. 4 of the *Sentences*, dis. 43, q. 2).

[1071]

now is to uphold his denial of this fact by insisting that being is not conceivable by us. In this case, I reply that to deny being as conceivable is to deny all thought to human beings. Such a denial affirms that thought is an illusion, and does not, therefore, exist. In fact, nothing is left to be the object of thought; to say that something is the object of thought is to say that the knowledge of being is present. The sceptic's insistence annihilates and renders impossible all thought.

Scepticism of this nature should reduce the sceptic to total silence; his mind should be completely incapacitated because in speaking or thinking he would give the lie to himself. It is not a question of thinking truly or falsely; it is a question of thinking or not thinking. If you think (well or badly, truly or falsely), you think something, and to say that you think something is to say that you think being. We find ourselves at that precise point where *knowledge* and *certainty* become the same (cf. 1059–1060).

1072. The sceptic has no right to assail truth in such an extreme fashion. His first step in this direction becomes an exercise in self-defeat because the possibility of thought lies beyond every assault. To attack the possibility of thought you would have to begin by not thinking. But you do not attack anything by not thinking. Your only achievement is to cut yourself off from mankind and place yourself in an animal, mineral or vegetable world.

1073. The proposition, 'possibility of thought', is identical with 'the thinkability of being'; thought, as we have said, is a mental operation which has being for its object.

Being, conceived under this aspect as the universal object of thought, is secure and beyond the range of any argument for this simple reason: in order to attack being, you must use thought. And because no one can contemporaneously *attack* and *not attack*, *think* and *not think*, no one can deny the intuition of being in all its universality.

The intuition of being therefore is necessarily admitted by everyone. Being as thinkable is a pure *fact*, not subject to our will. We contemplate it, and admit it mentally with the same necessity by which we are. It does not seek our consent or our dissent. It is. We either do not think, or we think being; thinking against being is absurd. Anyone imagining that he does think contrary to being simply does not understand what he is about; he believes he is doing what he is not doing. It is impossible for anyone to understand the significance of 'conceiving being in all its universality' and deny it. Denying it is to affirm it. It is impossible to doubt it as an illusion because it could not be even an illusion if it were not true and real. It is impossible to affirm as illusory that which is simple in the extreme[27] and ends in itself.

§3. *Corollaries of this teaching*

1074. We shall now synthesize our teaching in different words by reducing it to some simple principles already established (cf. vol. 2, 398–470). We said that:

1. Being is that element which enters into all our ideas.

2. Being is that which remains in our ideas after all possible abstractions have been made on them. The final abstraction leads us to being, pure and simple. If this were removed, every idea would be destroyed (cf. vol. 2, 410, 411).

Therefore, either we decide not to think or, if we think, we think being. We cannot deny the thinkability of being without thinking being in the very denial, and thus establishing it.

1075. The following propositions are corollaries of this teaching:

I. The idea of being, if it is the constitutive element of any

---

[27] The Pyrrhonists who, according to Sextus, admitted *appearances* would have been in contradiction with themselves if it were true, as Aenesidemus says, that they doubted about everything, including *being*: *Immo neque verum neque falsum, neque ENS neque NON ENS, sed idem, ut sic dicatur, non potius verum esse quam falsum: aut probabile potius quam improbabile: aut ens, quam non ens: aut tum quidem tale, alias vero aliusmodi: aut uni tale, mox alteri etiam non tale* [Indeed nothing is true or false, nothing is ENS or NOT ENS. All is the same so that nothing is true rather than false, or probable rather than improbable, or ens rather than not ens, or something at one moment and something else at another, or something relative to one thing which it is not to another]. This teaching, expounded by Aenesidemus in bk. 1 of the eight he wrote on the system of Pyrrho, is quoted by Photius in *Biblioth.*, c. 212.

idea whatsoever that we have,[28] must be the *unchangeable* element in every idea. Every other element can cease to be present to the mind.

1076. II. If the conception of being is *unchangeable* and the other elements in any of our ideas[29] changeable, differences of opinion can never be related to the idea of being. They can refer only to the determinations attributed to being, or to the subsistence of particular beings.

1077. III. For the same reason, when we say that the mass of people form inexact concepts of things, or when we note imprecision or some other defect in anyone's ideas, we never intend, nor can we intend, to criticize the idea of being or of ens, which is invariable and essential and the point of convergence for all who think. Our strictures are always concerned with the other elements which form part of the ideas which we are criticizing.

Article 4

The second sceptical doubt:
'How can we perceive something different from ourselves?'

§1. *Reply*

1078. The intuition of being, and even the conception of *some undetermined thing*,[30] is a simple, undeniable FACT offering no succour to the illusion and deception feared by sceptics (cf. 1069, 1070). Here we are dealing not with a judgment, but with a factual intuition lacking affirmation or denial — only the possibility of denial or affirmation is seen.

But when I think something, without determining further the object of my thought, I conceive two cases in which this 'something' is possible: it may be either in me, or outside me.

---

[28] I have shown that the idea of being can exist in us on its own (cf. vol. 2, 412).

[29] Even in those of sceptics.

[30] This phrase is perfectly synonymous with *some undetermined ens*.

But then sceptics go on to say that it is impossible for me to be aware of something outside me because I can never go outside myself.

1079. Perhaps what the sceptic says is true. At least let us take it momentarily for granted that we cannot verify with certainty whether anything exists outside ourselves.

What I am affirming here, however, is limited to this: I can conceive and imagine something outside myself. I am not ascertaining whether what I conceive is truly outside myself or not. Nevertheless, from the moment I ask: 'Does some ens exist outside of me', I already conceive the notion of some possible ens both outside and inside me. We need to remember the definition of possibility. When I say that an ens can be outside myself, I am simply affirming that I can think of an object different from me and outside me even if I am unable to verify whether it is truly outside me.

When sceptics, therefore, deny that I can be aware of an ens outside myself, their very denial shows that they, too, possess at least the concept of an ens outside or inside me, and different from or identical with me.

But the perception of being in all its universality contains nothing more than this concept.

When I think an undetermined ens, I neither think nor affirm that something truly exists outside myself. I only conceive that this is possible. In a word, I simply possess the notion of *different* and *equal*, of *outside* and *inside*, without applying it through the affirmation or denial of anything whatsoever.

The sceptics' objection, 'How can you know something different from yourself or outside yourself?', leaves the idea of being totally undisturbed. It even establishes and presupposes this idea, and by doing so shows that it stands apart from any assault. The sceptics themselves admit it, therefore, as something alien to controversy and outside discussion.

This confirms my previous observation that no one, not even sceptics, can put the idea of being in all its universality under attack in any argument whatsoever. This idea is presupposed and tacitly admitted by everyone as beyond dispute and as prior and superior to discussion because it is simply the possibility of discussion itself, a possibility confirmed when discussion takes place.

[1079]

§2. *Continuation.* — *Further clarification of the notion of object*

1080. The teaching developed in the previous number is re-assumed in a proposition already established by me: 'Being in all its universality is the *object* of the understanding' (cf. vol. 2, 539–557).

When, and in so far as, I consider an entity, it is the object of my consideration.

Whatever the thing may be, the fact that it is an object means that it is considered by me in itself, without any relationship with me or others.

This is a simple description of the way in which we mentally conceive. When I say that I think an entity, I say that I am thinking the entity in itself (in so far as it is) without relationship with anything else.[31]

There is no doubt, therefore, that in analysing the thought of 'something' we discover that what is thought stands before us independently of its relationship with us. When I think of this object I do not think that it may be something in me, or of me, because I am not thinking of myself in any way whatsoever.

If I am not thinking that the thing is in me, but in itself, it follows that I possess the notion of things as they are in themselves. I may indeed err in applying this notion, but this does not detract from my really thinking the possibility of the thing in itself, independently of me.

It cannot be objected that I deceive myself with such a notion. It cannot be said that I only imagine I have the notion of something different from myself, or equal to me. If I did not have it, as I said, I could not on the one hand speak of it, nor on the other hand be contradicted. If I did not have it, I could not deceive myself.

---

[31] We must make no mistake about this fact. It is indeed the case that what we *positively* know in things depends upon an action exercised over us by these things. Our act of understanding, however, is such that we conceive the *thing* itself, the *ens* itself that does the action, as a result of the *action* we experience. This is what I mean by *conceiving the thing in itself*, not in relationship with ourselves.

Anyone calling such a notion into doubt, therefore, is certainly mistaken about the object of his doubt. If he understood what it was, he would realise that he is attempting to doubt what cannot be doubted. The sceptics' arsenal could perhaps inflict damage on the proposition, 'I know that an object subsists outside myself', but it cannot harm this next proposition: 'I understand and conceive perfectly the meaning of "an object different from, and outside myself".'

But, as we said, the conception of being does not include the first of these two propositions; only the second is present in some way in the conception. Conceiving being means 'conceiving something undetermined in itself', and consequently not in me. Implicit in my conception, therefore, is the notion of something different from me. What I possess is without doubt an *object* of thought, different by nature from what is purely *subject*.

§3. *Important corollaries*

1081. The following are corollaries of what has been said:

I. The idea of being in all its universality is that idea through which we think the thing in itself.

Thinking something in itself means thinking it as independent of the subject, that is, independent of *ourselves*. When we think something as independent of ourselves, we think it as having a mode of existence different from our own (subjective). The idea of being, therefore, constitutes our possibility of going outside ourselves, as it were. It establishes the possibility of our thinking things different from ourselves.

1082. II. It is absurd, therefore, to ask how we can go outside ourselves, or what is the bridge enabling us to pass from ourselves to things different from us. Metaphorical expressions such as 'going outside' and 'communicating bridge' confuse the sense and make the question impossible to resolve. We are searching for a material or mechanical solution to a purely spiritual fact. We cannot go outside ourselves; no 'bridge' can be set up between us and that which is not us. We have to reduce the question to its proper terms and see it transformed in them.

The human being thinks of things as they are in themselves. This is the fact. He may or may not deceive himself with these thoughts of his, but his thought itself is such that its objects are present to him in themselves, that is, as objects, and not as subjects. This comes about as follows.

The innate idea of being in all its universality forms human intelligence. Possessing this idea is equivalent to possessing the possibility of seeing things in themselves. Human beings, therefore, have in some way innate in themselves this communicating 'bridge', if we want to use such a phrase, because they perceive ens in itself. Ens is the most common and essential quality of all things, which makes them what they are, independent of ourselves and separate from us subjects.[32]

From the first moment of its existence, therefore, the intelligent spirit has an aptitude for thinking things as they are in themselves, and not as they are in us. Our spirit has the concept of this diversity, this exteriority, or better this *objectiv*ity of things. We still have to see how the spirit can pass from conceiving a thing merely *possible* in itself to something really *subsisting* in itself and not in the spirit; here, we can deceive ourselves. But this is another question, which will be answered by seeing whether the human spirit can have any sure sign of something different from itself and outside its body. For the moment we state without doubt that the human spirit can simply think things. The innate idea of being in all its universality, by its own proper nature, makes the human spirit apt for this.

[32] The phrase 'outside ourselves' expresses some relationship with things exterior to our bodies, as we have said (cf. vol. 2, 834 ss.). It is equivalent to the other expression, 'different from our body'. The question: 'How can we be sure of what is   *outside* ourselves?' was engendered by sensistic philosophy and soon applied to spiritual matters. This application to spiritual things of metaphors taken from sense experience, a habit introduced by the sensists, accustomed us to phrases such as: 'All our thought went outside ourselves.' At this point transcendentalism appeared. Kant no longer asked: 'How can we be sure of what is *outside* ourselves?' (that is, outside our bodies), but generalised by applying the question to the spirit. He asked: 'How can we be sure of the objects of our spirit?', that is, 'How can we be sure of what is *different* from ourselves?' This final question gave rise to *critical scepticism*, which we are refuting here.

Article 5

The third sceptical doubt:
'Perhaps the spirit communicates its own forms
to what it sees, altering and transforming things
from what they are?'

1083. The sceptic will press his point, granting perhaps that
the human understanding has the capacity of thinking things
objectively and hence as they are in themselves, as we have
said. On the other hand, while conceding that the understanding can prescind from relationships expressing difference or
non-difference from the thinking subject, or expressing an
inside or outside to the thinking subject, he may ask whether
this property itself is subjective? If so, it is a pure form imposed
on things by the subject itself.

§1. *Reply*

1084. Let us imagine that this sceptical doubt is true, and that
the subject communicates to the things perceived a form which
differs from the form they have in themselves. It follows that
our apperception is not genuine and has no power to provide us
with certain knowledge of things.

My reply is that this doubt, even if conceivable relative to the
sense perceptions of our body, cannot be applied to the intuition our spirit has of being, or ens.

It is true, of course, that our bodily organs are moulded and
configured in a specific way, and play their part in any effect
produced in them. Such an effect, however, is the result not of
one, but of two concomitant causes: the external agent, and the
nature, quality and disposition of the organs themselves (cf. vol.
2, 878–905).

But to draw an analogy between what happens in corporeal
perception and what could happen in the direct, spiritual intuition of being in all its universality is contrary to correct philosophical method, and leads to the very error that we are
opposing. This error would never have occurred if *analogies*

had been set aside completely and attention had been concentrated directly upon the object of the spiritual intuition we are considering, that is, upon being in all its universality.

Anyone examining being in all its universality will notice immediately the contradiction in terms when we say that such being could be a production of our subjective mind, or something informed and determined by the mind itself. *Being in all its universality* means *that which is exempt from any form or mode of being*, whatever its genus or nature.

1085. Analysis of the sceptical supposition we have hypothetically granted shows that it includes two forms or modes of being: 1. that of the thing in itself, unknown to us; 2. that of the thing in so far as it is perceived by us, a mode which, according to the sceptics, emanates from us as perceivers, and is known to ourselves alone.

These two modes of anything — the one *real*, the other *appare*nt, the one necessarily unknown, the other known to us — are both possible, that is, thinkable by us. But note that we say *thinkable*, not *verifiable*. Let us grant for the moment that I cannot know if these two modes really exist in the thing. This means that I cannot *verify them* in nature. But I can know that they could exist, that is, I can *think them*. The sceptics, in fact, by proposing their doubt, already presuppose that I can think both the *apparent* and the *real* mode of anything. If I am to doubt whether the *mode* that I see in something is not real, but different from what is real, the concept of the possibility of the two modes has to be granted, that is, they have to be thought. But this supposition has no possible application whatsoever to the idea of being.

The *idea* of being in all its universality contains no judgment on the *mode* of being and, as completely undetermined, is receptive, with perfect impartiality and indifference, to any one of all the thinkable modes of being. And because the *mode* is thinkable but, according to the fears of the sceptics, is necessarily hidden, it too can be received by the unlimited universal nature of being.

It is absurd, therefore, that being in all its universality, intuited by our mind, can possess a mode or form determined by the nature of our mind, to which it presents itself divested of all modes. Such a doubt cannot originate in the mind of anyone considering the proper character of being in all its universality. We repeat: this being has neither mode nor form, but constitutes the possibility of all the modes and forms which we think and imagine.

1086. This property of the idea of being forms our intelligence; it is what I call *undetermination* and *universality* (cf. vol. 2, 428, 434). It also forms and proves the perfect *immateriality* of our intelligence.

§2. *Corollaries*

1087. Hence the following corollaries:

I. If *myself*, that is, the subject, is perfectly determined (anything subsisting in the real mode must be *determined*), and if BEING intuited naturally by the subject is perfectly *undetermined*, it follows that being, an *essentially objective* conception, cannot be called a *subjective* conception. It constitutes the OBJECT of the spirit and differs from the spirit itself (the SUBJECT), which is the contrary of the object [*App.*, no. 3].

Similarly, if *myself* is limited and *particular*, while BEING, naturally intuited by us, is unlimited and *universal*, *being* is not an effect or emanation of the spirit. The spirit, as a nature disparate from being, is incapable of causing and producing it.

1088. II. If *being* is the only idea we have in our spirit by nature, and all other ideas are *acquired*, it follows that our spirit adds to things only the concept of *being*. Being, however, is justified of itself because it is without any particular mode or form. Our spirit therefore (in so far as it is intellective) adds no mode or form to the things it perceives.

The subject does not falsify the things it perceives because it neither adds anything to them nor changes them; it perceives them exactly as they *present*[33] themselves.

---

[33] As I said, *intelligence* perceives things just as they *present* themselves without changing or falsifying them. I did not say, however, that things *present* themselves just as they are. Things are *presented* to our intelligence by internal and external sense in the first place, and we are entitled to ask if feeling *presents* them without altering, falsifying, restricting and limiting

Intelligence, therefore, is not a fallacious, deceitful faculty when it intuits being in all its universality or any other of its perceptions; it is essentially sincere, essentially truthful.

1089. III. This shows the foolishness of the sceptics' unease about *reason*, and the futility of their search for a *critique* of *reason* as though there could be something above reason that were not *reason*, yet could judge reason. *Reason*, or better *intelligence*, cannot be transcended by reasoning. In this sense, a *transcendental philosophy* is intrinsically absurd and repugnant.

It is a blatant contradiction to affirm that, because reason can be limited to some particular form, doubt about reason's deceptiveness could be above reason. What faculty enables us to think the possibility of another form different from that of reason? Only a superior reason with a more extended form could embrace both the form of reason and some other form. In this case, reason is simultaneously more and less extended than it actually is. But reason is one only. It is, therefore, less and more extended at the same time.

All these things show Kantianism to be founded upon the play of the imagination which first creates for itself a limited reason which it then judges and criticises. It is not reason as complete which judges and causes doubt. Complete reason embraces not only the imaginary, criticised faculty, but also the criticising faculty. Reason embraces the whole possibility of things.

them according to its own form and nature. But these are questions that I shall deal with later when I speak about the certainty of our materiated knowledge, that is, of knowledge as a mixture of matter and form. At the moment, I am speaking simply of pure, solely intellective, *formal* knowledge. Relative to this kind of knowledge, I think I have shown quite clearly against the *critical school* that the intelligent spirit possesses no restrictive form with which it may alter and falsify the things it perceives. It has only one, unlimited form. This is *the form of all possible forms*, totally undetermined and indifferent, and hence perfectly apt to receive all forms. It is impartial, without fraud or deceit, if I may put it that way. This utterly universal and genuine form is TRUTH itself, as I have shown (cf. 1062–1064).

[1089]

Article 6

The confutation of the sceptics is re-affirmed

1090. From what has been said it is clear that we should consider the famous question, 'How can an ens perceive something different from itself?', as alien to the discussion about knowledge and human certainty. We cannot plumb the depths of this question without exceeding the limits of solid knowledge.

The legitimate method of sound philosophy requires attentive observation of facts, which have to be classified and ordered, and reduced, as far as possible, to some primordial fact on which all the rest depend. Anyone who remains unsatisfied after discovering this primordial fact, and imagines that he has to carry on searching for some further explanation, leaves himself open to the danger of endless, vain hypotheses or sterile speculation. As a final step, he will also throw a suffocating blanket of scepticism over every other aspect of knowledge simply because he has not succeeded in finding something which, because it does not exist, he should never have looked for.[34]

1091. In our discussion, the primordial fact is the intuition of being in all its universality. This intuition draws us to an act terminating beyond ourselves as *subjects*, and ending in an undetermined *objects*.

The way in which we see being in all its universality as something in itself, objectively and independently of ourselves, is another incontrovertible fact. When this has been recognised, the whole difficulty experienced in explaining innumerable, particular facts is lifted. I am speaking about the difficulty

---

[34] I refer to the *final logical reason* presented to us by the fact of our first intuition. In the logical order, there can be no reason beyond this, although there can be other kinds of reasons (final, ontological reasons) in whose series we never attain the vision of the final reason. But we do see the final reason in a series of logical reasons because this is essential to *reason*. St. Augustine's celebrated phrase, *Quidquid super illam (rationalem creaturam) est, iam Creator est* [Whatever is superior to that (the rational creature) is *ipso facto* the Creator], has to be understood of this rational order.

arising from the question: 'How can we perceive something different from ourselves?'

The intuition of being in all its universality shows the possibility of seeing things in themselves, and actually constitutes the potency and act of this vision precisely because being, when intuited, is intuited in itself.

Wanting to explain this *primary fact* by means of yet another preceding fact in the same logical order is as intemperate as wanting to simplify further a number already reduced to unity, that is, to its first, simple element.

1092. Sceptics abuse this process by reasoning along the following lines: 'We cannot understand how an ens can perceive something different from itself. When a human being or any other intellective ens, seems to perceive something different from itself, we have to say that it only perceives something apparently different from itself. In reality, it does not perceive anything different from itself; it perceives itself and nothing more.'

In this kind of reasoning we see *theory* assailing and destroying *fact*; *ignorance* erasing *truth*.

My reply to the sceptics runs as follows. You say that we conceive being as different from ourselves in appearance only; in reality it is not different from us. But if, as you say, being *appears* to me as different from myself, I must *conceive* it as different from me. *Appearing* to me means *being conceived* by me. Note that I am not affirming that this being which I perceive in itself is different from or identical with me. I am simply saying that I *conceive* it as *different* from me. I am establishing the fact which you yourselves grant me. There is only one difference between us: the use we make of the fact we both admit. I say that if I conceive being as something different from myself, I have the faculty of conceiving things different from me. I do in fact conceive one thing in this way, and in it and with it conceive all other things. I am not asking whether this faculty of mine is deceptive. It is enough for me to affirm that my mind has an object independent of itself, whatever the truth or falsehood of this object. You begin by establishing, prior to every fact, that it is impossible for my mind to go outside itself and conceive something as independent of itself. You go on to conclude that being, conceived as different from the mind, cannot be different from the mind which, therefore, deceives itself. But can't you see that you have thus overstepped the limits of the question? The difficulty, and the question itself, consists simply in knowing whether the mind conceives anything different from itself. We are not asking if what it conceives corresponds or not to its conception. In declaring that it does not correspond, you grant that its conception terminates in something outside itself and different from itself. The object, as conceived by the mind, is not the mind itself. You cannot therefore deny the nature of this conception nor, in this case, distinguish *conceiving* from *appearing*; here, *appearing* is *conceiving*. Moreover, saying that the object, in so far as it is not conceived by the mind, does not correspond to the concept the mind has of it, is to pass judgment on something not conceived, and consequently totally unknown. You have exceeded the limits of your capacity.

1093. However, let this pass for now. I want to follow you in your imaginings and hypotheses. Let us grant, therefore, that the object conceived by the mind is not different from the mind itself, that is, from the perceiving subject. In this case, doesn't the *subject* itself, when you think it, become the *object* of your thought? When something is the object of our thought, therefore, it does not change its nature. Notwithstanding its status as object, it still remains what it was before. It can remain *subject*, and nevertheless be simultaneously the *object* of our thought.

If this is so, the phrase, 'The mind thinks things different from itself', can only mean that it thinks things as its objects. But how can these two expressions, 'thinking things different from itself' and 'things being objects of its thought', be synonymous?

Object of thought means that something is present to us in itself. 'Something in itself' means 'something in its own existsence'; and since existing and being present is different from acting, the *object* of thought is essentially something different from us in so far as we are thinking.

This is true even when I think about myself. In that act I, the subject, become the object of my thought, and in thinking about myself I consider myself in so far as I exist in me, and no more. The essence, therefore, of thought is that it terminate in an *object*, that is, in something different from the *thinking subject* as such. Ens, as the object of thought, that is, as different from the subject, cannot bring the authority and veracity of thought into question. On the contrary, we are so imbued with conceiving things different from ourselves that we cannot even conceive ourselves intellectually without considering ourselves as objectivised and different from the actually thinking subjects.

1094. The sceptics' arguments would be valid for other entia, if there were any, furnished with a manner of mental conception totally different from our own. These entia would have to conceive things not in their objective existence, but as identical with themselves as conceiving subjects. An intellective ens of this nature could affirm on behalf of them all: 'We conceive all things as part of ourselves. But that is impossible. Rather, we should be prepared to believe that things conceived in this way are created in the very act by which we conceive them. These conceptions of ours cannot possibly be true.'

Such a doubt, however, could never in fact arise in the minds of one of these entia. It could be prompted only in an ens possessing the faculty of seeing things as they are. Sceptics themselves, therefore, must have the faculty to conceive something different from themselves in order to bring the existence of this faculty into doubt. But a *conception* which does not exit from the subject is a concept in conflict with itself. It is at one and the same time a conception and not a conception.

1095. Finally, the legitimacy of thought is evident of itself if its nature is considered attentively. This nature consists in thinking things in themselves, as we do in fact think them. It is identical with thinking things in their own existence which, in turn, is called the *truth* of our conception.

In brief, according to the sceptics, things have two existences: 1. as perceived by us; 2. as not perceived by us. The *perceived existence* is existence *in se*, objective existence, and hence concerns the way in which things appear to us objectively. According to the sceptics, this perceived existence is false and illusory. The *real* existence, that is, as not perceived by us, must therefore be existence identical with ourselves precisely because we perceive only subjectively.

But these propositions are obviously contradictory. If *existence in itself* is perceived by us, and *existence imagined as subjective* is not perceived by us, is not the true existence that which we perceive? And the false or rather null existence, that is, the chimera brought to birth by the sceptics themselves, is it not the existence we do not perceive?[35]

Article 7

The argument developed so far is contained in the teaching of Christian tradition

1096. We have resolved the three fundamental doubts of the sceptics through the analysis of *truth*, or *idea of being*, which provides three characteristics, each of which is suitable for refuting one of the doubts. These three characteristics of being intuited by us are: 1. its *simplicity* (it represents itself alone); 2. its *objectivity*, and 3. its perfect *undetermination*.

In its *simplicity*, it neither represents anything outside itself, nor contains any judgment; its presence to us is a *fact*. In other words, it cannot be the source of illusion or deceit. The first doubt is resolved.

In its *objectivity*, it is different from and contrary to the

---

[35] The sceptics' error arises also because they confuse *existence* with the *specific essence* of anything. When I say that I affirm something as it *exists in itself*, I do *not* mean that I perceive it in its real *specific essence*. Perfect objectivity consists only in perceiving the first of these two things, that is, *existence*. In other words, it consists in applying the *idea of being in all its universality* to things. This idea is the source of objectivity and indeed that which properly speaking constitutes *objectivity*. On the other hand, our perception of the *essence* of things could be mixed with something *subjective*. This is true especially of our perception of bodies, as we have seen in volume 2. We repeat, therefore that the *known essence* of anything is not always the intact, pure, *real, specific essence* of that thing. Something can be lacking to known *essences*, as in the case of generic essences (cf. vol. 2, 646 ss.) or *nominal* essences especially. Some known essences can also contain subjective elements which, however, it is always possible for us to discern and separate from the objective element, thanks to our faculty of objective perception.

subject which perceives it. It constitutes the subject's intellect, that is, a power without subjective reference which sees things outside place and time. The second doubt, about the intellect's capacity for getting outside itself, is resolved. This doubt is founded upon a metaphor taken from bodily images which, when translated into appropriate expressions, is proved meaningless. The doubt then collapses of its own accord without need of further reflection.

In its *undeterminedness*,[36] being cannot determine anything, although it can receive determinations furnished by the things presented to it. It is impossible, therefore, and contrary to fact, to assert that our knowledge of things can receive from our intellect a subjective mode or particular form different from that which things have in themselves.

Finally, I showed that these doubts could not have arisen in the mind of any philosopher who had followed the path of facts and rejected a false method of vain hypotheses and vague, confused creations of the imagination.

1097. But, I am happy to say, my confutation of modern sceptics is not original. It is contained in the deposit of ancient Christian tradition, together with the method which starts from primordial, secure facts, and reasons about them. Abandoning that method, sophists[37] have plunged us, all unawares, into

[36] Here, I am consistently referring to ideal being, that is, to the idea of being, not of subsistent being.

[37] I have said elsewhere that the great merit of modern times, which began with Leonardo and Galileo, is to have publicised and popularised the method dependent upon facts. The defect of modern times lies in not practising this method. Many authors are clearly intent on following it and are to be commended for their resolution, although unwittingly they often abandon it. The majority, however, make fools of themselves with their endless boasting about following a method which they practise in appearance only. Their tasteless pride will certainly be mocked in the near future, if not altogether forgotten, by those who come after them. For myself, I am content to note that we do not always carry out what we believe we want and believe we do; much less do we actually carry out what we say we want. As far as arguing according to this method is concerned, I am prepared to affirm that knowing the method in principle is one thing; understanding how to use it in fact is another. We should not give credence too easily to those who insist they know how to follow it; we should first check their ability to do so before entrusting ourselves to beautiful, but possibly empty words.

ignorance, doubt and every kind of mental unease. Proof of this will be found in a brief exposition of Christian philosophy about the nature of the knowledge of truth, and of the truth's relationship with the spirit.

1098. According to this philosophy, the method to be followed in coming to understand the soul requires us: 1. to start from the *fact* of knowledge; and 2. to proceed from the examination of this *fact* to establish what the soul can or cannot do, that is, to decide its properties, faculties, and so on.[38]

In this way the philosophy we are examining moves from the same point as ourselves, that is, from the fact of the existence of knowledge which, on analysis, is reduced to perfect simplicity, that is, to the fact of being in all its universality which cannot contain any illusion in itself.

Analysing this fact of intellective knowledge, antiquity found, as we have, that it was primarily *objective*: 'The act of cognition,' says St. Thomas, 'extends to things outside the knower.'[39] This is the primordial fact. St. Thomas and those like him did not say, as the moderns do: 'This fact is impossible and is, therefore, only an appearance.' They said: 'This fact exists and is, therefore, true and real.' They did not ask: 'How can the knower go outside himself?' but: 'We have found that the knower goes outside himself. This is, therefore, possible.'

1099. They carried on reasoning in the following way. Knowledge, if it is *objective*, is not confined to the subject, but considers things in their own existence, not in the existence of the subject as though they were modifications of the subject. Knowledge, therefore, must be *universal*, that is, able to extend to all things which have or can have their own proper existence,

---

[38] St. Thomas establishes this method in *De Verit.*, 10, 8. The sceptical followers of transcendental philosophy do the opposite. Instead of saying: 'The mind does this; therefore it has the power to do it,' they say: 'The mind does not have the power to do this; therefore it can do it only apparently.' They arbitrarily and hypothetically restrict the power of the mind, and on the basis of these arbitrary assumptions declare the facts connected with the mind to be *appearances*. What they dare not deny plainly and clearly, they deny by equivocation. If the fact exists, it is real and valid; to grant a fact of this kind, and declare it worthless, is a contradiction, as we have said over and over again.

[39] *S.T.*, I, q. 84, art. 2.

and hence to every possible thing. They then concluded that bodies cannot know because they are determined to a sole, particular form; the intelligent subject, on the other hand, must be immaterial, that is, void of every bodily determination and restrictive form. St. Thomas affirms: 'Through matter, the form of any thing is determined and restricted to a particular being. It is clear, therefore, that the concept of *knowledge* is precisely the opposite of the concept of *materiality*. It is equally impossible also for things which receive their form only materially, such as plants, to be intelligent.'[40]

Moreover, if we examine the nature of intellective knowledge, we see that the characteristic of *universality*, which is comprised in that of *objectivity* and revealed as a result of the analysis of objectivity, is also seen directly. We know not only *different*, but *contrary* things. This led antiquity to affirm that the mind was capable of perceiving all things (*intellectus omnia cognoscit*). And indeed whoever can perceive the 'Yes' and 'No' of anything is not determined towards nothing. There is no middle case between two contraries to determine anyone who perceives. This was a fact noted even in classical philosophy. Empedocles, who had considered it only imperfectly, thought he could explain it by supposing the soul to be composed of the elements of all things. I say that he had observed it imperfectly because he had restricted himself to noting that 'the soul knows different things'. He overlooked the fact that the soul 1. knows not only the elements of things, but things themselves; 2. knows not only *different* but *contrary* things, and consequently is disposed to know equally well both the *yes* and *no* of anything whatsoever.

1100. Empedocles' error (I am speaking of his teaching as Aristotle seems to have understood it) is common to all materialists who imagine that ideas are similar in substance to things. The idea of light, for example, would be formed of some kind of phosphorus (as the Englishman, Hook, maintained), and so on for other ideas.

As far as I know antiquity did not dispute this aspect of the matter with Empedocles. But it did rebuke him for imperfect observation of the universality of knowledge, and especially

[40] *Ibid.*

for the first of his two imperfect observations by which he overlooked the fact that knowledge enables us to know not only the principles of things, but things themselves. Philosophers of antiquity maintained, in reply to Empedocles, that if the soul were to be composed of all the (physical) principles which make up things (this would indeed be the case if everything had to be known by means of its own likeness), the soul itself would have to result from as many tiny bodies or entia as there are knowable bodies and things, as well as from the principles of bodies. Consequently Anaxagoras, followed by Aristotle, maintained against Empedocles that the soul had to be immaterial, unmixed with anything else, and totally free from corporeal determinations if it were to be capable of knowing all things.

We are dealing, therefore, with a single fact, admitted by all: the *universality* of knowledge. Some later Greek authors explained this fact differently from their predecessors. All agreed, however, that the universality of knowledge required a *univer*sal power in the soul, that is, a power which could extend to all possible things. The earlier philosophers conceived the universal power only in a material way, and hence imagined it as made up of all the elements; the later philosophers, realising the futility of this explanation, saw that the opposite must be true. According to them, this power of the soul was universal in so far as it was not composed of anything coming from *determined* things. These philosophers affirmed this universality of the soul, therefore, as a power determined in itself to nothing, and hence capable of being determined in its effects. It thus gave rise to the knowledge of all possible things indifferently. This accounts for Aristotle's *tabula rasa*.

1101. In modern times, the opposite has taken place. The *fact* of universal knowledge has been declared impossible not because it could be denied (it could not), but because it is considered a deception. The presupposition of modern times requires a determined soul determining its own acts of knowledge. Such a process of reasoning is the effective annihilation of all good sense. Universal knowledge is first granted; then it is affirmed that the soul determines and limits its own knowledge, stamping it with the seal of universality. Such reasoning disregards the fact that predicating universality of knowledge is the opposite of determining and limiting it, and of rendering it *subjective*.

1102. St. Thomas says:

> Our intellect is ordered to the understanding of all things sensible and corporeal. Hence, it must be devoid of every corporal nature, just as the sense of sight is void of all colour precisely because it is made to perceive colours. If it had some kind of colour, it would be prevented from seeing other colours. In the same way, if the intellect possessed some determined nature, the congenital nature would prevent its knowing other natures."[41]

According to St. Thomas, the *universality* of knowledge is a fact rendering absurd Kant's restrictive forms. As we said, it is a clear contradiction to maintain that the *universality* of knowledge is the work of restrictive forms. The forms that produce universality do not restrict knowledge in any way; rather they remove every restriction and determination.

1103. Every error, however, is a camouflaged or mistaken truth, and in this case it is not difficult to see that Kant abused the truth of St. Thomas' principle: 'The intellect makes the species or ideas like itself because every agent produces what is similar to itself.'[42] But how did subjective forms take their origin from this badly understood truth?

It was first supposed and then affirmed that in communicating its own nature to ideas and giving them its form, the intellect furnished ideas with a particular, restrictive and subjective form. This supposition, the result of our modern materialism, resulted from taking the concept of form from corporeal forms, which are indeed restrictive and particular. For St.

---

[41] *De An.*, III, bk. 8. See also *S.T.*, I, q. 75, art. 2: *Quod (intellectus) potest cognoscere aliqua, oportet ut nihil eorum habeat in sua natura: quia illud quod inesset ei naturaliter, impedieret cognitionem aliorum. Sicut videmus, quod lingua infirmi, quae infecta est cholerico et amaro humore, non potest percipere aliquid dulce, sed omnia videntur ei amara* [For it (the intellect) to be able to know something, it must have nothing of what it knows in its nature. Anything naturally present to it would block its knowledge of other things. As we see, the tongue of a sick person, covered with bitter saliva of cholic, cannot taste anything sweet. Everything is bitter for it].'

[42] *Tales autem facit eas (intellectus agens species intelligibiles), qualis est ipse: nam omne agens agit sibi simile* (*C. Gentes.*, II, q. 76).

Thomas, however, the opposite is true. The form of which he speaks, with which the intellect informs its own perceptions and makes them like itself, is of a nature directly opposed to that of bodily form. It is a universal, not a particular form; it does not impose, but removes restrictions. The act by which the intellect communicates its own form to our perceptions is the very act by which its *universalises* them (cf. vol. 2, 490). In this way, the intellect considers things in their own proper, objective (not subjective) being. Hence St. Thomas affirms that the *immateriality* of this form constitutes the power of understanding.[43] This form is not, therefore, a *form* according to present-day understanding, as our moderns obviously consider it, but in the sense used by antiquity, which consists in the privation of every *form* understood in the modern sense. If the form of the intellect is universal, that is, perfectly *undetermined*, and hence perfectly indifferent to the perception of all possible beings, and such that this form is only the intuition of possibility itself,[44] then (and this is the conclusion of the writers of antiquity whom we have in mind) the intellect receives an unrestricted, *infinite* power.

St. Thomas says: 'The infinite is found in potency in our intellect' (the form of the intellect, because it is undetermined, has *per se* no actual knowledge of anything real, although it can have such knowledge). 'Hence, our intellect can never understand so many things that it cannot understand more again.' Again: 'The intellect knows the infinite in so far as the intellect is infinite according to the power it possesses' (its form). 'The intellect's power is infinite because… it is cognitive in relationship to what is universal…; consequently the intellect does not

[43] *Habet enim substantia animae humanae immaterialitatem; et, sicut ex dictis patet, ex hoc habet naturam intellectualem, quia omnis substantia immaterialis* (that is, devoid of restrictive and particular form) *est huiusmodi* ['The substance of the human soul possesses its own immateriality and therefore an intellectual nature, as we have made clear. Every immaterial substance' (that is, devoid of restrictive and particular form) 'is of this kind'] (*C. Gent.*, II, q. 7).

[44] *Intellectus respicit suum objectum secundum communem rationem entis, eo quo intellectus possibilis est, quo est omnia fieri* [The intellect, as the possible intellect by which all things come to be, regards its object according to the common notion of being] (*S. T.*, I, q. 79, a. 7).

terminate in some individual, but relative to itself[45] extends to infinite individuals.'[46]

1104. Having taken careful note of the fact that intellective knowledge is universal and infinite because limitlessly extended to everything, they also realised that it is and must be *necessary*: 'The form of what is understood is furnished at the level of intellect with universality, immateriality and unchangeableness. This becomes clear when we observe the activity itself of the intellect which understands *universally* and *necessarily*.'[47]

1105. Provided we note carefully that *universality* is only the *possibility* of anything, it is easy to see that the two qualities, *necessity* and *universality*, spring from one another. What is *necessary* has its origin in what is *possible*: we call *necessary* that which unites in itself every possibility in such a way that anything contrary to it is impossible.

We can see this in the following proposition: 'My friend Maurice is either alive or not alive.' This is a *necessary* proposition because the two contrary cases, alive or not alive, permit no

---

[45] He says 'relative to itself', because the intellect never attains to the knowledge of infinite individuals — individuals themselves never exist in an infinite number. Moreover, the intellect, although not limited *per se*, is limited by *sense*, which *presents* the intellect with the signs of entia the intellect then comes to know, as I have indicated in my *Saggio sui confini dell'umana ragione* (*Teodicea*, 150 ss.). This truth, that sense *presents* the intellect with the real terms of its activity, also forms part of St. Thomas' teaching. He notes that the *universality* of form and of the intellect, which consists in a lack of particular forms, is insufficient to allow us to know real things. *Ex hoc nondum* (that is, because the form of the intellect is universal or immaterial) *(intellectus) habet quod assimiletur huic vel illi rei determinatae, quod requiritur ad hoc quod anima nostra hanc vel illam rem determinate cognoscat. — Remanet rerum cognoscibilium a nobis, quae sunt naturae rerum sensibilium: et has quidem determinatas naturas rerum sensibilium* PRAESENTANT *nobis phantasmata, etc.* ['Hence' (that is, because the form of the intellect is *universal or immaterial*), '(the intellect) is still void of what assimilates it to one determined thing or another. But this is needed if our soul is to know in a determined way one thing or another... The intellective soul, therefore, remains in potency to determined likenesses of things we can know, that is, to the natures of sensible things. It is the phantasms which PRESENT us with the determined natures of sensible things, etc.'] (*C. Gentes*, II, q. 77).

[46] *S.T.*, I, q. 86, art. 2.

[47] *Itin. mentis in Deum.*

middle case. Necessity, therefore, is that which includes within itself every possibility in such a way that nothing contrary is possible. But the form of the intellect is precisely *total possibility*. The intellect, therefore, understands *necessarily*, that is, it sees the relationship between possibility and everything understood, and its intellection becomes necessary by means of the relationship.

1106. This explains the insistence of the Fathers of the Church, who maintain that the intelligent spirit is furnished with an *uncircumscribed light* (one without any particular, restrictive form) or, equivalently, furnished with a form which is 1. *universal*, undetermined, immaterial, infinite (words which have more or less the same meaning); and 2. *necessary* (hence, unchangeable, and per se everlasting).

Moreover, the Fathers saw and noted *unity* in the *universality* and *necessity* of knowledge. *Universality* is founded upon the knowledge provided by a single species of some thing or quality multiplied infinitely in an infinite number of individuals. Consequently, the *unity* of the species brings together and unites the multiplicity of things. Similarly, *necessity* is formed only by the one supreme species of form which represents the most common quality (if we may call it that) of things. In other words, it is formed by being, which unites and reduces to unity all particular possibilities.

As a result of their analysis of human knowledge, Church writers discovered that in its final form[48] knowledge was perfectly

---

[48] This explains St. Thomas' affirmation: *Si attendantur rationes universales sensibilium, omnes scientiae sunt de necessariis, si autem attendantur ipsae res, sic quaedam scientia est de necessariis, quaedam vero de contingentibus* [If we consider the universal notions of sensible things, all knowledge is about what is necessary; but if we consider the things themselves, some knowledge is about what is necessary, some about what is contingent] (*S.T.*, I, q. 86, art. 3). This shows that for St. Thomas the *necessity* of our cognitions comes from their *universality*. However, this necessity is not total, but relative only to the *formal* part of our cognitions. He explains this at greater length as follows: *Necessitas consequitur rationem formae, quia ea, quae consequuntur ad formam, ex necessitate insunt. — Ratio autem universalis accipitur secundum abstractionem formae a materia particulari. Dictum est autem supra, quod per se et directe intellectus est universalium. — Sic igitur contingentia prout sunt contingentia, cognoscuntur directe quidem a sensu, indirecte autem ab intellectu* [Necessity results from the notion which

one, universal or uncircumscribed, *immaterial, infinite, necessary, unchangeable, eternal.*

1107. Having established this fact,[49] they concluded that it could not come from the feelings nor from our spirit, that is, from the subject.[50] It does not come from the senses because sensations have neither *unity, universality, necessity, unchangeableness,* nor any of the characteristics listed above. It does not come from ourselves as knowing subjects because we are limited, contingent and changeable, and cannot therefore give to others what we do not possess. The attributes of our knowledge are contrary to our own subjective attributes, and surpass in dignity not only our own power, but that of any finite being whatsoever.

1108. St. Augustine, having analysed intellective knowledge and found that it consists essentially in *judging*,[51] soon realised

governs the form, because things which follow as a result of the form are necessarily contained therein... A universal notion arises when a form is abstracted from some particular matter. But, as we said above, understanding is *per se* and directly about universals... Contingent things as such are known directly therefore by feeling, but indirectly by the intellect] (*ibid.*).

[49] Aristotle ridicules the method used by Plato in establishing his theory of ideas. It seemed to Aristotle that Plato, instead of starting from obvious facts and from what we know in order to explain what we do not know, began from what we do not know to explain what we do know. St. Thomas repeats the admonition, against which Plato would have had no difficulty in defending himself: 'It is ridiculous to bring in other *entia* as middle terms in order to know things which are evident, etc.' (*S.T.*, I, q. 84, art. 1). But St. Thomas' words could be applied more reasonably against Kant who hypothetically introduces unknown forms which are not only incapable of explaining the obvious fact of knowledge, but are contrary to it. Kant describes them as characteristically subjective and restrictive, although knowledge is characterised essentially by its objectivity and absoluteness.

[50] See the moving passage from the *Itinerarium* quoted in the footnote to 1087 [*App.*, no. 3] where both senses and spirit are excluded as sources of formal knowledge.

[51] In his *De Vera Religione* St. Augustine establishes this important proposition: the specific difference between the senses and intellect is the power of *judgment* possessed by the intellect, but not by the senses: *Iudicare de corporibus, non sentientis tantum vitae, sed etiam ratiocinantis est* [Judgment about bodies requires a being that reasons as well as feels] (29). From this principle he deduces that a judgment is hidden in all intellective knowledge, and discovers along with this truth that not all those who judge, judge equally well. Good judgment depends upon the art of judgment which

as he proceeded with the analysis that knowledge contains a fundamental *unity*, because no judgment can be made without *unity*. He concludes, therefore, that such knowledge cannot come from the senses because, as he says, 'no one, on examining a body, can... ever find it truly and simply *one*. All bodies change their appearance or their location, and are made up of parts, each in its own place, and divided and scattered in different spaces by means of these places. It is certain... that a true, first unity is understood and seen only with the mind, never with the eyes of the body or any other sense.'[52]

1109. The great masters of whom we have been speaking go on to show that the formal element of our intellective

he then undertakes to examine: *Sed quia clarum est eam (naturam iudicantem) esse mutabilem, quando nunc perita nunc imperita invenitur; tanto autem melius judicat quanto est peritior; et tanto est peritior quanto alicuius artis — particeps est; ipsius artis natura quaerenda est* [It is clear that judging is carried out by a changeable nature which sometimes possesses and sometimes lacks skill in judgment. The greater the skill, the better the judgment. The level of skill, however, depends on the level of the art of judgment... in the one who judges. What is the nature of this art, therefore?] (30). Having analysed the *art* of judgment, he discovers that it depends upon a *rule* superior to human beings, that is, on *truth*, which is essentially united with all intellects. Having thus purified and separated from the rest of knowledge the formal element (this rule, this first form, this *truth*) by which we judge, St. Augustine demonstrates its superiority to human beings. As independent of them, it is not *subjective*, but essentially objective and divine.

[52] Shortly after Locke, the problem arose: 'How does the soul unite several sensations in a single subject? (vol. 1, 66)'. We explained this fact by means of 1. the *identity* of space relative to the senses (vol. 2, 941 ss.) and 2. the unity of *being* relative to the spirit (vol. 2, 961 ss). Relative to the spirit, however, appropriate simplicity and unity are essential. This seems to have been recognised by all modern philosophers who also seem to accept without doubt that unity of perception does not spring from the external senses, but from the internal nature of our spirit. C. Vittore Bonstetten has this to say about the perception of a tree in his paper, *Saggio analitico sul fenomeno della sensazione* in the *Biblioth. universelle etc., rédigée... Genève* (March 1830): 'The action of the interior sense when modified by the organisation produces the feeling which then gives rise to the idea of the tree. It is the feeling which, on the canvas prepared by the external organ, chooses the rays designating the tree, and gives to the image of the tree that *totally spiritual unity*, entirely immaterial, which forms a single whole of the tree. By means of speech we can then move the whole tree around mentally, and from it form thoughts, relationships, abstractions and principles — in a word, everything that the spirit can produce through sensation.'

knowledge cannot be an emanation of our limited nature. The author of the *Itinerarium* argues from the *unchangeableness* of knowledge and the changeableness of our nature as follows:

> Because our mind is changeable, it cannot see truth, which shines *unchangeably*, except by means of another altogether unchangeable light. This light cannot be a changeable creature.[53]

St. Thomas uses the perfect *undetermination* and *universality* of formal knowledge to show that it cannot be the essence of some limited nature, that is, it cannot be any *finite, determined* being.

Neither the essence of angels nor that of human beings can emit from itself the undetermined, universal knowledge of which we are speaking.

> That by which we know anything must be like what is known. If, then, the angel's power were such that it could know all things of itself, this power would indeed be the likeness and act of all things

— which cannot, of course, be granted.

> It is, therefore, necessary for other intelligible species to be added in the role of likenesses to the intellective power of angels. By means of these likenesses angels can know what they come to understand.[54]

St. Thomas goes on to conclude it is impossible to make formal knowledge emanate from the *essence* itself of the spirit. This can be predicated only of God whose essence is infinite and the universal principle of all things.[55]

[53] *Sed cum ipsa mens nostra sit commutabilis, illam (veritatem) sic incommutabiliter relucentem non potest videre, nisi per aliquam aliam lucem omnino incommutabiliter radiantem, quam impossibile est esse creaturam mutabilem* (*Itin. ment. etc,* 3).

[54] *Si potentia angeli per seipsam cognosceret omnia, — esset similitudo et actus omnium. Unde oportet quod superaddantur potentiae intellectivae ipsius aliquae species intelligibiles, quae sint similitudines rerum intellectarum* (*S.T.,* I-II, q. 51, art. 1, ad 2).

[55] *Quaelibet creatura habet esse finitum ac determinatum. Unde essentia superioris creaturae etsi habet quamdam similitudinem inferioris creaturae, prout comunicant in aliquo genere, non tamen complete habet similitudinem*

This passage enables us to understand how St. Thomas' perspicacity foresaw the conclusion we have already reproved in modern critical philosophy which, by drawing the form of knowledge from the human spirit, 'makes a god of the human being'. This impotent, but always foolhardy human spirit will be the new god of the universe, like the king tragically begged from Jove by Aesop's frogs.

1110. St. Augustine, on the basis of his observation (observation is another point from which we must begin) that the form of knowledge is the *rule* with which we judge not only all other things, but even ourselves as *subjects*, deduces that formal knowledge cannot emanate from the essence of the subject. Subjects cannot be the cause or judge of such a rule, which in any case does not depend upon them. They have to receive it just as it is, and they must submit to it. This form, or supreme rule of judgment, is properly named *truth*.

> Since this *law* governing all that can be done is totally *unchangeable*, and since the human mind, granted the vision of this law, is capable of the change wrought by error, it is clear that there is a law superior to our mind, a law called TRUTH.

He goes on:

> When the soul feels that it cannot of itself judge the beauty and movement of bodies... it must realise that the nature according to which it judges, and about which it can form no judgment, is far superior to itself.

---

illius: quia determinatur ad aliquam speciem, praeter quam est species inferioris creaturae (hence, the essence of a creature cannot furnish knowledge of things). *Sed essentia Dei est perfecta similitudo omnium, quantum ad omnia quae in rebus inveniuntur, sicut universale principium omnium* (so that God alone can understand all things through his *essence*) ['Any creature whatsoever has only finite, determined being. The essence of a higher creature, therefore, has some kind of likeness to that of a lower creature because they communicate in some genus, but not a complete likeness. The higher creature is determined to some species beyond that of the lower creature' (hence, the essence of a creature cannot furnish knowledge of things). 'But God's essence, as the universal principle of all things, is the perfect likeness of all elements found in things' (so that God alone can understand all things through his *essence*)] (*S.T.*, I, q. 84, art. 2).

[1110]

Again:

> We ourselves, and all rational souls, judge rightly when we judge according to *truth*; and truth alone judges us when we adhere to it.[56]

Note that this truth, so superior to ourselves, according to which we judge things and by which we are judged, has nothing superior to itself by which it can be judged, and is the very form in which, according to St. Augustine, we *know* all things. This form in turn is the *idea of being in all its universality*, which we have discovered through our analysis of human acts of knowledge: 'If both of us see that what you say is true and what I say is true, where do we see this? I certainly do not see it in you, nor you in me. We both see it in the same immutable *truth* which is above our minds.'[57]

1111. Reasons of this kind stimulated the ancient sages to make it their first concern to show that human nature cannot be the cause of truth, and to rid the human race of the profound absurdity finally embraced by modern philosophy which has despoiled truth of its attributes and surrendered them to the human spirit. Making the changeable unchangeable and the unchangeable changeable is to set up mankind as a hideous idol. This is the work that the cunning ruler of darkness has been able to renew in the current light of Christian history. But those are safe from this error who listen attentively and lovingly to the great tradition of the Church which proclaims unceasingly and unanimously to human beings: 'Do not think that you yourself are the light.'[58]

---

[56] *Haec autem lex omnium artium cum sit omnino incommutabilis, mens vero humana, cui talem legem videre concessum est, mutabilitatem pati possit erroris, satis apparet supra mentem nostram esse legem, quae veritas dicitur. — Itaque cum se anima sentiat, nec corporum speciem motumque iudicare secundum seipsam, simul oportet agnoscat... praestare sibi eam naturam, secundum quam iudicat, et de qua iudicare nullo modo potest. — Ut enim nos et omnes animae rationales, secundum veritatem de inferioribus recte iudicamus, sic de nobis, quando eidem cohaeremus, sola ipsa veritas iudicat* (*De V. Relig.*, cc. 30, 31).

[57] *Conf.*, bk. 12, c. 25.

[58] St. Augustine, *In Ps.*: *Noli putare te ipsam esse lucem* [Do not think that you are your own light]. — *Dic quia tu tibi lumen non es* [Say that you are not light to yourself (St. Aug., Serm. 8, *De verbis Domini*).

[1111]

CHAPTER 2

Truth, or the idea of being, as the means of knowing all other things[59]

Article 1

The connection between what has been said and what follows

1112. So far I have considered the idea of being in itself, and have shown that it is an intuition immune from all sceptical doubt. I must now show how the total certainty of things rests upon this solid base of the intellectual world.

We must therefore consider the idea of being in its application to things.

We shall begin by considering its aptitude for application. And because the title 'truth' depends upon this aptitude, we shall make 'truth' the subject of this chapter.

---

[59] We naturally see being, but in order to know that this being is the light which makes us know all things, that is, *truth*, we have to turn our attention to being itself and, after much reflection, come to know its extraordinary property and relationship with all things, by which it makes them known and evident. Only when we have obtained this knowledge, can we say we know the *truth* shining in us. We conceive being therefore with a *direct*, natural act, but under its relationship with *truth* we conceive it only by an act of reflection, which does not come about until long after the former conception. St. Thomas notes perceptively that 'because ens falls within the concept of truth, but not vice versa, we cannot apprehend *truth* without apprehending the concept of *ens*. He continues: 'Similarly when we compare what is intelligible with ens: ens can be understood only because it is intelligible. However, ens can be understood without reflecting on its intelligibility. In the same way, *ens as understood* is truth. But it does not follow, that when we understand ens, we understand truth' (*S. T.*, I, q. 16, art. 3, ad 3).

Article 2

Different uses of the word 'truth'

§1. *Most general meaning of 'truth'*

1113. Individual authors, in giving various meanings to a word, may be guilty of improper use of language. The same cannot be said when different meanings depend upon mankind's use of a word. There would seem to be no impropriety here. Rather, there will be something common to all the different meanings. This common notion, found in all the various senses of the word, will be its most general meaning and the unique essence of whatever the word signifies. If we examine the different meanings normally given by common parlance to the word 'truth', we can see that its most extensive meaning, its general notion, and the unique essence properly indicated by it, is that of *exemplar*. I have therefore defined truth as the *exemplar of things*.[60]

§2. *Distinction between truth and true things*

1114. The concept of *exemplar* includes a relationship with what is drawn from the exemplar, that is, with its *copy*. The *copy* is 'true' when it is perfectly *like* its exemplar. Hence, we must distinguish between *truth* and *true things*: truth is the exemplar; things are true when they conform to their exemplar, that is, when they share in truth.

§3. *Meanings of the expression, 'truth of things'*

1115. We also speak of 'the truth of a thing', and mean the *likeness* of the thing with its exemplar. We use this meaning because the *likeness* of the thing with its exemplar is its *truth*;

[60] Cf. *Saggio sull'Idillio e sulla nuova letteratura italiana* (*Opusc. Filos.*, vol. 1, pp. 321 ss.). This meaning of the word 'truth' is clearly present in the writings of some authors; for example, in the following passage of Cicero: 'Truth overrides imitation in everything' (*De Orat.*, 3, 57). Here, *imitation* is the opposite of *truth*; *copy*, the opposite of *original* or exemplar.

through this truth, the thing is *true* and shares in the content of the exemplar from which it has been drawn.

To possess a clear concept of truth, therefore, we must first have in our mind an exact, clear concept of *likeness*. How superficial the mind of those philosophers who supposed that the *likeness* of things could easily be understood, and at the same time supposed that it was very difficult to indicate the origin of universal concepts, particularly of the truth of things (vol. 1, 180–187)! On the contrary, *likeness* is the only concept by which we understand how things are true or false. We must therefore examine this concept a little, profiting from what I have already established regarding the nature of the *likeness* of things.

1116. Any *object* whatsoever, even external, can be considered as an *exemplar*, provided we consider it in its relationship as norm or type of other beings which must be formed according to it and like it.

In this sense, we say that the whole of nature is an *exemplar* for the artist, who copies and portrays its different parts. The events of human society and patterns of behaviour are an *exemplar* for the tragic or comic poet. A book transposed into another language can be correctly called 'exemplar' relative to the translation, which must agree perfectly with the original text.

Hence, *nature* is the *truth* of works by artists who have imitated and copied her. So we say: 'This is a true portrait', 'There is much truth in this picture'. In the same way we say a tragic or comic scene fully presents the truth, if it resembles what happens in fact. St. Jerome, using a similar propriety of speech, says that having kept his translation in line with the Hebrew text, he has rendered it according to the Hebrew *truth*.[61]

---

[61] Cf. in his Proemium: *Quamquam mihi omnino conscius non sim, mutasse me quidpiam de hebraica veritate* [Although I am not at all conscious of having changed anything of the Hebrew truth]; in the letter to Paulinus: *Quamquam iuxta hebraicam veritatem utrumque de eruditis possit intelligi* [Although both learned interpretations can be understood according to the Hebrew truth].

§4. *Truth properly speaking means an idea*

1117. We must now turn our attention to an important observation.

I have shown elsewhere that external things, in so far as they exist outside our mind, cannot be compared with one another; each stands by itself. Their likeness or unlikeness is simply a relationship they have with the mind that perceives them.[62] This relationship consists in our perception of many real entia by means of one single idea or *species*. Thus, their likeness can be defined as: 'Their aptitude for being thought by an intelligent mind by means of one single species'[63] (we are speaking solely of the part in which they are similar). For example, a carpenter does not compare two planks of wood simply by the external act of placing them side be side to see if they have the same size and shape. He compares them by the internal act of his mind at the moment they are side by side — the external, sensible conjunction of the planks is only an aid to the comparison.

When I compare a beautifully painted landscape with the panorama it depicts, and find that the painting possesses perfect truth, I am not comparing it with anything outside me — I cannot insert the painting into nature itself and make it one with nature, or even place the painting and nature side by side, as the carpenter does with the two planks. However, although I cannot compare nature with the painting I see and admire, because nature exists in itself outside me and unperceived by me, I can

---

[62] In order to understand this very important truth, the reader should recall what was said in volume 1 (cf. the footnote to paragraph 107, and paragraphs 180–187).

[63] The reply to the question: 'How can a single *idea* produce knowledge of many things?', is: 'By adding to it the *judgment about the subsistence of the thing.*' This judgment is referred to each thing in particular, and therefore individualises, as it were, the species. An act with which a word is pronounced internally can always be reduced to this formula: 'The thing I am thinking with my present idea subsists,' and 'subsists so many times' (this is the number of individuals) (cf. vol. 2, 402 ss.). Because the *judgment* is stimulated by *sensations* (vol. 2, 528 ss.), we can have many *intellective perceptions* based on one single *idea*. These *perceptions* are distinguished among themselves by different acts of judgment, all made with one idea and determined by *sensations*, as I have said.

nevertheless compare it with the idea and images I have of nature, or at least with nature in the way I think it. This is so true that I can carry out the comparison even in total darkness when no natural panorama is sensed before me, or even in a place where I see only a strange, ugly nature, totally different from the idyll of the painting with its gentle hills and rich plains in brilliant sunshine. Comparison therefore is always a function of my thought which, although simple, can compare many perceptions with a single species, noting where the perceptions form a single species, and where the species themselves are multiplied. The same argument can be put forward about any external thing whatsoever used as an exemplar: in order to be called 'exemplar', it must always be present in the mind; in short, it must be an idea.

An exemplar therefore is simply an *idea*, often accompanied by its image, because only a mental conception can serve as an exemplar.[64]

1118. This observation allows us to perfect the definition we have given of truth and reduce it to this simple form: 'Truth is an idea in so far as an idea is an exemplar of things.'[65]

---

[64] I have noted (cf. vol. 2, 648 ss.) that any contingent thing whatsoever can be thought in a more or less imperfect state. If I compare the ideas I have of something in a state of perfection and a state of imperfection, the sole difference I see is that the idea I have of the imperfect thing is the same as the idea of the perfect thing, but lacking some quality. In so far as both these ideas have something positive, they are one idea, not two. I use the *idea* of the thing considered in its perfect state in order to think the thing in all its possible states; I find everything positive in the perfect idea, and in order to think the thing imperfect, I need only subtract some part of what I am thinking. The name 'exemplar', therefore, should be used principally of the idea of the thing in its most perfect state. However, when we have not succeeded in forming the type of perfection, our exemplar is the most perfect idea we can have of things we know — in the arts the ability to form this near-perfect idea is found only in the most consummate artists. Furthermore, the degree of perfection of our taste and the degree of accuracy of our judgments about works of art depend on the degree of perfection of the exemplar which we have formed to guide our judgment. Properly speaking *truth* is this exemplar, in so far as it contains the total perfection of things. We are now in a position to understand the definition of truth given by Avicenna: 'The truth of a thing is that property of its being which is permanent to the thing' (*Metaphys.*, bk. 11, c. 2).

[65] St. Thomas notes that truth properly speaking is in the intellect, and less properly in things, just as we say a medicine is healthy, although health

§5. *The meaning of the word 'truth'*
when we say that there are many truths

1119. There are as many *truths* as there are exemplar-ideas of things. This is the only sense in which the word 'truth' is used in the plural, as for example, when we say: 'Truths are diminished among the children of men',[66] or we speak of a special truth: 'This is an important truth', or when Dante says:

> How beautiful the *truth* that I was shown,
> Its sweet form savoured and resavoured.[67]

1120. *Per se*, the exemplar-ideas of things correspond in number to the *full specific ideas* (cf. vol. 2, 646–656) which allow us to know things positively and fully. But relative to ourselves we can say that there are as many exemplar-ideas as the fullest ideas we can have of each thing.[68] This explains why we say that each thing has its truth in its species. The masters teach that 'where several things are true, there are several truths, but in the case of

strictly speaking is only in the animal (cf. *De Verit.*, q. 1, art. 4). My own teaching, confirmed by this observation of St. Thomas, was first taught openly by St. Augustine. We have seen that the essence of anything is that which is thought in the idea of the thing (cf. vol. 2, 648). St. Augustine teaches that the *essence* of anything is precisely the *truth* of the thing: *Veritas non est proprium essentiae: quia si sic, qua ratione dicitur: veritas est proprietas essentiae, posset dici e conservo, CUM OMNINO IDEM SINT* [Truth is not something proper to essence. If it were, the same reason for saying that it is a property of essence could be used in a contrary sense, ALTHOUGH THEY ARE ENTIRELY THE SAME THING] (*Solit.*, bk. 2, c. 5).

[66] Ps. 11.

[67] *Par.* 3.

[68] The *perfect exemplar* of things is *per se* the *full specific* and *absolute idea*. But we cannot possess this exemplar or archetype. The *exemplar* or *rule* we must use for judging the truth of things and propositions is the best specific or generic idea we have. If the only idea we have is a *negative generic idea*, with which we think merely a *nominal essence*, we have to use it alone, and judge things relative to it because we have no better idea of them. However, all our imperfect ideas are always true and a part of the most perfect idea (truth or supreme exemplar and rule of things), as we have said (cf. vol. 2, 648 ss.). The extent of our faculty to judge what is true or false, therefore, depends on how much of the most perfect exemplar is present in the norm we use for judging.

one thing there is only one truth'.[69] In the same way we must affirm that all the individual things belonging to an idea have a single truth because, as we have said, they have a single exemplar, a single idea that represents them perfectly and makes them known (cf. vol. 2, 501 ss.).

§6. *The meaning of 'truth'*
when used in the singular and absolutely

1121. All these *truths* are *specific* or *generic*[70] and as such refer to the class of things that each truth determines and forms with its own unity.[71]

'Truth' is also used in ordinary language with an absolute sense, and always in the singular. The sceptics themselves give it this meaning when they say: 'Truth cannot be known, or does not exist', or something similar. But what sense has mankind given to the word when it is used in this way?

A specific idea is an *exemplar* of, and limited to a class of entia it represents or makes known to us; individuals of the same species have a determined mode and degree of being which limits

---

[69] St. Thomas, *De Verit.*, q. 1, art. 4.

[70] In themselves, *truths* of finite things are always *specific*. However, a *generic idea*, if it is the only idea we have of something, takes the place of truth for us, and becomes the exemplar according to which, for lack of anything better, we judge. In such a case, our judgments, in order to be accurate, must fall within the sphere of what we know generically; they are valueless for specific characteristics whose exemplar or *rule* for judging is lacking.

[71] We should carefully distinguish the three meanings of the expression, 'the truth of a thing'. It can mean the *exemplar-idea of the thing*; this is the proper, natural sense of the expression. It can also mean 'the truth contained in the thing'. In this sense, 'the truth of a thing' means exactly the same as 'true thing', and expresses the perfect correspondence between the *thing* and its exemplar; in other words, between its idea and its *truth*. Finally, if the true thing is either considered or is in fact an exemplar, the expression, 'the truth of this thing', corresponds exactly to 'this truth'. Thus, in the following passage of Boccaccio: 'No one attained the truth of the fact' (Gior., 8, p. 4), the fact is taken as the exemplar, the truth itself, and means: no one was able to discover or know the truth, that is, this fact.

and specifies them. But things, whatever their species, have something in which they are equal. This element is being itself (prescinding from its modes and degrees), because they all *are*. The idea of *being* therefore is that which represents all entia of any species whatever, and by which all entia are known. It is the *idea* to which all species are reduced, and could for this reason be called the *species of* species.[72]

The idea of *being* also differs from all species and genera in that all species and genera are this same idea, but with limitations.

Hence, if every species and genus of things has its particular exemplar, that is, its truth in the specific or generic idea, and if above this exemplar there is another idea, which is the exemplar and therefore the truth of all possible species, and if finally this idea is the idea of pure *being*, then the idea of being is the *truth* of all things.

The idea of being therefore can be called 'truth' when it is considered as the *exemplar* of things in so far as they are known by us, as I have said elsewhere.

Hence, the idea of being is the one, universal, absolute *truth* by which we know all things, because it is the universal exemplar, and expresses that in which all things are equal.

1122. St. Augustine gave truth this absolute sense when he defined it as: 'That which indicates being.' He is speaking therefore of the *idea of being*, because this idea makes known and indicates what is. *Veritas est qua ostenditur id quod est* [Truth is that which manifests what is].[73] St. Hilary's definition has the same sense: *Verum est declarativum, aut manifestativum esse* [Truth is being in so far as being indicates and manifests],[74] that is, being considered as that which declares and manifests things. This is being that we intuit, being as it is in our mind — in a word, the *idea* of being. When St. Anselm said: 'Truth is related

---

[72] The thought of *being* can be found in two modes: either *imperfect*, when we have only a simple *notion* of being (this mode is innate); or *perfect*, when all the properties consequent on the notion of being would also be known. We do not have the second mode. This distinction will be clarified later under *The Forces Present in* a priori *Reasoning*.

[73] *De vera Relig., c. 36.*

[74] Bk. 5, *De Trinit.*

to all true things as time is related to all temporal things,'[75] he was speaking about the one, absolute truth, about the 'incorporeal light in which, as St. Augustine says, the mind sees everything it knows.'[76]

Article 3

Extracts from the author of the *Itinerary* and from St. Thomas to show that the idea of being is truth

1123. Knowledge results from sharing in truth. It will be sufficient, therefore, to investigate the means by and in which we know things in order to have found truth.

The following extract contains the teaching of the author of the *Itinerary* on this point:

> The action of the intellective power lies in the intellect's perception of terms, propositions and conclusion. The intellect understands the meaning of terms only when it comprehends what each thing is by means of the thing's definition. But no definition can be given without the use of higher notions, which in turn are obtained by means of still higher notions, and so on until we reach the highest and most general notions. If we do not know these supreme notions, the inferior notions cannot be definitively understood. Hence, we have to know what ENS is in itself in order to know fully the definition of any particular substance.[77]

According to this great man, therefore, all knowledge is ultimately resolved in the knowledge of *ens in itself*. In other

[75] *De Verit.*, c. 14.

[76] *De Trinit.*, 12, c. 15.

[77] *Operatio autem virtutis intellectivae est in perceptione intellectus terminorum, propositionum et illationum. Capit autem intellectus terminorum significata, cum comprehendit quid est unumquodque per definitionem. Sed definitio habet fieri per superiora, et illa per superiora definiri habent, usquequo veniatur ad suprema et generalissima, quibus ignoratis, non possunt intelligi definitive inferiora. Nisi igitur cognoscatur quid est ENS per se, non potest plene sciri definitio alicuius specialis substantiae (Itiner. mentis in Deum, c. 3).*

words, through the knowledge of ens we know everything else. Consequently, the idea of being, as the means by which we know things, is truth.

Let us now turn to St. Thomas, another luminary of Italy and of the Catholic Church. He says:

> Just as demonstrable things must ultimately be reduced to a few principles known to the intellect in themselves, so must the investigation of the quiddity of any thing; otherwise, we would continue *ad infinitum*, with the consequent loss of all knowledge and understanding of things. But that which the intellect conceives FIRST as MOST EXTENSIVELY KNOWN, and in which it resolves ALL its mental conceptions, is ENS...[78] All other conceptions, therefore, must be obtained by adding something to ens. But we cannot add anything to ens that is naturally outside ens, in the way we can add difference to a genus, or accident to a subject, because every nature is essentially ens.[79] Nevertheless some things can be added to being in so far as they express A MODE of ens which is not expressed in the word 'ens'... Thus the conformity of ens to the intellect is expressed by the word[80] 'TRUE'.[81]

[78] I think it helpful here to amass references to important authorities, which enables us to see how this important, basic truth of philosophy was generally known by the most observant, lucid thinkers. Note, for example, that the same observation is found in Avicenna (*Metaphysics*, bk. 1, c. 9), whom St. Thomas cites here in confirmation of his own opinion.

[79] What is not being is nothing, and cannot in itself form the object of knowledge. All knowledge without exception therefore has only being or ens for its object.

[80] The word 'TRUE' properly speaking expresses a *true thing*, that is, the conformity of an individual, subsistent being to the intellect. 'Truth', however, is *ideal ens* or the *idea of ens*.

[81] *Sicut in demonstrabilibus oportet fieri reductionem in aliqua principia per se intellectui nota, ita investigando quid est unumquodque; alias utrobique in infinitum iretur, et sic periret omnino scientia, et cognitio rerum. Illud autem quod PRIMO intellectus concipit quasi NOTISSIMUM, et in quo omnes conceptiones resolvit, est ENS. — Unde oportet quod omnes aliae conceptiones intellectus accipiantur ex additione ad ens. Sed enti non potest addi aliquid quasi extranea natura, per modum quo differentia additur generi, vel accidens subiecto: quia QUAELIBET NATURA ESSENTIALITER EST ENS: — sed secundum hoc aliqua dicuntur addere supra ens, inquantum exprimunt ipsius MODUM, qui nomine ipsius entis non exprimitur. —*

1124. St. Thomas continues by showing that truth is the cause of knowledge:

> All knowledge is accomplished by an assimilation[82] of the knower[83] to the thing known, in such a way that the assimilation is called cause of the knowledge... The first comparison of ens to the intellect, therefore, requires that ens should correspond to the intellect. This correspondence is the proportion between the thing and the intellect,[84] and in this correspondence the concept of *true* is formally accomplished.[85] This conformity or proportion between the thing and the intellect, therefore, is what is added by the meaning of the word *true* to the meaning of the word *ens*. And, as we have said, knowledge of the thing depends upon this conformity. Hence, the entity of the thing (for me, 'being

Convenientiam vero entis ad intellectum exprimit hoc nomen VERUM (*De Verit.*, q. 1, art. 1).

[82] In fact the *idea of being* expresses and represents, that is, makes known, what is present in every real ens. There is a similarity therefore between being as *subsisting* and being as *ideal*: the former is possible being, the latter, the same being, but in act. From this comes the well-known distinction made by the whole of antiquity between *potency* and *act*. The distinction is certainly mysterious and difficult to grasp, but that does not entitle us to deny it. It is a fact acknowledged throughout history and by all peoples and schools. We have to begin from it as from a primary fact. Although extraordinary and obscure to us, it is a fact, and therefore an undoubtable truth. A false method of philosophy, boastful ignorance and proud modesty may harm itself by refusing to recognise this fact, but it cannot eliminate it.

[83] 'Of the knower', that is, of the *idea* in the knower. This idea is intimately and formally joined to the human spirit, and therefore all that belongs to the idea is attributed to the spirit. Hence, Aristotle says: 'The soul is in some way all things' (*De Anima*, bk. 3, test. 37). The uncertainty of this opinion is evident by his inclusion of 'in some way', which indicates a kind of uncertainty in the concept. The opinion, expressed in clear, appropriate words, would be: 'The idea of being, innate in the intelligent soul and essential to it, is or rather becomes all things in their state of possibility.'

[84] That is, with the idea of the thing. This idea is in the intellect.

[85] In so far as the idea is occasioned or determined in us by that *ens*, the relationship between a subsistent being and its idea constitutes truth, that is, makes the object *true*. But the *idea* itself, as perfect and specific, and considered in its relationship with the *entia* referred to it, is the *truth* of these *entia*.

[1124]

in itself') precedes the concept of truth, but KNOWLEDGE[86] IS AN EFFECT OF TRUTH.[87]

Article 4
Another demonstration that the idea of being is truth

§1. *Different ways of speaking seem to give rise to many kinds of scepticism*

1125. A concept expressed in new language is easily taken for a new concept. This explains the great number of apparent objections to truth on the part of sceptics and many sceptical sects. If, however, we carefully examine the concept of scepticism, we see that it and its philosophy are only one, just as truth itself, which the sceptics attack or at least think they are attacking, is one.

In order to counter this error or travesty of the mind and this pathetic display of imagination, we must show what scepticism is in itself, without any of its trappings, and reduce it to its ultimate expression.

---

[86] Things present us with knowledge of themselves according to the degree of their metaphysical *truth*, that is, of their correspondence to the *exemplar-idea* (in the Creator) whence they originate. But we would still be unable to know things even if *true*, were they not *true* relative to us; we know them, that is, only if an *exemplar-idea* is in us to make them known, that is, a truth which is the *innate idea of being*.

[87] *Omnis autem cognitio perficitur per assimilationem congnoscentis ad rem cognitam, ita quod assimilatio dicta est causa cognitionis. — Prima ergo comparatio entis ad intellectum est ut ens intellectui correspondeat: quae quidem correspondentia, adaequatio rei et intellectus dicitur: et in hoc formaliter ratio veri perficitur. Hoc est ergo quod addit verum supra ens, scilicet conformitatem, sive adaequationem rei et intellectus; ad quam conformitatem ut dictum est, sequitur cognitio rei. Sic ergo entitas rei praecedit rationem veritatis sed COGNITIO EST QUIDAM VERITATIS EFFECTUS* (*De Verit.*, 1, 1).

§2. *Apparent forms of scepticism*

1126. Scepticism has appeared under four principal forms:

1. Some sceptics say that truth does not exist.

2. Some limit themselves to saying that truth cannot be known.

3. Some say that only a truth relative to us, a subjective truth, is known. And finally

4. Some assert nothing but say they are doubtful about everything, even about the existence of truth.

§3. *Suitably expressed, scepticism can have only one form*

1127. The third of these forms maintains simply a *subjective truth*. But *subjective truth* is not truth; this is a misuse of the word, and the misuse of a word cannot summarise a system.

To grant knowledge of a *subjective truth* means not granting knowledge of any truth. Consequently, the third system, in which the question is discussed only apparently and by misusing words, must be reduced to one of the first two. We have to be ready therefore either to deny human beings *knowledge* of truth (the second form), or go further and deny the existence of truth (the first form) [*App.*, no. 4].

1128. However, the first and second systems differ only in expression, not in reality.

If I say I have not the slightest knowledge of truth, I cannot affirm its existence, precisely because I know nothing about it. The second system, therefore, ultimately leaves the existence of truth in doubt, affirming only that its existence cannot be known.

The first system comes to mean the same: anyone affirming that truth does not exist, affirms that he does not know truth. But if he has not the slightest knowledge of truth, he cannot deny it. This system also must be reduced to affirming that truth is not known while leaving its existence in doubt.

1129. This system, composed of an affirmation and a doubt, was easy to refute because of the contradiction in its terms.

Thus, we find in antiquity an unanswerable refutation of such an absurd system. For example, we read in Lucretius:

Denique nil sciri si quis putat, id quoque nescit,
An sciri possit, quum se nil scire fatetur:
Hunc igitur contra mittam contendere causam,
Qui capite ipse suo instituit vestigia retro.
Et tamen hoc quoque uti concedam scire; at id ipsum
Quaeram, quum in rebus veri nil viderit ante,
Unde sciat, quid sit scire, et nescire vicissim.

[He who thinks that nothing can be known,
Does not know whether what he says can be known.
I would be ready to enter the fray against such a person
Who has mentally followed his argument backwards.
I would even be prepared to grant that he knows all this.
But because he could not see truth in previous things,
I would ask him how he comes to know
The difference between knowing and not knowing.][88]

This ancient confutation of the sceptics is irrefutable. We can only wonder why scepticism continues to reappear, until we remember that it is not a philosophy but a disease, a frenzy enslaving humanity.

1130. In fact, the formula, 'Truth cannot be known' (to which

---

[88] Bk. 4. — Lucretius' last reason is subtle and worth analysing. In effect he says: if you deny truth, you deny knowledge. It is clear that you contradict yourself not only by affirming you do not know truth, when the affirmation means presenting a proposition as true, but also by using the words 'truth' and 'falsity', 'to know' and 'not to know'. If you know the meaning of these words, you already know what truth and falsity are, what to know and not to know are. Can you know all that when, according to yourself, truth, falsity, knowing, or not knowing cannot be known? Truth in fact is not something outside the intellect; it is in the intellect. If you have some knowledge in your intellect, you have some truth. Remove this *truth* and you remove the *knowledge*. And if you remove the knowledge, you remove language. You simply become ignorant, like mute animals, incapable of defending or attacking truth. You are no longer a sect of philosophers or even human beings, but brute animals. This is the only possible effect of scepticism coherent with itself. It cannot ask any more questions; it is dumb; its system affects only itself. To declare oneself a sceptic is synonymous with self-degradation and annihilation.

we have reduced scepticism), cannot be emended in any way whatsoever. It must be eliminated. No matter how it is expressed or modified, it remains essentially absurd and contradictory, as I shall now explain.

Let us change the formula to another well-known form: 'The only truth that can be known is that truth cannot be known.'

The truth exempted by scepticism is: 'Truth cannot be known.' But, if some truth can be known, it is false that, absolutely speaking, truth cannot be known. The truth exempted by scepticism is itself, therefore, a false proposition. For the exempt proposition to be true, it must contain the exception by which alone scepticism affirms the proposition to be true. But if the exception itself must be contained in the exempt proposition, we have a formula incapable of completion, since it would continue *ad infinitum*. For example: 'No truth can be known except this truth that "No truth can be known except this truth" that "No truth can be known except this truth"', and so on *ad infinitum*. Because we would never reach the end, scepticism's formula is intrinsically impossible; if the formula cannot be stated, neither can it be thought. By force of its own system scepticism is condemned to pronounce its formula for the duration of its life, a formula that has meaning only when finally completed. But like any endless formula, it can never be finally pronounced. Thus, scepticism, unable to formulate its thought but eternally engaged in doing so, is in a state in which it can no longer think, because no thought can be expressed until it is completed.

1131. This observation had been made, and ancient scepticism had collapsed, when Pyrrho emerged and connived a more refined form of scepticism, the scepticism of *doubt*.[89] He said he

---

[89] According to etymology, 'sceptic' (from σκέπτω) expresses one who *observes*, *investigates* without any definite conclusion. If we consider that the philosophical disputes are concerned with *highly reflective knowledge*, and that *reflection* is subject to disturbance by an infinite number of causes (which must have been the case especially in pagan times) we cannot wonder that scepticism came into being at such a period. Scepticism developed from the exaggeration of a good principle, from a kind of diffidence, a just doubt of oneself, a prudent suspension of judgment, which, according to Socrates, is the form of wisdom itself. Pyrrho's *practical reason*, which directs the human being to act according to necessity and the probable advantages of life, disguises the right principle that 'we must often decide to act upon mere

neither denied nor affirmed anything, but doubted everything. He thought he had thus avoided the contradiction directed against the sceptics who preceded him. This form of *doubt* is the only apparent form that scepticism can have. We must therefore discuss it.

§4. *What is required if the scepticism of doubt is to be coherent*

1132. The sophisticated sceptic desires to avoid at all costs the contradiction found among cruder sceptics who resolutely affirm their denial of the possibility of any affirmation whatsoever. He knows he must avoid every contradiction, honing his mind to keep scepticism in fashion and present it as a system without any intrinsic contradiction. Hence he recognises at least the principle of contradiction and presupposes some sure truth within the system of doubt. It was in fact this sure truth which guided our sceptic in forming his system. His sole desire that the system of doubt should be free of all contradiction led him into contradiction from the beginning!

1133. Let us accept that these convolutions and knots with which scepticism strangles itself to death are silken threads keeping it alive and topical. This kind of scepticism does not affirm that truth cannot be known, because it sees the contradiction in such an affirmation. However, if the doubt must not contain an affirmation, such a system of scepticism will end by eating its own words.

When sceptics of this kind say 'I doubt', they have pronounced an affirmation, because they have *affirmed that they doubt*. But if every affirmation is to be excluded from their *doubt*, they must doubt their doubt, and say 'I doubt that I doubt'. In which case, they must go back another step and make their doubt fall on the very doubt about the doubt; they will doubt whether they doubted their doubt. The formula has now added another link and become: 'I doubt whether I doubt that I

probabilities'. This fact proves our free activity and, because following our will as a norm is a practical assent, indicates the influence of the will in our practical assent to a proposition.

[1132–1133]

doubt.' But this is no better; the proposition still affirms, at least with the third verb if not with the first and second.

The sceptics must surely see how difficult it is to exclude every affirmation from their doubt. If now they add a further link, the formula becomes: 'I doubt whether I doubt that I doubt my doubt,' which is certainly more sceptical but still an affirmation — the difficulty has been pushed back one step, not solved. In short, the difficulty remains as long as we apply this scepticism to an infinite series of doubt-links in which the final term, even if it were reached, would still be an affirmation. All we can say, therefore, is that the formula proper to this kind of scepticism must be an endless series. It would no longer be scepticism if the formula were to come to an end. The result must be a series of doubts of the following form: 'I doubt that I doubt that I doubt that I doubt' etc, *ad infinitum.*

Such a formula affirms nothing because we can never pronounce the completed formula, never find the final term. If the final term were found, the formula would end, which is contrary to the hypothesis. The affirmation, therefore, pronounced at the start of the formula, can never be completed, and we are left with a suspended affirmation. And a suspended affirmation means a suspended thought, because to think is to affirm.

We see from this formula that the theme of the sceptic's teaching could alone fill every book on earth. When no more books are left, it must add an 'etcetera' because its extraordinary fecundity never comes, nor can come to an end. Young students who enter the school of the sceptics can be certain that for the whole of their life they will never hear completely even the simple title of the sublime philosophy they desire to know [*App.*, no. 5].

If some divinity came down on this earth to judge the different schools of philosophy, something very strange would happen to the sceptics. The first question asked of the assembled philosophers would be: 'What is your opinion?' After hearing the statements of the other schools and rightly judging them according to their merit, our divinity would finally come to the sceptics. Each, in reply to his question, 'What is your opinion?', would begin to recite the one, real form of their system: 'I doubt that I doubt…' And each would continue for all eternity, crazily pursuing the infinite series of doubts to the scorn of the divine judge and of their fellow-creatures. Would that such scorn were the only punishment meted out to them!

§5. *Scepticism is the impossibility of thought*

1134. When scepticism is thus taken to its ultimate and inevitable expression, it renders all thought impossible, unless it accepts defeat by affirming truth.[90]

Scepticism accepts only one thought, and this cannot be activated.

§6. *The idea of being, and the truth according to which we judge things, are the same*

1135. Granted what has been said so far, I can demonstrate this as follows.

I first discussed the *idea of being* (cf. 1065 ss.), and then *truth* (cf. 1112 ss.). I started from each concept and ended at precisely the same place, although by seemingly different routes.

Discussing the *idea of being*, I found that it constitutes the *possibility* of thought (cf. 1090 ss.), and that sceptics who deny *being* have rendered thought impossible, and thus contradicted themselves with the first thought they presumed to make.

In the case of *truth*, I found that sceptics who deny it are reduced finally to the same result: they render thought impossible (cf. 1134).

Consequently, to deny *truth* is to render thought impossible. To render thought impossible is to deny the *idea of being*. The idea of being is, therefore, truth. And this is what I proposed to demonstrate in this Article.

[90] Hence the opinion of St. Thomas that it is impossible for a human being to think that truth does not exist: *Nullus potest cogitare veritatem non esse* [No one can think that truth is not] (*De Verit.*, q. 10, art. 12). To think and simultaneously to deny truth is a contradiction. The true sceptic cannot exist, and those who claim to be such, either do not know what they are saying, or are lying, as will be clearly seen later.

CHAPTER 3

Possible[91] application of the idea of being

Article 1

Application of the idea of being generates
the first four principles of reasoning

1136. As soon as the idea of being is applied to things, it changes into the principle by means of which we know things (cf. vol. 2, 558 ss.). According to the aspect under which this application is considered and the difference in the applications themselves, the idea of being, although one, is expressed in several principles and even seems to multiple itself (cf. vol. 2, 570 ss.).

The first four principles were deduced from the idea of being in *New Essay*, vol. 2, 557 ss. They are 1. the principle of knowledge; 2. the principle of contradiction; 3. the principle of substance; and 4. the principle of cause. It was shown that these principles are simply the applied idea of being. The justification given for the idea of being is therefore valid for these principles also, and the certainty of the idea is equally the certainty of the principles.[92]

---

[91] Note that in this chapter we are still not dealing with the application of the idea of being to exterior things, but with the explanation of the *possibility* of this application. We are speaking of a *possible*, not an actual *application*.

[92] St. Thomas notes in a certain passage the very strict union that exists between the *first principles* and *being*. Sometimes he affirms that the intellect cannot err about the first principles, just as it cannot err about the being of things: *Intellectus semper est rectus secundum quod intellectus est principiorum, circa quae non decipitur EX EADEM CAUSA, qua non decipitur circa quod quid est* [The intellect is always right in so far as it is that which understands principles. It is not deceived relative to the principles for the SAME REASON that it is not deceived about that which is] (that is, about the *quiddity*, the being of things) (*S.T.*, I, q. 17, art. 3, ad 2).

Article 2

The general principle of the application of the idea of being considered in its objective value relative to things outside the mind

1137. What has been said so far already includes the principle mentioned in the title of this article. My intention therefore is not to indicate something new, but to express more clearly and explicitly what I have already noted. In fact, when I showed that the idea of being is *objective*, I also proved its power of arriving with certainty at conclusions about things outside the mind which are known by us in that idea. Kant and his followers denied this power to human intelligence.

Kant did not note the principle by which the application of the idea of being becomes valid when made to things not apparent to the senses but considered simply in themselves. This principle states: 'That which my internal reasoning concludes about exterior things through necessary deduction must be true relative to the things themselves. If it were not true, my internal reasoning could not exist. But it does exist.'

1138. Let me explain. My internal reasoning exists, and possesses an intrinsic necessity. This is granted by Kant himself. But he goes on to add that this intrinsic necessity is altogether ideal, and cannot therefore be applied to things *considered in themselves*. My reply is that our internal reasoning, if presumed to have no force relative to things considered in themselves, cannot be true and necessary even in the simple order of ideas.

We are certain of external things, therefore, because this certainty is a *necessary condition* already included in the certainty we have about ideal relationships. The internal, ideal order is necessary of its own nature. It cannot be doubted; it must be granted. The external, real order is a condition without which the ideal order could not be what it is. By means of our necessary certainty in the ideal order, therefore, we are also certain of what we know in the order of real things.

The opposite seemed true because certainty, which is one, had been divided in two by the distinction made between *internal* and *external certainty*. It was not noticed that internal certainty would not be in any way, unless that which is pronounced internally is verified externally. *Certainty*, therefore, is one, and consists in the correspondence between what is thought and what is.

1139. This results from the essential objectivity of knowledge, as we explained earlier. But I ask once more, what is the meaning of *objective*? It means that knowledge terminates in an object, that knowledge does not finish in itself or in an act of one who knows, but in some different entity which may be ideal or real. Because knowledge is objective, the truth of this object is essential to knowledge. There are not, therefore, two certainties, one belonging to knowledge and the other to the object of knowledge. Object and knowledge are synthesized so that when I make my judgment and affirm that my knowledge has the object it actually possesses, certainty is an attribute of my judgment. To say 'My judgment is necessary' is equivalent to stating that the object known by me must *necessarily* be in the way knowledge presents it to me, and cannot be otherwise. The intrinsic, essential *necessity* that I experience in my knowledge is therefore certain proof of the truth of the objects of my knowledge itself.

1140. The principle of knowledge[93] and that of contradiction[94] presuppose *possible being* as a different essence from that of the subject, and as opposite to the subject. The intrinsic necessity felt in these principles, therefore, enables us to draw conclusions about being considered in itself and separate from every affection of our own. In other words, what our knowledge affirms as *necessary* is as follows: 'The act by which we exist subjectively is altogether different from the act by which being exists as thought.' This knowledge, therefore, can only be necessary if the essential distinction between *being* and *ourselves* is also necessary.

1141. The same can be said about the other two principles of substance and cause.

As a result of perceiving some accident, I conclude that a substance exists; as a result of some happening, I conclude that a cause really exists. That this substance and this cause really

[93] I formulated it as: 'The object of thought is being' (vol. 2, 559 ss.).

[94] 'Being and non-being is not the object of thought' (*ibid.*).

subsist is contained in the necessity proper to my first cognition. Let us grant that I have not perceived the substance with my senses, nor perceived the cause directly; it is nevertheless sufficient for me to have perceived the accident and the event or happening. If I am certain of what I have perceived, I am also certain about that which I have not perceived with my senses (that is, the substance and cause) simply because what I have not perceived is a necessary condition of my knowledge. The truth of external things is assured at the same level as my internal knowledge because it is a necessary condition of my internal knowledge. In fact, if the external substance and cause were not real, the internal proposition, 'Given the accident or happening, the substance or cause must exist', would be false. But this proposition is as true and necessary as the principles of contradiction and knowledge. These principles, in turn, are as true and necessary as the idea of being, the source of necessary certainty. If, therefore, it is agreed that these principles are essentially true, it must also be agreed that they are valid for application to things different from the mind and noted in themselves. The second conception is the same as the first, or at least indivisible from it.

1142. It will be maintained that this whole argument supposes that the *perception* of real sensible things is true. This is of course correct, but it cannot be impugned by those who agree about the internal value of knowledge. Perception is internal, and it is in our internal experience that we find both 1. modifications of ourselves, and 2. something which is not ourselves. This second element, foreign to ourselves, is revealed to us in a fact internal to ourselves, that is, in the fact of our *experience*, an extraordinary fact that reveals in us something different from us.

CHAPTER 4

Persuasion relative to the idea of being or truth, and to the principles of reasoning

Article 1

Every human being has a necessary persuasion about truth and about the first principles of reasoning

1143. Certainty is 'a firm and reasonable persuasion that conforms to the truth' (cf. 1044).

This definition contains two principal elements, 1. truth and 2. persuasion.

Until now I have spoken about truth; I shall now speak about persuasion.

Persuasion is not completely subject to the human will. A basic persuasion has been inserted in us by nature along with the act by which nature has infused being or truth and attached it to our souls [*App.*, no. 6]. With this being or truth we judge things.

However, this persuasion of the first truth is neither imposed upon us nor extracted from us against our will. Nor is it blind persuasion. It arises from the presence of truth in all its clarity. Truth is so obvious that human beings, once they have seen it, know it of themselves as true. There can be nothing more true than truth. This follows from what we have said about the characteristic and proper nature of being in all its universality which demands nothing from us, but stands in its own right as a single, extremely simple fact.

1144. If we wish to find some proof that human beings are of their nature persuaded of the first principles of reasoning, we need look no further than the history of scepticism. As we have seen, any scepticism which truly denied the principles of reasoning would destroy the possibility of thought and of reasoning. But there has never been a sceptic really prepared to abandon reasoning for the sake of immersing himself in total mental and verbal silence. All sceptics have used reason to propagate their opinion. By this very fact they admit and use the first principles of reasoning without being conscious of what they are doing. Moreover, they do this naturally because the first principles cannot be denied. The very act of denial presupposes and requires them.

Article 2

The first principles of reasoning are also called common conceptions

1145. Because every human being possesses the first principles of reasoning by nature and follows them, they are also called *common conceptions*. Note, however, that they are *common* because they possess an intrinsic power and force that renders them immediately known and immediately received by every individual of the human race. They do not possess their force of invincible persuasion from the fact that they are common, as one author seemed to maintain recently.[95]

Article 3

The nature of common sense

1146. It is these principles, therefore, which form what is called *common sense*. This phrase includes all those consequences which, derivable from the principles, are so immediate and so plain that any person, however unlearned, could deduce them for himself. Because they are so *easy* and obvious, they are seen and granted by all human beings without exception.[96]

[95] Lammenais.

[96] Reid, the first proponent of the philosophy of *common sense*, defined it as 'the degree of judgment common to people with whom we can talk and conduct affairs' (*Essay on the powers of the human mind*, etc., vol. 2, p. 175). Shortly afterwards, he affirms: 'All cognition and knowledge must be built up on principles which are self-evident. *Each person* possessing common sense is a competent judge of such principles when he conceives them

This definition enables us to see that *common sense* is only that reasoning which each person arrives at of himself. The word *sense* has no other meaning here.[97]

1147. *Common sense* should not be confused, therefore, with *common beliefs*, or with *true and false traditions* (error, too, has its traditions) which are passed on from generation to generation, and received according to the faith and authority of the ancestors who have transmitted them.

When we rebuke someone for 'having lost his common sense', therefore, we are certainly not rebuking him for 'not accepting common beliefs'. Anyone arguing against the affirmations of *common sense* is necessarily arguing badly, or rather has lost the use of reason. He does not see and does not know what can be seen and known with that thread of reason possessed by all human beings who have attained a sufficient stage of development. Hence, insanity consists in constantly deducing consequences opposed to those of human common sense.

This is not the case with those who oppose *common beliefs*. Their opposition does not normally lead to their being called

distinctly. Consequently arguments often conclude with an appeal to common sense' (*ibid.*, p. 178). This appeal is also made for the sake of strengthening good faith in a hesitant adversary when he does not wish to yield to evidence. We use common sense to shame him, as it were, in his obstinacy, if he goes on resisting when everyone else has ceded to the clarity of obvious truth. In other words, this is an argument from shame. Considered like this, *common sense* is not even an *authority*. It is not used as an argument intended to convince the understanding, but as a penalty imposed upon human repugnance to profess the truth. Later on, we shall consider *common sense* under the aspect of *authority*. Here it is sufficient to note that making common sense consist in a judgment given by human beings on any argument whatsoever is a misapplication of language. In philosophical terms common sense can only be the judgment rendered by all, not by a great part of mankind, about the first principles and their immediate consequences. Other parts of human knowledge which are remote consequences of the first principles are altogether foreign to *common sense*. And what a disaster it would be if the only certain knowledge we had were solely of those things that everyone knows and knows with certainty!

[97] The understanding's direct intuition of truth is a *spiritual sense* (cf. vol. 2, 553 ss.). Hence the word *sense* is not used correctly in the expression *common sense* which refers only to truths seen directly or almost directly by the spirit. The general use of the expression, *common sense*, confirms our teaching on the *sense* which we admit in the spirit.

insane. If the beliefs they reject have the weight of legitimate authority in their favour, such dissidents are said to be unreasonable; if the beliefs are holy and pious, such dissidents are said to be impious. On the other hand, those who oppose common, false or impious beliefs, such as idolatrous superstitions, are reasonably and laudably entitled to the description 'enemies of common prejudices'.

Article 4

An objection against the universal persuasion of first principles

1148. One objection laid against the affirmation that human beings cannot disavow first principles by a law of nature is as follows: 'In some periods, especially in our own, people can be found who deny these principles. These persons must lack persuasion about them, therefore, and have no experience of the conviction you are describing.'

Article 5

Reply: the distinction between direct and reflective knowledge

1149. I acknowledge the fact described. Moreover, I believe there are people who in some way are persuaded they have eliminated even the first principles of reasoning. I need to explain this fact; its explanation will in turn provide an answer to the consequence, wrongly drawn from the same fact, about the lack of universal persuasion concerning first principles.

We have to distinguish two kinds of knowledge in human beings, *direct* and *reflective*. This distinction is of the highest importance, and has been mentioned several times in volume 2 of this work.[98]

[98] Cf. especially vol. 2, 469 ss. and 547 ss. — St. Thomas notes explicitly: 'Every act of the understanding is unknown to itself', and affirms that no act of our understanding can be known without another act, an act of *reflection* upon the prior act of knowledge: *Alius est actus quo intellectus intelligit*

1150. Imagine that I am asked whether I know a given thing or accept a given principle. When replying I do not use *direct* but *reflective knowledge*. When I affirm or deny that I accept a given principle, I turn my gaze upon myself and examine the state of my understanding. I then acknowledge that the principle is approved or disapproved by my understanding. Let us suppose that I do approve some principle; this is direct knowledge. Examining myself and the state of my understanding, I find that my understanding approves the principle; this is reflective knowledge.

In affirming that I accept or do not accept a principle, I cannot possibly use the same knowledge with which my understanding accepts the validity of the principle. I must make use of the knowledge resulting from the examination of my state of understanding relative to the principle. By means of my scrutiny I acknowledge the state of my opinions and decide whether I approve or disapprove the principle. The knowledge resulting from my turning back on my understanding in order to know its state is *reflective knowledge*; the prior knowledge with which I intend simply to approve or disapprove of the principle is *direct* knowledge.

1151. The distinction between *direct* and *reflective knowledge* is now clear. We must add that the latter does not always harmonise with the former. It can in fact deceive us about the state of our direct knowledge. This happens when we turn back upon our mind and decide to examine its state relative to some principle, but then carry out the scrutiny inaccurately, or hurriedly, or perhaps allow our judgment to be formed by some hidden prejudice rather than by careful examination. In these cases I can deceive myself, and believe and affirm that my mind does not approve the principle even though it does approve it, and vice versa. Such limitation in our self-knowledge seems strange at first sight, but is nonetheless true: it is a fact.

1152. Granted this, the continual contradiction of the sceptics is easily explained. When they reason, they use and accept in the act of reasoning all the first principles of reason. But they do not

lapidem, et alius est actus quo intelligit se intelligere lapidem [There is one act by which the intellect knows a stone, and another act by which it understands that it understands the stone] (cf. *S.T.*, I, q. 87, art. 3).

[1150–1152]

realise they are doing this.[99] In fact, they think they are doing the opposite, and take the destruction of first principles as the basis of discussion and the aim of their arguments. At the same time, they assert their disbelief in these principles, whose defence and justification they reject. Throughout this whole process they show their open use and admission of such principles (which are necessary in all their reasoning — there could be no reasoning without them) in their *direct knowledge*.[100] In their *reflective knowledge*, however, they openly deny assent to the principles which they undertake to overthrow. But reflective knowledge, when contrary to direct knowledge, is inevitably false and deceptive.

Article 6

The danger of believing those who assert that they are not persuaded of first principles

1153. Those who assert that they are not persuaded of first principles, therefore, are either deceived or deceive. Others, however, may not suspect such wickedness or this extraordinary possibility of error about what we know. If this is the case, and there is no firm hold on the truths we have explained, some may be inclined too easily to believe these totally false affirmations of oversubtle sceptics, and be drawn, even by their own good nature, into a serious and certain danger of becoming unsuited to defend the cause of truth. Anyone who undertakes to believe that there could be people in the world who truly doubt about first principles, as though these principles were not firmly established and secured in our souls by the bountiful hand of nature, will inevitably come to a bad end.

[99] Kant, for example, after having denied the objective force of the *principle of cause*, uses it unbeknown to himself to establish the forms of the human spirit, as we have seen above.

[100] The solid tradition of antiquity has always taught that it is impossible for human beings to think that the first principles of reasoning are false. *Ea quae naturaliter rationi sunt insita, verissima esse constat, in tantum ut nec ea esse falsa SIT POSSIBILE COGITARE* [It is clear that the things naturally posited in reason are totally true in such a way that IT IS IMPOSSIBLE EVEN TO THINK they are false] (*C. Gent.*, I, q. 7).

Associating with sceptics, people like this will no longer find any fixed point of persuasion in human reason; the entire range of truth will be totally devoid, for them, of any undeniable element, and will remain entirely undefended against human rashness. They will find themselves capable of doubting their own existence, the existence of everything else, and the existence of God. God himself, wishing to reveal truths to the human heart, will be unable to provide it with a secure, infallible proof of the veracity of his own divine words. Any unconscious fellow-traveller with sceptics will constantly be subject to the fear of fatal illusion and *false evidence*, as it is called, because interiorly he bears no impression of any eternal rule and inextinguishable splendour, but only lights he himself can quench.

He may not be a sceptic himself. Indeed, he may wish to oppose scepticism. Nevertheless, having granted so much to sceptics, he will be forced to go a great deal further along their path, and seek the firm point he needs outside the territory of truth. He will seek something that satisfies him, as the sceptics do, something more absolute and more firm than truth itself, and he will place the supreme principle of certainty in blind instinct, or some irresistible urge to believe, or natural suggestion, or in mere authority which, unsupported, ceases to be authority. In a word, his search will take him anywhere, but always outside truth. In such a case, the new *criterion* is never justified because unenlightened by truth. A principle of this kind may indeed be able to produce in the human being a forced, unworthy assent, but never a reasonable assent, which is serenely produced and attained by the sole force of truth, never by any other element.[101]

Article 7

The first means for rectifying the reflective knowledge
of those who deny first principles is to show that they are
in contradiction with their own direct knowledge

1154. When a human being has arrived at such a pitch of self-deceit that he believes he does not give assent to first

[101] This is Lammenais' case.

principles, but impugns them, his belief has to be shown false by his being drawn to consider the self-contradiction in which all his reasoning involves him.

His *reflective knowledge* will be rectified when he is brought to observe more accurately in himself the natural, *direct* knowledge to which reflective knowledge, an indication of direct knowledge, must conform.

Article 8

The second means for rectifying the reflective knowledge
of those who deny first principles, or fail to reason correctly
about the most obvious things, is the authority of others,
which could therefore be called
a criterion of reflective knowledge

1155. An appeal to the authority of others, by which we make use of the natural human inclination to believe others, is of great assistance in rectifying reflective knowledge.

Moreover, our human need to listen to others can be reinforced in various ways when two people are in disagreement about even the most obvious things. One can always say to the other: 'As human beings we are furnished with reason. This means that all our fellow human beings are furnished with reason just as we are. My reason, however, reaches a conclusion exactly opposite to yours. Could we not ask ourselves therefore what conclusion is reached by others? If one of us is wrong (and we cannot both be right), a comparison on the same point with the conclusion of many others will help us to discover who is mistaken.'

1156. If one person surrenders to the authority of others in this way, correction is at hand. However, the authority of others has not been the *criterion of certainty* in general, but simply the *criterion of reflective knowledge*. Although the first principles of reasoning have not been placed in us by the use of this criterion, the prejudice and bias preventing our acknowledging them has been removed. We are now able to see that which we have always possessed and accepted with our natural, *direct* knowledge, but rejected and opposed with our *reflective knowledge*.

Others' authority in primary matters, that is, in matters appertaining to *common sense* (cf. 1146, 1147) as we have described them above, is an excellent rule and a safe haven from error and danger in our first steps. For this reason nature itself, after giving us being, has not left us isolated on earth. We are born into the midst of society so that we may be helped and supported as we take our first steps in reasoning, as well as in those proper to our tiny bodies.

1157. But if the human evil of which we are speaking were disdain and rejection of all authority, our state would be perilous in the extreme. Some confirmation of what I have said can, however, be found in experience drawn from the care of insane people whose reasoning about the most obvious things in human life can only be described as weird. Considerable progress, which sometimes results in complete cure, is made when they are obliged by the presence of a force much greater than their own to conform to the regular habits and reasonings of other people.[102]

---

[102] What I have said presupposes that people have not reached such a disturbed state of reflection that they perjure themselves as a body by denying the first principles of reason. Such degradation of mankind is impossible in the particular, extraordinary conditions in which the human race presently finds itself; Christianity will always save mankind from *universal* scepticism. We must keep in mind that divine providence has taken mankind into its care, and in this sense it is true that the truth is always found in mankind as a whole. On the other hand, long, dispassionate meditation on the condition of individuals and of people taken as a whole will show that of themselves, without supernatural assistance, they are far more desolate and unhappy than is normally believed because we see humanity sustained by God in a most wonderful manner. For myself, long meditation has convinced me that humanity without revelation is devoid of sufficient moral force to preserve it from total lapse into the most abject idolatry. Humanity is subject to such mental debility that it finds scepticism impossible for one reason alone: the doctrine of scepticism is proper to a philosophical faction, and itself requires some use of reason. Humanity would not have time to surrender itself entirely to scepticism before giving in to self-annihilation and extinction at a level more wretched than that of brutes.

PART THREE

APPLICATION OF THE CRITERION TO DEMONSTRATE THE TRUTH OF NON-PURE, OR MATERIATED KNOWLEDGE

CHAPTER 1
The fact in general

Article 1
The connection with what has been said

1158. I have already shown that the intuition of being is an undeniable fact, immune from every possibility of deception. It constitutes the faculty by which we know what is different from and independent of ourselves.[103]

I also pointed out, however, that as long as we restrict the argument to possible being alone we do not affirm anything as subsistent. In such a case we grasp, through the idea of being, only the possibility of being. In other words, we have the concept in all its universality. When presented with this concept we are simply given the possibility or faculty of knowing things in their mode of being independent of ourselves (cf. 1078 ss.). We still have to learn how the *concept* of subsistent entia, different from us in general, can lead us to affirm individual, subsistent

---

[103] Cf. 1065–1111. — Our knowledge is made up of: 1. *being*, which we conceive in all our acts of knowledge (this is the formal part of knowledge); 2. *determinations* of being (this is the material part). As I have indicated on several occasions, I restrict myself to saying that our knowledge is perfectly objective in its *formal* part, without extending the same assertion to the material part.

entia. We need to know how we can pass from the simple faculty of knowledge, given to us by nature in the idea of being, to the possession of actual cognitions of real entia different from ourselves.

We have prepared the way for this discovery by establishing an unshakeable *principle* regarding the communication between things considered *per se* and the necessary judgment which we make upon their subsistence:[104] 'The things we judge to subsist by a necessary deduction must subsist. If they did not subsist of themselves and in reality, our interior judgment would not be true and necessary. Consequently our intuition of being would not be, as in fact it is, true and necessary' (cf. 1137–1142). As we said, the internal necessity of being requires necessarily that external things be as we judge them — in themselves, in a mode different from our own.

This principle, which constitutes the *possible application* of the idea of being to subsistent things considered in themselves, has its root, as we also affirmed, in that marvellous property of being, absolute *objectivity*. Indeed, the possible application of the idea of being is properly speaking only its objectivity manifested in its particular relationship with things that exist outside the mind. The objectivity of being — if I may repeat myself yet again, but in other words — consists in this: *being* which the mind sees or intuits is essentially different from the *act* of the mind with which it sees or intuits it. An accurate analysis of the primal fact, the intuition of being, indicates the presence of two elements, the *act* of the intuiting or seeing subject, and *being*, which is seen or intuited. These two elements cannot be confused; the act of the mind is essentially different from being, intuited by that act. If, therefore, the intuition of being is such that being is not presented to us as dependent on our mind, but rather totally independent from and foreign to it, we have to say that in this intuition (which we must not abandon) we possess from the very beginning two acts, that of the subject and that of being. This second act maintains being present to the subject, and forces the subject to intuit it. In this intuition, therefore,

---

[104] I do not say between *things* and *ideas*. Ideas alone do not include the subsistence of things, but only their possibility. I say between *subsistent things* and the *judgment about their subsistence*.

being informs, and the subject intuiting it is in its turn *informed* by being.[105]

Natural and logical necessity are both present, gently and without any coercion, in this presentation of being and in its acceptance by the intuiting subject. *Logical necessity*, therefore, springs from something essentially different from the mind, although seen by the mind. This necessity refers to the object, not to the act of the mind. But we judge, with a necessary deduction, of the subsistence of an object different from the mind by means of *logical necessity* which is unique, and which I have described as totally present in being in all its universality.

Our judgment tells us that if the external thing did not subsist as we judge it, *being* would not be. But being is, evidently and necessarily. The external object (the substance, the cause) must also subsist, therefore, because that internal necessity requires it as its condition; the sight of this relationship is in fact what causes us to pronounce our judgment. The principle of the *possible application* of the idea of being to subsistent things is therefore well established, and as certain as the idea of being itself.

1159. But this principle requires and supposes further data if it is to be used in a worthwhile and practical way. It supposes that our spirit sees that the intrinsic necessity possessed by being of itself is also possessed by the judgment with which we judge that a substance or cause subsists.

But how does our spirit conceive a strict, necessary union between subsistent things and the idea of being so that the subsistence of the former is proved by the necessity of the latter? What are the conditions in which the spirit must be found if it is to see the necessity of pronouncing such a judgment upon the subsistence of something external to the mind and to ourselves? If the spirit remains with the idea of being alone, it has of course already gone out of itself because being is something other than the spirit. Nevertheless, it will not have gone beyond the possibility of things. Some change must take place in it, therefore, or some element at least must fall under its consideration which enables it to pass from the region of merely possible things to that of subsistent things. What is this change? What is this new

---

[105] Hence we affirmed that the faculty of intuiting *being* is a *spiritual sense*. Sense perceives by experiencing passively, as it were, that is, by receiving.

element leading the spirit to move in such a way? What constitutes the link between this element, the idea of being, and subsistent things? What is the link, that is, enabling the spirit, prompted by the necessity originally lying in being, to judge that these things subsist? We still have to answer these questions.

But this undertaking presupposes another. Our search reaches out for the *principle* justifying the judgment we make about the existence of things. But judgment on the subsistence of things presupposes the idea of things, or at least that the idea be co-existent with the judgment, as we have already shown to be the fact in perception (cf. vol. 2, 405–407). This gives rise to another question, with which the application of being is really completed: 'How do we acquire the ideas of things?' This was the subject of the whole of volume 2, to which we refer the reader, but we still have to show the relationship of our present question with the three preceding queries by indicating the place it holds in the search for the criterion of certainty.

The three preceding questions were intended to illustrate how the mind can perceive things outside itself (supposing that ideas have been granted it). The fourth question asks how things outside the mind can be presented to the mind in such a way that it perceives them? This last question is concerned with the origin of acquired ideas; the first three constitute the search for the criterion of certainty.

1160. If we wish, we can express the first three questions in another way:

First question. 'What is the *principle* by which the human spirit knows what is in all its universality different from itself?' As we have said, this principle is the idea of being in all its universality because *being* (object) is that which constitutes what is *different* from the spirit (subject). That is to say, whatever is *different* is always included in *being*.

Second question. 'What is the *principle* by which the human spirit knows with certainty what is different from itself and really subsisting?' As we have said, this principle consists in the link or bond of identity between the real subsistence of things and ideal being so that the real subsistence shares in the necessity of ideal being. This happens in such a way that the necessity of being contains, supposes and requires the external reality which it judges to be present through a necessary deduction of identification.

Third question. 'What is the *principle* by which the subsistence of real things is seen bound to the ideal necessity internal to ourselves?' This is the question we intend to answer in our present chapter.

1161. It is clear that this third question presupposes as present in us, as we said, the idea of whatever it is we judge to be subsistent. In other words, it presupposes the solution to the question of the origin of ideas. We have to re-examine the origin of acquired ideas, therefore, and in this origin find the justification of the judgment made by our mind on the subsistence of things.

When we acquire a new idea, we always acquire at the same time a new, partial determination of being in all in universality.[106] We have until now called such a partial determination of the idea of being in all its universality the *matter* of our acts of knowledge. The first two questions, therefore, were concerned with only the *form* of knowledge; with the third, we descend to materiated knowledge whose legitimacy and validity we have to demonstrate in the present chapter.

All matter of knowledge, therefore, is either particular and determined, or something contained in what is particular and determined. We shall include the matter of our knowledge under the general determination, *fact.*

Let us now proceed immediately to speak of the certainty of our knowledge of this fact, considered generally, that is, of all that is or happens. I begin as follows.

---

[106] If we possessed a positive idea of God (which is naturally impossible for us here on earth), we would not have acquired any materiated knowledge, but increased our formal or objective knowledge. All that we know positively about God is *form* and pure object of our mind and knowledge. The same is true of heavenly beings which possess the vision of God. This explains St. Thomas' beautiful phrase: *Cum aliquis intellectus creatus videt Deum per essentiam, ipsa essentia Dei fit forma intelligibilis intellectus* [When any created intellect sees God in his essence, the very essence of God becomes the intelligible form of the intellect].

Article 2

The fact in itself, neither felt nor understood

1162. It is clear that there can be no knowledge or certainty about a fact which is neither felt nor understood. We cannot ask, therefore, how we are certain of such a fact. To be certain of something, we must first know it. Nevertheless, a comment may be useful at this point.

When we know a fact, two elements are present in our knowledge: knowledge (the act of our knowledge), and the fact itself (the object of our knowledge). By means of an abstraction we can separate the knowledge of the fact from the fact itself and so conceive that the fact exists in itself even when unknown. This shows that our notion of the act by which an ens exists (a fact) presents this act as having a nature independent (relative to our mode of mental conception) of knowledge. Relative to us, therefore, *knowing* and *existing* are two separate and incommunicable elements; and this separation and incommunicability is a condition of our *knowing*. I mean that if *knowing* and *existing* were not two incommunicable elements, our knowing would be impossible. It is the analysis of our act of knowledge which provides us with the separation of these two elements: *knowing* cries out, as it were, that it is not *being as known*, and witnesses that it must stand apart.

1163. Consideration of this proposition allows us to understand 1. that the efforts of the German transcendental school to make *knowing* and *being*, that is, the intellective act and the object of that act,[107] interpenetrate and identify are vain; 2. and that transcendental idealism is therefore absurd because it removes the one condition which makes knowledge possible, that is, the essential separation between *knowledge* and *existence*. It makes knowing impossible because it destroys being in itself, and consequently truth.

---

[107] The *intellective act* (intuition), the *idea* (the ideal, possible object), the *sensitive act* (sensation, sense-perception), the *term of the sensitive act* (matter), the *rational act* (intellective perception) and *real ens* (the real object to which the idea refers) are six different things and every care must be taken to avoid confusing them.

Article 3

The fact when felt but not understood

1164. The fact when felt but not understood is either *feeling*, or the *corporeal matter* of feeling if the feeling is material (cf. vol. 2, 1005 ss.). If we suppose this fact to be *felt* only and not *understood*, it is not yet the object of any act of knowledge. We cannot therefore ask: 'How can we be certain of such a fact?' because certainty is only an attribute of *knowledge*. If knowledge is absent, certainty is also absent.

As we have said so many times, *feeling* is unknown to itself. Only through abstraction, by which we separate all knowledge from feeling and consider it apart, in itself, do we come to know the existence of an *unknown feeling*. But considering the fact of feeling, in this way, we can reasonably conclude that *feeling* is an element separate from *knowledge*, as we said a short time ago about *being*. This separation between *feeling* and *knowledge* is another condition necessary for *knowledge*. Only *knowledge* renders feeling an object; it is not such *per se*. If the *act* of knowing and its *object* were not essentially distinct, knowing would be impossible because it is essential to knowing that the two things be separate. It is impossible, therefore, to identify *knowing* and *feeling*, or to make *knowing* emanate from *feeling* as though it were some development of feeling. The efforts of Schelling and the systematists have their origin solely in the lack of a careful examination of the fact of knowledge

1165. We have to say, therefore, that our knowing can only subsist on condition that three distinct activities are posited: 1. the activity of being; 2. the activity of feeling; 3. the activity of knowing. But the way these three activities are united in a single ens and bound together to form a single substance is a question altogether too profound for me to attempt to answer in this current work.

Article 4

How the matter of knowledge is shown to our spirit

1166. *Being* has two modes, the *ideal mode* and the *real mode*.

Ideal being is the *form* of knowledge.
Real being is the *matter* of knowledge.
In this chapter we call the matter of knowledge *fact*.

We have seen that the *fact* which forms the matter of our act of knowledge is distinguished into two primal species. One consists in the *activity of non-sensitive being*, the other in the *activity of feeling*. These can be called two species of *real being*.

The matter of knowledge, that is, *non-sensitive being* and *feeling* cannot of themselves provide a basis for reasoning about their certainty as long as they remain *unknown* and have not been made objects of the third activity, *knowing*. Certainty is an attribute only of knowledge, which is not present in this case.

How, then, is the matter of knowledge (*non-sensitive being* and *feeling*) presented to our intelligent spirit? How does it become the object of our knowledge?

1167. The *matter* of our knowledge is presented to our spirit by feeling itself. This arises from the identity between ourselves as *sensitive* beings and ourselves as *intelligent* beings. By nature we are already furnished with 1. a fundamental feeling; 2. the vision of being in general. Nature itself, therefore, has presented us with the the *form* and *first matter* of our knowledge (cf. vol. 2, 722). Our acquired matter is only a modification of the first, originating matter (of the fundamental feeling) (cf. vol. 2, 705).

1168. It may be objected that although this serves to explain how the part of the matter of our acts of knowledge which consists in feeling is presented to our intelligent spirit, it does not explain the part of the matter that consists in the simple activity of real ens which lacks feeling. In other words, how do we form for ourselves the idea of inanimate entia?

This idea comes to us from the *matter* of feeling. The idea of inanimate entia is composed of 1. the matter of feeling; 2. those forces which, modifying the matter of this feeling, suppose no activity other than that which is found in the matter of feeling, according to the old tag: 'Every agent acts according to its own likeness.'

Article 5

The universal principle governing every application
of the form of reason to facts presented by feeling

1169. The universal principle governing every application of
the form of reason to facts provided by feeling is the following:
'The known fact must form an equation with the form of
reason.'[108]

But it is clear that if knowledge of a fact is equal to the form of
knowledge, knowledge of a fact is equally justified and certain
when the form of knowledge is justified.

The principle, therefore, has to be verified but, before we can
do that, relevant clarifications are called for.

Article 6

Explanation of the universal principle stated above

1170. The equation which has to exist between the *matter* of
knowledge (considered in knowledge itself) and the *form* of
knowledge requires that everything *explicitly* and particularly
comprised in materiated knowledge be already comprised
implicitly and universally in the form.

1171. Let us set this out syllogistically. 'Every human being
possesses reason; Andrew is a human being; therefore Andrew
possesses reason.' The major of these three propositions, 'Every
human being possesses reason', refers to the possible world and
tells us, in a general and implicit way, that the particular human
being, Andrew, possesses reason. If all human beings possess

---

[108] We have already indicated this (cf. 1160 ss.). Here we are dealing more
fully with the second of the three questions indicated in those numbers.
Aquinas caught sight of this when he wrote: *Ens quod est* PRIMUM *per
communitatem, cum* SIT IDEM PER ESSENTIAM REI CUILIBET (this is the
equation), *nullius proportionem excidit; et ideo in cognitione cuiuslibet rei
cognoscitur* ['Ens, which is FIRST because of its commonality, is never
disproportionate because it is the SAME IN ESSENCE FOR ANYTHING
WHATSOEVER' (this is the equation). 'It is known, therefore, when we know
anything whatsoever'] (*De Ver.*, q. 10, art. 11).

[1169–1171]

reason, each one must possess reason, whatever his name. The third proposition, therefore, is comprised implicitly and generally in the first. It is in this sense that I affirm an equation between the third and first propositions, in so far as that which is asserted in the third is already asserted in the first. No new assertion is made; the particular proposition is identified with the general.

1172. Let me explain more clearly.

In the first proposition, 'All human beings possess reason,' something general is affirmed. This general proposition comprises a quantity of particular propositions which, however, are not distinguished individually in our minds. Because they are not distinguished, and because we do not know the subjects to which they refer, we say that we know them only implicitly. But when feeling presents their particular subjects, these particular propositions are completed and rendered clear and distinct. We now know them in a particular way with the same light with which we formerly knew them in a universal way. In other words, a proposition, when materiated and complete, makes a perfect equation not with the universal proposition, but with the particular proposition which, although present in the universal, remained there unseen and confused. We ourselves could not distinguish it because we did not know the subject of which it was predicated.

In the syllogism used in our example, we know implicitly, as a result of the first proposition, 'Every human being possesses reason,' that an individual human being called Andrew possesses reason. But how can our knowledge that Andrew possesses reason be in us if we do not know Andrew? It is a blind, indistinct proposition, enveloped in the general proposition and there absorbed, but with a virtual, not an actual existence. It is in this sense that the universal proposition forms a perfect equation with the particular proposition. As soon as we have a perception of Andrew, and come to know the particular proposition, or rather in knowing it, we also know that it was already present (without our knowing this) in the universal.

The universal proposition, therefore, is capable, by means of its virtuality, of forming simultaneously as many equations as there are particular propositions. In other words, the general proposition takes on in each equation the special relationship it holds towards the particular proposition with which it is compared.

1173. Everything is reduced, therefore, to *perception*, as we said. Given perception, we know the individual subject and hence possess the *particular proposition* which forms an equation with the general proposition. Perception, however, has already been justified by us. We also showed that while all this is accomplished within us, the nature of *experience* also shows that not everything within us appertains to us. It is possible for an element essentially foreign to us to be in us, and this is precisely what occurs in perception. In the fact of *intuition* there is no contradiction present in our knowing something different from us (that which is *ideal*). Equally in the fact of *perception* there is no contradiction in our knowing something different from us (that which is *real*).

Article 7

An objection resolved

1174. But at this point we are faced with an extremely difficult question: 'How can the *matter* of knowledge be identified with the *form*? And if the matter is not identified with the form, how can it be said to be contained in the form and make with it a perfect equation?'

I answer that the *matter*, considered in itself, is never identified with the form of knowledge.[109] On the contrary, we have already shown that the matter in itself (the fact, being considered simply and feeling) is an activity different from knowing, and even more different from the form of knowledge (cf. 1164 ss.). We also said that the matter of knowledge, when separate from knowledge itself, remains unknown and outside the question of certainty, which is only an attribute of knowledge. It is the *matter* of knowledge as *known* which is identified with the form of knowledge. In this fact, the spirit simply considers the matter relatively to being, and sees it contained in being as an actuation and term of being itself.

---

[109] We can apply here the ancient adage: 'Contingent things are not; God alone is.'

There is no identification before the matter is united with being. The matter is such that nothing can be said about it before we know it. But when it has been united with being and thus objectivised and become known to us, it has acquired through our act of knowledge a relationship, form and predicate that it previously lacked. In this predicate consists its identification with being. Being is predicated of it, and our act of knowledge consists in this predication.

When we go on to consider the *matter* as already *known*, we imagine that it has in itself something totally common to all things. This most common quality, as common, is however acquired for it by the mind and received by the mind. It is a relationship it has with the act of the mind; it is not something real in the matter, but real only in the mind itself.

This was insufficiently considered by Aristotle and others like him, and led to their thinking that the mind could obtain for itself the idea of being by abstracting what was most common in things. But it is the mind itself which places this most common quality in things, and in retrieving the quality only takes back what is its own. As I have said, that which is *common* in things is only the result of the relationship that they have with the intelligent mind.[110]

---

[110] Certain passages in St. Thomas show, I think, that this great man had seen these two important things: 1. that *universality* is not drawn out of things, but placed in them by the mind; 2. that the essence of knowing consists in the mind's adding *universality* to felt things. This teaching seems clearly expressed by the Saint in the following passage: *Cum dicitur universale abstractum, duo intelliguntur, scilicet ipsa natura rei, et abstractio SEU UNIVERSALITAS* (abstraction for Aquinas is, therefore, the same as the universality of something). *Ipsa igitur natura cui accidit vel intelligi vel abstrahi, vel intentio universalitatis* (note how three synonyms are used: being understood, being abstracted, and the universality of the thing), *non est nisi in singularibus: sed hoc ipsum quod est INTELLIGI, VEL ABSTRAHI, VEL INTENTIO UNIVERSALITATIS, EST IN INTELLECTU* ['When we speak about the abstract universal, we understand two things, namely, the nature of the thing, and abstraction or UNIVERSALITY' (abstraction for Aquinas is, therefore, the same as the universality of something). 'The nature of the thing which happens to be understood or abstracted, or the underlying universality' (note how three synonyms are used: being understood, being abstracted, and the universality of the thing) 'is not present in individual things. BEING UNDERSTOOD, OR BEING ABSTRACTED, OR THE UNDERLYING UNIVERSALITY, IS IN THE INTELLECT'] (*S. T.*, I, q. 85, art. 2). There is, however, one reasonable

1175. It should be noted that when we established, on the basis of the equation between them, the principle that the certainty of a *particular proposition* (which refers to what is real) is the same as the certainty of the *general proposition* (which refers to what is possible), we were speaking of propositions equally composed of *matter* and *form*. We were not speaking of an equation between *matter separated from form* and *form* itself.

If this is true, the matter of knowledge, the fact, may of itself prove to be something highly mysterious and covert. I would not disagree with this in any way, but add that this mysterious, covert activity included in the fact is the root of knowledge itself. This activity itself is in the last analysis a fact owing its origin to the supreme necessity beginning in the highest of all natures, before which the philosopher must bow his head in humble adoration.

difficulty which will occur to those who remember the distinction St. Thomas makes between the two operations he assigns to the intellect and which he sometimes calls 1. illuminating the phantasms and 2. abstracting the phantasms, and which I have explained in vol. 2. 495 fn. But in the passage quoted above, St. Thomas uses the word *abstrahere* [to abstract] to indicate the action which elsewhere he calls *illustrari phantasmata* [illuminating the phantasms]. He does in fact distinguish two kinds of abstraction, the first of which he describes with the phrase *per modum simplicitatis* [in a simple way], a perfect synonym for *illustrari phantasmata* which is the meaning given here to *abstrahere*. The second kind of abstraction he describes as done *per modum compositionis et divisionis* [by adding to and taking from]. This is *abstrahere* properly speaking, which is contrasted in other places with *illustrari*.

[1175]

CHAPTER 2

A further explanation of the principle justifying
materiated knowledge in general. The formal part

1176. We cannot seek a reason for the primary fact of know-ledge outside the fact itself. It will help, therefore, if we analyse the fact further in order to grasp its internal reason. This we shall do in the present and following chapters. First we shall consider the formal part of perception and knowledge, and then perception itself.

Article 1

The nature of the imperfect state of innate being
in the human mind

1177. I have already said that *being* is present to our spirit in an imperfect manner.[111] Let us analyse this initial, fundamental intuition in order to discover what accounts for this im-perfection.

It is not difficult to see that the perfection of the being we intuit by nature depends upon the presence of its *terms*. We conceive the activity called *being*, but we see neither where it originates nor where it terminates. It is as though we saw a man working, but without knowing whether his action will produce a statue, a picture or something else.

1178. Because we do not know by nature where this activity, which we conceive and which we call *being*, terminates, we find that:

1. The intuition of this activity cannot bring us to the knowledge of anything real because each real thing is the term of the activity called *being*.[112]

---

[111] *Being* cannot, of course, find itself in an imperfect state relative to itself. I mean that it is present to us in such a way that we cannot absorb and see it perfectly with the eye of our mind, but must perceive it imperfectly. The limitation and imperfection is entirely ours.

[112] Hence, if we knew being perfectly, that is, with all its terms, we would know everything, says St. Thomas. *Quicumque cognoscit perfecte aliquam*

2. Being naturally intuited by us is *undetermined*, that is, void of its terms; *universal*, in so far as it is disposed for receiving the terms which it does not have; *possible*, or in potency, in so far as it has no terminated or absolutised act, but only a principle of act. In a word, by this single observation, we can conclude that 'what we see by nature is the first activity, but devoid of its terms with which alone it takes its place in nature and forms a real subsistence'. We see only those qualities which we have attributed in volume 2 to being in all its universality, the foundation of reason and human knowledge.

3. If being were to reveal itself more clearly to our mind, transmit its own activity from within and thus terminate and complete itself, we would see God. But until this takes place, and as long as we see being so imperfectly by nature — this first activity which conceals its term from us — we can only agree with St. Augustine when he says so impressively that in this life *certa, quamvis adhuc tenuissima forma cognitionis, attingimus Deum* [we reach God with a sure but very poor form of knowledge][113]

4. Finally, we see that the other activity given us by feeling is essentially separate and distinct from being itself (the form of the intelligence) because it does not come from the interior of being, but from elsewhere.[114] Nevertheless, this activity is judged by means of being, and is known as dependent on it. We know it as a partial, contingent term of being which cannot be confused with being. It is a term whose origin,[115] considered in itself, is inexplicable, although it receives from its relationship with *being* (the form of reason) a new condition enabling it to enter the class of entia. In other words, we realise that it is a fact which has come to share ineffably in being.

---

naturam universalem, cognoscit modum quo natura illa potest haberi [Anyone who knows some universal nature perfectly, knows how that nature is able to present itself], — and *ex diverso modo existendi constituuntur diversi gradus entium* [that the different grades of entia are constituted from their different ways of existing] (*C. G.*, I, q. 50).

[113] *De Lib. Arbitr.*, bk. 2, c. 15.

[114] This shows clearly that pantheism is absurd.

[115] Creation is essentially inexplicable to the human being, as I shall show elsewhere.

1179. We can therefore say of everything presented to us by feeling, that is, of all the matter of knowledge, 'that it is not an activity emanating from the essence of being, the form of knowledge, in such a way that it is an essential term of being. On the contrary, it is such that, although extraneous to the essence of being (the form of knowledge), it is neither subsistent, nor perceivable as subsistent, except as term of the activity of being itself'.

We necessarily acknowledge being which is the form of knowledge, therefore, as furnished with a twofold activity. Its *essential* activity, with which it constitutes and absolutises itself, terminates in a way unknown to us; the other activity terminates in other contingent beings outside and distinct from it. These beings are presented as terms to our perception by feeling.[116]

These conclusions are not the result of reasoning, but of simple observation and analysis of our knowledge. In order to understand them well, the reader has no need to follow some long, difficult series of argument. It is sufficient to concentrate and focus one's attention on self to see and note clearly all that is contained in human knowledge.

Article 2

Likeness

1180. We see being by nature. This is the primary fact.

Our vision of being is imperfect. This imperfection consists in our seeing the activity called being in its principle, not in the terms in which it fulfils and absolutises itself (cf. 1177 ss.).

Being, unfulfilled and unabsolutised, is *most common* being and as such can terminate in infinite things either essential or inessential to it. The inessential terms of being perceived by us are all real, finite things.

Our feeling, or any modification we experience of this feeling, is one of the terms of being naturally intuited by us. We know things, therefore, or the terms of being itself, through feeling.

---

[116] Creation, therefore, is not necessary, despite recent teaching in France.

1181. But a given feeling comes, goes and returns. In some cases, therefore, being can repeat the same term an indefinite number of times. When we see being terminated in a feeling, we perceive (by means of sense) a real ens. This is what we have called *perception*. But when we consider this feeling (the term of being) simply as *possibly* renewable an indefinite number of times, we have the *idea* or species of something, and with it we know a given term in which being can terminate, although we do not know if it does in fact terminate there. In this *idea* we possess the (knowable) *essence* of any thing.

Essence is always the ideal thing. It is an incomplete actuation and determination of being because *essence* can itself terminate in one or sometimes in infinite, real individuals. These realities actuate and complete the essence, and thus even being, determined by the essence. They are presented to us by feeling alone in the case of real, finite and contingent entia.

Logically considered, the first step taken by *being* with its activity is towards the full specific *essence* which determines it. It then arrives at *subsistence*, its final term. This is the completed act of the essence: being, most common being, is simply the thing in remote potency, the *initial being* of things; *determined essence* is the thing in proximate potency.

1182. If we find the torso of an ancient statue, and later dig up a head, two arms and two legs, we need only compare the other parts with the torso to see if they belong to it. The same is true relative to that *initial being* we possess by nature. When we experience a feeling, that is, any action whatsoever, we acknowledge this action as the completion and term of that being which we already have naturally. The nature of knowledge consists in this confrontation and awareness.

The idea of anything is the thing itself devoid of the act which makes it subsist. But just as we know the hands and feet when we know the torso of the statue, so we know real, subsistent things through their ideas when these things are *felt* as acting on us. They are recognised as subsistent entia, that is, as actuations of that being which is already known by nature. What is known first in potency (in the mind), is then recognised in act (outside the mind) as really subsisting in itself. And this comes about through feeling which, in its *passivity*, implies and contains that which differs. This twofold mode of being which things possess (in the mind and in themselves) is the source of the concept of likeness, as I mentioned elsewhere, and provides the explanation of the ancient dictum: 'Every act of knowledge arises as a result of likeness.'

1183. The *likeness* through which we know things is, according to antiquity, that which exists between an essence in potency and an essence in act. We are dealing with one and the same thing, but in different modes. This is the clear teaching of the ancient sages, which they prove by their exquisite analysis of the nature of likeness. St. Bonaventure, one of our greatest Italian thinkers, whose words I have used in volume 2 to illustrate so many noble truths, says: 'A thing is not so identified with its likeness that it is numerically one with it; nor is it so different that it differs in number. — Hence, it remains that the likeness of anything belongs in the same genus as the thing. Leaving the thing, it differs from the thing, but it does not pass into another genus. Here I am speaking of likeness as likeness, not according to the intent of the one using it. I am speaking, that is, of likeness in so far as it comes from the subject and at the same time does not leave it, as brightness coming from light does not abandon light.'[117]

In this passage from St. Bonaventure, likeness (in the mind) does not differ numerically (this must be noted carefully) from the thing (subsisting outside the mind). It is nevertheless different. This is explained by considering it as an actuation, completion and term of the possible essence existing in the mind

1184. St. Thomas' teaching is the same. According to him, 'the intelligible likeness, by means of which something is understood in its substance, must be of the same species as the thing understood, or rather THE SPECIES ITSELF'.[118]

---

[117] *Res non habet tantam identitatem cum sua similitudine, ut sint unum numero: nec tantam diversitatem ut differant numero. — Et ideo similitudo rei in eodem genere est per reductionem cum eo cuius est similitudo. Quia enim egreditur, ideo differt; sed non transit in aliud genus. Et loquor de similitudine secundum rationem similitudinis, non intentionis, id est prout a subiecto exit et non recedit, ut splendor a luce* (I *Sent.*, dist. 3, part. 2, art. 1, q. 1).

[118] *Similitudo intelligibilis, per quam intelligitur aliquid secundum suam substantiam, oportet quod sit eiusdem speciei, VEL MAGIS SPECIES EIUS* (C. G., III, q. 49).

These last words are very illuminating. The idea with which we know some thing is the *species* itself; it is determined being, but as yet devoid of its term,[119] that is, the real, subsistent thing outside the act of the mind. Considered in itself, therefore, the idea is not the *real individual*, but the *species* in so far as its act can be renewed and repeated in an indefinite number of individuals.

1185. This explains the perfect unity between the one who understands and the thing understood, of which St. Thomas speaks so often. It is the unity between the idea and the subsistent thing which joins itself to us through feeling. Once joined to us through its action in our feeling, it can be seen by us internally as joined with its likeness or potency, that is, with innate being. 'That which is understood,' says St. Thomas, 'must be in the one who understands.'[120] And again: 'That which is actually intelligible must form a single thing with the intellect which actually understands,[121] just as that which is actually feelable is feeling itself in act.[122] In so far as what is intelligible is distinguished from the intellect, however, both' (that is, the intellect and the thing) 'are in potency, as we find in sense. The sense proper to the eye does not actually see nor is what is visible actually seen, until the sense is informed by the visible species in such a way that one single thing results from what is visible and from the act of sight itself.'[123] All this flows from the analysis of the act by which the mind knows and sense feels.

1186. These outstanding men whom we quote deduced all this from an extremely perspicacious analysis of the act of knowledge, whose nature they examined with great care. They

[119] We are speaking of contingent things.

[120] *Intellectum oportet esse in intelligente* (*C. G.*, I, q. 51).

[121] That is, with the *idea* proper to the intellect, with the *essence* seen by the intellect.

[122] There is a foreign entity in the experience undergone by sense. The understanding perceives this element as distinct, which it is, from the act of feeling and of knowing.

[123] *Intelligibile in actu, est intellectus in actu sicut et sensibile in actu est sensus in actu; secundum vero quod intelligibile ab intellectu distinguitur, est utrumque in potentia, sicut et in sensu patet: neque enim visus est videns actu, neque visibile videtur actu, nisi cum visus informatur visibili specie, ut sic ex visibili et visu unum fiat* (*C. G.*, I, q. 51).

concluded that the *likenesses* described above are *intellectual lights*, and that *universal likeness, being in all its universality*, is — to use the words of the author of the *Itinerarium*, — 'the light of truth which shines so brilliantly before the face of the mind'.[124]

1187. But what is the effect of this analysis of the manner in which we come to know? Basically, it simplifies the difficulty of understanding the unique fact of knowledge. The analysis reduces all the species and varieties of knowledge to a single, ultimate fact which explains all the others although itself remains mysterious and obscure for us to the end.

The first question, 'How can the mind know subsistent entia through ideas?', presents no further difficulty when two things are granted and held firmly: 1. we see *being* naturally; 2. the being we see is one with entia themselves when they are considered in potency. Consequently these entia, in so far as they subsist, are simply the terms and completions of that being which we already see.

1188. The second question, 'How can these terms and completions of being which are seen as independent of us be known by us?', also receives considerable light when we consider that each of us is a subsistent ens and one of those terms and completions of being which we see. We are in ourselves in such a way that we who see being also feel ourselves. As sensitive, subsistent entia, we are subjects joined to and communicating with all other entia which, exercising their action upon us, modify our feeling. As a result we know things *acting* in us as entia foreign to ourselves.

1189. All this is clear, granted our intuition of being in all its

---

[124] *...ubi (in intelligentia) ad modum candelabri relucet lux veritatis in facie nostrae mentis* (*Itin. mentis in Deum*, c. 3). St. Bonaventure goes on to confirm what had already been said by the author of *De Coelesti Hierarchia*, namely that 'intellectual substances are such because they are lights' (that is, they possess light in themselves); that 'the perfection and completion of the intellectual substance is spiritual light'; that 'that potency which, in the intellect, is a consequence of the nature of the soul, is a kind of light in the soul'. By means of this light St. Bonaventure explains the famous acting intellect, and states that such teaching is *super verba philosophica et catholica fundatus* [founded upon philosophical and catholic expressions] (II *Sent.*, dist. 24, p. 2, art. 1, q. 1).

universality, the first fact whose explanation must not be sought in any other preceding fact. We have to conclude, therefore, relative to this fact, that *being* is knowable of itself. In other words, its marvellous prerogative consists in being able to exist in minds and constitute them. St. Thomas had already arrived at this conclusion which, when well understood, provides the final, tranquil goal for those seeking the nature of human knowledge.

'The intelligible species in which our intellect shares are reduced as it were to their first cause in some principle which is INTELLIGIBLE OF ITS VERY OWN ESSENCE.'[125] The *essential intelligibility* of this principle of understanding is precisely the ultimate fact of which we are speaking where every search ends in final satisfaction. St. Thomas' words can be explained in these equivalent terms: 'On examining and analysing the nature of knowledge, we find that every difficulty is finally reduced to seeking how we can perceive being. But there is no other reason except the fact that we understand being and all other things through being because they are being. We have to say therefore that being has a nature capable of existing in our minds. In other words, being alone must be intelligible of its very own essence.'

Article 3

The refutation of the fundamental error of the German school is strengthened (vol. 1, 331 ss.)

1190. The fundamental error of the German school is found at three levels: the absolute identification of things 1. with ideas; 2. then with intellect, and finally 3. with human beings. Our concern must be with the first level, the root of the other two.

1191. Kant, the originator of this school, initiated[126] the error of which we are speaking as a result of a difficulty he saw but

---

[125] *S.T.*, I, q. 84, art. 4.

[126] I say 'initiated' because he identified only the formal part of things with ideas, leaving their *matter* doubtfully distinct from them. Fichte completed the identification by making matter arise from the nature of ideas or of the spirit.

could not resolve. I shall express this difficulty once more with all the force of which I am capable.

When Kant examined the way in which our spirit perceives intellectually, he thought he noted that the predicate which we give to the object when we perceive it is already contained in the object. For example, when we think of a sizeable house, *size*, which is the predicate, is, according to Kant, already inherent in the house itself. It is not we who add something to it with our thought. On the other hand, the concept, *size*, which is applicable to different subjects, must of itself be found in those subjects although we do not think of them without the use of the senses which present them to us. When we do perceive those subjects through the use of the senses, we see that they are so bound to the concept of size that this concept would be empty and have no meaning without them.

As result of these observations, Kant concluded that there is a perfect *identity* between the *concept* in the mind and the *attribute* of the thing outside the mind. It is as though he reasoned in this way: 'When I discover an *attribute*, for example, *size*, in a given object, I do this through a judgment, that is, I apply my mental *concept* of size to the sensible object. When I apply this concept, I come to consider this concept of size as adhering essentially to the object itself. For example, when I say this object is large, I attribute to it the same size that I first thought as separate from it. But if the size that I attribute to a sensible object is that which I was thinking previously, this *attribute* of the object must be identical with my *idea*, and my idea, or concept — which is the same — must be a necessary *ingredient* in forming the objects which I perceive and which I then think as different from me. Indeed if the size that I see in the object is not that which I think, how could I use my concept of size to know that object? How could I be aided in knowing the object by means of a concept which has nothing to do with what is in the object?

There is nothing to be gained by my applying to the object a predicate that is not its own. Such a predicate cannot help me to know the object's own predicate. In other words there cannot be a passage from what is in the mind to what is outside it in the object. I have to conclude, therefore, that my concepts, the qualities in my mind, form part of external objects as an element necessary to them.'

1192. Anyone who understands the teaching we have developed above will not be dissuaded by this difficulty which at first sight is undeniably ingenious. But what we have explained becomes perfectly clear when we have carefully understood the following facts which are provided by an analysis of human knowledge.

1. Every contingent thing has two modes of being, in the mind and outside the mind.

2. The mode of being in the mind is in *potency*, and outside the mind is the *act* of the same identical essence which is seen by the mind.

3. Hence there is in the mind a complete *likeness* with the thing outside the mind, and although this likeness is not identical with the thing relative to its act of reality, it does not differ in number from the thing to which that act belongs. It is the very beginning of the thing, and constitutes its *species* or *intelligibility*.

4. If we consider things (limited, contingent) as separate from the mind, they are unknown, or rather unknowable *per se*. Their relationship with the mind is not in them, but in the mind. Their likeness, found in the mind, is however only their ideal being, that is, some determination of being in all its universality which, as knowable *per se*, is the fount of all ideas and all knowability.[127]

5. Limited, contingent things, because they are only acts and terms of most common being intuited by the mind, can be considered apart from this being. As separate, they are said to subsist outside the mind, and are called *real things*.

6. Finally, even if the *reality* and *ideality* of a thing were to be identified, which is not the case (only the *thing* is identical, not the *mode* of being), the thing would never be confused with the act of the mind or the subject which possesses it because the *idea* as such is *per se* an object distinct from the thinking subject and contrary to it.

1193. *Real things* cannot therefore be confused in any way with ideas without doing violence to language. Still less can they be confused with the mind perceiving them because the

---

[127] Because limited things of themselves *are* not, they have no *knowability* of themselves.

separation and real distinction of these three entities is contained in their very definition.

CHAPTER 3

The certainty of perception,
especially of the perception of ourselves

Article 1

What we perceive

1194. We must now discuss the importance of intellective perception. In this life we perceive only two kinds of real things: 1. ourselves; and 2. bodies. We begin with the certainty of the perception of ourselves.

Article 2

The feeling of *myself* is a substantial feeling

1195. *Myself* is a being who thinks, and is therefore a *substance*. *Myself* as substance is a *feeling*, because *myself* feels, and always feels the same in all the actions it does. When it is not acting, it still feels because it is alive and essentially feels that it is alive.

1196. *Myself* is, therefore, a *fundamental feeling* because all its feelings are rooted in it.[128] It needs no other sensations; it is of itself. 'We' can never be without ourselves. All other sensations

---

[128] I demonstrated and explained this in vol. 2, 692 ss. *Substantial feeling* corresponds to what St. Augustine says in bk. 9 of his work on the *Trinity*: SUBSTANTIALITER *notitia (sui) inest menti* [Information about itself is SUBSTANTIALLY in our mind]. In fact, the soul, in order to perceive itself immediately, needs only to turn its attention to its own feeling. However, this action of turning our intellective attention to our own feeling is not innate. Hence St. Thomas says that the mind has only an *habitual notion* of itself necessarily and substantially: *Notitia qua anima se ipsam novit, non est in genere accidentis, quantum ad id quo* HABITUALITER *cognoscitur, sed solum quantum ad actum cognitionis* [The information with which the soul knows itself is not classified as an accident relative to that by which it is HABITUALLY known, but only relative to the act of knowledge] (*De Verit.*, 10, 8).

need our essential feeling because all possible sensations are simply modifications of ourselves.

With the feeling *myself*, therefore, we feel an ens, a substance, a subject (that is, a living, feeling principle). Consequently, if we think this feeling, we perceive a substance. There is therefore a substance which we perceive directly, and we are this substance.

Article 3

We perceive ourselves without an intermediary principle

1197. When we perceive *ourselves* with our understanding, we have no need of any intermediagment. Conscious of the fundamental feeling, we say to ourselves: 'We exist', meaning: 'It is *us*', that is, it is this feeling, which is a substance, an ens which subsists with an internal energy. In fact, in the feeling of *myself* the human being feels precisely the energy in which he is, the energy through which he is distinguished from all other existing substances.[129]

Because our particular subsistence is understood in the feeling *ourself*, our understanding, in order to perceive *ourself*, has only to turn its attention to *ourself* and acknowledge the real, subjective existence already present in the feeling. We do not need integration or induction to do this because the acknowledgement is carried out by means of the notion of objective being which is in the understanding.

Article 4

The certainty of the perception of *MYSELF*

1198. If the perception of *myself* were not granted, I could not ask whether it were certain. However, whether true or illusory,

---

[129] Nevertheless, when we analyse the perception of ourselves (and of all other subsistent things), we find that pure *being* is a different activity from *feeling*. Hence, we who are a *feeling* have *being*, not from ourselves but from elsewhere. Thus, the expression used by some German and French philosophers, 'We exist through ourselves', is incorrect. Indeed, our observation clearly makes true the opinion of St. Augustine and other Fathers that creatures, absolutely speaking, are not.

it is given by nature because composed of two primitive facts: 1. the form or idea of being; 2. the matter or fundamental feeling, perceived of itself and indicated by the monosyllable 'I'. Granted, therefore, that it is given, is the perception of *myself* true and certain?

The idea of existence, the first part of the perception, is verified *per se*, as I have shown earlier (cf. 1065 ss.).

We wish to verify whether the feeling given by nature (*myself*) which we judge to exist, is the judgment which constitutes the intellective perception of *myself*. We can therefore express the question, 'Is the perception of *myself* certain?', as follows: 'Does my understanding judge correctly when it applies the universal predicate of existence to my feeling?'

1199. The answer is contained in the general principle of the application of the form of reason (predicate) to the matter (subject), a principle discussed in the preceding chapter. We saw that every activity, every feeling, is simply an actuation, or a term of the actuation, of *being*. The predicate is therefore correctly applied to the feeling constituting *myself*, and because this perception of *myself* is the most direct, and also the condition of all other perceptions (of contingent things), it is the most certain.

Article 5

St Augustine uses the certainty of the perception of ourselves to refute the Academicians

1200. In his refutation of the Academicians, St. Augustine begins with the undeniable fact of the perception of *myself* [*App.*, no. 7]. He argues:

> In this (that is, in our judging that we are alive) we have no fear of being deceived by some likeness of truth, because even the person who is deceived is undoubtedly alive. Our seeing this cannot be impugned by the objections brought against external vision. Objections of this kind suggest that we are perhaps deceived in the same way that our eye is deceived when it sees a stick bent in water, or when sailors appear to see towers move, and an infinite number of other things which differ from the way they are seen. But

the truth under discussion is not seen by the bodily eye; the knowledge by which we know that we live is much deeper. The Academician cannot say: 'Perhaps you are asleep, and without knowing it, you dream that you see.' Certainly the things we see in dreams resemble very closely what we see when awake; we all know that. But the certainty of our knowledge of being alive does not make us say: 'I know I am awake', but 'I know I am alive'. Whether we are asleep or awake, we are alive. Dreams cannot deceive us relative to this knowledge because both sleeping and seeing things in dreams is the act of one who is alive. Nor can the Academician attack such knowledge by saying: 'You're a raving lunatic, and don't know that you are.' Things seen by healthy people are very much like those seen by lunatics. A lunatic is alive! And in answer to the Academicians we do not say: 'I know I am not a lunatic', but: 'I know I am alive' Hence, people who say that they are alive can never be deceived or lie. Anyone who says: 'I know I am alive' may perhaps be accused of a thousand kinds of false visions, but that does not disturb him because anyone who is deceived is alive.[130]

Article 6

Other truths that share in the certainty of the perception of *myself*

1201. St. Augustine goes on to deduce many other truths from the unshakeable certainty of our being alive and of our being:

If such were the only things found in human knowledge, they would be very few. However, they multiply so much in every way that they are no longer few but reach an infinite number. The person who says: 'I know I am alive', says he knows one thing. But if he says: 'I know that I know I am alive', he says he knows two things. And to know that we know these two things is to know a third truth. In this way we could add the fourth, the fifth and innumerable other truths, if we were able. But because it is not possible to understand an indefinite number by adding

---

[130] *De Trinitate*, bk. 15, c. 12.

one at a time, nor to go on stating numbers interminably, we at least certainly understand and say that the series is true and that it is so countless that we truly cannot understand and state its infinite number.

The same can be said of the certainty of our will. It is surely imprudent to reply 'Perhaps you are deceived?' to someone who says 'I want to be happy'. If the person says: 'I know what I want, and I know that I know it', a third affirmation that the person knows these two truths can be added. And then a fourth that they know that they know the two truths, and so on indefinitely.[131] Thus, if someone says: 'I do not want to make a mistake', whether he errs or not, it will always be true that he does not want to err. It would be the height of impudence to reply to such a person: 'Perhaps you are deceived'. Even if he were deceived, he is not deceived in wishing not to be deceived! And if he adds that he knows it, he can add as many such truths as he wishes, aware that the number of truths is infinite. The person who says: 'I do not wish to be deceived, and I know I do not

---

[131] We must not think that St. Augustine's observation is a clever but vain subtlety, and that these truths he speaks of are differences only in words and not in reality. Anyone who understands will surely find the observation very acute and helpful in knowing the nature of human cognitions. St. Augustine distinguishes the *different reflections* our mind carries out on its own cognitions. He notes that every reflection is a new act of the mind, differing from the preceding reflection and producing some new knowledge. It is of the greatest importance to recognise this, particularly when it is applied to explain facts of the mind. In this work I have frequently been obliged to make use of the distinction between *reflective* and *direct* knowledge, demonstrating that they are not the same. They are entirely distinct and sometimes contradict each other (cf, amongst other places, 1149–1157). A reflection on the knowledge we have, that is, knowing that we know, so increases our knowledge that the new knowledge relates to the former in the way that more relates to less, or even the infinite to the finite. With reflective knowledge we rule and control direct knowledge as we will; only reflective knowledge brings direct knowledge under our free will. We would never have discovered the *art of writing* if we had not reflected on *language*. *Numbers* are an invention arising from the reflection on the *ideas* of numbers. Algebraic *letters* are the result of a reflection on numbers. *Analytical functions* arose from a third reflection on algebraic letters. This is the real meaning of the apparent play on words: 'We know that we know that we know'! It is the simplest formula expressing the order of ideas, to which the Analytical Functions of Lagrange belong.

wish to be deceived. I know that I know', can indicate, even if clumsily expressed, an infinite number of truths.

And other things can be found which firmly refute the Academicians, who maintain that the human being is unable to know anything.[132]

Article 7

An observation on the intellective perceptions of feelings

1202. As a conclusion to this chapter, I observe that what is presented to our understanding cannot in any way be different from what we know. To be presented with something means we must feel it; it is the thing in so far as it is known and perceived by us. As felt, it must be identical to itself when known directly, that is, perceived intellectively. To perceive it is simply to know or affirm to ourselves that we feel it. Thus the intellective perception has the same *identical* term as the sensation, which is its proximate object. In this kind of knowledge, deformity or falsity cannot be present in anything of itself. This confirmation of intellective perception arises from the simplicity of the spirit, which, as a single principle, unites feeling and intellection.

---

[132] *De Trinit.*, bk. 15, c. 12.

CHAPTER 4

The certainty of the perception of bodies

Article 1

Difficulty in demonstrating the certainty
of the perception of bodies[133]

1203. In the perception of ourselves, the two terms composing the judgment are given us entirely by nature. They are the predicate, being in all its universality, and the subject, *myself*, a real, substantial being. United in the unity of the perceiving subject, they form the intellective perception of *myself*. We cannot doubt this kind of intellective perception because the idea of being is an idea justified of itself — it is truth — and *myself* is the matter of our knowledge. This matter is not changed by our perception of it, because it is a feeling which is naturally just what it appears to be — because appearing is feeling. The simple perception of *myself* therefore admits only the application of the first principle of all knowledge, without any intermediate reasoning or use of a middle principle.

1204. The perception of bodies, however, is not so simple.

---

[133] The sceptics directed their whole armoury against the perception of bodies, as I have already said. St. Augustine writes: *Cum enim duo sint genera rerum quae sciuntur, unum earum quae per sensus corporis percipit animus, alterum earum quae per se ipsum* (here we see how well St. Augustine distinguishes the two kinds of perception I have posited, which are the two sources of the matter of cognitions): *multa illi philosophi garrierunt contra corporis sensus; animi autem quasdam firmissimas per se ipsum perceptiones rerum verarum, quale illud est quod dixi, Scio me vivere, nequaquam in dubium vocare potuerunt* ['Two kinds of things are known, one of which is perceived by the spirit through the bodily senses, the other by the spirit through itself' (here we see how well St. Augustine distinguishes the two kinds of perception I have posited, which are the two sources of the matter of cognitions). 'Those philosophers have said many things against the bodily senses but have been unable to cast any doubt on the clear perceptions of true things which the spirit has through itself, such as the example I have given, "I know I am alive"'] (*De Trinit.*, bk. 15, c. 12).

When we feel bodies, we experience an *action*, an activity, carried out in us. But the agent is not presented to us as an ens simply in itself, independently of every relationship with any other ens. Feeling and all corporeal sensations make us feel this substance called body in its activity in us; we feel it in its special relationship with us, not simply in so far as it *is*, but in so far as it acts.

It is indeed true, therefore, that we perceive the *action* of a body solely as an *experience*; this is the way *feeling* presents the action to us. The understanding, however, sees this experience not from the point of view of one who experiences (this is the way sense experiences it) but from the point of view of one who acts, and therefore changes the experience into action for itself. It recognises contemporaneously an acting principle different from itself, and an ens or substance, whose only proper characteristic is action.

An ens is therefore supplied as something known solely by its action, not in itself. The mind supposes it because whatever acts must have the first act constituting it an *ens*; an act performed on another is a second act rooted in a first act. The fact that the second act entails the first is seen in being, because it is a truth belonging to the intrinsic order of being.

We must therefore find some justification for these intellective operations.

Article 2

Our understanding sees an action in the experiences undergone by our sense

1205. I have shown elsewhere that 'experience' and 'action' express two relationships of the same thing. I have also shown that the *understanding* perceives an action in the experience undergone by *feeling* (cf. vol. 2, 666 ss.). This teaching gives rise to the following difficulty: 'Feeling perceives experience but not action. The understanding cannot perceive experience without action because, you say, the latter is included in the former. This seems to be a contradiction.'

I reply: 'It is true that feeling perceives experience but not action, because experience has a different existence from action. The understanding, however, perceives experience with the *concept* of experience. This *concept* cannot exist unless the *concept* of action is included in it. These are relative concepts: one is reciprocally included in the other'. In order to know what this *concept* of experience is, and how the understanding forms it, we will briefly recall the teaching given in volume 2.

Article 3

The human spirit perceives and knows a corporeal substance through the experience undergone by the feeling

1206. The principle of knowledge states: 'The object of the intellect is being', or equivalently: 'If the intellect understands, it must understand something' (vol. 2, 602 ss.).

When we, who are endowed with intellect, are conscious of a modification, we naturally say:[134] 'It is something which is not me.' We say this reasonably and necessarily: there must always be something, whatever it is, modifying us. We feel that a force is being applied, whether pleasantly or unpleasantly; and that which actually produces experience is not nothing. Therefore something or some entity is perceived.

At the same time we say: 'If something is present, a substance must be present, a first act which is the foundation of the ens', because every datum is in this sense either a substance or an appurtenance of substance — there is no middle term.[135] We see therefore that the perceived thing is in the experience undergone by feeling. It is an action in us, an agent, an acting agent in fact, because an agent can only be conceived as ens.

The difficulty therefore disappears. Sense can perceive the happening only as an experience, because the happening is not an objective potency. Sense can perceive an agent only by experiencing the agent; it cannot perceive it in any way with a

---

[134] As I have said, we are moved to do this by various needs and by our instincts (cf. vol. 2, 514 ss., 1030 ss.).

[135] I have amply shown the absolute necessity of this deduction in volume 2, 597 ss.

relationship of action. But the understanding, which is the faculty of seeing things in themselves, necessarily sees the ens that is acting. This ens *is*, in so far as anything is in itself which acts: action is a consequence of being. *Being* is an essential activity, the first activity on which all other activities depend. It is therefore proper to the intellect always to see an action in an experience, an agent in the action, and an ens in itself (substance) in the agent (cf. vol. 2, 578 ss.); one thing is implied in the other, and is seen with a single act. This act is called an act of perception.

1207. We can now understand the *concept* of experience. It is an action considered relatively to the ens undergoing the action. The *concept* of experience embraces the concept of action; the former issues from the latter, just as the latter issues from the concept of agent. We can therefore conclude as follows. The perception of *myself* is made by means of two elements given by nature and brought together in an ens without the intervention of any faculty other than that of *synthesis*. Similarly, the perception of bodies is made by means of the union of two elements, given by nature, which unite through the *faculty of synthesis* aided by the faculty of *integration*. To the *agent* actually revealed in the experience integration adds the first act, which is conceived in every ens as its necessary foundation, constituting it an ens.

This first act however is determined solely by the action[136] produced by the act in our feeling.

Article 4

Justification of the perception of bodies

1208. In the perception of bodies therefore we find: 1. the

---

[136] 'Body' expresses an *ens in so far as it carries out in us an action having a given mode* (extension). If we considered the *body ens*, independently of its action, we would no longer be considering what we call 'body'. We must note this carefully, because it explains the term 'perception of bodies'. We say 'perception' in so far as 'body' expresses an agent acting on us. We must not turn body into an abstract, unknown or non-sensible being; if we do, its notion is destroyed. Hence, the *physical effect* is beyond all doubt, because it is understood in the very definition of body.

perception of *myself* with its modification or feelable experience; 2. the understanding perceiving the experience and acquiring the concept of experience; 3. the concept of experience comprising as its co-relative the concept of action; 4. the concept of actual action comprising an act and, therefore, an agent; 5. the agent mentally integrated through the need to conceive it as an *ens*.

The perception of *myself* with its modifications was justified in the previous chapter.

No demonstration is needed to show that the concepts of experience, action and agent are present in each other by implication, and that the understanding cannot have one without having simultaneously and at least implicitly the other two.

All we need to know is how the understanding passes from the concept of *agent* to the concept of *ens*. But we have already shown that being, naturally present to the human mind, is the universal means of knowing. We need only consider therefore that an *agent* is unknown if not conceived as an *ens*. This is the essential, universal function of the human mind. Thus, in the perception of bodies, the conception of the *ens* is logically anterior to that of agent, action and experience.

We said, however, that this fact involved some kind of *integration*, and in the following way. Because we need to conceive an *agent*, we have to unite *being* to the agent and thus apprehend it as an ens. But the mere concept of agent does not contain all that constitutes the ens; the first act is lacking because the ens first *is*, before acting in something different.

Thus, we add not only being in all its universality but the ens or basic first act of a body; this addition is an integration.

Note carefully that this first act, added to the agent through our need to conceive it, is nothing positive. The agent is always determined by its *sensible action*, which is the sole positive element we know in the perception of bodies. Hence, corporeal substance is *specified* by its *sensible* action alone, not by what we add to it through the need to conceive it. This *sensible* action is what takes the place of substance in bodies, and by its means they are what they are and receive their definition.

Because of this, we refrain from saying that the intellective perception of bodies involves an application of the principle of substance. What we understand as substance in them is not supplied; this is what is *perceived* by the senses. This perceived element is therefore the *first specific act* of bodies. The previous act, the pure form of ens, common to all entia, remains, but without specifying any ens.

At the same time it is clear that a *body* as perceived by a human being is an imperfect ens. It presents not the act by which it is an ens in itself, but the act by which it is an ens relative to feeling. This is why I call it *extrasubjective ens*.

CHAPTER 5

The certainty of entia which are not perceived but deduced from entia which are perceived

Article 1

The kind of entia we know by reasoning but not by perception

1209. Just as there are two kinds of entia that we perceive (the human soul and the body),[137] so there are two kinds of supra-sensible entia, angels[138] and God, which our mind arrives at by reasoning.

Article 2

The distinction between the idea and the judgment on the subsistence of these entia

1210. Two things must be explained about our knowledge of these entia: the conception or idea we have of them, and our judgment on their subsistence.

---

[137] We perceive OURSELVES, and from this perception we abstract the idea of the human soul by separating our *judgment* on the subsistence of a thing from the *real apprehension* of the thing (as I have often described in vol. 2). In the same way we perceive our *body* and all *bodies* acting directly on ours. From these perceptions we obtain by abstraction the concept both of organic and animal body, and inorganic body.

[138] Angels provided a great deal of material for ancient philosophies. It is not my intention to discuss whether we can demonstrate their subsistence rigorously by pure reason. It is sufficient that we form some idea of them, even though we may have no certain proof of their subsistence.

Article 3

The origin of the conception of these entia

1211. The conception (whatever it may be) arises from our abstraction and synthesis of the ideas of the things we have perceived, and from the idea of being in all its universality.

The notion of human intelligence is the nearest to these conceptions. If we strip human intelligence from the body and conceive an intelligence that is not ordered to inform any body, we have some concept of the angels.

If we strip human intelligence of all its limitations, we can obtain some kind of notion of God.

Article 4

Judgment on the existence of God

1212. It is not my intention to discuss the arguments used to establish the existence of angelic intelligences.

The existence of God is deduced in many ways, but the most common is that which establishes a *cause of the universe*. I have given the justification for the *principle of cause*, showing that it forms a perfect equation with the *principle of knowledge* and with the form of reason (cf. vol. 2, 558–573). I need only justify its particular application to divine existence.

The perception of the natures which compose the universe has been justified in the preceding chapters.

These natures *are* not being, but *have* being. Thus they *receive* being, because all that is not being (but nevertheless has being) must receive it from whoever is being.

Therefore, whoever is *being* must give being to the natures which compose the universe and are perceived by us.

But that which is *being* and gives being to creatures is cause, that is, God.

In this argument, analysis of perception provides us with these two facts: 1. natures exist, that is, *have* being; 2. natures *are* not themselves being.

If we apply the idea of being, we conclude as follows.

Being is added to natures and therefore natures begin to be, because 'to be added to' or 'to begin'[139] is the same thing.

But for natures to begin to be, or to have being added to them is an action (a change). But according to the principle of cause (*ibid.*), a first action (change) requires an immovable ens that has produced the action.

The *principle of cause*, therefore, is aptly applied to deduce the existence of God. The existence of God, arrived at in this way, is a perfect equation (cf. 1169) with the principle of cause; it is one of those particular cases for all of which the principle of cause has already given a universal conclusion which is valid relative not only to the mind but also to the subsistent thing.

---

[139] I would not like the true meaning of 'begins' to be misunderstood. 'To begin' does not mean that the nature did not exist in the preceding moment. 'To begin' refers to the instant in which the thing begins, not to the previous instant. Thus, if a nature lasts continuously for centuries, we can say that it begins at every moment because at every moment it needs to receive the energy which makes it subsist, that is, the activity of being.

CHAPTER 6
Knowledge of essences

Article 1
The sense in which we are said to know the essences of things

1213. Essence is that which is thought in the idea of anything (cf. vol. 2, 646). We know as many essences, therefore, as there are things about which we have some idea.

In saying that we know essences in this sense, we are speaking accurately, as the following observation will show.

When we say 'the essence of something', for example, of a *tree, human being, colour, size*, etc., we use words like *tree, human being, colour, size*, etc., to indicate the thing whose essence we are seeking. But how are names imposed on things? We have already seen that words are imposed on things in so far as we know things (cf. vol. 2, 679). If words are given a more extensive meaning, they are abused rather than used. They either obscure our vision, or exist as figments of our imagination. When I say *tree, human being, colour, size*, etc., I name things in so far as they are known to me. If they were not known by me, I could not name them. What do we mean, therefore, when we say that we are looking for the essence of *tree, human being, colour, size*, etc.? Simply that we are examining the meaning of these words in order to understand the ideas that human beings have applied to the names *tree, human being, colour*, size, etc. But perhaps I am looking for something that people have not attached to these names? In this case, we are no longer searching for the essence of *tree, human being*, etc., but the essence of some other unnamed and unknown thing for which we should not even search.

1214. It may be objected that essence described in this way is neither more nor less than what is comprised in the definition of anything. But this is precisely how antiquity understood essence: *Essentia*, says St. Thomas, *comprehendit in se illa tantum, quae cadunt in definitione speciei* [Essence includes within itself only that which falls within the definition of a species].[140]

Thus the Lockian school of philosophers were rash in mocking antiquity for maintaining that human beings know the essences of things. Quite possibly Locke's school did not even try to understand their predecessors.

1215. Another possible objection is that essence may not be what is thought in the idea of something, but rather that property which is first thought of in the thing and from which every other property depends. In fact, the essence is indeed the *first property*, and as such confirms and proves the knowledge of essences, rather than eliminates it. Moreover, careful attention shows that our definition is simpler and at the same time more rigorous.

We are said to have an idea of something as soon as we form some concept of it. We have the idea of a tree, for example, neither before nor after but as soon as we have conceived that quality, whatever it may be, to which human beings have given the name 'tree'. Not before, because we knew nothing of the tree before we had the concept of that property.[141] Not after, because everything added to the notion or property of which tree is the proper name, is something that does not belong to the meaning of the name. The additions are other essences, perhaps *accidentals*, which although they determine or actuate the essence of tree in a particular tree, are not tree taken simply as such. Every simple idea, therefore, contains an essence, and equally every composite idea contains an essence. And all the elements[142] which make a composite idea what it is, distinguished from everything else, are essential to it.

---

[140] *S.T.*, I, q. 3, art. 3. — *Species* is only the *idea*.

[141] Hence, *essences* are simple and, as antiquity reminds us, there is no middle state between knowing them and not knowing them. St Thomas says: 'Anyone not grasping the *essence* of some simple thing' (such as things in the first apprehension we have of them) 'is altogether ignorant of it. He cannot know a part of the essence and not know some other part of it. It is not made up of parts' (*In Metaph.* Arist., bk. 9, less. 11).

[142] Even those which, considered apart, would be accidental. For example, 'the essence of a red piece of cloth' is not only that it be cloth, but red as well. Otherwise it would not be red cloth any longer, but something else, which would have to be defined differently.

[1215]

Article 2

Why modern philosophers have denied
the knowledge of essences

1216. I have already said that this comes about because they have given the word 'essence' an improper meaning (cf. 1213–1215). Modern philosophers have understood in the word 'essence' not that which we know in something, but also that which could be unknown in it. For example, in bodies there could be present, besides the properties we know, another totally unknown property on which the others depend. We have called this the corporeal principle, not the corporeal essence (cf. vol. 2, 855). Let me explain more clearly.

We know a body through an action it exercises on us. We know therefore an activity determined by its effect, and this activity is the essence of our idea of body. But could it not be that such an activity was a partial potency of some other activity unknown to us? We can neither affirm nor deny this. This totally unknown activity has no name. Nevertheless, because it is not contradictory, it caused some thinkers to maintain that we do not know the essence of bodies, instead of saying that we do not know if the essence we call body depends on and is rooted in some other unknown essence as its special potency. There is a great divide between these two affirmations. In the second, we do not say that body is unknown to us, but that there is something different from body on which the body depends.

1217. Here too we can gain some idea of how, through haste and intemperance, clever people become rash in their research. They skip over and abandon the very things they are looking for. We have already seen in general how some people become sceptics; others seem to be fellow-travellers, as it were, with sceptics. Instead of taking the truth as their terminus and source of satisfaction, they go on, looking for something other than truth which would provide them with greater satisfaction. In our present case, some go beyond the definition of essence. Instead of stopping at it, they go on to form a gratuitous, frivolous concept of essence for the sake of which they struggle with their own imagination to prove that human beings have no knowledge of essence — the only thing which they do in fact know![143]

Article 3

The truth of essences which are known in general

1218. Known essences are simply that activity of a thing which is comprehended in the idea of the thing.

But every idea is contained by being, which is truth. Every idea, therefore, is a determined truth.

Error can be imported only into the *judgment* which we make about our ideas, that is, we can err in so far as we judge that more is comprehended in our ideas than is in fact comprehended. Let us see, therefore, what is required if there is to be no mistake in our judgment.

Article 4

Limits to our natural knowledge of essences

1219. We can ask two series of questions about the knowledge of essences. The first concerns my individual knowledge, the second the knowledge possessed by human nature.

About my particular knowledge I can ask whether I know a given thing, and whether I possess all the knowledge that is granted to human nature.

About the second kind of knowledge I can ask: 1. What are

[143] If a new, previously unknown principle, unable to be discerned by the senses, were somehow to be discovered in an object, and all the other properties were to originate from this, we would know a new essence, but it would not be that which we designate with the word 'body'. If we were to call the new principle body, this word would have changed its meaning. Nevertheless, because of the radical act of being, it would seem in such a case that we had come to know better the nature of *body*. This would indeed be true. We should not wonder, therefore, that the infinite mind knows all things in a single essence.

the means by which human nature comes to know? 2. How much does each means contribute in providing ideas and conceptions of things? 3. What are the universal impediments which sometimes prevent things knowable in themselves from being known by us? 4. How far are things themselves knowable?

The first series of questions is proper not to philosophy but to the prudence of each individual who wishes to evaluate his knowledge rightly and without presumption. The second is a matter for philosophy, and we shall deal with each of the questions belonging to this series by summarising what we have expounded elsewhere.

1220. *First question*: What are the means by which human nature knows *essences*, that is, forms the ideas of things?

Reply: There are four means: 1. *perception*, 2. *analysis* and *synthesis*, 3. the perception of either natural or conventional signs, especially the conventional sign of *speech*, and 4. *integration*.

1221. *Second question*: How much force and strength has each of these means in providing the ideas of things? In other words, which of them provides more *perfect* ideas of any thing?

Reply: The most perfect ideas that a human being can have are those acquired through *perception*. In these *ideas* the specific essence[144] is known *positively*, that is, the thing itself is known. It is this essence, when present, which is expressed by the names imposed on things, and it this which is unfolded in the definition given to a thing. Later, by means of analysis and synthesis, the specific essence takes three modes, each of which we have indicated respectively with the expressions, *perfect specific essence, abstract specific essence*, and *imperfect specific essence*.[145]

Analysis, which pertains to the second means of knowing, dissects *specific essences* (the foundation of all human knowledge) and thus forms abstract, partial essences such as *real and mental generic* essences. *Synthesis*, which also pertains to the

---

[144] The reader should recall the classification of the different *essences* intuited by human beings (cf. vol. 2, 646 ss.).

[145] We must note that the only truly simple mode amongst these three is that of abstract specific essence. The others are a composite of many accidental and substantial essences.

second means of knowing, provides only *complex essences* and adds some kind of union amongst the more simple essences.

The third means of knowing, through *signs*, presents us with even more imperfect ideas. This means enables us to have more or less positive *mental generic* ideas.[146]

Finally, the fourth method of knowing, *integration*, sometimes gives us negative ideas entirely devoid of matter. Such ideas make us know the existence of an ens, but provide no information about it other than that of its existence and a *relationship* with something else known to us. This is sufficient to determine the ens and prevent its confusion with any other ens.

1222. We then have to consider that *perception* constitutes the *maximum* limit of our knowledge of things. It truly constitutes what we call the *positive* element of any idea which has as its basis the *direct, real action* of anything on us or, to put it in another way, that part of a thing which is *really* communicated to us and inexists in us. This perceptive knowledge serves us as a rule with which to recognise the degrees and perfection of the ideas of things. The other means of conceiving (*analysis* and *synthesis*, *signs* and *integration*) cannot provide us with everything administered to us by perception. If one person himself perceives something, and another only hears the same thing described by the one who has perceived it, there is no doubt that the perceiver has a more perfect, lively and rich idea of the thing than the other who knows the thing only orally or nominally.[147] Consequently, when we compare the essences of things received through the various means we have described, we say that the full knowledge possible to a human being can only be obtained in the case of an idea procured with the first means, perception.

1223. *Third question*: What are the impediments which

---

[146] When we have the idea of the *species*, we possess in it also the characteristics that form the *genera*. If someone told us, therefore, that a new species had been found belonging to a genus known to us, the idea of that species in its *positive* part would be *generic* only because we would not know the characteristics that distinguish this species from others. It would, however, be specific in its *negative* part. We see from this that nominal and *negative essences* can be specific, generic and universal.

[147] We are speaking of a *thing* specifically different from the other things which have fallen under the perception of this second person.

prevent things knowable in themselves from being fully known by human beings?

Reply: They can only be summed up as those obstacles which prevent the thing from exercising on a human being the action of which it is capable. Things draw near to us and act in us with the force of which they are capable, independently of us. The proximity and the action depend upon an altogether different cause, totally outside human capacity and the capacity of every other creature. We have to list amongst the essential limitations of human knowing that 'the human mind cannot produce for itself any knowledge unless the objects of that knowledge are presented to the mind by some other ens' (cf. *Teodicea*, 85–115).

1224. *Fourth question*: How far are things themselves knowable?

Reply: Only being is known of itself, and constitutes knowability (cf. 1203 ss.). Hence, as our ancestors said, things are knowable in so far as they share in being.[148] If we consider our knowledge carefully, we notice an obvious and infinite distinction between the *intuition* of being and the *perception* of real things, the traces of which are finally resolved in feelings caused in us. We see that it is impossible to intuit being and not understand it; to intuit it is precisely to understand it. Feelings, however, are not understood *per se*. They begin to be understood only when we see them in relationship with being, that is, when we see them as a term of being itself. Hence, there is a difference between the *knowability* of things of themselves and their *knowability* in so far as it is participated, just as being is either *per se*, or participated being. As participated, the nature of the perception that we can have of real things varies. And it is this varying nature of *perception* that we must now consider somewhat more attentively.

---

[148] *Unumquodque cognoscibile est in quantum est ens* (St. Thomas, *In I Phys.*, c. 1).

Article 5

The subjective and objective part in the knowledge of essences

1225. *Perception* is the means providing us with the *maximum* degree of knowledge of things. It is therefore the rule according to which we judge the quantity of our knowing. We say that we have a *perfect conception* of anything if we have *perceived* it, and that our conception is not perfect if we have not perceived it.

But our *perception* of things differs from one thing to another. Some things we know intimately and fully, others more superficially. This variety in perception depends upon several causes which we must examine carefully. First, we shall speak of the variety of fullness in perception, which depends on the differing knowableness of things themselves and on our essential constitution.

In the first place, therefore, what we conceive through perceiving things is in part *objective* and in part *subjective*. We have to note and distinguish carefully these two elements[149] and first show that their necessity depends upon an essential limitation of human nature.

Being is the *object* itself. Everything that is not being, therefore, is *per se* unknown, and must be made known by being. But what are we? We are certainly not being. We see being and we conceive it, but at the same time we feel that we conceive it as something that is present to us but is not us. In us as intelligent beings, therefore, we have to distinguish two essentially distinct elements: 1. the *being* that we see; 2. ourselves who see *being*.

Being as seen by us is *knowledge*; we are *feeling*. *Knowledge* need not be known through any other means precisely because it is knowledge; feeling needs an act of knowledge in order that it be known. *Being* is the object, and we are the subject. It is always necessary, therefore, that something *subjective* (which

[149] If we neglect the *subjective* element, as some classes of dogmatists do, we become overbearing and pretentious, which certainly does not become us. If we neglect the *objective* element, as the critical school of sceptics did, we find ourselves debased and despoiled of true and real knowledge. Our investigation is very important, therefore, if we are to avoid this twofold danger in philosophy.

constitutes the matter of our knowledge) be mingled with something *objective* (that constitutes the form of knowledge).

In this way we can formulate the principle for discerning the objective from the subjective part of perceptions: 'Everything in our conception of a thing which comes from being is objective; everything placed there by our feeling as such[150] is subjective.'

1226. This principle is equivalent to saying: 'Ourselves and our modifications are the subjective part. If, therefore, something remains in the conception of a thing when we remove the conception of ourselves and the modifications of ourselves, it is here that we must look for the objective part of perception. We can be sure that this has not been posited by us, but is found in the thing perceived. For example, when I perceive something, its existence is not my existence; it is not subjective; its energy is not my energy.' In a word, everything that I am forced to grant in the thing in virtue simply of the idea of being is its objective part.

1227. We can now ask if the subjective part is the misleading part and the objective the truthful part.

First, provided we do not change one for the other, neither the subjective nor the objective part is *misleading*. If we apply what belongs only to us to things different from us, we deceive ourselves. But we are certainly not constrained by nature to take such a step. Although we possess an inclination towards sense, we also have the means for withstanding its attraction. If, therefore, we take subjective knowledge for subjective, and objective for objective, we shall not mislead ourselves, and even the subjective knowledge will be true and useful for us.

What is the means enabling us to distinguish safely between the subjective and objective parts of knowledge? We have

[150] I say 'by our feeling as such' because *being* is already added in the intellective perception, that is, we recognise in this perception an act or term of being. Hence (cf. vol. 2, 880 ss.) I distinguished and separated the *extrasubjective* from the *subjective* part in the perception of bodies by means of a principle which is only a particular application of the general principle given here. By means of that principle I found three *extrasubjective* elements in the perception of external bodies: 1. the existence of a force; 2. multiplicity; and 3. continuous extension. These elements are things essentially different from us (subject).

already seen that this is the power essential to being itself which, as object, and objectivity itself, is essentially independent of us. What we conclude about things in virtue of being — in other words, what we do not receive from ourselves — is the *objective* part of knowledge; the *subjective* part comes from ourselves, not from being. Those who do not see that being is an essence in itself, absolute and totally different from our own, and that we conceive it as such, confuse the object with the subject, and call all human knowledge subjective.

1228. *Secondly*, we must note that the *subject* feels itself as *subject*, and that if we take this *feeling* in the place of *knowledge*, we imagine we have some subjective knowledge. But this is not knowledge. We can have *objective* knowledge even of the subject. This knowledge does not delude us, although it can indeed be called subjective knowledge in so far as through it we know the subject. In a word, we are the source of the subjective part of knowledge, just as *being* is the source of objective knowledge. Knowing ourselves for the subjects that we are is to know ourselves truly. The knowledge that can delude us is only that which we have of other things which differ from being and from ourselves as subjects because they are not contained in the subject with their very own entity.

Limited things different from us are subjects if, like us, they have a power of feeling or of understanding; but if they are without the power of feeling, they are neither an *object per se* nor a *subject*. We are therefore obliged to indicate them negatively as *extrasubjective*. This word means simply that their first act, which constitutes them as real entia, remains unknown to us and must be supplied by us if we are to be able to understand it, as we said about bodies. But that which is *extrasubjective* is not perceived by us except through its sense-arousing action upon us. Nevertheless as we perceive it, we mingle with it something *subjective*, that is, something of our own feeling which must be separated out if we are to avoid delusion.

Article 6

Consequences of the nature of our knowledge of essences

1229. Being therefore has an absolute and essential *knowability*. We (the subject) possess knowability through being; things different from us and from being have their knowability by means of us and of being, that is, in so far as they exercise some force on us while we, who know ourselves through being, know also the activities modifying us.

This teaching gives rise to several consequences which throw light on the intimate nature of human knowledge.

1. Because the subject varies, different *intelligent subjects* have a different perception of their own subject. The variation in subjects must also provide variety in the perceptions of things which, different from being and from the subject, can give, as we said, only a mixed perception made up of what is extrasubjective and objective.

1230. 2. *Being* which shines in the mind does not present itself as subsistent and complete in itself. It is, as a result, *most common*. But all other things are knowable only through *being*. The knowledge we have in our present state is, therefore, essentially *universal*; our intellect does not attain to any subsistent, individual ens. In fact, there is not a single ens in the world which is knowable of itself; each needs to be made knowable through its relationship with most common being. If *being* which shines in our minds were complete with its essential terms, it would be an individual essentially perceived by our understanding because being is knowable of its nature and indeed constitutes knowledge [*App.*, no. 8]: it would be God.

Hence, although our feelings are particular, our knowledge of them always contains what is universal. Knowing a feeling simply means perceiving it in its possibility and considering it as an essence which can very often be actuated in an indefinite number of individuals.

1231. 3. As a result, our perceptions of different things can be reduced to an equivalent number of formulae which express their nature.

I. The intuition of being provides this formula: 'Being is intuited of itself, and cannot be intuited in any other way'.

II. The general perception of all other things is covered by the following formula: 'A determined ens is perceived by means of feeling.' This formula is rendered more particular according to the different ways of perceiving things, and is expressed in the following formulae:

a) In the idea of the soul we know an ens determined by a substantial feeling that constitutes our substance, *ourselves*.

b) In the idea of our body we know an ens determined by some kind of action on our substantial feeling (on *ourselves*). This action is considered by us as *knowable substance*.

1232. 4. Because all *things* are seen as terms, actuations and *effects* of being (although we may not see exactly how they are effects), we can say in general that 'the essences we know are the effects of being'. We ourselves are an effect of being because our essence could not be realised in a real subsistence except by our receiving the act of being. And we know other things through their effects upon us.[151]

Article 7

The imperfection of objective intuition

1233. Although the intuition of *being* is objective and the same as the intuition of *truth*, it can vary according to the degrees of light by which being is manifested to the mind and renders it capable of acts of knowledge. These degrees of greater light are the perfection of the very essence of creatures because they are the perfection of the creatures' form. Perhaps this explains one of the causes (the first and greatest?) of differing intellectual capacities.

I do not know, however, if the degrees in the clarity of light which being reveals to minds are something different from the

[151] God, however, knows the particulars in all things, because his knowledge is not produced by things different from being, by effects, but by being itself, the *cause* of things, as St. Thomas states so well (*C.G.*, I, q. 65).

degrees of the quantity of that which being in itself and of itself can reveal to intelligences.

Article 8

Positive and negative essences

1234. The distinction between positive and negative cognitions draws its origin from the distinction between the objective part of perception and the subjective and extrasubjective part of perception.

But encountering the phrase *negative essence* or *knowledge* immediately makes us ask how we can possibly have negative knowledge. We either know or do not know. If we know something, our knowledge is positive of its own nature. It is impossible for any knowledge to be called *negative*.

This apparent difficulty vanishes if we have learned to understand the nature of the differing cognitions we can have of anything. We must remember that knowledge of any subsistent thing is composed of 1. what issues from the idea of being; 2. what we feel or perceive with our feeling of the real thing. For example, knowledge that a thing subsists issues from the idea of being as a result of the sense experience we have of this thing. We cannot know, however, whether this thing is a tree, or possesses a certain kind of trunk, leaves or fruit or any other sort of essential and accidental qualities unless we have perceived all these things with our senses, either together or a little at a time. If we had never seen or felt anything like these qualities of a tree, we could never in any way imagine or conceive anything about them. It is our sense perception that renders the idea of the subsistent *tree* full and vivid, that is, positive. The tree in this perception is presented to us in the active form and state it can have relative to us. And although a great deal of what is extrasubjective and subjective (which we can, however, distinguish and separate from what is objective) comes to us through such perception and representation, we experience all the activity that the tree can exert on us as sentient entia. Hence we apprehend and receive the real, *effective connection* that the nature of the tree has with our own nature.

[1234]

We must, therefore, distinguish *judgment about the subsistence* of the tree from the *representation* of the tree. The former is entirely objective because it reaches out to judge something of the tree's subsistence (and apply the idea of being); the latter is made up of three elements: that which is objective, that which is extrasubjective, and that which is subjective.

Let us imagine now that we have never perceived this thing we call *tree*. Could we know if a tree subsisted? We certainly could if someone told us. But how can we know whether that which subsists is a *tree*? I cannot know this for certain, but I do know that *something* called *tree* subsists. My knowledge is simply that a thing exists (this is completely objective knowledge because the idea of thing is universal and undetermined), and that this thing is called *tree* by human beings. The name determines the thing exactly without however providing me with any representation of it marked by a relationship that has something real in itself: the relationship is created simply by the human mind which gives the thing its name.

1235. However, the relationship of which we are speaking could possess something real instead of being merely nominal, without its providing me with any representation of the thing. I may know some fruit without knowing more than that it has been produced by something in this world. This ens, the cause of the fruit, is known by me through its effect, that is, through a real relationship suitable for determining the thing perfectly for me, but without providing me with any representation of it. This representation consists solely in the *connection between the inherent activity of the thing and my feeling*, that is, in the experience I have of that activity when I feel its effect as it causes a modification of my feeling.

1236. In these two cases, therefore, I know the thing only through an *arbitrary* or *natural relationship*, not by any perception of the thing. We must notice here that the *relationship* is always constituted by the idea of being and as such belongs to the objective part of knowledge. Not only the relationship of *cause*, but that of *sign*, and any other relationship suitable for determining for me something unknown of itself, appertains to the objective part of knowledge.

Knowing that a thing is, knowing a relationship that determines it, does not mean that we possess some representation of it, as we said. Such knowledge, therefore, does not provide a positive idea of a thing. This is constituted, I must repeat, 'by the immediate action of the thing on us as sentient *entia*, and our consciousness of this action which provides knowledge of the representation itself'.

The idea as we have described it, void of representation, is rightly called *negative* because, in all that it makes known, it contains no representation of the thing. This idea appertains completely to the idea of being and its applications. It is *per se* extraneous to the nature of the thing which, when it becomes known, participates in the idea.

Article 9

The negative idea of God

1237. Although a long tradition tells us that our idea of God is negative, there are several difficulties connected with this which can usefully be discussed here.

The first difficulty. Objectors say that we form the idea of the supreme, infinite spirit by starting from the idea of the soul, stripping it of all its limitations, and adding to it all possible worth. But if the idea of the soul is positive, and we add so much to it, the resulting idea must be much more positive.

Reply. It is not true that we form the idea of God by starting from the soul in the way indicated.

In ideas we have to distinguish the two parts mentioned in the preceding article. 1. The part which contains a subsistence, and some determination by means of a *relationship*. This part provides only a negative idea and presents us with nothing about the thing itself (which is not offered to our perception). 2. The part which represents the thing. This part makes us feel *the force that the thing has to act in us*, and hence to produce a perception of itself. This second part is positive. It is the vital part, if I may call it that. In comparison with this, the first part is only a sketch of an idea, or fundamental outline within which the idea must be found. It is not the idea itself.

In the idea we have of God in this life, we possess the first part through the relationships of cause and effect, of limited and

[1237]

unlimited, of imperfect and perfect, and so on. But however many these *relationships* may be, they can provide us only with the first of the parts we have described.

1238. Nature, however, does not allow us to be truly satisfied with such an idea of a non-sensible thing. We have an essential, profound need within us, the first need of human nature, which continually prompts us to desire a full, positive idea of God. We want to perceive him, to have a direct vision of him. But such longings of nature cannot be entirely satisfied here on earth. Incapable of perceiving God himself by natural means, we have recourse to analogies of him, the best of which we find in intelligent spirits such as the human soul. We bring these analogies together, and from them compose the concept as well as we can. This explains why religions themselves have recourse to symbols, a necessary supplement for the positive, beatifying idea of God which we lack here on earth, but to which we aspire unendingly without knowing it, stimulated by means of a wonderful instinct of our human nature [*App.*, no. 9].

The symbols we have of God do not, therefore, give us any perception of the divine essence. These likenesses and symbols possess nothing more than distant analogy with God.

It is true that the idea we have of an ens is greater and fuller if we consider this ens with all its known perfections united in it. Nevertheless, it is still totally inadequate, defective and nothing in comparison with the representation of God. This will become more clear if we consider that, having accumulated all possible perfections in an ens, we have still not found the *single act* through which they all subsist. This act related to God must be such that each of these perfections, and all of them taken together, are contained and made one in it. No example of such perfect simplicity and unity is to be found in nature. This unity and simplicity of being form the divine essence, and until we see the subsistent being which is one in this way we have no positive idea of God (cf. *Teodicea*, 55–60).

1239. *Second difficulty.* If our knowledge of God is negative, it is not knowledge. God will never be found when we turn our attention and affection towards him; we shall never know to whom we are directing our attention. In such a situation, it is as though God did not exist for us.

Reply. This difficulty also vanishes when the negative idea we have been describing is understood. But we need to explain it in other words.

Let us imagine something that we have never known either through perception, or by likeness, analogy of nature, or relationship with any other thing we have perceived.

What we are imagining is altogether unknown to us. But its *existence* is then revealed to us. We begin to know something about it, without however knowing anything of its *essence*. In a word, we know that something unknown to us exists.

What else could we know about this thing without at the same time knowing its essence?

We could know all the infinite *relationships* it can have with things known to us.

When we speak of God, we are talking of one who has relationships with *real things*, with *feelings* and with *ideas*, the three activities we have previously distinguished.

With *real things*, he has the relationship of cause. We know this because we know the effects of God, as we call this thing *unknown* to us. It is true that the effects do not reveal the cause itself, which remains veiled, as it were. But it is also true that these effects are so proper to this cause that they are impossible to any other. Consequently, through them, as through a sure sign, we have delineated the cause in such a way that we cannot mistake or confuse it with any other. We have some sure datum which involves the positive concept, although our limitation prevents our drawing it out. In fact, the notion 'creatures' implicitly contains the notion of God which we would find if we were able to understand fully what is expressed by the word 'creation'. The divine origin of this word becomes obvious when we consider its hidden meaning. Such a word, whose meaning cannot be fully understood by reason, would require for its understanding the prior positive idea of God which it implies.

With *feelings*, God has the relationship of *supreme good*. We continually desire happiness, of which we have only a universal notion. In the same way, we desire the hidden being, whose possession forms happiness.

With *ideas*, God has the relationship of *being which is per se intelligible*.

We have the idea of being in which is comprised *something*

[1239]

infinite in potency. As a result, in any series of things we never come to a term beyond which we can pass to attain the infinite number. This capacity for taking yet another step, however many we have already taken, makes us comprehend that all the things of which these series are composed are essentially limited. But the concept of limited things is relative to something unlimited and absolute. Therefore, although we do not know this unlimited and absolute being, we do understand its possibility. We understand that it is the opposite of what we know (that is, what is limited). In contradistinction to what is limited, we think what is real and unlimited, but only *negatively*.

When we accumulate in an ens all the degrees and qualities of perfection that we know, we have no doubt that we are still engaged with a limited ens. But we mentally reach out from this to its contrary, and maintain that an ens is possible contrary to this limited ens in which my imagination is confined.[152] But if someone asks us what this ens is, we have to say that we do not know it. We only know that it is the opposite of all that one can think, that is, the opposite of all that is limited. Through this opposition, therefore, and through this negation of *limited ens*, what is unknown is contradistinguished and established in such a way that it cannot be confused at all with any other ens. As the mind progresses, it sets aside all limited entia apart from which only the unlimited can exist. God therefore is formed through the exclusion of every other possible being distinct from him, and consequently by means of negations.

1240. The mind, however, has a more proximate knowledge of God, although this, too, is negative. It knows separately 1. possible being, 2. some specific essences, and 3. the *act* by which these essences exist, that is, some limited substances. But essence, in so far as it is distinct from being, is a limitation of being. Limits, however, are impossible in God. By such an observation we draw up a formula with which we express only God: 'Being thought as complete in act is God.' This formula is true, but unintelligible to human beings in so far as they cannot think being itself in its perfect, complete act.

This is the *ineffable name* of God, that is, a formula that can express only God. Although we cannot understand this

---

[152] Here we are speaking of the *concept* of God, not of his *existence*.

formula in its unity, it can be understood in its elements. This is sufficient to enable us to use it in marking and naming God separately from all other things, in none of which we find these elements bound together in the way they are expressed in our formula.

1241. Our negative knowledge of God, therefore, is such that through it, we know, without admixture of error, the one to whom we have to turn. We can without hesitation adore our *cause*, know in practice the *source of goodness*, and in the *light proper to minds* terminate our desire for knowledge. How stupid and vain is the effort of this world's sages who, simply because they misuse the phrase 'incomprehensible being', would want to restrain and turn away mankind from approaching this inexhaustible spring of all good!

Article 10

Conclusion

1242. I shall conclude this chapter on our knowledge of essences with three observations.

1. The same names are applied to every kind of idea that we have, whether these ideas are positive or negative. Ideas therefore, relative to language, are indicated identically and all seem to express equally full, positive essences. This, however, is not the case. We need to note this carefully in order not to change a mental or purely nominal ens into a real ens [*App.*, no. 10].

1243. 2. With the simple idea of anything, according to which we think its essence, we affirm nothing about the subsistence of entia; we are still in the world of possibilities. From the moment essences are conceived by us, they show themselves to us as possible by their nature because being possible is equivalent to being thinkable. This explains why antiquity maintained that there could be no error in the simple apprehension of things (ideas). And St. Thomas approves Aristotle's dictum which defines *intelligence* as the faculty of what is *indivisible*, in which (faculty) falsity cannot be found.[153]

---

[153] Arist., *De Anima*, bk. 3.

1244. 3. We have seen that only essences, the objects of various branches of knowledge, can be the particular principles of the branches of knowledge (cf. vol. 2, 570 ss.). Sciences, or branches of knowledge, therefore, have principles about which error is impossible.

PART FOUR

ERRORS
TO WHICH HUMAN KNOWLEDGE
IS SUBJECT

CHAPTER 1

A summary of all the cognitions in which nature itself protects us from every error

1245. If truth and certainty had been committed to the care of human free will, they would have languished and in all probability soon been annihilated by human perversity. For this reason we saw that the first truths were entrusted by creative Providence to human nature, not to an individual human being. Human nature, essentially intelligent, sees the first truths essentially. Human beings cannot but see them, nor can they annihilate them. Just as they have no power to create anything, they have no power to destroy anything that has received existence from God [*App.*, no. 11].

1246. Let us therefore briefly summarise all that nature does to ensure that human beings possess truth and are protected from error. We will thus confirm that genuine scepticism is impossible; that it is simply a lie told by an alienated human being to himself or others; and that in intelligent natures truth has a possession or even a dominion which cannot be taken away, although free human nature can sin against truth.

I. First, a human being naturally has the permanent vision of *being* in general. Being is the *light* of reason, the final *reason* of human reasoning; it always convinces while remaining unconquered itself.[154] This final *reason* is *truth*, so that

---

[154] St. Thomas teaches that the human being cannot in any way err about being. He says: *Proprium obiectum intellectus est quod quid est* (this means

all things are true in so far they share in it. The human being therefore possesses truth by nature.

II. The first principles of reason are the idea of *being* as applied (cf. vol. 2, 480 ss.) and, like the idea of being, are immune from error.[155]

These first truths are the sources of all human cognitions, but there are also truths of fact about which we cannot err. They are:

III. Human beings cannot be deceived about their own existence.[156]

IV. They cannot err about the direct consciousness of their principal modifications[157]

V. When our understanding receives solely what the senses give, they do not draw it into error [*App.*, no. 12]. This witness of the senses is a part of the consciousness whose certainty was indicated in IV.

VI. Abstraction, which draws ideas from perceptions, that is, knowledge of the *essences* of things or, as the ancient writers called it, *simple apprehension*, is also immune from error.[158] As we have seen, these *essences* are the *particular*

being, the *essence* of things): *unde* CIRCA HOC NON DECIPITUR INTELLECTUS ['The proper object of the intellect is that something is' (this means *being*, the *essence* of things). 'Hence the INTELLECT IS NOT DECEIVED IN THIS'] (*Contra G.*, I, q. 58).

[155] St. Thomas says: *Intellectus* IN PRIMIS PRINCIPIIS NON ERRAT, *sed in conclusionibus interdum, ad quas ex primis principiis ratiocinando procedit* [The intellect DOES NOT ERR ABOUT FIRST PRINCIPLES, but errs in the conclusions it reaches when reasoning from first principles] (*Contra G.*, I, q. 61).

[156] St. Thomas says: NULLUS ERRAVIT UNQUAM IN HOC QUOD NON PERCIPERE SE VIVERE [NOBODY HAS EVER ERRED BY NOT PERCEIVING THAT HE IS ALIVE] (*De Verit.*, q. 10, art. 8).

[157] It was from this fact that Descartes' 'I think' (consciousness of thought) began, and *evidence* of this kind is the foundation of the whole Cartesian edifice. We have noted that although this foundation is solid, its solidity is due to the principles of reason; it cannot therefore be the first stone of the edifice of knowledge. Descartes' error is that he did not start to build from the foundations. It was the weak point which gave way against the assaults on Cartesian philosophy.

[158] This also was taught by St. Thomas (*De Anima*, bk. 3, less. 11): 'There is an action of the intellect by which it perceives *what is indivisible*' (that is, simple essences), 'for example, when it understands human nature, or the ox, or anything like this amongst non-composite objects. Such understanding is

principles of the branches of knowledge, and correspond to the *preconceptions* or προλήψεις of Epicurus.

Such then are the natural, unbreakable bonds by which truth is united and secured with our nature, a nature made for truth. However, we have reviewed only the limits placed on the temerity of human reason, limits within which reason's assaults against truth are defeated and repulsed. We must also consider the extent of error conceded to human beings within which they can harm themselves.

about things in which there is no falsehood both because non-composite things are neither true nor false, and because the intellect does not deceive itself about the being of things. But in those intelligible things which contain what is true and what is false, a kind of composition of understood things is present, as for instance, when a single thing is formed from many' (composite ideas are formed by the operation of synthesis). The *non-composite* things St. Thomas speaks of are *pure ideas*, devoid of judgment about real, subsistent things. There is nothing false or true in them because they are exemplars and truths of things. Truth and falsehood are present in things in the measure that the things correspond or not to their exemplar-ideas. If, therefore, we are not thinking of real things but only of ideas and possibilities of things, we never judge the correspondence of things to ideas. Truth and falsehood, and the possibility of error, are in this judgment.

[1246]

CHAPTER 2
The nature of human errors

Article 1
The distinction between investigating the nature of error and investigating the nature of its cause

1247. A discussion about the *cause* of errors can easily be substituted for a discussion about their *nature*. In fact, when we have described the *nature* of error, how it comes about, and in what it consists, we seem to have found its cause as well. This happens because, in order to describe the nature of error and how it comes about, we must also describe the act by which our understanding falls into error. It is this act, we are told, that is precisely the *cause* of error.

All this is indeed true, but the act is the proximate, not the *final cause* moving our understanding to perform the operation with which it produces error for itself. Error consists in a mistaken act of the understanding. The nature of error, the way it comes about, and even its proximate cause, are in the act of the understanding. But what moves the understanding to this act? This question differs from the first; we want to know the first cause which inclines and stimulates human beings to error. Because both causes, the proximate and the remote, are intimately bound together, we will first say a word about the proximate cause, in which the *nature* of error consists, and then investigate the less proximate or remote *cause*, which is the true, efficient cause of our errors.

Article 2
Error is solely in the understanding

1248. To say that the senses deceive, and to attribute errors to the imagination is inexact and false, as we said.

In order to be true, such expressions have to mean that the senses and imagination simply furnish the matter and occasion of error. A square tower seen from a distance appears to be round, but our eye does not tell us the tower is round; it only tells us that the term of our sensation is a *round, felt experience* (or rather it *has* a round, felt experience — it does not *tell* us this). The understanding adds its judgment and concludes from the *round, felt experience* that it sees a round tower. It is the understanding that deceives itself; the intellect judges as probable or certain the rich reward vividly presented by the imagination. The vividness of the image is real, but the understanding errs in deducing probability or certainty from it.

Everyone knows this truth, but writers have never been willing to abandon equivocal expressions about errors of the senses, the imagination, etc., in order to state that only the occasion of the deceptions is in the senses and imagination.[159]

Article 3

Error is in judgments posterior to perceptions

1249. Only the understanding is subject to error (cf. vol. 1, 124). If we wish to know which particular function of the

---

[159] 'For the same reason,' Bossuet says, 'only the understanding can err. Properly speaking, error is not in feeling, which always does what it must do; it is designed to act according to the dispositions of both objects and organs. The understanding must judge of the organs themselves and draw the necessary consequences from sensations. If it allows itself to be taken by surprise, it alone is deceiving itself' (*De la connaissance de Dieu et de soi-même*, c. 1, 7). Earlier, St. Thomas had taught that feeling perceives neither *truth* nor *falsity*, which concern the intellect alone. Thus, the expression 'sense errors' should be understood to mean either that sense furnishes the *occasion* of *self-deception* to the intellect, or that the expression is true or false in the way non-sensible things are true or false relative to the intellect which *apprehends* things as they are: *Falsitas non (est) in sensu, sicut in cognoscente verum et falsum. — Falsitas non est quaerenda in sensu nisi sicuti ibi est veritas. Veritas autem non sic est in sensu, ut sensus cognoscat veritatem sed in quantum veram apprehensionem habet de sensibilibus* [Falsehood (is) not in feeling in the way that true and false are in the one who knows… Falsehood is to be sought in feeling only to the extent that truth is there. But truth is not in feeling in order that feeling may know truth: it is there in so far as feeling has a true apprehension of sensible things] (*S.T.*, I, q. 17, art. 2).

understanding is subject to error, we quickly see that it is the *judgment*. Error is a *deficiency*[160] in our judgments by which we assert what is false rather than what is true.

But the first judgments, that is, our perceptions, together with the ideas we draw from them (which the ancient writers called *simple apprehensions*) are immune from error. These first actions are carried out by our intelligent nature, which does not err (cf. 1213 ss.).

The seat of error therefore lies in the *judgments* made by our *reason* after our perceptions of things; and in these judgments two objects are always united.[161]

1250. The union of two objects can be called a synthesis. Hence we could reduce the general formula for errors to the following: 'Error always consists in a badly made synthesis of objects.'

1251. One of the two objects is *subject* of the judgment, the other *predicate*. Thus every error consists in the wrong union of a *predicate* and *subject*. We err either by 1. matching a predicate to a subject to which the predicate does not belong, or 2. denying a predicate to a subject to which the predicate does belong. Matching a predicate to a subject is a kind of union; denying a predicate, a kind of mental division. Hence, ancient writers said that the understanding is subject to error only when it unites or divides.[162]

---

[160] *Error*, like any evil, is a *negative* not a *positive* thing, according to the well-known observation of that great Father of the Church, St. Augustine: *Si verum est id quod est, falsum non esse uspiam concludetur quovis repugnante* [If that which is true is that which is, we must conclude that what is false is not, whatever the objections' (*Solil*, 2, 8).

[161] This is the characteristic of such *judgments*, which distinguishes them from judgments that are also *perceptions*. The latter are not composed of two objects but of an object and a *something sensed*, as we have shown (cf. vol. 1, 119, 120 and fn.).

[162] We can say that the understanding is subject to error in composition and division for the reason given. But these two operations can be reduced to one, that is, *composition*. *Division* can take the form of composition because the *composition* of a negative predicate with a subject is true division under the form of composition, as in the case of algebraic addition when the quantities of opposite signs are united. Hence St. Thomas sometimes simply says: 'Falsehood proper to the intellect concerns *per se* only composition', without more ado (*S. T.*, I, q. 17, art. 3). Aristotle says the same (cf. bk. 3, *De*

Article 4

Explanation of the particular kind of errors caused by the misuse of language

1252. We can give a general meaning to a word,[163] or a meaning different from that given it by common use. But unless we first define its meaning and say that we are using it not as an accepted, current sign, but as an arbitrary sign of some idea of our own, we infallibly lead ourselves and others into error. We then have to take great care throughout our discourse to keep to the given definition of the word. We must not revert to the normal use, to which we are drawn continually by the practice and example of others.

1253. Sometimes, however, we do not change the meaning of words advertently and intentionally. We unconsciously use them in a more or less general sense, or differently from the meaning they have, so that error enters unnoticed into our discourses.

Anima, test. 21, 22). At other times St. Thomas says that falsity is found where the intellect either composes or divides: 'We are not deceived about the essence of things... But we can be deceived when composing or dividing, if we attribute to the thing whose essence we understand anything which does not necessarily belong to that essence, or is contrary to it': *circa quod quid est intellectus non decipitur. — In componendo vero vel dividendo potest decipi, dum attribuit rei, cuius quidditatem intelligit, aliquid quod eam non consequitur, vel quo ei opponitur (S.T.*, I, q. 17, art. 3).

[163] It is generally thought that a determined sense is not given to words in common use. This is false — if it were true, an author's first qualification, which is to use words *properly*, would cease. We are led to think that common sense (which is principally responsible for determining the meaning of words) does not give us a determined sense for these two apparent reasons: 1. we notice that individuals often *misuse* language in their arguments; and 2. the majority of people are incapable of defining any word when we ask them. The first reason demonstrates the opposite of what it is intended to prove; we would be unable to know any particular *misuse* of language unless we knew the *proper*, determined sense of a word. The second reason demonstrates nothing provided we note the existence of *popular* and *scientific* knowledge. Both of these are true, but only *scientific* knowledge (characterised by St. Thomas as *fit per studiosam inquisitionem* [acquired by studious research] (*S.T.*, I, a. 87, art. 2)) provides *definitions*, whose composition requires analysis, comparisons, a separation between what is common and the *difference*. Cf. vol. 2, *App.*, no. 14.

In fact we cannot always keep to the new meaning we improperly gave the word at the beginning. From time to time, as our discourse advances, we slip back into the common meaning of the word and come close to normal speech. Even if we were able to keep to the false meaning which we have given inadvertently or as a result of some bias (something totally impossible), other people would certainly not understand us. We would intend the meaning that we had assigned the word, while they would understand the meaning given by common use. This kind of misunderstanding is the source of infinite controversies among educated people.

1254. Analysing the error we have described, we find it consists in making two objects out of one. Any misused word signifies two things: 1. the meaning fixed for it by use (which has not been withdrawn by some particular declaration, nor can be withdrawn without such a declaration); and 2. the meaning given by the speaker, who applies his own words to the object thought by him as expressed in the word. At this point, there are good grounds for confusing two essences, two objects, by attributing to one object what belongs to the other. This at least is how the listener certainly understands it.

1255. Two classes of error can be found in the fact we have described. The speaker, if he intends to speak about one object but expresses another through the word he uses, errs by attributing the definition of one thing to another.

If, on the other hand, he mistakenly takes the word first in one sense and then in another, he makes one object out of two, grotesquely uniting in one single ens parts of both objects. Thus, for example, reason may first be predicated of an object. Later some quality attributable only to brute animals (such as the necessity of following instinct alone) may be predicated of the same object. Rousseau did this when he made the phrase 'state of nature' (that is, human nature) mean 'state natural to animals' (perhaps as a satire on his time, or to express his own profound sadness), and concluded that a wild, bestial life was more fitting for human nature.

1256. Antiquity had said that the understanding, when coming to know the being of things, is subject *per accidens* to error. As a result of careful analysis, we can see that these errors originate from a wrong use of language. When language is used incorrectly, it multiplies and mixes entia, producing a genuine, intellectual synthesis.[164]

Article 5

Why error is only in judgments posterior to perceptions and first ideas

1257. Error comes about in an act of the spirit posterior to perceptions and first ideas. Perceptions, like all actions in which the understanding does not err (cf. 1246), *necessarily* happen in us. This is a fact of intelligent nature, and intelligent nature does not err.[165] We therefore either have or do not have *perceptions*, but when we have them, we are never mistaken. This is also true of the *ideas of things contained in perceptions*.

Article 6

Direct knowledge and reflective knowledge — continuation

1258. I must however explain more carefully the two kinds of knowledge, *direct* and *reflective*, already mentioned many

---

[164] Cf. *S.T.*, I, q. 17, art. 3 where St. Thomas begins: *Quia vero falsitas intellectus per se, solum circa compositionem intellectus est,* per accidens *etiam in operatione intellectus, qua cognoscit quod quid est, potest esse falsitas, IN QUANTUM IBI COMPOSITIO INTELLECTUS ADMISCETUR* [Although falsehood proper to the intellect *per se* concerns solely composition by the intellect, falsehood can be present *per accidens* in the intellect's activity by which it knows that something is, IN SO FAR AS COMPOSITION BY THE INTELLECT IS MIXED WITH THE INTELLECT'S ACTIVITY]. He goes on to explain the two classes of errors we have considered. Strictly speaking, however, even these errors arise solely by means of some *composition* by the intellect, occasioned by language. It seems clearer, therefore, and less subject to equivocation if, instead of saying that here also the understanding errs only *per accidens* in its apprehension, we say that it errs in its composition and not in its apprehension, as I have observed elsewhere.

[165] St. Thomas also gives this reason. He says: *Res naturalis non deficit ab esse, quod sibi competit secundum suam formam* [A natural thing is not defective in being which belongs to it according to its form] (*S.T.*, I, q. 17, art. 3).

times. I do this because our purpose is to know the intellectual acts in which error consists.

We saw that when we come into this world, void of all ideas of things, we are affected by sensations, which leave some phenomena in our phantasy (images). Our understanding has perceptions from these sensations, and by means of the images has ideas, as I have explained.[166]

The understanding forms perceptions and the ideas posterior to perceptions in a natural, instinctive way. Hence, because nature does not err, the understanding is not subject to error (cf. 1257).

These *first*, unwilled *acts of knowledge* however must be distinguished from subsequent, willed acts. The former make up *direct* knowledge, the second, *reflective knowledge*.

1259. The greatest philosophers were always aware of the distinction between these two kinds of human acts of knowledge. Only sensist philosophy lost sight of such an important distinction in the tradition of knowledge.

Direct knowledge is purely *synthetical*, whereas reflective knowledge is also *analytical*. By reflection we turn back upon what we have first directly perceived; we analyse it and break it down, considering each part. When we have broken it down, we recompose it as we want. In perception, on the contrary, we fully grasp the whole thing with a simple act, as if it were a simple object. In this first intellectual apprehension we do not distinguish anything in particular about the thing.

The nature of our intelligence is limited by the law that 'it needs multiple acts to distinguish multiple things, nor can it distinguish one thing from another without negation which follows affirmation'. We first perceive the whole thing, and then analyse it by means of subsequent *reflection*. Considering things in their parts gives us new insights; on the other hand, the first, all-encompassing perception appears confused and imperfect.[167] This explains why the first perception escapes the

---

[166] Cf. vol. 2, 528 ss. for an explanation of how the understanding has perception of feelable things, and vol. 2, 519, 520 for how it separates ideas from perception. [*App.*, no. 13].

[167] St. Thomas says: *Tanto enim perfectius congnoscimus, quanto differentias eius (rei cognitae) ad alia plenius intuemur* [The more perfectly we know, the more fully we intuit the differences (in the thing known) from

observation of those who do not attentively consider how the fact of thought originates in their consciousness.

1260. Aristotle clearly noted the nature of this part of direct knowledge relative to the ideas or intuitions of essences. According to him, the intellective act which he calls *intelligence* consists of this knowledge. Moreover, he knew that the object intuited by this act is presented in its totality, without division between one part and another, so that in this first apprehension the object is simple and indivisible. He also noted that this first apprehension comes about by a spontaneous movement of nature, and is immune from error.[168]

St. Thomas, following the same path, distinguishes two kinds of knowledge. The first is that of *indivisibles* where there is no error (this is the direct knowledge of essences under discussion). The second is that of things divided or composed by the understanding (this is *reflective* knowledge). In this knowledge, the understanding reflects on its first perceptions or ideas, analysing and breaking them down. It is precisely in these operations that error arises.

According to St. Thomas, the first thing apprehended by the understanding is the *essences of things*.[169] These essences

other things]. The reason he offers is very significant: *Habet enim res unaquaeque in seipsa esse proprium ab omnibus aliis distinctum* [Every thing whatsoever has within itself its own being distinct from all others] (*C.G.*, I, q. 58). The first perception of things is confused because it grasps as a single thing many things at once. When Laromiguière defined an idea as 'a distinct feeling developed from other feelings', he saw the truth we are discussing but did not observe that an idea and perception exists in a confused state before it exists in a distinct state, and that even in its first state it differs essentially from *feelings* (cf. vol. 2, 966 ss.).

[168] *Intelligentia est indivisibilium in quibus non est falsum* [Intelligence is concerned with what is indivisible, in which there is no falsehood] (*De An.*, 3).

[169] *Intellectus humanus non statim in prima apprehensione capit perfectam rei cognitionem: sed primo apprehendit aliquid de ipsa, puta* QUIDDITATEM *ipsius rei, quae est primum et proprium obiectum intellectus, et deinde intelligit proprietates et accidentia et habitudines circumstantes rei essentiam* [The human intellect, in the first apprehension of a thing, does not immediately attain perfect knowledge of the thing. It first apprehends something of the thing, that is, its QUIDDITY, which is the first and proper object of the intellect. It then understands the properties, accidents and dispositions enveloping the essence of the thing] (*S.T.*, I, q. 85, art. 5).

correspond to the *first ideas*, that is, to the ideas contained in the intellective perceptions. *Reflection* follows and, as it analyses these *ideas* of things, notes and distinguishes in each part its different properties. This operation adds nothing to first, *direct* knowledge except greater light, making us note what was first contained in direct knowledge. It has been said rightly therefore that the essence of things (ideas) is the proper object of the intellect; pure reflection produces no new object but only examines and *acknowledges* the object already apprehended.

1261. For this reason, reflective knowledge is more an *acknowledgement* than an *act of knowledge*. As Tertullian most fittingly said: *Nos definimus Deum primum natura COGNOSCENDUM, deinde doctrina RECOGNOSCENDUM* [We define that God is first naturally KNOWN and then doctrinally ACKNOWLEDGED]'.[170] Here we see how well this ancient writer of the Church had noticed that human beings, after knowing things by a first, natural intellection, turn in upon themselves and by reflection acknowledge and analyse the same things, giving them distinction and clarity — the form taken by *teaching* and every branch of knowledge. Averroes was of the same opinion: he distinguished two kinds of acts of knowledge, one 'according to the way of information', the other 'according to the way of verification'.

1262. We have seen that according to St. Thomas the essences or ideas of things belong to direct knowledge, and that these essences or ideas are the *principles* of the branches of knowledge dealing with the same things. *Direct knowledge* therefore is the germ, rule and criterion of reflective knowledge. Reflection refers to perception or direct apprehension as the norm and exemplar, to which it must adapt itself if it is to be true. In this respect, Epicurus himself distinguished direct from reflective knowledge.

His *preconceptions* (προλήψεις) are well known. They are simply Aristotle's *indivisibles*, St. Thomas' *essences*, Tertullian's *act of knowledge*, and Averroes' *formation*-knowledge. In a word all these expressions are names given to first, *direct* knowledge according to the various aspects under which it was considered by different thinkers at different times. Epicurus placed the principles of reasoning in *preconceptions*; without these we could not investigate, doubt, decide or name anything, nor

---

[170] *Contr. Marc.*, bk. 1.

make an act of *reflection*. Reflection always turns back on that which is first found in the mind. It does not add to, but analyses, acknowledges and verifies. Thus, by virtue of nature, it is necessary that we receive intellective perceptions without our knowledge or will so that by an act of will we can move our understanding to think about perceptions and ideas. This second operation is more commonly noticed; the spontaneous, first operation eludes our observation. This explains why in common speech the word 'reflect' is used to express any operation whatsoever of the mind. We reduce every use of the intellective faculty to reflection.

1263. I have mentioned these authorities so that the distinction between *direct* and *reflective* knowledge may be firmly understood and considered under its different aspects. Such a distinction, which so many illustrious men have noted and considered as the necessary foundation of human cognitions, cannot be thought meaningless. It is truly necessary for knowing the nature and cause of error. Because error is found only in *reflective knowledge*, we need to know what reflective knowledge is, and not confuse it with the first kind of knowledge. Only in this way can we penetrate the nature, seat and origin of error. And in order to do this, it will be helpful if I say a few words about the distinction between *popular* and *philosophical* knowledge, which must not be confused with the distinction between *direct* and *reflective* knowledge

Article 7

Popular knowledge and philosophical knowledge

1264. *Direct knowledge* consists in intellective perceptions and in ideas separated from perceptions. *Reflection*, stimulated by language, is then immediately activated, and in its first stages notes the *immediate* and quasi-immediate *relationships* of things perceived and apprehended. This first operation of *reflection* does not *analyse* the individual ideas and perceptions of things.[171] It leaves them complete, as they are when first

---

[171] Analysis must take place to some extent before the immediate relationships of things are observed, because a relationship presupposes a

acquired, and contemplates them together. This is a synthetical operation, of which every human being is capable. Hence it constitutes principally, if not totally, common, *popular knowledge*.

1265. *Philosophical knowledge* begins with the analysis of individual objects. When we submit the things we have perceived to analysis, we acquire a marvellous light, which makes the teaching of great thinkers so wonderful. Analysis can be considered as the point of departure of philosophy. Using it as our starting point we can confirm the important relationships between beings observed as it were intuitively by the great mass of human beings.

1266. Thus, *popular knowledge* lies between purely *direct* knowledge and *philosophical knowledge*. It starts from a first reflection, whereas philosophical knowledge comes about by means of a second reflection.[172] Although the strong *first reflection* of popular knowledge discovers new, immediate relationships, it does not add any new matter to knowledge. Further reflections make known the *relationships* between preceding acts of knowledge.

1267. *Direct knowledge* is free from error. This is not wholly true of *popular* knowledge, because it is partly produced by reflection (we ignore the role of imagination). *Philosophical*

---

distinct vision of particular things. This first *analysis* of real things is made on things as a whole, not on each individually. In the first perception, real things are fused into a whole; for example, the visual universe is a single perception. *Analysis* follows and distinguishes one ens from another. It is at this point that the *synthesis* we are discussing takes place. Hence *analysis* and *synthesis* are closely related operations. *Reflection* certainly begins with *analysis*, but this analysis does not produce knowledge worthy of the name; popular knowledge is completed by the addition of the first *synthesis*. Thus, properly speaking, what I call *first reflection* and the *cause* of popular knowledge is composed of two operations: 1. analysis that distinguishes real entia which are at first confused in the perception; 2. synthesis that understands and, as it were, directly perceives the important relationships. We can say the same about philosophical knowledge: it begins with *analysis*, but is called philosophical knowledge only when synthesis follows to complete it and give it a distinct and important characteristic.

172 What I call 'first' and 'second' reflection is calculated from the proper objects of the first and second reflection, not from the first and second acts of reflection. The objects specify the two reflections I am discussing.

knowledge, however, is even more subject to error than other kinds, because it originates from more remote reflection.

1268. Those who confuse *direct* with *popular knowledge* bestow infallibility on people, because they attribute to popular knowledge what can only be predicated of direct knowledge. Entire nations, the whole of humanity in fact, is alas subject to error. We read: 'Every man is a liar';[173] and: 'They are all gone aside, they are become unprofitable together; there is none that doth good, no, not one.'[174] Thus, while the masses, from whom errors originated, were absolved, the philosophers, to whom all errors were attributed, considered themselves unjustly treated and accused their adversaries of popular prejudices.

1269. The passage of Tertullian quoted above rightly indicates that reflection is an operation different from simple knowledge. I used the passage for this reason. An examination of the kind of *reflection* he is discussing shows that he is not opposing philosophical, learned reflection to purely direct knowledge, but to popular knowledge. On earth our knowledge of God is not *direct* knowledge, because God is perceived *reflectively*, not directly; we perceive him with that first reflection which generates the popular knowledge that consists in noting the relationships of things perceived. But, as I have said, our idea of *God* is of an ens who is principle and cause of the universe.

Elsewhere Tertullian distinguishes *popular* from *philosophical knowledge*. In fact the whole of his book, *Testimony of the Soul*, is an attempt to establish this distinction. He tries to show how the soul with its first reflections rises naturally to the sound teachings of the Christian faith. He notes how invocations such as 'God help me!', 'Immortal God', 'God knows and sees', etc., are often heard on the lips of all human beings. And after mentioning these forms of expression, he adds:

> Everybody considers such movements of the soul to be the teaching of nature and a silent hymn of our connatural or innate consciousness. Our soul certainly existed before literature, speech before books, feeling before style, and the human being before the philosopher and poet. Do we really think that human beings were mute,

[173] Ps 115: 11 [Douai].
[174] Ps 13: 3 [Douai].

and never uttered a syllable before the spread of writing?
The soul certainly did not learn from philosophy or litera-
ture, or from books or study. Despite its simplicity and
lack of polish, despite its ignorance of higher education
and learning, the soul knew these basic things without being taught except by nature.

Few other passages could be found in antiquity that express
so well the distinction between *popular* and *philosophi*cal
knowledge.

1270. The very ancient distinction between *direct* and *reflective* knowledge has appeared again in modern times, but, as so
easily happens, direct knowledge has been confused with *popular* knowledge which springs from initial reflection on things
directly perceived. This first reflection sees things as a whole,
and encompasses them all with their relationships in one great
unity. It was very easy therefore for such first reflection to be
confused with the *direct* act of intelligence. The direct act is
undemonstrative and unobserved; the first reflection is resplen-
dent and, like a crowd, vociferous. Let me quote a passage from
an eloquent philosopher in which he expertly leads his readers
to observe *direct* knowledge (which *per se* is so elusive) and to
separate it from reflective knowledge:

> You want to think, and you think. But don't you some-
> times find yourself thinking without having wished to
> think? Return directly to the first fact of your intelligence,
> because your intelligence must have had its first fact, a
> phenomenon in which it revealed itself for the first time.
> Before this first fact you did not exist for yourselves, or if
> you did exist for yourselves, you did not know that you
> were an existence which could develop; your intelligence
> was not yet developed. Intelligence reveals itself only
> through its acts, or at least one act, and prior to this act you
> were not capable of suspecting its presence; you were ab-
> solutely ignorant of it. Clearly then, when your intelli-
> gence revealed itself for the first time, it did not do so by
> force of your will. But it did manifest itself, and in some
> way you were vividly aware of this manifestation.
> Try to surprise yourselves thinking, without having
> wanted to think. You will find yourselves where your in-
> telligence started, and you will be able to see even now
> with some degree of precision what happened or had to

happen in that first fact of your intelligence, although it no longer exists or can return. To think is to affirm.[175] The first affirmation, in which the will, and consequently reflection, has played no part, cannot be an affirmation mixed with negation, because we never start with a negation. Our starting point is an affirmation without negation, an instinctive perception of *truth*,[176] a wholly instinctive development[177] of thought. Your thought develops, whether you intervene or not, because the power proper to thought is to think.[178] The power is an affirmation, therefore, a pure affirmation and apperception, unmixed with negation.

In this first intuition we find everything that will later be present in reflection, but at the moment is present under other conditions. We do not begin by looking for ourselves, because that would presuppose that we know our own existence.

But on a certain day, at a certain hour and moment — a solemn moment in our existence — we discover ourselves without any searching. Thought, in its instinctive development, discovers that we are. We affirm ourselves with a profound certainty unmixed with any negation whatsoever. We perceive ourselves, but do not discern with total clarity of reflection our proper characteristic of being limited. We do not distinguish ourselves with total precision from the world, and we do not distinctly identify the

---

[175] To affirm is to judge, and therefore to think is to judge. This truth is the foundation of this *New Essay*.

[176] I have already said that the *ideas* of things are their *truth*. — I agree that the first act of thought, which is undoubtedly perception, is an *affirmation* without *negation*, but not, I add, without *limits*. These *limits* are present in the object of our judgment without our observing them separately, and thus without their requiring any negation from us. *Negation* cannot be in our judgment, unless we have first noted the limits in the object affirmed.

[177] This instinct however is not entirely hidden; it is not a fact totally isolated and unconnected with any other fact. Cf. my explanation in 1258 [*App.*, no. 13].

[178] But not without the subject, because it is the subject who thinks. The fact of thought does not mean that it is a power independent of the subject. However, it is true that thought develops without the *deliberate will* of the subject. The individuality of the subject is essential to the generality of thought. We do not need to look further than these facts. They are indeed facts, and we have to reconcile them with theory, which I think will be a little difficult for our author.

characteristics of the world: we find ourselves and we find
the world. We also perceive 'something other', to which
naturally and instinctively we relate ourselves and the
world. We distinguish all this, but without any strict separation. Thus, our intelligence, in its development, perceives everything but not at first in a reflective, distinct,
negative way. If our intelligence perceives everything with
a perfect certainty, it does so in a confused way.[179]

1271. Throughout this extract the author seems intent on distinguishing *direct* first knowledge from *reflective* knowledge.
Only a few sentences show a confusion between *direct* knowledge and *popular*, first-reflection knowledge;[180] the confusion is
more evident in what follows the extract. Because the distinction and clear indication of the limits of *direct knowledge*,
which alone is free from error, is of the highest importance, I
consider it helpful to indicate the particular characteristic which
enables us to distinguish securely between direct and popular
knowledge.

---

[179] This *confusion* arises to some extent from the multiplicity of parts
which compose the objects. Such multiplicity subdues the first act of our
intellective energy. We have seen how *multiplicity* causes confusion in
perception (cf. vol. 2, 902 ss.).

[180] This confusion is seen in the author's supposition that we perceive
contemporaneously ourselves, the world and something (the infinite)
outside the world. On the contrary: 1. We have the idea of being in all its
universality as a first, necessary and spontaneous intuition. This is the
infinite which excludes every *negation* and every *affirmation*, and as a first
act forms the intellective potency. 2. We perceive the external world with a
first synthesis (intellectual perception); at this point, although there are *limits*
in the object thus unfolded, *affirmation* alone, not *negation*, is present. 3. If
we abstract from this perception our judgment on the subsistence of things,
we are left with pure apprehension (idea). Other *limits* now appear, but
explicit *negation* is still not present, at least not necessarily. In our state as
intellective beings, we have that feeling later expressed by the personal
pronoun 'I', of which we soon acquire the intellective perception. *Direct
knowledge* is followed by first reflection, that is, by popular knowledge.
With this reflection we think 1. of a cause of everything (God); 2. of
other important relationships of things proffered by direct knowledge. Our
author, however, produces only one kind of knowledge out of all these
things; he calls it *spontaneous* and contrasts it with *reflective* knowledge. But
so-called *spontaneous* knowledge, we must note, has two parts: *direct* and
popular, which cannot be confused.

[1271]

First, the objects of *direct* knowledge are more particular than those of popular knowledge, which is a *first reflection* on what we have perceived. The act of reflection has of its nature a wider field than that of perception or of acts submitted to reflection in general. In fact, we perceive things either one at a time[181] or several together — when, for instance, we perceive simultaneously with eyes trained for the purpose on a whole panorama of things at a suitable distance. But even though we see all this at once, we still change the scene when we move; we can continually see and perceive new things. However, no matter how complex and multiple our actual perception may be, it cannot be extended to perceive past or future things, that is, things that are not actually present. Our perceptions succeed one another, and in doing so continually fade away.

But if the actual perception fades, its memory remains; all that we have perceived at any time is preserved in the deposit of memory. When we reflect, our gaze turns back over the entire treasure of information stored in our memory and even on consciousness itself. Times past, together with times present, are lined up before reflection, which embraces and comprehends them all. Other reflections and partial visions replace this universal gaze, and we have the real beginning of that analysis by which popular knowledge imperceptibly becomes philosophical knowledge.

1272. These characteristics of *particularity* in direct knowledge and of *generality* in popular knowledge mean that popular knowledge is better suited than direct knowledge to produce a sublime feeling in us.

A *sublime feeling* is always produced by a lively presentation of things whether it is dependent on their number or outstanding quality. The presentation increases in vivacity in proportion to its novelty and to the extent that human beings are endowed with a powerful, pristine imagination, which are factors present and united in the first infancy of mankind. This fact explains the noble characteristics of the ancient poets: their basic, popular

---

[181] Here I presuppose that the first perception, obtained by means of the first, natural analysis already discussed, is in some way rendered distinct. In other words, the *entia* which are distinct in reality have also been distinguished in our perception.

knowledge and their language, which delights us by its universality, grandeur, confidence, simplicity and enthusiasm.[182]

The first reflection of human beings 1. is *lively* precisely because phantasy is still fresh and vivacious, as it is in the youth of individuals, of nations and of humankind; 2. is *new* precisely because it is *first* reflection, discovering the relationships of things with a kind of creative inventiveness; 3. is *sublime* because it is necessarily concerned with relationships between the most important and necessary things, and indicates[183] invisible entia such as a *cause*, a God; 4. is *vast* because it has not yet learnt to halt before particular things and their minute parts where there is nothing to hold its attention, but gazes around once more, ranging eagerly over everything to which, still unsatisfied, it adds the infinite.

1273. Our author attributes enthusiasm to spontaneous, not reflective knowledge. He does so because he has failed to observe that enthusiasm cannot come from direct knowledge, no matter how spontaneous, but only from *first* and from *final* reflection. It arises from first reflection for the reasons I have given; one example is the excitement of deaf-mutes when they come to know the existence of God for the first time.[184] It arises from final reflection because when we have analysed, separated and detailed everything, and turned from our necessarily paltry, frigid considerations, we gradually put everything together again to find ourselves, after our long, exhausting journey, back where we had started. Once more we are at home with what is great, sublime and 'all' — but an 'all' now enriched with infinite clarity and light [*App.*, no. 14].

---

[182] See the observations on the state of early aesthetics in *Saggio sull'Idillio e sulla nuova Letteratura italiana* (*Opusc. Fil.*, 5, 1, pp. 304 ss.).

[183] The mind does not cease to perform this operation after receiving revelation. The natural bent of the mind strengthens belief in what revelation has revealed, making belief easier and deeper.

[184] Abbé, Sichard describes the kind of ecstasy that seized the deaf-mute Massieu when he understood that God existed. See also the biography of the deaf-mute Teresa Ferrari in *Memorie di Modena*, Continuation, vol. 2, by Ces. Galvani.

Article 8
A summary of what has been said about the seat of error

1274. First human knowledge is *direct*, and cannot be otherwise. It is stimulated by an instinct to satisfy our needs, and occasioned by sensations and images of external things.

Second knowledge is *reflective*, and pertains to first reflection. I have called it *popular* knowledge because it is common to all human beings. The only means for carrying out this first reflection is language received from society (cf. vol. 2, 514 ss.).

So far we have produced no analysis, or virtually no analysis; knowledge is eminently compact. Analysis initiates philosophical knowledge with a second or at least higher reflection. When we have somewhat confusedly embraced the whole, we want to recognise and elucidate what we know so that we can have clearer and more distinct knowledge. Hence we begin by analysing the parts and in so doing take the first steps towards philosophical knowledge.

1275. The philosopher therefore comes from the general mass of people, but at first necessarily retains something of the general mass. Analysis is an art, and like all arts, it is not known perfectly from the beginning. Hence philosophy begins with an imperfect analysis. But analysis perfects itself, and philosophy becomes more canny as it passes through a series of innumerable errors which sometimes humiliate, and at other times completely discourage and debase the human being.

Philosophy therefore starts from the *masses*. Later, when it realises that excessive confidence and facile explanation of the facts of nature lead it into gross errors, it seeks more subtle explanations and ingenious hypotheses, disdaining and distancing itself from the masses, and assuming a more serious and singular attitude. It declares itself content with few judgments, and from being popular becomes *erudite*, with *erudite* errors, because it never masters any particular truth without first giving countless demonstrations of human fallaciousness (cf. vol. 2, 29–34).

As soon as philosophy has enriched itself with particular

truths recognised by means of reflection and elucidated by analysis, it begins to recompose these truths into a whole, and, as we have said, returns to a synthesis which simply confirms the first, popular synthesis with the additional great light of its witness.

1276. Which, among all these kinds of knowledge, is the seat of error?

Direct knowledge is immune from error because it is a function of nature.

Popular knowledge starts as a function of the will, and it is here that error begins.

However, because popular knowledge is limited, it is less subject to error than philosophical knowledge. Popular knowledge, consisting of a first reflection with which the important relationships of things are observed and grasped, embraces the totality of things, not their individual parts. 'The greatest danger of error arises from the ease with which the part is taken for the whole'; nearly every kind of error can be reduced to this simple formula. In addition, philosophical knowledge in its first stages reflects on popular knowledge and itself becomes susceptive of the errors of popular knowledge.

1277. But we must also note that *popular knowledge* in its initial stage is the effect of a natural, instinctive will, not of a deliberate will. As we have seen, we acquire mastery of our understanding solely by means of language (cf. vol. 2, 525 ss.). Language moves our understanding to the first reflection in a way similar to that by which the senses occasionally move it to intellective perception. The subject (*myself*), with its instinct for using all its forces to satisfy its needs, prompts the understanding to attend to the meanings of words. In this first operation the understanding apprehends necessary relationships, by which we learn to use our understanding as we will. Error cannot occur in this apprehension of the important, necessary relationships of things because our will has not yet taken part in the action; the understanding has necessarily apprehended and judged. Hence this part of *popular knowledge* is itself a function of nature, a perception of indivisible things, and hence free from all error. This first, involuntary and somewhat confused apprehension of the important relationships of things could very reasonably be called *common sense*, provided we mean that all philosophical speculation must be referred to common sense as to its exemplar.[185]

1278. After the first apprehension of the important relationships of things, we are free to give or deny assent to them. This second operation is not an acquisition of new knowledge; we still have no philosophical knowledge. Although the judgment may require some new reflection, our reflection is not of such a nature as to produce new knowledge or knowledge in a new form. It is simply a recognition of what has been apprehended, but leaves it in the same form under which it was apprehended. The effective sphere of error begins here; this is the gap allowing error to enter popular knowledge. Error always begins with the use of our will.

[185] Granting this to the modern supporters of common sense, I observe that in this case 'common sense' cannot be called the 'criterion of certainty' in the way that this phrase is understood in the philosophical question: 'What is the criterion of certainty?' The criterion of certainty sought here is a unique, *supreme principle* which serves as a *rule* for knowing whether a proposition is true or false. In order to understand the difference between the *criterion of certainty* sought by the philosopher and a criterion of certainty such as the deposit of truths preserved in common sense, let us suppose that an inspired book exists which contains the solutions to all the questions possible in a particular branch of knowledge. This book would certainly not be the desired *criterion* of the branch of knowledge but the branch of knowledge in all its perfection. Let us suppose that I am looking for a rule for measuring the height of a house. Someone gives me a measuring rod, and this becomes the rule with which I measure the height. But if I am given a length of string equal to the height of the house, the string is not a rule but the height itself. Similarly the teachings of common sense can never be the rule or supreme criterion sought by the logicians, although as true and even infallible teachings they can be used to refute philosophical opinions.

CHAPTER 3

The cause of human errors

Article 1

Error is willed

1279. Error can be found only in *reflection*, and at the point where reflection begins to be willed (cf. 1274, 1277). Error, therefore, is willed.

Article 2

Malebranche's splendid teaching about the cause of error

1280. Malebranche saw this truth, and posited the true *cause* of error in the human will itself. Everything else that combined to incline the will to error he called *occasions* or occasional causes of error.[186] He also made a distinction between the first and the second operations of the understanding. The first, which are not willed, cannot contain error, and are the norm, as

[186] In reducing everything to sense, which only perceives directly, modern philosophy has lost sight of this splendid truth. It no longer considers or understands the nature of reflection, the most difficult of the acts of the human spirit to be observed. And because it ignores the nature of *reflection*, modern philosophy has been unable to understand the difference between an *act* of the human spirit and *advertence* to this act, which is simply reflection upon the act itself. Consequently, we think that we advert to all that happens in our spirit, and that unadverted things do not exist. Nevertheless, we often fall into error without realising that our own act of will has led us to err. The usual argument is: 'If I am unaware that my will has moved my understanding to this error, my will has had no part in the error.' This is the common sophistry of ordinary people which we have opposed so many times in the course of this *New Essay*. Holy Scripture, however, speaks of *acts of will*, even culpable acts, of which we remain ignorant simply because we do not advert to them, and encourages us to beseech the Lord to cleanse us from our hidden sins: *Ab occultis meis munda me* [From my secret sins cleanse me] (Ps 18: 13 [Douai]).

Descartes had also made clear;[187] the second, which are willed, are to be weighed and verified by the first.

Malebranche saw that *first judgments* can be called mere perceptions. When the understanding reflects willingly on these first judgments and gives them its assent, its consequent *judgment* is a second operation that presupposes the preceding perception. Intellectual perception, in fact, which is carried out only by means of the primal judgment or synthesis, is not willed; the understanding, although active, is moved to make that synthesis naturally and instinctively.[188]

---

[187] We need to consider carefully the nature of Descartes' *clear idea* which he himself called the *criterion of certainty*. This is simply the *first idea* of things (the essence, as he sometimes called it). It is the idea contained in intellective perception or, if we are speaking of real relationships such as cause, in first reflection. In a word, Descartes' clear idea, whose nature we find by penetrating to the very heart of his philosophy, is *popular knowledge*. In fact, the whole of Cartesian philosophy starts from the *intellective perception of myself*, that is, from direct knowledge. Descartes then reflects on this perception of *myself* in order to acknowledge it, and concludes that 'I must admit in *myself* only that which I find in the first perception.' Having found this particular proposition, he generalises it, and uses it in the place of popular knowledge, that is, in the place of the important relationships between entia. He then establishes this rule: 'We must only grant that which is found to be contained in the first perception or idea of things.' The first perceptions, the first ideas, that is, popular, direct knowledge, become Descartes' criterion, just as they are the criterion for those who use *common sense* in a reasonable way. Descartes adds that in order not to fall into error we have first to assure ourselves of what is contained in the first perception or idea. In other words, we have to see it *clearly*. This rule of prudence is extremely acute, and of the greatest importance in avoiding error. We have to avoid any hostile attitude towards Descartes' genius, therefore, while attempting to perfect his system by clarifying it and correcting the defects which are never lacking in human works. This is what we shall try to do.

[188] Bk. 1, c. 2. However, Malebranche did not see that every intellectual operation must be a judgment. Consequently his usual order for acts of the understanding is 1. perceptions; 2. judgments; and 3. reasoning. In volume 2, I showed that intellectual perceptions are simply first judgments from which ideas are extracted in the way we have indicated. *Reasoning* is not included in *direct* knowledge, but begins to appear in knowledge dependent upon first reflection, *popular knowledge*, as I have called it. *Judgments* and *reasoning* have two states. At first they are instinctive and not willed, and their conclusions are similar to *intellective perceptions*. Through them, the understanding apprehends new things, and seems almost passive as it is borne necessarily to action. *Second judgments* and *reasoning*, which make up

Malebranche also recognised 1. that the seat of error consists solely in an act of the understanding, that is, in a judgment and 2. that the seat of error is not in all species of judgments, but in reflective, willed judgments.

1281. Error arises in these willed judgments, as Malebranche noted so well, when *we give our assent* (in which real judgment consists) to that which is not shown in any way by our understanding in its perceptions and ideas. We lie to ourselves by affirming as present in the first perceptions and ideas of our understanding that which is not present, or vice versa by refusing to accept that which is there. He says:

> All agree that rash judgments[189] are sins, and that every sin is willed. All must also agree, therefore, that in such a case it is the will that judges by acquiescing in confused, complex perceptions of the understanding.

He adds this acute comment on the intimate union between the will and the understanding:

> However, the question about understanding as the sole faculty of judgment and reasoning seems useless to me. It is more a question of words than anything else. I say 'the understanding... as the sole faculty' because it certainly plays the part I have assigned it in our judgments, in the sense that we must know or feel a thing before judging it or consenting to it. On the other hand, the understanding and the will is only the mind itself. Properly speaking, therefore, it is the mind that perceives, judges, reasons, wills, etc. I also use the word 'understanding' to indicate a passive faculty, that is, the capacity for receiving ideas.[190]

second reflection, are different. They do not resemble *perceptions*; they are *acknowledgments* or willed assents given to perceptions. As such they acquire their own exclusive expression as judgments and reasoning, and possess much greater light and clarity. On the other hand, it is only with great difficulty that we recognise and acknowledge our very first judgments and reasoning as part of our judgment and reason.

[189] Rash judgments are normally considered those which harm our neighbour. Every rash judgment, however, taken in the fullest sense of the word, presents some defect even if it is not related to our neighbour. Sometimes these defects arise within us from original corruption, and almost without our intervention.

[190] Bk. 1, c. 2.

[1281]

This passivity in the understanding is simply the necessity which impels the understanding towards perception in the case of *direct knowledge*, the first part of *popular knowledge*. The understanding which then reflects and acknowledges the judgments made is the willed activity of which Malebranche is speaking. This shows that the will and the understanding form together, as it were, a single potency. The intelligent soul is the will in so far as the soul is considered as an active force moving towards a known end, or choosing between several ends.

Malebranche goes on to note that if the very nature of our understanding were such that the understanding (and not the will, which gives its consent to something not presented by the understanding) drew us to error, God himself would have deceived us by providing us with a deceptive nature.[191] St. Thomas says very aptly: 'As far as our intellectual power in concerned, the intellect can never be said to be false; it is always true.'[192]

1282. There is, however, one objection to be resolved against this teaching on the cause of error. Some truths, such as almost all geometry theorems, are evident to the highest degree. Is our assent to such truths willed? It would seem not. But this makes it appear that assent does not depend upon the will, and is determined by truth itself.

Our answer is that an act of the *will* can be either determined or undetermined. If it is undetermined, the will is said to be

---

[191] Bk. 1, c. 2. — Because the will reaches out only for 'things known to the intellect, it necessarily reaches out for what is at least similar to that which is true and good. If it had no freedom in this matter, but were forced to reach for everything similar to that which is good and true, it would necessarily be involved in endless errors towards which it would hurtle headlong. That which is similar to what is true and good is not however true and good. In this case, its errors could with good reason be attributed to the supreme Creator from whom its existence originated.'

[192] *Virtus intellectualis est quaedam perfectio intellectus in cognoscendo. Secundum autem virtutem intellectualem non contingit intellectum falsum dicere, sed semper verum* [Our intellectual power is a kind of perfection of the intellect relative to our act of knowledge. As far as our intellectual power in concerned, the intellect can never be said to be false, but always true] (*C. G.*, I, q. 61). Aristotle says the same when he calls *understanding* 'the proper act of the intellect', that is, the first act made of itself by the intellect independently of the will; and he adds that the *understanding* cannot err.

free.[193] 'Will' is simply the power of acting for an end. If, by hypothesis, a possible end, a single good, were present, the will would be determined by this end; if several ends were present, the understanding could *choose* between them. It is true, therefore, that in giving its assent and expressly forming a judgment, the will is sometimes determined by the evidence presented by the truth, as in geometrical propositions. This, however, does not destroy the will; it simply ensures that in these cases the will is not free[194] — although, to speak truly, the will which in these

[193] In ordinary language 'free will' and 'free decision' [*liberum arbitrium*] are synonymous. But what is the proper force of 'decision'? (*arbitrium* in Latin, hence the Italian *libero arbitrio* [in English 'free decision' to distinguish it from 'free will']). 'Decision' means *judgment*. According to common human feeling, therefore, *free will* and *free judgment* are the same thing. This shows that according to popular knowledge the judgment made by the understanding is sometimes free, and that the nature of the will is simply to be a free judgment. In other words, 'the will is a power to give or to suspend assent to a proposition'. In the use of language itself, therefore, the intimate connection between the understanding and the will is expressed admirably.

The understanding is moved in three ways: 1. by the instinct called *myself* (in this way it is moved to perceptions and first ideas); 2. by a will which is not free, that is, by a known and experienced end which determines its action (in heaven the understanding is moved in this way by knowledge and experience of the supreme good); 3. by the free will, when the known and experienced good is imperfect and leaves the understanding with the faculty to propose some greater good to itself, and thus prevents its being determined by the prior good (this state is proper to our present life). The understanding is called *will* in so far as it moves itself with an end in view; free understanding (decision) is called *freedom* when the understanding is considered as present in that force by which it determines itself.

[194] However, the will, even when giving full assent to the most evident geometrical propositions, is often freer than we believe. Although the understanding apprehends these truths necessarily with its first reflection, it retains the energy enabling it to form a special assent that can ignore and deny these propositions, or at least make them the object of arguments and confrontation. Leibniz said: 'It is my belief that if geometrical truths had as great a role in human passions as moral truths, they too would be called into doubt and made as much a matter for dispute as moral truths.'

In modern times, our genius for evil has become aware that all truth is bound together, and that accepting a single part of truth leads inevitably to accepting all of it. As a result, truth has been denied *in toto*, and books have been written to assail even the truths of geometry, the foundations of which have been assailed by attempts to prove that they rested upon gratuitous and

cases seems not to be free to judge in one way or another remains free either to judge or to abstain from judging by turning the attention of the mind elsewhere. Malebranche's argument is, however, very relevant. Let us see, therefore, how it comes about that some propositions are presented to the mind with such evidence that they leave it without choice in its judgment, and determined to a single way of judging.

1283. Malebranche offers this reason:

> Note that things are not totally evident to our understanding until it has examined them from every angle and according to all their relationships. Only then can it arrive at some judgment about them. But at this point we have to take account of that sure law of the will which desires nothing without first knowing it. The will cannot now push the understanding further ahead, nor demand anything new relative to what has been put before the understanding, which has already examined the individual parts of the thing and finds nothing more to know in it. Now, finally, the will, which cannot pressurise and stimulate the understanding any further, must rest in what is offered to it by the understanding. Such full assent is judgment (in its proper meaning) and reasoning. Because the judgment relative to the most evident things is not free in us with the freedom called 'indifference', it seems to be independent of our will,

although it, too, really is an act of will.

> Assent can always be held back when some obscurity remains in things submitted for our examination, or when

altogether unproven principles. When it was found impossible to explain the force of the evidence exerted in us by those principles, it was then maintained that two sources of evidence were present, one true and the other illusory. The illusion, it was affirmed, absorbs all true evidence in such a way that human beings become delusions to themselves. Critical philosophy concluded, indeed, that such a universal illusion was necessary, and constituted the nature of things. Even belief in the 'nature of things' is part of the same illusion! The final boast of sceptics of every age, from biblical to modern times when sceptics simply call themselves 'indifferent', is to hold back or deny assent to all truth, even the most evident, and to desire not to give in to reason of any kind. Sceptics exist to sneer and to rejoice in their sneering! 'So I saw that there is nothing better than that a man should enjoy his work, for that is his lot. [Who can bring him to see what will be after him?]' (Eccles 3: 22).

something seems to be missing in the question under discussion. This often happens in difficult and as it were multiple subject-matter. The will can command the understanding to re-examine the matter, and this causes us to believe more easily that the judgments we make in such cases are freely willed.[195]

1284. But we also have to note that the careful examination to which the understanding submits things also depends on the will which, if it is not content with assenting to evident things, prevents the understanding from considering them. In this case, although the understanding has grasped them almost intuitively as it were, the will always has the possibility of considering them as true only in appearance. It has the capacity of supposing and believing from a general point of view that something still hidden could be found to uncover the deception of the evidence. In cases like this, the will which finds the truth distasteful knows how to be humble, and to withdraw itself from the pressure of any evidence whatsoever under the pretext of impotence and fallibility. Finally, even if we suppose that the will has commanded the understanding to examine the matter, and that the understanding has carried out fully what has been commanded, it is still possible, I think, when experience of feeling is lacking, for the will in its stubbornness to stand firm in wanting to continually disregard and deny the matter.

Article 3

Occasional causes of error

1285. We must now examine the occasional causes of error in order to understand better why it is more difficult for us to withhold our assent from geometrical than from moral truths.

'Error is a reflection by which the understanding, turning back to what it knows, willingly withholds its assent from this knowledge, and interiorly affirms that it has apprehended something other than that which it has really apprehended.'

Because error is an act of willed understanding, the occasional

---

[195] Bk. 1, c. 2.

causes of error must be found partly in the understanding and partly in the will.

1286. The understanding's part in error lies in its fabricating something either not perceived or not apprehended and judging this as perceived or apprehended. Consequently, fabrication is found in every error.

The will's part in error consists in moving the understanding to produce this simulation and to pronounce the false judgment.

Both intellect and will depend partly upon ourselves, and to this extent form our *free decision* or *free will*. Nevertheless they also depend partly upon their own laws to which they have to submit. From this point of view these faculties are not free. The laws to which, of their nature, they have to bow give rise to occasional causes of error, as we shall now describe.

1287. The understanding is subject to the following law: 'In reflecting on its cognitions, it is easier for the understanding to distinguish its cognitions (and we are speaking about them as a whole as well as about their parts), and more difficult to confuse them, in so far as they differ in themselves and from other imaginable cognitions or perceptions. Equally, it is easier for the understanding to mistake one of them for a true or imaginary object of knowledge in so far as one is like the other.' This law of the understanding enables us to conclude that the occasional cause of error from the point of view of the intellect is the *likeness* between some cognitions and perceptions (true or imagined) and others. We have already shown that the first idea is what we call the *truth* of the thing perceived or known. Hence St. Augustine and others say that the understanding errs because it takes something similar to what is true for the true thing itself.

1288. The will is subject to the following law: 'It receives an inclination towards one thing rather than another from several causes which conspire to make something present itself to the will in a more lively fashion and as a greater good than something else. These causes are principally 1. the good known in the object; 2. the liveliness and perfection of intellective cognition; 3. sensible experience; 4. instinct; 5. imagination; 6. passions; and 7. habits.'

1289. As free, this inclination of the will is unable to produce

[1286–1289]

deliberation in the will (unless an infinite good acts within it to determine it). Nevertheless, the inclination ensures that 'there is greater difficulty in moving the understanding to recognise and give full assent to a truth in so far as 1. this truth is contrary to the inclination already received in the will by the actions of the causes listed, and 2. the inclination already contracted is stronger.' Contrariwise, it is easier to give prompt, immediate and full consent to something similar to what is true (by exchanging it with what is true) in so far as the will's inclination is strong and assent is more in conformity with inclination. The occasional cause of error on the will's part is therefore the *inclination* it has contracted for giving assent readily to anything false which favours the inclination.

1290. Hence, there are two occasional causes of error: 1. the likeness between what is false and what is true; 2. the will's *inclination* to assent to what is similar to something true because such assent conforms with the inclination itself. We need to offer examples of each of these causes.

We said that two similar cognitions facilitate error on the part of the understanding. Such knowledge can have its source in any faculty whatsoever — in the imagination, in feeling or in the understanding itself. In this sense we can rightly say that there are as many sources of error as there are faculties.

1291. Let us take sensible perceptions and examine their misleading likeness to what is true. Two colours, tastes, scents, sounds or fine materials are easily confused and exchanged for one another if they are very alike. This does not mean that sense does not experience the difference.[196] Sense is in fact very delicate, and passively perceives even the smallest differences between things. The confusion arises because we do not *advert* to the difference with our reflection. Nevertheless, having *seemed* to have observed carefully enough, we conclude by confusing one perception with another, or rather by substituting both perceptions either with a somewhat confused

---

[196] Even if we suppose that sense could not entirely perceive the difference between two similar, but really different bodies, the error would still be in the understanding which, instead of considering the possible limitation of the sensory power, unconditionally denies every difference and thus acts rashly by positing an absolute judgment.

imaginary perception, or with one not so well defined that it descends to the slight, tiny differences between the perceptions.[197]

1292. The *likeness* which facilitates the mind's error lies in the matter itself of our cognitions, and is administered by internal and external sense; sense provides the matter of knowledge, and the intellect the form. On the other hand, the *similarity* or fabrication of what is true is not provided by sense, but added by the understanding. This takes place especially in the associations of complex ideas or perceptions through which a judgment is wrongly added to the sense-perception

Let us take as an example the judgment with which we judge the sun's movement. Sensible perception does not necessarily indicate real movement in the sun, but apparent movement only. However, the perception of the sun's apparent movement is similar to other perceptions of apparent movement which are connected with real movement. As a result, real and apparent movement produce a composite perception and association of ideas. This complex perception is taken and exchanged with the perception of apparent movement only, not with real movement.

The likeness in these two perceptions consists in this: apparent movement is present in both perceptions. Their difference depends upon the fact that in first, intellective perceptions apparent movement is also real movement. Error consists in judging that the perception of the sun's movement is amongst those perceptions to which real movement has to be added. The confusion of two similar perceptions forms the error. The deceptive *likeness* of what is true is therefore produced by the understanding which associates the real with the apparent movement and makes a single composite perception of these two things. It substitutes the perception of the sun's apparent movement, which is simple, with the composite perception, that is, with the perception to which has been added, besides the

---

[197] The *likeness* provided by the imagination is similar to that of the senses (the imagination is only an interior bodily feeling). If, therefore, someone produces an imitation of Virgil or any other great author, and judges that the reproduction of style is perfect, he could easily fall into error by *amour propre* as a result of a few similarities between his work and that of his great model.

appearance of movement, the real movement thought of by the understanding.

The same kind of error takes place whenever the understanding uses the principle of *analogy* and errs through an accidental exception to this principle.

1293. In general, error can be reduced to the following formula: it is 'a consequence that does not come from the premises'. The consequence is fabricated by the understanding and, through a likeness or relationship which it has with the premises, is declared to be contained in them.

1294. In considering the occasional cause of error on the part of the will, we need to give priority to clarifying the notion of will. We sometimes understand the will as 'the internal force determining human beings to act'. But this definition is too general, and includes instinct. I maintain that human beings possess two interior forces which determine their actions: 1. instinct, which they have in common with purely sensitive beings; 2. will, which is proper to intellectual beings. The best definition that I have found of instinct is Araldi's: 'Instinct's offspring are those actions in which the spirit concurs without the intervention of any kind of knowledge, and as a result of giving way to impulse and the attraction of some sensation' [*App.*, no. 15]. The definition of the will, however, runs as follows: 'It is an interior activity through which human beings determine themselves to action through knowledge of an end.'

Elsewhere I have noted that the potencies of *entia* are ordered according to a law which requires that a corresponding *active* potency is added to every *passive potency*. The passive potency of *feeling* has a corresponding active potency of *instinct*; the receptive potency of *intellect* has the corresponding active potency of *will*. The will, therefore, does not operate unless conditioned by a known good; if human beings do an action before they *know* its effect, they are determined by instinct. On the other hand, if we know only a single good, we are indeed determined towards it willingly because of our knowledge, but with a *will that has been determined* necessarily.[198] But if we know several good things, independently of one

---

[198] It cannot be said, in our hypothesis of a sole good, that we are free to suspend the act of will bearing us towards this good. We cannot willingly

another,[199] we can determine ourselves to choose amongst them. This human operation is carried out with *free* or *undetermined will*.

1295. Applying all these interior forces to the potency of understanding, we find that the understanding is moved 1. by instinct, 2. by non-free will, 3. by free will whose freedom is greater in proportion to the number of independent goods known to us.[200]

1296. As we were saying, we wished to see by way of example how the inclination of the will is the occasional cause of error in the understanding. To do this, and in order not to confuse them, we listed the three forces capable of moving the understanding. We noted that we were going to deal only with the third force. The first and second are immune from error: the first *per se*, and the second because the known good is one only and cannot therefore give rise to fabrication. Because error is an invention taking the place of truth (cf. 1286), it follows that 'error, of its very nature, requires the understanding to apprehend at least two things, one true, the other false (the latter being invented in place of what is true)'. Our hypothesis, however, posits one mental conception alone, not two.

1297. The will can receive its *inclination* to carry out a false judgment from any of the seven causes we have enumerated, but it would take too long to give examples of them all. Let us, therefore, consider simply the action of the passions on our judgment.

An ambitious person will be inclined to judge that the post he desires can be obtained easily, although he never achieves it and his false judgment makes him the butt of the whole nation; an

suspend this act without proposing this as our end, and consequently without knowing the suspension as good. But such knowledge is posterior to knowledge of the good of the act itself. The latter is *respectively* direct knowledge; the former *respectively* reflective knowledge, that is, it requires a reflection on the suspension of the act.

[199] If the good involved were the supreme good, and were perceived as such, it would include all the others, which could not, therefore, be said to be independent.

[200] We could also distinguish *deliberating will* from *free will*, despite their being confused by serious authorities, but we do not wish to prolong the discussion.

avaricious person will overstate the possible damage to his self-made fortune from slight and distant dangers; 'love that dupes the clear eye' will judge the beloved's defects as beauty, and will see in her demise 'great public loss, and darkness for our world'.

1298. In order to withstand the *inclination* received in the will towards false judgment from the causes we have described, and to support it against falling into such a lie, we have to use as a bulwark our highest human faculty, the *free* will constituted by the intimate energy we experience in ourselves. In persons constantly ready and determined to oppose the evil inclination taken on by the will, the *degree* of merit is equal to the degree of *free activity* they have had to use to overcome it.

1299. From what has been said, we can at last draw this important conclusion: 'Error is extremely probable when 1. what is true is extremely *similar* to what is false, and it is highly difficult to discern between the two; and 2. the *inclination* of the will to take what is false for what is true, or simply to judge immediately, is at a such a high level that the greatest use of *freedom* is required to determine oneself to what is true rather than to what is false, or to suspend the judgment until true and false are adequately distinguished.'

1300. Another conclusion is: 'If such a judgment has to be made by the mass of people, error can be predicted with certainty because the mass does not have the power needed to avoid it.' The mass of people, at least as they are constituted now (and always have been), are incapable of making great use of their own freedom either to grasp something true which their will seeks to avoid or to abandon something false to which their will is inclined, or even to suspend their judgment until they discover the clear distinction between what is true and what is false — a distinction that will perhaps always elude them because of the proximity of what is false.[201]

---

[201] This incapacity for suspending assent has always been noted in the masses. Hence Cicero's *Vulgus ex veritate pauca, ex opinione multa existimat* [The populace relies very little on truth, but a great deal on opinion] (*Pro Roscio* 10).

[1298–1300]

Article 4

Why it seems that we are necessitated when giving our assent to some truths, such as geometric truths, that are furnished with evidence leading to certainty

1301. Having discovered the occasional causes of errors, we can turn back to the fact indicated in the title of this article and explain it better. We do not hesitate, in fact, to give assent to some truths furnished with evidence leading to certainty, such as geometric truths, because for most of the time they are unaccompanied by occasional causes of error; that is to say:

1. They are so distinct and precise that they are altogether dissimilar[202] and of very differing natures.

---

[202] When there is some similarity between these truths, however, mathematicians do err. This is one of the causes of error amongst mathematicians. Another is mistakes in *speech* or in *writing*. When the tongue or the hand err in some calculation, error enters inevitably. In this case the instruments used for the calculation are the *occasional causes* of error. We can, therefore, establish in general 'that all the powers and instruments used by the understanding in reaching the conclusion made by its judgment can be occasional causes of error (although more remote causes than those we have already listed)'. However, the remoter occasional causes have no efficacy in producing error of themselves without the intervention of less remote causes, just as these in their turn do not necessarily lead us to err unless the will consents negatively or even positively. We can see that fallibility on the part of the powers and instruments does not necessarily produce error without the co-operation of the will if we consider, for example, what happens when my hand writes either willingly or mechanically a *b* in place of an *a*. If my hand is determined mechanically to write *b*, the will's co-operation is simply *negative*, that is, the error has occurred because the will did not direct my hand throughout the calculation as it should have done, but let it act of its own accord. This is a defect. If the hand is determined willingly to write *b*, the will's co-operation is, moreover, positive. However, in the case of the negative co-operation of the will, the error can be called purely *material* and would begin to be formal only at the end of the calculation if the final judgment about the result were held as absolute and infallible. A mathematician does not fall into formal error, therefore, if at the end of the calculation he says: 'This is the answer, provided that my hand or speech has not erred, etc.' This kind of prudence, which is often taken for granted, removes formal and willing error, and gives rise to mistakes which are not true errors.

2. Our will is not previously inclined to one result rather than another.

Article 5

Human beings are absolved of many errors

1302. The nature of the assent that we give or deny to a proposition deserves every attention.

In the first place, the will may or may not make a decision, but if it does actually posit its decision it can only move in one of two absolute directions; it can say either 'Yes' or 'No'. If its decision is suspended, there would be no decision, which is against our hypothesis.

Secondly, we are obliged in an infinite number of cases every day to make positive or negative decisions if we wish to act, or even go on existing. For instance, unless we decide to believe that the food we are offered is not contaminated and can safely be eaten, we would die of hunger, or live in such continual fear that our life would be an unending misery. We are obliged to make these decisions and judgments, however, before we have acquired apodictic certainty of the truth in question. In our everyday life we would be dead long before we made such judgments if we had first to be apodictically certain of them. More often than not, we have to make our decisions on the basis of *probable* arguments, resolving not to worry about the tiny probabilities that stand against our decision — at least if we do not wish to be intolerable burdens to ourselves. If our preoccupation or fear about such probabilities reaches a certain level, we become obsessed and live at odds with others who marginalise us as troublesome in the extreme. We cannot say, therefore, that the will, in all these cases where it assents fully without worry or other concern to matters which are only highly probable, is continually in error or exposed to error. What we have to do instead is to consider another accidental characteristic of the full assent given by the will to things which are only highly probable.

1303. The understanding or the will (we can speak of either here, as we have seen) can give an *assent* which is on the one hand *full* in some way, and on the other more or less *provisional*. In these cases, the provisional character of the assent is what distinguishes the wise man's act of assent from that of the rash and thoughtless person.

I am speaking about *assent* which is *full* in some way, and by this I mean a decision that halts and terminates in the conclusion made by the judgment, without proceeding further. The search for a decision is not prolonged, and no anxious thought is given to possible cases, which could go on *ad infinitum*. In other words, there is no trace in the spirit of any fear of something opposed to the decision, as there would be in the mind and heart of persons for whom the case is not yet closed and finished, but held open undeterminedly. People of this kind are continually anxious, and necessarily fuel their own doubt and anxiety.

Nevertheless this *assent*, which is *full* in some way because the mind has abandoned further search and come to rest in a conclusion, can be simply *provisional*. This is what distinguishes the assent given by prudent people in the probable matters of life from that given by fools. [203] But what do we mean by the phrase '*provisional* assent'?

Simply this: if some reasonable cause is present, the person who has given his *assent* and has therefore completed his mental search, is ready to resume the search and maintain it for as long as circumstances show that it is prudent to do so. We have all experienced the modesty and reserve shown by wise people about the least dubious of matters: 'As far as I can see, that's the situation', 'I think so, but I could be mistaken', 'This is my

[203] Antiquity saw that there are two ways of giving assent to what is false. The first was defined as: *Qualiscumque existimatio levis qua aliquis adhaeret falso tanquam vero, SINE ASSENSU CREDULITATIS* [Any slight thought by which a person adheres to what is false as though it were true, but WITHOUT THE ASSENT THAT SPRINGS FROM BELIEF]. The second was defined as 'firm belief'. These authors saw, as we do, the need to distinguish two false assents in human beings, and their distinction coincides in great part with ours. We said that the first kind of assent was not always rash, and could not be imputed to any fault in the human will. In some cases it is necessary if we are going to act, and is neither *firm* nor *firm belief* (cf. St. Thomas., *S. T.*, I, q. 94, art. 4). The Academicians also knew about the necessity of provisional assent, but did not develop it further.

opinion, but more clear-sighted people may see the matter differently', and so on. And we can see how wise people are ready to listen courteously to a contrary opinion, and even seek it. They are eager also to receive light from others even in matters in which they themselves are acknowledged experts. The way they reserve their judgment, their readiness to listen, their careful reflection on the things they have heard, their desire to benefit even from the unlearned in matters where they have already formed an opinion — all this shows that their assent, although *full* in the sense that it closes a question and shuts out hesitation from the spirit, is indeed *provisional*. In other words, the matter has been closed, but not without some predisposition to reopen it, if need be, and appeal against the decision. This kind of conclusion, which leaves the spirit always disposed to re-examine the matter if some just motive draws it to do so, absolves such people from error because assent given in this way is just what it should be, neither more nor less, and also because the will has not acted rashly or precipitously.

1304. If we look at certainty from the point of view of *persuasion* and assent, the state of a mind which has reached the kind of assent we are dealing with can reasonably be called a state of *certainty* because the mind no longer hesitates fearfully in the face of doubts. It is not suspended, but already resting in a certain, determined and completed opinion; its opinion is not *uncertain*, that is, it is not vague and hesitant. And this is *normal certainty*.

1305. The great majority of people, however, are under the unfortunate influence of the hasty, deplorable rashness they receive as part of human inheritance. They simply do not know how to find that state of *provisional* certainty which constitutes the golden mean. All they desire are *absolute*, uncontestable opinions. This is especially the case with youth, whose lack of experience prevents them from understanding the fallibility and short-sightedness of the human mind. They fail to see how easy it is to fall into error through hasty and over-confident judgments, nor do they understand the immensity of the harm that error causes.

Such presumption and unhappy security of judgment overrides both the docility with which the wise spirit should be prepared to reflect on questions already resolved, and the diffident awareness that senses the possibility of some mistake in every first judgment. There is no longer any ready willingness to listen to what others have to say about such judgments. This attitude is obviously the source of many private and public disagreements and confrontations that divide and sunder the human race despite its destiny as a single family. Often two brothers with different opinions cannot live together. On the other hand, wisdom in the discreet person is the mother of charity, and reconciles spirits even when minds differ.

1306. Prudent people, therefore, avoid many dangers by frequently employing in daily life assent which is both *full* and *provisional*. 1. On the one hand, assent when *full*, that is, finished and complete, does not leave the mind in suspense and disquiet as doubt naturally does; it produces a state of certainty, makes human actions possible, and gives rise to solid frankness and the resolution necessary for action in one's undertakings. 2. On the other hand, because this assent is *provisional* in the sense explained, it avoids error (which would not be possible in the case of an absolute, immobile assent) and leaves the way open to progress in spirit by assisting quiet, wholesome communication between human beings. Effective union between many individuals is brought about by means of courtesy and tolerance in the midst of varying opinions.[204]

---

[204] As I said, such restraint is the way to prevent *material* error from becoming true, formal error. Material error, which is sometimes inevitable, does not depend upon our will, and hence is not produced by us. For example, in measuring a piece of ground, I use a rule made by a person on whom I can normally depend. A slight discrepancy in the rule, however, provides me with a false result. I could be the cause of this error only if people thought that I, like a quality inspector, were obliged to check the rule I use. Maintaining this in an absolute sense would mean that everyone had to undertake everyone else's job, which would be impossible and highly damaging. It would be superior 1. to our energy of will, that can stay alert only for a determined time; 2. to the time available; and 3. it would moreover be *harmful* to submit things to the scrupulous examination needed to avoid material error. *Material* error, therefore, which does not depend upon an act of human will, often cannot and must not be avoided. But we can and must prevent its becoming formal by giving a *definitive*, but simultaneously *provisional* assent at the end of our calculations. In other words, we conclude with the implicit condition: 'Provided a better examination does not produce some other conclusion'.

Article 6

Although we cannot always avoid material error, we can avoid the harm springing from it

1307. We can, therefore, avoid *formal error*, that is, error which is an act of our will. At the same time, we have to infer from what has been said that we cannot avoid *material error*, that is, an erroneous judgment which we make on the basis of data that does not depend upon us, and that cannot and must not depend upon us.[205] But can we avoid the *harm* resulting from *material error*?

1308. If we mean true, final and total harm, we can avoid it and eliminate all fear about it by firm belief in the existence of a God and of divine providence. The existence of God is an immediate consequence of the form of reason, a consequence implicitly contained in the form of reason itself.[206]

Granted the presence of an all-beneficent providence over things, we can trust in it for assurance that the material error in which we necessarily fall without our intervention is one of the many accidents directed by the all-wise and all-powerful goodness governing all things. The true part of Descartes' principle lies here: on the truth of the divine existence depends the

[205] In the way that *precision* in instruments made by experts does not depend on us, according to the preceding footnote. This precision must reasonably be presupposed, and taken from the beginning as our standard of judgment. If we then note some sign of imprecision, it can and must be rectified. Imagine, for example, that we always had to check instruments before using them. We could do this only by using more dependable instruments as norms. But often it is impossible to go back to the initial standards. For instance, we cannot measure the degree of longitude every time we want to make some geodetic observation.

[206] This does not exclude the possibility of God's having manifested himself from the beginning by means of revelation. Philosophy recognises that the *first reflections* could not have been made easily by human beings without the use of a *language*. This language could, however, have been communicated without any positive manifestation of the existence of God. The necessity of this positive manifestation must, therefore, be deduced from other principles, not from those dependent upon some absolute need of this manifestation to promote the *first* human *reflections*.

assurance we have, not that we shall avoid mistakes, but that our unwilled errors will not harm us.

Persons who do not admit a supreme guide cannot reasonably believe they will avoid errors, nor that someone will free them from the harm arising from errors. The result is inevitably a distrusting and exaggeratedly meticulous spirit in such people. Moreover, God does not deliver from the damage caused by error those who set themselves apart and want to work out everything for themselves.

Article 7

The limits within which material error can occur

1309. Several times we have mentioned *material* and *formal error*. It will help if we consider more carefully the differences between these two kinds of error, especially the limits within which *material error* can occur, before we take our argument further.

I note therefore that we always judge on the basis of *data*. But data are such that either error has no place in them or doubt about them is possible. Intellective perceptions which form *direct* knowledge are examples of the first kind of data; *data which depend* partly upon blind faculties such as instinct are examples of the second kind.

For example, I carry out some written calculation in algebra. My hand writes 2 instead of 3, and the whole calculation is mistaken. There is no doubt that 2 was written in a moment of distraction or suspension of attention. My hand, moving casually as a result of a combination of the direction of the preceding movement and mechanical and instinctive laws, writes 2 where it should have written 3.

Could this momentary suspension of attention be avoided? We cannot say, but we do know perfectly well that continual watch over our attention causes fatigue, and that prolonged effort cannot be maintained indefinitely with complete success. This fact of experience enables us to conclude that as a result of limited watch over our attention, we are not absolute masters of our attention, and cannot always have the degree of power over it that we would wish. On the other hand, the momentary distraction of attention when my hand writes 2 is so slight and brief that I do not advert to it in any way nor retain any trace of it in my memory. *Noticing it* afterwards is, therefore, completely impossible for me.

The defect committed by my hand can therefore be dependent upon a lack of attention which comes from some limitation of my willed energy rather than from me; it can come from some deficiency not adverted to by me, nor able to be adverted to, because of the limitation to which the energy of my will is subject. In this case I have no more reason to believe that I have erred than I have in any other case, and it certainly cannot be desirable that I should check this step on the grounds of the general possibility that some mistake could be present. If this were so, I should have to review every other step *ad infinitum* without hope of conclusion. I would always be going back to the beginning and playing the sad, impossible game of the sceptics. I have to conclude that I cannot take precautions against some material errors. Which errors are these, according to the line of argument we have been following?

1310. Two causes concur in producing the error we have described above: 1. the suspension of intellectual attention; 2. an instinctive or habitual force which moves the hand independently of the understanding's attention. But these two causes play different roles in the production of the mistake. The intellective will concurs negatively, and is therefore only the *occasion* of error; the movement of the hand is the true efficient *cause*.

This analysis enables us to conclude that 'the cause of true knowledge is the understanding; the cause of material error is not the understanding but some *blind* potency that continues to operate even when the understanding has suspended its functions, and in operating produces an erroneous datum on the basis of which the understanding then judges'.

1311. The *blind potency* which produces the erroneous *datum* on the basis of which the understanding judges is not, however, the only cause of material error. Some *data* are produced not by any blind potency, nor by any potency of one's own, but on the authority of others[207] which allows the data to be admitted as

---

[207] When I use mathematical instruments made by a craftsman and I rely on them for my calculations, I base myself on the *authority* of the craftsman

true without further examination. Hence the error. Often the understanding acts with perfect consistency in willing to skip further examination of the data. These are the frequent cases in which the understanding must reasonably give its *full* though *provisional* assent because the contrary would entail, for itself or someone else, greater harm than the damage the understanding is trying to avoid through meticulous examination of the data.

1312. We can conclude, therefore. that there are two causes of material errors: 1. basing one's judgment upon a *datum* provided by some blind power; or 2. basing one's judgment upon fallible *authority*. These are purely material errors whenever it is necessary for the understanding to accept the data as satisfactory without further need to verify them.

1313. Granted this knowledge of the causes of *material error*, we can now easily delineate the limits within which such error can occur. We say that *material error* is limited to those judgments which rest upon *data* that are not absolutely certain, but admitted without further examination to avoid greater harm. If, on the contrary, the understanding judges upon the basis of data which is 1. independent of fallible authority and 2. not the effect of a blind faculty such as instinct or habit which moves the hand, then the understanding alone produces the judgment without co-operation from anything else. Only formal errors are present in these circumstances.

1314. The following truth is a result of what has been said, and is worthy of consideration: 'Material error can occur in mathematical and physical sciences, but in moral and metaphysical sciences only formal errors are possible.'

The reason is clear from what has been said. Moral and metaphysical sciences arise only from reflection on our first interior knowledge and on all that is present in our consciousness. The *data* therefore are infallible. They depend neither upon the authority of others nor upon *blind forces*, but simply upon nature, or on the understanding itself. In such judgments nothing can be done when the action of the understanding is impeded or suspended because no other force can act during such

which assures me that the instruments function as they should. The authority is founded in the known expertise of his work.

suspension by positing a new datum or the signs of some decision. Hence the understanding is either present with its actual
attention and judges or, if it is not present, the work of reasoning makes no further progress.[208]

Article 8

The sense in which the Scriptures and
the Fathers of the Church say that truths are obvious,
and that everyone who wishes can come to possess them

1315. The truths necessary for human beings are metaphysical and moral. Only formal error, which is caused by the human
will, can occur in such truths. They must be taken as the point
of reference in those passages of the Scriptures and the Fathers
of the Church which affirm that ignorance of the truth is
dependent on human beings themselves, who reject the invita-
tions of wisdom.

In the book of Proverbs we read:

> Wisdom cries aloud in the street;
> in the markets she raises her voice;
> on the top of the walls she cries out;
> at the entrance of the city gates she speaks:
> 'How long, O simple ones, will you love being simple?
> How long will scoffers delight in their scoffing
> and fools hate knowledge?
> Give heed to my reproof;
> behold, I will pour out my thoughts to you;
> I will make my words known to you.
> Because I have called and you refused to listen,
> have stretched out my hand and no one has heeded'.[209]

It is, alas, the evil disposition of the will that holds us back and
distances us from the principal truths that form wisdom.

In another place, Scripture requires that we search for the

---

[208] The possibility of our falling *necessarily* into a formal error, that is,
without our having the freedom to avoid it, is a delicate and very difficult
question.

[209] Prov 1: 20–24.

truth with the same longing and eager desire with which we look for riches, and promises that we shall not fail to find it:

> If you seek it like silver
> and search for it as for hidden treasures;
> then you will understand the fear of the LORD
> and find the knowledge of God.[210]

This knowledge is precisely the knowledge of those metaphysical and moral truths of which we are speaking.

Scripture then puts on wisdom's lips:

> I love those who love me,
> and those who seek me diligently find me.[211]

These places, and innumerable others, show clearly that the condition which Scripture requires in one who is to find wisdom, 'whose mouth will utter truth',[212] is that he has a good and perfect will, eager and solicitous in seeking the truth.

1316. The teaching of the Fathers derives from that of Scripture. Perhaps the most familiar and best expressed of St. Augustine's opinions is that human beings without the truth have only themselves to blame. The truth replies to everyone of us because we carry it within, where we can all consult it.

> Everywhere, O Truth, you preside over those who consult you, and you reply to all, even when they seek knowledge of different things. You reply clearly, but not all hear clearly. All ask about whatever they want, but not all hear what they want to hear. Your best minister is the one who no longer pays attention in order to hear from you what he wants, but rather wants what he hears from you.[213]

A good rule for finding the truth is to draw near it with a

---

[210] *Ibid.*, 2: 4, 5.

[211] *Ibid.*, 8: 17.

[212] *Ibid.*, 8: 7.

[213] *Ubique, Veritas, praesides omnibus consulentibus te, simulque respondes omnibus etiam diversa consulentibus. Liquide tu respondes, sed non liquide omnes audiunt. Omnes unde volunt consulunt, sed non semper quod volunt audiunt. Optimus minister tuus est, qui non magis intuetur hoc a te audire quod ipse voluerit, sed potius hoc velle quod a te audierit* (Conf., bk. 10, c. 26).

unprejudiced mind and a will equally disposed to receive whatever the truth has to give — if we do not approach in this way, we hear not what it says to us, but what we want to hear. When we consult the truth, we should receive and love in the same spirit everything that it has to say to us. Indeed, we should love whatever we love only because the truth has said it.

1317. According to St. Augustine, therefore, each one who wishes finds the truth in himself.[214] As we have seen, everyone has the innate light of truth, and moreover direct knowledge, which is immune from error. By reflecting on this he can acknowledge for himself the great metaphysical and moral truths. But we do need to be aware that in the passage we have quoted, St. Augustine is not speaking about the supernatural truth which God communicates to souls with grace. Note, therefore, that this holy Doctor says that the truth is open even to the wicked if they wish to acknowledge it. They can see it simply by reflecting within themselves:

> The wicked themselves, while fleeing from the unchangeable light of truth, are touched by it. Hence the wicked too think of eternity, and rightly reprove or praise many things in human activity. With what standards do they finally judge except those by which they see how all should live, although they themselves do not in fact live in this way?[215]

1318. St. Augustine gives two reasons for our refusal to acknowledge truth, although it is within us, and for our falling into error. These reasons correspond with what we have said about the similarity between what is true and what is false, and about the passions which dispose the will to take what is false

---

[214] This *truth* that we have in ourselves does not always provide particular truths already fashioned and prepared for us. But it does show us the way and indicates sure means for finding them. When, for instance, we feel the need to seek assistance from others in order to be instructed in some branch of knowledge or to have some item of truth clarified, it is truth existing in us which sends us to them. Interior truth does not close us up within ourselves, nor does it exclude authority or other means in the search for what is true. Rather, it is that which shows us the necessity of such means, and guides us to them.

[215] *De Trinit.*, bk. 14, c. 15.

for what is true when what is false is desired and resembles what is true. He speaks of these occasional causes of error in his book *De Vera Religione* and says:

> Falsehood does not arise from the things that deceive us. They show us only the degree of beauty they have themselves received. — Nor does it originate with the senses which announce to the spirit presiding over them only the changes by which they themselves are affected according to the nature of the bodily organs. It is sins which deceive the soul as it searches for what is true while abandoning and neglecting the truth.[216]

Shortly afterwards, he goes on:

> No one can be cast out by the truth unless he has been possessed by some likeness of the truth. You ask what it is that is so attractive in bodily desire? It is nothing other than what is agreeable. Things which resist us cause pain, and agreeable things produce pleasure.

Observing that we know what is agreeable when it pleases us to do so, St. Augustine argues that we can, when we want to, easily know even what is supremely agreeable, that is, God, and that this truth depends upon our good or evil will. 'Acknowledge what is supremely agreeable,' says the Saint. 'Do not desire to go outside yourself; turn back to yourself. TRUTH DWELLS WITHIN' [*App.*, no. 16] and we reach it, he says, 'by searching not in the space occupied by things, but in the desire proper to the mind.'[217]

1319. The same teaching is found in other Fathers and Doctors of the Church. To avoid endless quotations, I shall choose as my witness the author of the *Itinerarium*, whom I have already cited on several occasions. He says that we have within

---

[216] C. 36.

[217] C. 39. St. Augustine went to such lengths in professing this truth, and was so aware that error in the principles of metaphysics and morals was brought about only by assent dependent upon the will, that in his *Retractationes* (bk. 1, c. 13) he wrote with great acuteness: *Et ille qui peccat ignorans, voluntate utique facit, quod cum faciendum non sit, putat esse faciendum* [He who sins while ignorant, does so willingly. Although something is not to be done, he thinks that it is to be done].

ourselves the possibility of discovering the truth provided we want to and do not allow ourselves to be deceived by sensible things that dispose our wills to consent to error. He says:

> It is obvious that our intellect is joined to eternal truth because only by means of such a teacher could it understand anything true with certainty. YOU ARE ABLE THEREFORE OF YOURSELF TO SEE TRUTH which teaches you, provided that concupiscence and phantasies do not impede you by placing themselves like clouds between you and the ray of truth.[218]

1320. Finally, it is a common place amongst antiquity that the human soul darkened by passions is not suited for finding the truth by reflecting upon itself. *Purification* of soul, which all the famous, ancient schools of philosophy taught and required from their disciples to prepare them for understanding the teaching they were to receive, has no other foundation than the truth we are describing. And our divine Master also required hearers whose ears of the heart were open: *Qui habet aures audiendi, audiat* [He who has ears to hear, let him hear].[219]

---

[218] *Ex quo manifeste apparet, quod coniunctus sit intellectus noster ipsi aeternae veritati, dum non nisi per illam docentem nihil verum potest certitudinaliter capere. VIDERE IGITUR PER TE POTES VERITATEM, quae te docet, si te concupiscentiae et phantasmata non impediant et se tanquam nubes inter te et veritatis radium non interponant* (*Itin.* bk. 3).

[219] Matt 11: 15. The argument in this article concerns *reflective knowledge* only, which does not consist in the *first perception* of things (direct knowledge) but in the *acknowledgement* of things. However, *ignorance* can occur in direct knowledge, although *error* cannot; that is, we can lack knowledge because we have to receive it from outside, and in dependence upon other things. Hence we need: 1. external sensible things, which provide the matter of knowledge; and 2. the internal requirements of organisation, which are in all probability the first occasion through which the understanding is moved to perceive external things. The sources of *first reflection*, which produces *popular knowledge*, are themselves partly external to us, that is, they are 1. language, the cause occasioning the act of reflection; and 2. the things communicated by language, which are the objects of reflection (these can even be supernatural matters, such as the content of divine revelation). However, the true *cause* of understanding and reflection is always within us. Hence, St.Bonaventure's *VIDERE IGITUR PER TE POTES VERITATEM* [YOU ARE ABLE THEREFORE OF YOURSELF TO SEE TRUTH], where we have to understand 'granted the necessary conditions for reflective activity'.

Article 9

St. Augustine's teaching on idolatry indicates an example of error in common, popular knowledge

1321. As we have seen, the will, by surrendering to the inclination towards error, especially when what is false shows considerable similarity to what is true, is the cause of formal error. For the sake of greater light and evidence on the matter, we must now apply this teaching to some really serious error. St. Augustine, whose teaching it is, provides us with a suitable example.

We have distinguished two kinds of knowledge, *popular* knowledge which is concerned with first reflection, and *philosophical* knowledge which is concerned with further reflection.

We have seen that error is far more likely to intrude in the second kind of reflection than the first where, however, it is sometimes present precisely because reflection is present. St. Augustine gives us an example of common, popular error and of philosophical error. He shows how both spring from the weakness and degradation of the human will as it allows itself to be influenced and corrupted to the greatest degree by the passions.

St. Augustine's example, drawn from popular knowledge, is of idolatry, a capital, universal error. I shall quote the whole passage in which he describes the origin of this error because of the great care he takes to show how the minds of the human race (the whole human race, we may say without exaggeration) were detached from the truth in this respect, and plunged into the darkness of perdition.

> Because human beings *loved* (here he indicates desire, which occasions error) what was made more than the maker and his art, they were afflicted with THIS ERROR (of idolatry) which made them seek the maker and his art in the works themselves. Unable to find him (because God, who stands above our very minds, does not fall under our bodily senses), they judge that the works themselves are the maker and his art. This is the source of all impiety, not only of those who sin, but also of those who are damned through their sins.

[1321]

The Saint then describes the progress of idolatry, which goes hand in hand with that of corruption. The greater the likeness between what is false and what is true, the easier it is to fall into error; less disorder is required in the will for it to commit error in the case of similarity than for it to take as true something very different from what is true. But as the will becomes more corrupt, the mind is blinded and the error degenerates until, at the most corrupt level of all, the will is incapable of using its understanding, even for things which are highly dissimilar.

It seems that this kind of progress can be noted in idolatry. In his description, St. Augustine observes that human beings began with the *love* of creatures, and then went over willingly to *serve* them. This points to progress along the path of corruption. As the error of idolatry develops, the same kind of progress is encountered. Idolatry began when the most beautiful creatures were taken for the Creator because they seemed more like him; but the mind's confusion was then extended to the ugliest of creatures, and things which did not have even the least apparent likeness with the divinity and its perfection were cherished as divinities.

We need to hear St. Augustine on this point:

> People look up to created things against the commandment of God, and love them in place of the law and the truth… But they add damnation to damnation not only by wanting to *love*, but even by wanting to *serve* creatures in preference to the Creator, and to worship them in both their highest and their most degraded aspects.

The two levels of corruption are clearly indicated, and these correspond to the degrees of error. First the understanding is deceived by taking for God the things most like God:

> Some maintain they should worship the soul as a supreme God. They worship the first intellective creature which the Father made by means of truth in order that the soul might have its gaze fixed on truth, and might know itself through truth, to which it is extremely SIMILAR.[220]

---

[220] Note how St. Augustine teaches constantly that the soul needs *truth* (the first idea) in order to know itself. Feeling is not sufficient. In a word, the soul is not known to itself through itself.

The second, grosser error is to take for God the things most unlike God. St. Augustine continues:

> Then they (human beings) begin to worship genital life, through which the eternal, incommunicable God enables visible, temporal things to generate. Next, they descend to animals, and from these to the worship of brute bodies. They first choose the most beautiful, which are certainly the heavenly bodies. The sun is the most obvious, and some are content with this. Others believe that the moon in her splendour is also worthy of worship. As they say, it is nearer us and demonstrates a beauty nearer ours. Other people add the bodies of other stars, and the whole of heaven with its stars. Some include the atmosphere along with the heaven above us, and submit their own souls to these two bodily elements. The most religious in their own eyes, however, are those who encompass all creatures, that is to say, the world with all the things that it contains, and the life which gives breath and animation to some (life which some believe is corporeal, others incorporeal). In a word, they believe that this whole complex is some great God, of whom other things are parts. And all this because they did not know the author and founder of every creature. They descended to what was like him, and from the works of God abased themselves in their own works which again are visible.[221]

And St. Augustine rightly notes greater error in the kind of idolatry that traffics in these likenesses than in the idolatry of nature. Nature is, after all, far greater and more sublime than human works, and is in some way more similar to God because it is the work of God.

Article 10

St. Augustine's teaching on disbelief indicates an example of error in philosophical knowledge

1322. St. Augustine, after speaking of idolatry as an error present in *popular* knowledge, goes on to speak of disbelief, a

[221] *De V. R.*, c. 37.

good example of error in *philosophical* knowledge. This, too, he describes as the effect of a will bent towards evil and surrendering to it.

> There is a lower and more desolate worship of likenesses by which human beings cultivate their phantasies and honour under the name of religion whatever occurs to their ERRING spirit, and whatever pride and hubris places before their imagination. They arrive at such a point that they imagine they have to worship nothing at all, and that others who do worship have wrapped themselves in superstition and the misery of *servitude*.

According to St. Augustine, therefore, the desire for unrestrained *freedom*, which removes human beings from the just dominion of God, is the germ of disbelief. This is indeed what can be seen in every age; it is the entire story of disbelief from the giants who lived before the flood to our present-day sophists.

> But their counsel is in vain. They do not succeed in avoiding service. The vices that have made them think in this way remain to provide them with a cult. They aim at a threefold passion of pleasure, of power, or of lustful gazes. Amongst those who believe that nothing is to be worshipped, I deny that there are any who escape subjection either to the pleasures of the flesh, or the search for power, or the madness of the delights offered by some vain spectacles... And because the world is full of these things, those drawn by love of the world to disbelieve in worship of any kind bow down before every part of the world.[222]

1323. St. Augustine concludes from all these things that 'there COULD HAVE BEEN NO ERROR in religion if human beings had not given their affection and worship to the spirit, or the body, or their own phantasies instead of to God.'[223]

1324. But human beings who fall into the fatal error of which we are speaking are mentally confused, and no longer capable of

---

[222] *De V. R.*, c. 38.

[223] *Quamobrem sit tibi manifestum atque perceptum, NULLUM ERROREM in Religione esse potuisse, si anima pro Deo suo non coleret animam, aut corpus, aut phantasmata sua (De V. R.*, c. 10).

calmly acknowledging the truth. Their return to the truth must begin, therefore, from *faith* much more than from *reasoning*, and this, as we have said (cf. 1155 ss.), is the great service that *authority* provides. Authority makes up for the debility of reflection, disturbed and uncertain as it is by the badly disposed will. Our great author goes on: 'Although these miserable people have reached this extremity and succumbed to the dominion of vices... they can, as long as they live, renew the battle and conquer once more.' But only on condition that 'they first believe that which they cannot as yet understand.'[224]

Article 11

Continuation of the analysis of error: error presupposes mental confusion

1325. Material error arises from *erroneous data* not dependent on ourselves. Formal error depends entirely upon ourselves, and arises only after prior mental *confusion*.[225]

---

[224] *De V. R.*, c. 38. — *Si prius credant quod intelligere nondum valent.*

[225] We have already explained how a blind potency can provide *erroneous data*, even though there is neither error nor truth in what is blind. The blind potency can provide *conventional signs* from which error comes. For example, in the case of a hand that is moved mechanically to write *4* in a calculation where it should write *3*, the *4* written by the hand contains the error. It is true that the figure *4*, considered in its own existence, contains neither error nor truth, and it is this existence which is produced by the blind potency. Consequently the blind potency producing the number does not insert error or truth into it, properly speaking. Nevertheless, we consider that figure as a sign of four units resulting from the calculation, and then, without the intervention of our will, add to it what we call 'material' error. In doing this, we simply take this figure as an indication of what it conventionally expresses. And we act correctly because it is right that we should give each sign its conventional value. We cannot, in fact, do otherwise. But what we do, although right of itself and free from error, is associated with the blind act of the hand which again cannot be called error, and results in an *error* at the end of the calculation. This error consists 'in taking the result as something done by an intelligent faculty, although it was the work not only of such a faculty, but also of a blind faculty'.

In fact, this error takes place when we reflect upon our perceptions and ideas, and put one idea or perception in the place of another, that is, we confuse them. We can see this better if we reduce error to its most common formula: 'Error is present when we attribute to a subject a predicate not belonging to it.'[226] Examining this formula it is easy to see how it can be reduced equivalently to the following: 'Error is present when we take one intellection for another.'

When I attribute to a subject a predicate not belonging to it, I am merely formulating for that subject a concept different from what is true. In other words, I think the subject is something which it is not; I think it has a predicate that it has not. My mind, therefore, has two possible intellections: one is the true concept of the thing, that is, I conceive the thing itself without the predicate; the other is the false concept, that is, I conceive the same thing with the predicate. With both concepts before me, I choose the second instead of the first. For example, I say: 'This thing I have named, or the thing that produced this feeling in me or determined me in some other way, has the predicate we are speaking of.' Some exchange or confusion between the two intellections takes place in my mind; I create a union that does not exist, and I affirm its existence.

1326. It is clear that in reflecting on the things in my mind, I cannot see either what is not there, or something different from what is there, unless the eye of my reflection, guided by the will, affirms that it sees what it does not see, that is, unless the eye of my reflection *lies*. If it seems to see, then what it seems to see must be an idol created by itself. But genuine creation is beyond the powers of the human spirit, and alien to it. When we say that we create something for ourselves, we can only mean that what previously existed in our mind is now wrongly united. There is still no error, however, as a result of this mistaken conjunction provided that we realise that it is our own work, and we do not take it as something produced in our mind by nature — in other words, we do not take it as the truth about the thing in question.

---

[226] As we have said, it is clear that this formula can also include the kind of error that consists in denying a predicate to a subject that belongs to it, provided that the predicate is taken as an unknown value that can be either negative or positive.

On the one hand, there is what we *conceive directly*, and on the other what we *fabricate*; error lies in taking the fabrication for what is conceived directly. In positing the fabrication in place of the perception,[227] we do two things: 1. we fabricate; 2. we put this fabrication in the place of the truth (the perception, the direct concepts), by ignoring and rejecting the truth. This rejection of the truth we actually have in mind, perfects and informs our error.

1327. The activity by which we fall into error must necessarily be produced as a result of darkness and confusion of ideas, as our very nature shows us. The act of reflection has to be turned away from the vision of what nature places in our mind, and fixed on its own fabrication and artifice. Truth and fabrication are then made to compenetrate and become one, or rather we intellectually draw the fabrication like a veil over the truth. In other words, we attempt to destroy what is true, if that were possible. This attempt is, however, frustrated by immovable nature, even though the disturbance in our reflection can increase indefinitely and render reflection incapable of discerning any truth which reflection itself has tried to hide and deny for a long time. Our state of reflection, already *confused* and *dark*, now becomes habitual, and can rightly be called a state of *lethargy* and mental *blindness*.

Article 12

Error results from an unjust suspension of assent

1328. As a result of our analysis of error in relationship to the understanding, we found that error consists in a *confusion* of ideas, one of which is exchanged for another.[228] Let us now

---

[227] Or in place of the *relationships* of perceptions and of all the consequences determined by the perceptions and virtually contained in them.

[228] It is *myself*, the subject, that exchanges one idea for another, but it carries out this operation with its faculty of *word*, not with that of *ideas*. This occurs as follows. The faculty of ideas has for its term the universal idea; the faculty of word fixes and determines the *particular* in the universal, that is, pronounces, and in pronouncing posits something particular in the

examine error in its relationship with the will which moves the understanding to produce error.

We can express the nature of this act with the following formula: 'Error arises from making a judgment when the ideas of our mind are still in an indistinct, confused state, in which it is easy to exchange one idea for another.'

1329. Let us imagine that we have two ideas, one a predicate and one a subject. These ideas, and the idea of their connection, are perfectly distinguished from one another.[229] As long as the mind remains in this state, it is totally impossible for us to consent to error sincerely, as we have said in speaking about the evidence of geometrical propositions (cf. 1293 ss.). If bad will is present, however, which hates a truth and loves its contrary error, we make ourselves capable of surrendering to error.

What we do is this. We look for some seemingly true argument — some sophism — which enables us to *suspend* our judgment and confuse our ideas a little. Our former clarity is now slightly distorted. Normally, it is not difficult to achieve this. There are always general reasons more or less suitable for making us suspend our assent. Many people are so attached to their own opinion, for example, that they are prepared to confess their own ignorance rather than give in. More often than not, they end an argument by bringing forward the ignorance and

---

universal. The *faculty of word*, therefore, is that of judgment, and error resides only in the interior judgment (cf. 1249 ss.), that is, in the *result* of the judgment. This result can also be expressed by means of an external word because it is not a simple apprehension, but an effect of the energy of the subject who, when roused to a greater effort, embodies, as it were, what had previously been conceived languidly, and determines it with all the determinations necessary for true *subsistence* and for being expressed. Human nature has been granted one, single thing comparable to the act of creation: the creation of error.

[229] Ideas are distinct in themselves, and cannot be confused. In our argument, however, we are speaking of *reflection* which twists and turns, as it were, in search of one idea or another. As it does so, it sometimes alights and rests on one idea rather than another, exchanging them without finding what it was looking for. Moreover, composite ideas, which are the work of reflection, sometimes involve in their make-up entire opinions of which we are unaware. The *confusion* to which our mind is subject has its proper seat, therefore, in the faculty of reflection guided by the will. Confusion is not generated by the object (ideas), but by the subject (the act of reflection).

[1329]

fallibility of human reason itself, and take on the air — for that moment alone — of modest, humble-minded investigators.

The only benefit you will have obtained from your convincing, stringent arguments is to hear yourself gently admonished by general advice about moderation and sobriety in thought and research; they will remind you very seriously that there is a limit to human knowledge, and that you should avoid what is inscrutable and obscure. This is, of course, ridiculous, but it is very frequent, and offers clear proof that those who do not want to assent to a proposition never will. There will always be some general reason, some 'Who knows?'; in other words, they appeal to their own ignorance or some affected scepticism, that they can use as protection in withholding their assent to the proposed truth.

1330. But we can leave this case of blatant obstinacy in error in order to point out that a person with at least a general will to know the truth can nevertheless make himself unduly meticulous and anxious in giving assent to an obvious truth if he is biased and worried by an over-anxious fear of error. One of the rules a person of this kind must use for avoiding error is the following: 'We must dispose our wills in such a way that we give our ready and complete assent to the known truth as soon as we know what is true.' This unsullied readiness to assent joyfully to the presence of what is true is what forms and characterises upright, virtuous people, who seem endowed with exquisite good sense in discerning and knowing the truth precisely because they surrender immediately and unresistingly to its light.

On the other hand, affected suspension of one's assent or the exaggerated hesitation produced by excessive fear of error is often sufficient to cause error [*App.*, no. 17] by providing time for the mind to confuse itself and the reflection to lose its balance.

—

Article 13

Error sometimes results from haste or undue alacrity in giving assent

1331. Error occurs when the mind is in a state of confusion

(cf. 1328 ss.). However, even when our mind has reached a state in which ideas are clearly distinct, the will can still produce error (although not while the ideas remain distinct). Suspension of assent allows us to use a fleeting moment to overturn our calm serenity of mind and replace it with disturbance and confusion (*ibid.*).

If, however, the mind has not reached a state in which ideas are distinct from one another, and the will produces assent, an error arises from hastiness and undue alacrity in our judgment. We must speak now of this precipitate judgment.

Two motives can induce the will to hasten the assent and move the intellect to judge, before the mind has succeeded in distinguishing the ideas to be used in making its judgment: 1. love of error which draws the will to take advantage of the moment of confusion, embrace the error and introduce it into the spirit under the guise of truth; 2. a desire to finish the matter with an immediate decision rather than bear the burden caused by a state of suspension and uncertainty.

1332. We have already listed seven reasons capable of producing some kind of inclination in the will: 1. known good in the object;[230] 2. the perfection of intellective knowledge; 3. sensible experience; 4. imagination; 5. passions; 6. habits; 7. instinct (cf. 1288). The first five produce an inclination in the will towards or against the object, and through love or hatred for the object tend to encourage hastiness in judgment; in a word, through love of what is found in the error. The last two often produce in the will an inclination to hasty judgment, more as a result of the anguish we feel in holding our judgment suspended than through love or hatred of the object. This occurs when an instinct or habit of rash judgment incites and suddenly provokes us.

In fact, suspension of judgment naturally causes us anguish as long as our reflection has not shown us the need for such suspension. Only then do we begin to proceed more slowly when judging.

1333. Meanwhile, even from the beginning of our mental development, we find some instinct drawing us to conclusions on the basis of first appearances without our giving any prior thought to distinguishing our ideas. This instinct is produced,

[230] Or known evil.

as I have hinted elsewhere, by the needs of our animal life, which by means of the unity of the subject puts into action all the subject's forces, including its intellectual powers, for the sake of self-preservation. It is natural for this instinctive movement of reason, which springs from our natural needs, to be made hurriedly, on the spur of the moment. Sense brooks no delay; its essential property is hasty action.[231]

We begin to judge hastily through instinct, therefore, almost from the day of our birth, and thus acquire a habit of undue alacrity in judging. This is particularly the case with an entire people as such. Hasty judgment is a vice that is corrected only through culture, study or lengthy reflection.[232]

1334. But error certainly does not arise if the will, although inclined to move the intellect to false judgment, refuses to cede either to love of error and hatred of its contrary truth, or to the desire to settle something quickly and remove the burden caused by prolonging a decision. Hence, anyone who loves the truth in general, although not totally lacking in passions and impulses contrary to equanimity of judgment, must take as his shield the first of Descartes' four rules of method (the rule against hasty judgment). I would formulate it as follows:

---

[231] This occurs because sense is drawn to its particular aim without perceiving anything outside that aim, and hence without regard for anything extraneous to its satisfaction in acting.

[232] We can see wonderful uprightness of judgment in children, and often in the honest, just judgments of peoples (taken as a whole) free from agitators. Children's uprightness arises from their lack of passions, or lack of subjection to them, as well as from their freedom from bad habits, prejudices, and so on; the uprightness of a people depends necessarily on their being free from *sophisticated* passions, and from the considerations and sophistries of cultured human beings, which find their source and development in the possibilities open to the powerful. However, uprightness of judgment on the part of children and peoples does not prevent their falling into error. It is different for the truly wise, who unite virtue and experience of human affairs with the search for knowledge. Prudent persons of this kind are more easily on their guard against error because they have no love for it. Using reflection illuminated by experience, which has informed them about the danger of error, they put a brake on their passions and simultaneously rule the natural instinct drawing them towards hasty judgment. As a result, they form a habit of suspending their judgment when necessary, and of examining matters coolly and accurately before pronouncing on them.

[1334]

'Let the judgment be suspended until the ideas of the predicate, the subject and their connection are distinct and clear in the mind. Every care must be taken to achieve this, however. Only when these ideas have been rendered distinct and clear, should the judgment be concluded.'

CHAPTER 4

Reflective persuasion of truth and error

1335. After discussing the natural, spontaneous *persuasion* of the first principles (cf. 1143 ss.), I think it will be helpful to say something about the willed, reflective persuasion we form when we consent to truth or error. This is 'persuasion' in the exact sense of the word.

Article 1

Reflective persuasion in general

1336. What we have said so far shows that the reflective *persuasion* which human beings acquire about an opinion is the joint effect of will and reason.

'Such persuasion is the understanding's final rest in an assent given by the will to a proposition.'

The will moves and as it were envelops the understanding, which adheres to and comes to rest in a proposition. It is here that this kind of persuasion arises.

1337. When the proposition is formally false, the persuasion is more an act of the will than of the understanding. The will desires the proposition and, profiting from whatever confusion remains in the ideas, forces the understanding to a *belief* whose falsehood is not clearly seen by the understanding. In place of truth, the understanding easily *believes* and approves the confused falsehood. It will be helpful therefore if we recall the different levels at which the will's action produces persuasion in various cases of assent.

Article 2

Evidence, and the persuasion produced
by the first criterion of certainty in the principles

1338. Our apprehension of, and assent to the first principles is necessary, not free.

The apprehension is natural because carried out in us by *nature* itself. The assent which we irresistibly give the first principles is determined by their *evidence*.

1339. *Evidence* has its origin in the universality and necessity of the idea of being, in which the first principles are rooted. A thing can only be in the mode conveyed by this idea, which encompasses every possibility within itself and indeed is possibility. Our mind is necessitated to form all its true and false judgments according to this perfectly simple idea (the supreme rule of logic). False judgments however do not depend on this infallible rule but on the wrong use that the *subject* makes of it.

1340. The word 'evidence' deserves further explanation. It has been much abused by the different meanings given it. Its etymology, which expresses clear vision or perception, has been partly responsible for this abuse and for the uncertainty of philosophers about its meaning. Simple vision or perception is only a contingent fact, and we do not see how that which is contingent and accidental requires a necessary consent. Indeed, there have always been philosophers who posited erroneous and truthful evidence, and believed that they should enquire about the criterion of evidence.

In fact, the clear vision of anything does not generally speaking include a judgment. And there is a substantial difference between the vision and the thing seen. When our judgment about the thing seen is based solely on our vision of it, deception is possible: the vision, although distinct and *clear*, could be erroneous, that is, apt to make us believe the thing to be different from what it is.

To avoid these equivocations which change intellective evidence into a simple vision similar to that of external sight, we must explain the nature of *intellective evidence* and show that it includes the concept both of a *clear* and of a *necessary apprehension* of some thing. I define intellective evidence as follows: 'Intellective evidence is the apprehension of the *necessity* of a proposition.'

Understood in this way, *intellective evidence* presents not only the fact of *perception* but also the *reason* which irresistibly causes our assent and determines our judgment. This reason, having within itself intellective evidence, is the necessity of the proposition to which we assent.

1341. On the part of the understanding, the persuasion of intellective evidence is greatest in the first principles and eludes the forces of human freedom, which, as we have said, is unable to oppose nature or deny what the understanding necessarily sees.

Article 3

Persuasion produced by the criterion of certainty found in consequences

1342. Intellective evidence is always a *necessity* seen by the understanding in a proposition (cf. 1338 ss.). The necessity of first propositions is of such a kind that it must be felt. But a number of consequential propositions do not manifest any necessity. Is there any *intellective evidence* for these propositions? The question can be answered only be examining the nature of the evidence of consequential propositions. 'The intellective evidence of consequential propositions is present when the propositions are seen in the principles'. This means that we clearly see the connection of a consequential proposition with the supreme principle, and that if the proposition were false, the supreme principle would also be false, which is impossible to be thought.

1343. A consequential proposition can be contained in the supreme, *per se* evident principle in two ways: 1. by its very nature, or 2. because of some fact or contingent condition. In the first case the proposition has an *apodictic* necessity and therefore *apodictic* evidence. In the second, the proposition has a *hypothetical* necessity and therefore *hypothetical* evidence. We can illustrate this by two examples.

The proposition, 'At this moment I must be moving or standing still', is said to be a *necessary* proposition; 'I am moving' is said to be a *contingent* proposition because the contrary is possible.

The propositions are correctly named provided they are considered abstractly as possible propositions. But if they are considered actually in a subject who has assented to both of them, the *certainty* which the subject has of both propositions equally contains some necessity. In the case of the first proposition, the necessity is *apodictic*; in the case of the second, *hypothetical*. Both propositions, joined to the reasonable assent given them, become necessary, but the first apodictically, the second hypothetically.

What I am saying can be better understood if the assent given to the necessity of the two propositions is expressed at the time they are made. In which case they become:

'I am *certain* that at this moment I must be moving or standing still,' and

'I am *certain* that I am moving.'

1344. The origin of the *certainty* expressed in the two propositions is simply a *necessity*.

The necessity of the assent given to the first proposition is the absolute necessity of the proposition. We see that it is impossible to think something different from that which the proposition states because there are only two *possible* opposite cases, movement or rest. The proposition includes all *possibilities*, and therefore constitutes apodictic necessity; it is an example of the *principle of knowledge*.

The necessity of the assent given to the second proposition does not originate in the proposition itself, which has nothing necessary within it. It arises from an implicit fact, that is, from the awareness I have of my movement and from the direct, natural perception which my understanding has of what is happening in my consciousness.[233] Granted the fact of the intellective

---

[233] Hence antiquity said that intellective knowledge always concerns that which is necessary. *Intellectus*, says Aristotle, *et sapientia et scientia non sunt contingentium sed necessarium* [Understanding, wisdom and knowledge concern necessary, not contingent things] (*Eth.*, bk. 6, c. 6). St. Thomas says that the *things* treated by the branches of knowledge are sometimes contingent, but are not the sciences themselves, that is, not the *universal reasons* used for considering contingent things: *Nihil enim est adeo contingens, quin in se aliquid necessarium habeat. Sicut hoc ipsum quod est Sortem currere, in se quidem contingens est, sed habitudo cursus ad motum est necessaria. Necessarium enim est Sortem moveri, si currit* [Nothing is so contingent that it does not have in itself something necessary. The fact, for example, that Socrates is running is in itself contingent, but the ability to run is necessary for motion. It is necessary for Socrates to move if he runs]. He shows that the necessary element in contingent things comes from the intellect, which always considers them in relationship to its universal concepts (*S.T.*, I. q. 86, art. 3).

perception of the movement, the movement is undeniable, because it is an element of the fact itself (cf. 1158 ss.). If my movement, at the time I perceive it intellectively, could not be, it would simultaneously be and not be. By means of the fact of perception, the *per se* contingent proposition becomes necessary; this is a particular instance of the *principle of contradiction*.

We can conclude, therefore, 1. that *apodictic* certainty is present when the necessity of the proposition, which constitutes its evidence, derives solely from the *form of truth* or the first principles without need of anything else; and 2. that *hypothetical* certainty derives from the first principles applied to a contingent fact of consciousness.

1345. Persuasion of deduced propositions is strong when they are seen in the principles. In this case, persuasion is produced more by the understanding than the will. But if the deduction is drawn out and the certainty depends on many contingent facts, the will has scope to make the understanding suspend its assent, and by confusing its ideas, disturb it in its vision.

Article 4

Our state of mind when we are persuaded
by the first criterion of certainty,
according to St. Thomas and the author of the *Itinerary*

1346. We need to describe carefully the state of our mind when it possesses truth through the first criterion of certainty, and actually sees truth. The description of this state is ultimately the criterion by which we are *certain* and, after reflection on our certainty, *know* we are certain, and can repeatedly tell ourselves so. The result is greater interior confirmation and satisfaction which completes our persuasion of truth and makes it unmovable.

1347. People who have not drawn a careful distinction between *direct*[234] and *reflective* knowledge, but confined their

---

[234] Any knowledge whatsoever (even that which *per se* is reflective) can be called *relatively direct* when it is considered relative to another reflection upon it.

attention to the latter, have discussed only a partial criterion of certainty. Instead of the true, *universal criterion*, they offer a *partial criterion of reflective certainty*, that is, they describe a *state* of the mind already in possession of certainty. They do not consider that a mind in possession of certainty must have already made use of some criterion. Hence the description of a state of mind in possession of certainty can constitute a *criterion valid* only for *reflection*. Such a criterion allows us to be aware of our previous possession of certainty and to confirm it.

1348. These thinkers, in order to describe this state of the mind, were content to have recourse to *evidence* as the criterion of certainty. But the various meanings of the word 'evidence' gave rise to many disputes which could be settled only by determining the characteristic of *intellective evidence* and thus avoiding confusion between the evidence of the senses and the evidence of the understanding. Such confusion is still present today in the miserably limited systems of materialists and sensists.

This is not the case among the greatest of the scholastics such as St. Thomas and the author of the *Itinerary*, where we do not find any confusion about the state of the mind in possession of certainty. For them the characteristic of intellective evidence is the *necessity* of any thing, that is, the intuition of the impossibility of its contrary. They located this state in the mind's clear vision that what is thought IMPOSSIBILE EST ALITER SE HABERE [CANNOT POSSIBLY BE OTHERWISE THAN AS THOUGHT].[235]

---

[235] The following is the whole passage in the *Itinerary* where the author describes the state of the mind in possession of intellectual evidence through the first criterion: *Tunc intellectus noster dicitur veraciter comprehendere (propositiones) cum certitudinaliter scit illas veras esse: et hoc scire est scire: QUONIAM NON POTEST FALLI IN ILLA COMPREHENSIONE, scit enim quod veritas illa NON POTEST ALITER SE HABERE. Scit igitur veritatem illam esse incommutabilem* [The human intellect is truly said to comprehend (propositions) when it knows with certainty that they are true. To know this is to know THAT THE INTELLECT CANNOT ERR IN THE COMPREHENSION. IT KNOWS THAT THE TRUTH CANNOT BE OTHERWISE, that the truth is unchangeable] (*Itin. mentis* etc., 3). St. Thomas makes *necessity* the characteristic note of intellective evidence when he writes: *scire est causam rei cognoscere, et quoniam IMPOSSIBILE EST ALITER SE HABERE* [To know is to know the cause of a thing, that is, to know that IT CANNOT POSSIBLY BE OTHERWISE] (*De Verit.*, q. 10, art. 10).

Now, having described in this way the state of the mind in possession of certainty through use of the first criterion, we have arrived at that final link and proposition for which we cannot justifiably seek another reason or criterion.[236]

Article 5

Persuasion produced by the extrinsic criterion of certainty, and especially by authority

1349. Certainty acquired by an *extrinsic* criterion consists in the knowledge of a secure *sign* of a proposition (authority, for example), but not in the vision of the *final reason* or of the *necessity* of the proposition.

The action of the *will* is more present in the *assent* which produces persuasion of this kind of certainty than in the assent which is given to the vision of an intrinsic necessity in a proposition.

1350. Nevertheless when the *sign* and its connection with the proposition that it indicates are both certain, necessity is present inducing the understanding to assent. The will however can easily remove the evidence provided by the sign and the connection, and so produce confusion of ideas. In this state the understanding can be enveloped by the will and easily suspend or even deny its adhesion and assent.

If persuasion is founded on an infallible authority, *certainty* can be stronger, relative to the persuasion and adhesion by the will, than the certainty of the first principles. But not relative to the understanding, which is more necessitated by the vision of the first principles than by authority, even infallible authority.[237]

---

[236] Anyone looking for the criterion of intellective evidence would be looking for the impossible, because the criterion would either have, or not have intellective evidence. If it did not have intellective evidence, it would be valueless. If it had such evidence, we would have returned to the first criterion, *idem per idem*. Thus the Schools very aptly said in this regard: *Ratio non est quaerenda eorum quorum non est ratio* [A reason must not be sought for things which have no reason] (Jn. Duns, *Quodl.*, q. 16).

[237] *Assent* is produced by two causes: 1. the force of the motive determining the understanding; and 2. the force of the will. The will acts

Article 6

Persuasion about the first principles, deduced from an extrinsic criterion

1351. Because the first principles are contained in the supreme criterion itself of certainty, they have an intellective evidence or intrinsic necessity which compels the reason of every individual, in whom it induces an inescapable persuasion. But can these first principles be proved by the extrinsic, second criterion — in other words, in addition to the *intrinsic necessity* which makes the first principles intellectively evident, is there a *secure sign* which contradistinguishes them and enables them to be known separately?

more noticeably than the understanding in producing *Christian faith*. And its action also acquires the nature of virtue precisely because it is an action of the will. On the other hand, the assent of the understanding is determined more directly by the first principles than by infallible authority. To understand how reliable these distinctions are, we must note the difference between *certainty* and *truth*. There are indeed no degrees in truth because truth is simple and immutable. But certainty is truth perceived by us, that is, it is 'a firm, reasonable persuasion that conforms to the truth'. Degrees of greater intension and firmness can therefore be assigned to our perception of, and adhesion to truth, in other words, to our *persuasion*. We cannot therefore assign degrees in *certainty* relative to truth, but relative only to the act of our powers. This teaching is held by the two perceptive Italians whom we have quoted many times. One of them, St. Bonaventure, compares the certainty of faith with the certainty of reason as follows: *DE CERTITUDINE ADHAESIONIS* (which means relative to the will) *verum est fidem esse certiorem scientia philosophica. Si autem loquamur de CERTITUDINE SPECULATIONIS, quae quidem respicit ipsum intellectum* (and therefore not the will) *et nudam veritatem, sic concedi potest quod maior est certitudo in aliqua scientia ita certitudinaliter nosse quod nullo modo discredere, nec in corde suo ullo modo contradicere potest, sicut patet in cognitione dignitatum et primorum principiorum* ['RELATIVE TO THE CERTAINTY OF ADHESION' (which means relative to the will) 'it is true that faith is more certain than philosophical knowledge. But if we are talking about the CERTAINTY OF SPECULATION, which concerns the intellect' (and therefore not the will) 'and pure truth, it can be granted that certainty in some branches of knowledge is greater than in faith, simply because by means of knowledge someone can know something with certainty which he cannot in any way disbelieve, or contradict in his heart, as is clear in the knowledge of values and the first principles'] (*In 3 Sent.*, D. 23, art. 1, q. 4). We see the same teaching in St. Thomas' *De Veritate*, q. 10, art. 2.

At first glance the question appears absurd. We have said that a *secure sign* cannot exist unless the *first principles* have already been used to recognise it as such. However, on closer examination, the question is not entirely meaningless if we keep in mind the distinction between direct and reflective knowledge. Reflection alone is subject to disturbance and confusion, and consequently provides a home for error. Through reflection we can deny what we know directly. Sceptics do this when they deny the first principles with an operation appertaining to reflection, although it is impossible for them to lack direct knowledge of, or even avoid using, the same principles to deny their very existence; in fact they have to use them in whatever they think.

But the first principles, necessarily granted by each individual human being, are therefore granted by all. This universal, human consent forms common sense, which is a *sign* of the principles. For this reason I said that *common sense* is an excellent rule for those whose mind has become so confused, and their reflection so disturbed, that they *believe* they doubt the principles. This *rule* is however a particular case of the extrinsic, secondary criterion of certainty. It is valid for the certainty of the first principles relative to reflective knowledge but not for their certainty in general. The rule can confirm and certify the reflective knowledge of the first principles, and by means of reflection discern these principles from all others.

1352. We need to note carefully that the consent of the human race can be called common sense only when it is produced by the truth. Although a first truth essential to human beings must undoubtedly produce the effect of common consent in mankind, a similar effect can sometimes be produced without intrinsic contradiction by an error, because both the *individual* human being and the *masses* are fallible. Even if this were not granted in fact, it is still not intrinsically contradictory to human nature.[238]

---

[238] The case does not in fact take place because the light of revelation has prevented it, not because humanity has the essential power to avoid it. But the following case is found: 'A human being can find the same error present in all those people with whom he speaks and can speak during his whole life.' Thus there is no way in which he can know of the existence of other human beings who hold a different opinion, or that other times will come when a different opinion is held. For many slaves in the ancient world and for many

How, then, do we say that the general consent of human beings can discern the first principles for someone who has erred? And how therefore can this consent be called a criterion suitable for use as a guide for reflection? I answer as follows.

1353. Even though our reflection is disturbed and confused, the first principles are always seen clearly with direct knowledge; they are never extinguished in us. I maintain that this light, which always lives in us in the first principles, can be made visible and brought before the distracted gaze of sceptics by the authority of others. The criterion of reflection for the first principles is not constituted by human *authority alone* but by the inextinguishable light of the principles aided and strengthened by human authority, which of itself could not certify anything; better, our vision is corrected to see the principles.

By the aid of the light remaining in us, therefore, we use the authority of the human race to confirm the first principles. We are thus able to restrict this authority, which tells us so many things, true and false, and proffers so many principles and consequences. We can, if we wish, discern among all the different cases those in which human authority pays suffrage to the first principles, and determine these alone as principles which, in addition to being approved by the human race, find in our mind a harmonious correspondence, a witness that serves as an interpreter of authority, just as authority in its turn interprets and enlightens that internal witness.

The authority of the human race therefore does not by itself form the criterion of the reflection we are discussing. Human authority and what we may call the remnant of reason left in fallen human nature, to which authority comes as a support, form a single criterion and rule of the truth.

Article 7

Persuasion about error is possible: the nature of this persuasion

1354. Persuasion about error is possible but it refers more to

in the hands of unbelievers in modern times, it was and still is impossible to find in the authority of one's fellows the means of ridding oneself of many errors.

the action of the will than to that of the understanding. This is the opposite of what we have said about the different kinds of persuasions dealt with so far; these spring from the truth of something, truth known with either the intrinsic or extrinsic principle of certainty.

1355. In producing persuasion, truth has within itself a force to determine the understanding. But when we persuade ourselves of what is false, we persuade ourselves of something which has no power to determine our understanding; it has no existence, because what is false does not exist. Truth exists of itself, and in direct knowledge, but what is false is found neither expressly nor virtually in direct knowledge.

What is false therefore is always *fabricated knowledge*, as I have said. And a *fabrication* is something created by the will, which moves the confused intellect. The intellect gives in to the will's movement, decides that what is false is true, and forms an idol from it. Like all fabrications, this false matter, determined by the understanding, is a purely mental entity. The action producing it appertains to the faculty of *word*, that is, of the judgment. Errors can therefore fittingly be called *false words* or interior lies.

1356. Mental entities, created by the mind, are not *per se* false, but become so 1. when we consider them as existing in themselves and not as mental; 2. when we take them as mental but judge they have a foundation in direct knowledge, which they do not have.

1357. Furthermore a *mental entity* always manifests the *limitation* of the human mind. This is the limitation of mental conception which, as a process, corresponds poorly to the nature of the thing conceived. Because of this, antiquity recognised a *subjective* element in cognitions, although it also noted that such an element does not necessarily deceive us or render our cognitions false. Our understanding, which is universal, allows us to know that this element is *subjective* without our being constrained to take it as *objective*, the only way in which it would be false.[239]

---

[239] St. Thomas distinguishes 1. the act or mode of understanding, which appertains to the subject and is conformed to the *subject*; and 2. the *object* of understanding, which is independent of the subject. For example, we

1358. Error therefore can arise in two ways:

Either 1. an entity is formed by the understanding which, contrary to fact, declares that the entity is indeed in the mind, as in the following proposition: 'An effect exists without any cause.' In this kind of error the ideal, mental entity is lacking.

Or 2. a mental entity is formed and declared to be something real and extrinsic, for example, 'Maurice is alive', when in reality he is dead. In this kind of error the extrinsic entity or reality is lacking.

Error is therefore an effort of the understanding to see an entity where no entity exists, or to see an entity different from that which exists. In such an action the term of understanding is a void, nothingness.[240]

understand material things with a simple, immaterial act, but we do not attribute simplicity and immateriality to the thing understood. On the other hand, we understand God with multiple acts, but do not attribute multiplicity to God. Our understanding, by means of its *universality*, is able to distinguish what we, the subject, add to our way of understanding, and what belongs to the thing. The known *thing* therefore is not altered by the knowing subject; it is not rendered subjective. Only the *mode* or *act* of understanding remains subjective. This brilliant distinction is sufficient to destroy critical scepticism. We see that critical philosophy is founded solely on a confusion of ideas. It has intermingled the *mode* or act of understanding with the object understood — two things which our predecessors had so carefully distinguished.

[240] I have distinguished three kinds of persuasion:

　　1. Persuasion dependent upon the first *criterion*, which shows a truth intrinsic to the proposition to which we assent. The understanding plays a large role in this kind of persuasion.

　　2. Persuasion coming from the second criterion, which shows that the proposition assented to is true, but that we know the truth through a *secure sign*, for example, infallible authority, and not as intrinsic to the proposition. The understanding is less involved here than in the first case; the will is more involved.

　　3. Persuasion coming from *error*. Here the principal action is that of the will; the understanding with a function of its own obeys the will, not vice versa.

St. Augustine deals with these three kinds of persuasion in his little work, *De utilitate credendi*. He calls them *understanding*, *believing*, and *guessing*.

Article 8

Continuation

1359. This explains why persuasion about error is fabricated. Error is entirely the action of the human being, a blow against nature, an attempt of the will to seduce the understanding which *per se* is attracted and determined only by the light of truth.

Hence, because direct knowledge is always true and indestructible, persuasion about error lies solely in reflection, which is an action added as it were to human nature. Truth, the foundation of our mind, precedes reflection and is always present, able to be seen. Those who err are never, perhaps, totally unmindful of it.

1360. Error is always superficial and never penetrates deep into human nature. Persuasion about error, no matter how well entrenched, is often full of uncertainties and doubts which, although apparently solved, continue to reappear. A mysterious *unrest* never really abandons those in the grip of error, although it has no strength in itself to turn them back to the peace of truth.

Article 9

Error is always a kind of ignorance

1361. An erroneous understanding terminates not in truth but in a fabricated object void of all entity (cf. 1354 ss.). As I said, the term of an erroneous understanding is *per se* nothingness. An erroneous understanding is without knowledge and does not acquire knowledge. Contrary to the understanding's *belief*, its term has no entity — the understanding *says* it sees, but in fact sees nothing and therefore lies to itself. Such is the empty knowledge of those in error.

1362. Error is always ignorance. However, while one kind of ignorance is a simple negation of knowledge, error adds to this negation the force of understanding moved by the will. The aim is to fabricate an empty being in place of absent knowledge, and thus allow ourselves to imagine that we know. But not knowing, and telling ourselves we do know, is a hidden lie of pride. Every formal error therefore is a secret act of pride; every error is essentially pride.[241]

Antiquity, in order to differentiate this *negation* of knowledge from simple ignorance, called it appropriately 'privation'.

[241] St. Augustine, who discerned the secrets of the human heart so well, made the same observation: '*To guess*' (which for Augustine means the same as to err) 'is reprehensible for two reasons: first, the person persuaded that he knows' (that is, someone in error) 'is unable to learn even that which he could otherwise learn, and second, temerity is in itself a sign that the desires in the spirit are not as they should be. — Therefore the *credulity* of those who guess that they know what they do not know is defective' (*De util. cred.*, 11). St. Thomas himself calls this presumption *mater erroris* [the mother of error] (*C.G.*, I, 5). Consequently, the accusation of *credulity* can be levelled only at those who *err*. Those who presume they believe nothing are in no way free from the defect of credulity: they are *credulous* of error, and in this alone, according to the great men we have quoted, defective *credulity* properly speaking consists.

PART FIVE

CONCLUSION

CHAPTER 1

The teachings we have developed are illustrated by St. Augustine's analysis of the materialists' error

1363. St. Augustine's analysis of the materialists' error shows that error is simply a *privation* of knowledge. Thus, when the materialist tells himself that his soul is body, he does not *know* this, he only *conjectures* it.[242]

We must distinguish the action of the mind when it really knows that a thing is what it is from its action when it *conjectures* that the thing is what it is. The second action of conjecturing, believing or guessing that a thing is what it is, without *knowing*, is subject to error. When a thing is not what we fancy it is, we have a false opinion; in other words we err.

1364. It is extremely important that we investigate 'how a mind which has no knowledge of a proposition can nevertheless assent to the proposition by telling itself that it knows what it does not know'. Furthermore, not only does the erroneous mind say it knows what it does not know, it affirms and conjectures the opposite of what it knows. Materialists are a case in point. St. Augustine claims that the spiritual nature of the soul is naturally known to every human being through the evidence of consciousness.[243] We must ask therefore: 'How does a human

---

[242] *Cum ergo verbi gratia mens aerem se putat, aerem intelligere putat, se tamen intelligere scit; aerem autem se esse non SCIT sed PUTAT* [When, for example, the mind thinks itself to be air, it thinks that air understands; it knows however that it understands. It does not KNOW but THINKS that it is air] (*De Trinit.*, 10).

[243] In Book 10 of *De Trinitate* St. Augustine shows at length that every human being, through the evidence of his own consciousness, knows that he

being *say* that he has a corporeal soul when he *knows* through his own consciousness that his soul is spiritual?'

1365. The materialist is subject to contradiction: 1. on the one hand he has an intimate *knowledge* of his own soul as living, feeling and understanding; 2. on the other, he *guesses* that his soul is body. This contradiction can be explained only by distinguishing the two functions of the soul: 1. apprehension of truth, the source of *direct* knowledge, and 2. reflection, the source of *reflective* knowledge. We know the *intellective*, spiritual nature of our soul by means of *direct knowledge* provided by our intimate feeling and our consciousness. But we disregard this intimate knowledge, and with another act of our understanding investigate what the soul is (as if we did not know), and declare it *material*, thereby rejecting the true knowledge we have.

1366. St. Augustine then presents the following difficulty: Why are we commanded to know ourselves when the soul naturally knows itself? He answers: 'The precept requires the soul to think about itself *ut se ipsam cogitet* [in order to know itself]. *Not knowing oneself* is different from *not thinking* about oneself'; we can *know ourselves* without thinking about ourselves, that is, without actually reflecting on what we know.[244]

1367. But how can *reflection* be so disturbed as to make us guess that the soul is corporeal? According to St. Augustine, we must note that

> those who are of the opinion that the soul is corporeal do not err simply because they fail to include the mind in their concept of the soul, but rather because they (arbitrarily) add to the concept the things without which they are incapable of conceiving any nature; they consider that

lives, feels and *understands*, and knowing this, knows his own soul, the subject, which lives, feels and understands. Error arises when something heterogeneous is added to this knowledge. The heterogeneous element is not supplied by the internal evidence of consciousness but by the external senses, which perceive only bodies, not the soul. Thus St. Augustine accepts *internal observation* as a legitimate source of knowledge of the soul.

[244] *Utquid ergo ei praeceptum est ut se ipsa cognoscat? Credo ut se cogitet: cum aliud sit non se NOSSE, aliud non se COGITARE* [I believe we are commanded to know ourselves in order that we may think about ourselves. KNOWING ourselves is different from THINKING about ourselves (*De Trinit.*, 10, 5).

thinking without corporeal images means they are thinking of nothing.[245]

1368. How is it that they can think only of bodies, and that
whenever they think of something, only corporeal images present themselves? Because when we direct our understanding to
reflect on anything, we need to know how to *direct* it carefully
to the object of its search. If we do not know how to direct our
understanding and reflection to what they seek, our reflection
will latch on to something different, take it for the thing itself
and so exchange one thing for another. Now, in doing this, the
understanding is principally guided by the *will* and its *habits*.
What therefore makes the understanding, or better, the materialists' reflection, seek the spirit but find only bodies, that is, find
only a corporeal soul while studiously seeking to perceive a
spiritual soul? St. Augustine answers that this occurs because
materialists have practised directing their reflection only towards bodies; their will is occupied and attracted solely by bodies. Hence they have never learnt the way to reach the spirit.
The spirit is not discovered in the same way as bodies which are
outside of us and discovered with external observation. The
spirit is discovered in the opposite way, that is, by turning
within and remaining inside ourselves:

> This explains why the mind does not seek itself as if it were
> absent from itself. Nothing is closer to thought than the
> mind; nothing is more present to the mind than the mind
> itself, and nothing could be more in the mind than the mind
> itself. But the mind, once accustomed to sensible
> (corporeal) things, on which it thinks lovingly, is unable to
> keep itself to itself without the images of these things.
> Hence, the shame of its error; the mind is no longer able to
> separate itself from the images of sensed things and see it-
> self alone. In some extraordinary way these things attach
> themselves to it with the adhesion proper to love. This is
> the mind's *stain*. Although it strives to think solely of it-
> self, it conjectures that it is part of that without which it
> cannot think of itself.[246]

[245] *De Trinit.*, 10, 7.

[246] *De Trinit.*, 10, 7, 8. — We are born with this kind of *stain*, which
increases with wrong use. It is a fact that the rational part of human beings is

1369. We see therefore that the *confusion* of ideas which error presupposes comes from the evil disposition of the will. The will is unable to move the understanding to make the necessary distinctions, and reaches its conclusions while ideas are still confused. The holy Doctor continues, examining acutely all the strands of the materialists' error:

> When our mind is commanded to know itself, it does not pursue its investigation as if it were separated from itself, but separates what it has added to itself. The mind is more interior than sensible things, which are clearly outside, and even more interior than their images, which nevertheless are in a part of the soul and also present in animals, even though animals are without intelligence, which belongs to the mind alone. Although the mind is internal, it comes out of itself in some way when it extends its affection of love to these traces of the many things it has understood... The mind can therefore know itself, and need not seek itself as if it were absent. Let the mind fix the attention of the will, by which it ranges over other things, upon itself, and think itself.[247] The mind will see that there never was a time when it did not know itself;[248] but it loved something else which it CONFUSED with itself and in a certain way added to itself. Thus, it imagined that the many things it gathered together were one, although they were different.[249]

1370. St. Augustine suggests two ways for bringing the materialists' vague and errant reflection back to the right road where it may find and reconsider itself, that is, its spirit. First, they must be taught to note these things about which all humans agree and disagree, and thus be led to see that certainty is proper to the former, and uncertainty proper to the latter.[250]

uncertain in its movement, while the senses are extremely active from infancy and, I would say, engage the whole person before reason has been able to control them.

[247] The mind *INTENTIONEM VOLUNTATIS, qua per alia vagabatur, statuat in semeipsam et se cogitet* [determines within itself the THE WILL'S ATTENTION by which it ranges through other things, and thinks of itself].

[248] With *direct* knowledge void of reflection.

[249] *De Trinit.*, 10, 8.

[250] *Secernat (mens) quod se PUTAT, cernat quod SCIT; hoc ei remaneat unde ne illi quidem dubitaverunt qui aliud atque aliud corpus esse mentem*

Second, they must be taught to note those things which cannot possibly be doubted, and those which can be doubted; they must be shown that error has to be sought in doubtful things gratuitously added to the truth; error consists in this addition.[251] We see therefore how St. Augustine acknowledges *common sense* and the *necessity* of intellective perception as two means of correcting wayward, errant *reflection*.

putaverunt. Neque enim omnis mens aerem se esse existimat, sed aliae ignem, aliae cerebrum, aliaeque aliud corpus et aliud aliae sicut supra commemoravi; OMNES tamen se intelligere noverunt et esse et vivere, sed intelligere ad quod intelligunt referunt, esse autem et vivere ad se ipsas, etc [Let (the mind) separate what it THINKS itself to be from what it KNOWS itself to be. It will be left with what cannot be doubted, even by those who have thought the mind to be some kind of body. Not every mind thinks itself to be air; some minds consider themselves fire, others the brain, others another body, and others something else, as I noted above. But THEY ALL know that they understand, and that they exist and live. They refer their understanding to that which they understand, but their being and living to themselves, etc.]. (*De Trin.*, 10, 10).

[251] *Sed quoniam de natura mentis agitur, removeamus a consideratione nostra omnes notitias quae capiuntur extrinsecus per sensus corporis, et ea quae posuimus omnes mentes de se ipsis nosse certasque esse diligentius attendamus. Utrum enim aeris sit vis vivendi, reminiscendi, intelligendi, volendi, cogitandi, sciendi, iudicandi; an ignis, an cerebri, an sanguinis, an atomorum, an praeter usitata quattuor elementa quinti nescio cuius corporis, an ipsius carnis nostrae compago vel temperamentum haec efficere valeat dubitaverunt homines, et alius hoc, alius illud affirmare conatus est. Vivere se tamen et meminisse et intelligere et velle et cogitare et scire et iudicare quis dubitet?... Non est igitur aliquid eorum. Totumque illud quod se iubetur ut noverit, ad hoc pertinet ut certa sit non se esse aliquid eorum de quibus incerta est, idque solum esse se certa sit quod solum esse se certa est* [Because we are dealing with the nature of the mind, we must omit from our consideration every notion received externally through our bodily senses, and diligently consider the things which, as we have seen, every mind knows about itself as certain. People have doubted whether air is the force of life or the power of remembering, understanding, willing, thinking, knowing, judging; or whether fire, brain, blood, atoms, or a fifth element of some kind of body (besides the usual four) has this power, or whether the composition and temperament of our flesh is able to effect all these things — different people affirm different things. But who doubts that he lives, remembers, understands, wills, thinks and knows? ... The mind therefore is none of these material things. The sum total of what the mind is commanded to know is that it is certain that it is none of those things of which it is uncertain, and that it is only that which it is certain that it is] (*De Trin.*, 10, 10).

1371. From all this we can also infer that persuasion in the case of error is never as firm as persuasion in truth, and never goes long unaccompanied by hesitation and doubt. Hence a person who has often tried to confirm his persuasion in error, and by experience sees that he wastes his time in fruitless effort, finally opts to believe that firm persuasion is impossible, and comes to rest in abject scepticism.

I cannot find a better example to demonstrate the inconstancy of persuasion of error than St. Augustine's observation on the divergence or mutability of opinions about those matters in which precisely materialists err:

> The command that the soul should know itself means simply that it must be certain that it is only those things of which it is certain, and none of those things about which it is uncertain. It thinks uncertainly that it is fire or air or any other body whatsoever. And it cannot think what it is in the same way that it thinks what it is not.[252] By means of the images of its phantasy, the soul thinks all these things: fire, air, this or that body, a part or composition and temperament, and says it is only one or other, but not all of them. But if it were one of them, it would certainly think this thing in a way different from all the others, that is, not through some imaginary fabrication (as we imagine absent things which are touched with our bodily sense or anything similar) but with an interior, true, unsimulated presence — nothing could be more present to itself than itself — like thinking it lives, remembers, understands and wills. It knows all these things within itself without imagining them outside itself and touched by the sense as all corporeal things are touched. If the soul takes nothing at all from these thoughts in order to add it deceptively to itself and believe it is itself, then all that is left to the soul in these thoughts (stripped of their external objects) is the soul itself.[253]

---

[252] The distinction between what is subjective and what is objective and extrasubjective is clearly visible in this discourse. As we have seen, confusing these elements is the origin of all materialism, (cf. vol. 2, 988 ss.).

[253] *De Trin.*, 10, 10.

CHAPTER 2

Epilogue on the criterion of truth

1372. We can summarise what has been discussed in this Section as follows. Knowledge is of two kinds, *direct* and *reflective*. The former, relative to the latter, is the truth[254] possessed by all human beings. Reflective knowledge simply develops, unites and analyses *direct* knowledge. It is *true* when it conforms to and is one with the latter, but false if it prefers to fabricate and create rather than be founded on and recognise what is in direct knowledge. *Error* therefore is a kind of creation carried out by human beings with the faculty of reflection.

First reflections constitute *popular knowledge*; second reflections, *philosophical knowledge*. Because knowledge is subject to error in proportion to the part played in it by *reflection*, philosophical knowledge is more subject to error than popular knowledge.

1373. Reflection adds *light* and perfection to human knowledge. Philosophical knowledge therefore has on the one hand the disadvantage of being very subject to error, and on the other the advantage of being endowed with much greater light and perfection than popular knowledge.

Reflection is the source of the most enlightened knowledge, and of what is generally understood as knowledge. Although it is moved by both instinct and will, we could simply say that it is moved by will because the will always co-operates, at least by means of habits or negatively. Hence a wayward or an upright will leads reflection into error or truth.

When the will is accustomed to directing reflection falsely, confusion arises so that reflection sees nothing more, not even what is evident. The human eye is darkened and, in this state, reflection denies even the first principles.

1374. But if *direct knowledge* is the rule or criterion to which

---

[254] The idea of being is simply called logical *truth*. First *ideas* or essences are *truths* or types with which we compare and identify the whole class of things included in the truths, and distinguished and known explicitly by analysis.

reflection must be referred, only intellective *evidence* renders knowledge of this kind capable of having such authority and force over reflective knowledge that we feel obliged to direct our reflections by its rule.

This evidence, which is not a subjective fact, is endowed with its own *obligating* force, precisely because it is intellective and not sensible. It has an intrinsic *logical necessity* through which we irrefutably understand and know that the contrary cannot possibly be thought.

The source of this necessity is the *idea of being*, the source of all intellective knowledge. This idea contains within itself all possibilities, which taken together form what we call necessity because all that is must be in them. We have to conclude therefore that the true and final principle of *certainty* is, and can only be, the *idea of being* present to our spirit and manifesting itself not only with the clarity of light but also with such intrinsic necessity that nothing else can be thought outside of it. Hence if human beings wish to find the truth, they must reason according to this principle

1375. When we go on to reflect, however, we are dealing with a question of mere contingent fact, and only careful historical observation of humankind enables us to see whether we reason naturally according to this supreme criterion. This explains why those who think philosophy is something very abstract and far removed from facts, readily say that this is not a question for philosophy. But whatever the case, I must say a few, even non-philosophical,words about the matter. They will be sufficient provided they are true. In my opinion the history of the human race presents a sad spectacle. Corruption of heart and confusion of mind is the heritage of all humanity. This is human history — St. Paul's 'corrupt lump' is the theory behind this history.[255]

Cicero writes:

> Scarcely have we been born and welcomed than we im-
> merse ourselves in every kind of wickedness and in the
> deepest perversity of opinions, as if we had sucked error
> with the milk of our nurse's breast. When we are returned
> to our parents and consigned to teachers, we imbibe such
> wayward errors that truth gives place to vanity, and nature

[255] Gal 5: 9 [Douai].

to ancient prejudice. Add to this the poets who offer an impressive appearance of learning and wisdom; we listen to these poets, read and learn them, fixing them deeply in our minds... Next come the people, apparently the best teacher (*quasi maximus quidem magister populus*), and the whole multitude consenting to vice of every kind. We burden ourselves entirely with waywardness, denying nature itself.[256]

1376. In the common sense of the *human race* therefore the individual finds no secure way of correcting his wayward, disturbed reflection. The opposite however must be said about *Christian society*. Here, in the authority of others (if we wish to choose them),[257] each one of us finds a secure way of confirming and reassuring his uncertain, timorous reflection. Those who do not use this way therefore are inexcusable. The truth is firmly founded not in the *society of the human race* but in *Christian society*. Only in Christian society, not elsewhere, do we find 'the pillar and ground of the truth' (to use a scriptural phrase).[258] Only divine help could render the stages of human reflection certain and safe, just as only divine power can strengthen the feet of a paralytic, or restore light to eyes that have lost it.[259]

1377. But it is not enough simply to assure the existence of truth among human beings in order to respond to their needs. Our *will* must also be improved; it is only *with our will* that we

---

[256] *Tusc.*, 3, 1. — Lamennais is clearly refuted here and in what follows.

[257] This choice can be made only with the light of reason, which remains in every corrupted person. Of itself, this light would be incapable of leading us to the truth, not because it is defective but because our eye, looking elsewhere, is defective. In this situation we have to associate our light with the light of others; we have to use what little power remains to us to discover faithful counsellors. In this way, neither an individual's own light, nor the light of others, comes to the aid of wayward individual. Instead, he receives assistance from a confederation of these two lights. Thus each person seeks counsel only after knowing the counsellors whom he then chooses not because they are *human beings*, but because of the *light* which he knows is in them.

[258] 1 Tim 3: 15 [Douai].

[259] It is the whole human race, not an individual, that St. Gregory compares to the man born blind and healed by Jesus Christ: *Caecum quippe est genus humanum* [The blind man is the human race] (cf. *Hom. 2 in Ev.*).

find the truth which, although we may not look at it, stands continually before our gaze. This is the way in which Christianity led human beings to the truth, corrected their behaviour and made them *good*. Human beings were *enlightened*, and culture and civilization sprang from the root of virtue. We fall short therefore if, in order to help our fellows, we simply indicate what the criterion of certainty is; we must also preach the *love of truth* and place it in their hearts.

Hence St. Augustine said: 'He alone is our true teacher who can impress the idea in us, fill us with light and impart VIRTUE to the heart of the listener.'

SECTION SEVEN

THE FORCES PRESENT IN *A PRIORI* REASONING

CHAPTER 1

What we mean by *a priori* reasoning

1378. I have distinguished the *form* of knowledge from *knowledge* in the strict sense,[260] and shown that the former is innate, and the latter acquired.

Knowledge is initially *direct*, and then *reflective*. Reflective knowledge of first reflection (*popular* knowledge) adds the notion of new entia to direct knowledge,[261] while knowledge from further reflection (*philosophical* knowledge) adds nothing — we simply acquire greater light about the objects we know, and a strong persuasion of truth deep within our spirit. This

---

[260] Philosophical language still lacks perfect determination. We sometimes have to use a single word with different meanings; perhaps the limited nature of language and the affinity of ideas do not permit us to do otherwise. Hence, when we use a word to which usage has given different meanings, we must note the meaning given in each place. I myself have sometimes included even the *form* of thought in the word 'knowledge', but I add the phrase 'in the strict sense' to note that the word is being used to mean *knowledge* obtained by a judgment. In general, people do not speak of the *form* of reason to distinguish it from everything else; when they do speak of it, they tend to call it 'light of reason'. If the etymology of the word 'intellect' shows they recognise in the power of understanding something essentially understood (*intellectum*), they never, as far as I know, use the word 'knowledge' to name what is first understood by the spirit. This explains the certain, universal persuasion found in antiquity (except for the few philosophers who stood out from the rest) that all *cognitions* are acquired through the senses.

[261] These entia are the cause of the universe, and generally speaking are invisible powers. But, as I have shown, we have only negative knowledge of them.

gives a kind of satisfaction which is as it were a foretaste of the happiness produced by truth itself when it is fully revealed to us.

Knowledge, whether direct or reflective of first reflection, which terminates in new objects, can be called 'fundamental'.[262] Hence knowledge of *further reflection* contains nothing which is not in *fundamental* knowledge. The analysis of *fundamental* knowledge will therefore be sufficient for us to distinguish *a priori* from *a posteriori* knowledge.

1379. *Fundamental knowledge*, like all other knowledge, is composed of two elements: 1. the idea of being, and 2. the mode of being. The idea of being contains possibility, which is the source of all that is necessary and universal in human knowledge. But *a priori* knowledge is qualified by *necessity* and *universality* (cf. vol. 1, 304–309). Therefore anything contained *a priori* in human knowledge is included in the idea of being in all its universality. All other knowledge shares *a priori* knowledge only in so far as the idea of being is present in it (cf. vol. 2, 408 ss.).

Any knowledge which is a mixture of the idea of being in all its universality and of the determinations or modes of being is not entirely *a priori*; it is mixed, and exists only when the two elements composing it are present. It needs sensible perceptions, and a kind of first attention devoted to them. This kind of knowledge can be said to acquire its existence *a posteriori*. We must therefore return to the idea of being where alone *pure*, *a priori* knowledge is found.

1380. Etymologically, the expressions '*a priori*' and '*a posteriori*' were coined to indicate reasoning rather than knowledge as such. They mean 'an argument deduced from what is anterior', and 'an argument deduced from what is posterior'. What is anterior was generally understood as cause; what is posterior, as effect. Thus, reasonings which moved from cause to effect were called '*a priori*', and those from effect to cause, '*a posteriori*'. But I take '*a priori* knowledge' in a stricter sense, where it means knowledge contained not in the efficient or any other cause of

---

[262] *Fundamental knowledge* is composed of *perceptions* which contain some kind of *positive* knowledge, and of reasonings which give some kind of *negative knowledge*.

the thing under discussion, but in the *formal cause of know-ledge* and of reason (or deduced from this formal cause alone). A formal cause is the *first fact*, anterior to all others in the order of acts of knowledge. This explains why *a priori* knowledge, taken in this sense, is qualified by necessity and universality.[263]

But is *a priori* reasoning possible in this sense? And if it is possible, what is its extent and bounds? These are the questions I now propose to discuss, to which the teaching I have already presented will serve as an introduction.

---

[263] Kant took *a priori knowledge* in a similar sense, as I indicated in vol. 1 (cf. footnote 229). But there is a difference between Kant and myself in the definition of *a priori* knowledge, and only clarity in discussion will indicate this difference. According to Kant, *a priori* knowledge has the two characteristics of *necessity* and *universality* as its distinguishing marks. My *a priori* knowledge also has these two characteristics, which however are the result of a previous characteristic that forms the essence of this knowledge. In fact, Kant finds *a priori* knowledge in the forms added by the spirit's own action to the perceptions of sensible things. Thus his *a priori* knowledge is properly speaking acquired, although it originates in the spirit whose forms are simply powers or special activities which of themselves add nothing to what is actually understood by the spirit. I affirm however that the spirit essentially understands something (being in all its universality). My *a priori* knowledge therefore is essential to the spirit because it is being in all its universality and everything being contains, although not in a state of analysis or of advertence. Hence Kant begins the development of our spirit with an accidental *act* of the spirit — I begin its development with an essentially *understood object* preceding all its *accidental acts*.

CHAPTER 2

The starting point of human knowledge according to some thinkers of the German school

Article 1

The purpose of this Chapter

1381. *A priori* reasoning is reasoning carried out on the idea of being in all its universality without the introduction of any other element (cf. vol. 1, 378 ss.). It is called 'a priori' because this idea is the first idea, independent of all others.

However, before we begin the difficult examination of the question, 'What reasoning can we carry out on this pure, universal idea, and where will such reasoning take us?', it will be helpful to confirm and defend the right of this idea to be the starting point of all human knowledge. I will therefore defend its *primacy* against the ingenuity of contemporary systems, all of which have their origin in Germany, a truly intellectual nation.

I have shown that Kant's many forms are infected with the original sin of subjectivism. Their only use is that they can all be reduced to the single objective form I have established. They are simply modes of application of this unique, true form which, when determined in a general way, results in Kant's particular forms. These, contrary to their appearance, are not *pure*, because they each contain something restrictive and partial (cf. vol. 1, 368–384).

Article 2

The principal difference between our unique form and the forms assigned by some modern thinkers to the intelligent spirit

1382. After Kant, some thinkers reduced the number of first forms of intelligence. But I must oppose these also and show that there cannot be more than one form.

First, however, it will be helpful if I indicate again the common, characteristic difference which separates the forms suggested by some modern thinkers from the unique form I have suggested. All the great minds, especially in Germany, who discussed the question, 'What is the principle of knowledge?', placed this principle not in the *object* of the spirit but in its *act*, and limited themselves to the analysis of the latter rather than the former. But their ignorance of the nature of human potencies, especially the intellective potency, contributed to their failure. I have attempted to establish that the nature of the *potencies* consists 'in a stable union with a term or object, called "form", which, as object and essential for the potency, draws the subject into the act terminating in the object'. This is the case of the intellect (cf. vol. 2, 1005 ss.). I found the nature of the intellective potency to consist in an essential, *first act* which terminates in an object also essential to the act and its form (truth). In other words, the act terminates in something to which it is itself receptive, and is determined and necessitated to this reception. The act does not move spontaneously, nor act upon an object passive in its regard.

I began from the analysis of the essential *object* of the intellect. Such a procedure was recognised as necessary by antiquity, but modern thinkers, as far as I can verify, have not risen to the same heights; they start solely from the *act* of the spirit, unaware that the object must precede this act, which is known only through the object, not vice versa, the object through the act.

Article 3.

The starting point of Kant's philosophy

1383. Let us now examine these systems. We will begin with Kant, in order not to interrupt the sequence of ideas.

Kant imagined that everything the spirit conceives has to be clothed with forms by the spirit itself. In this his research had indeed taken him a step further than his modern predecessors.

Descartes, for example, had begun from the minor of a syllogism, but had unknowingly presupposed the major (cf. vol. 2, 979 ss.).

Locke presupposed more than Descartes without giving any explanation. Because he did not divide mixed knowledge into its form and matter, his starting point was its matter — he completely presupposed its form and did not mention it.[264]

Condillac makes his statue reason from the very first sensations it receives. He fails to notice that principles are necessary for reasoning. His starting point therefore is also the *material*, not the *formal* element of knowledge. Consequently he does not even suspect the need for an explanation.

Kant, stimulated by the work of some English thinkers after Locke, and more so by the Scots, noted clearly the highest element of knowledge, its form, and believed it should be explained. His starting point therefore is higher than that of all the other modern philosophers.

1384. But, as I said, in order to explain the form of knowledge, he had recourse to the *act* and *nature of the intelligent spirit*. He should have gone further and reached the *essential object of the spirit*. This defect prevented him from discovering the *supreme form* of reason; he stopped at inferior, mixed, restrictive and subjective forms which depend on the first. He said that the spirit, in its act of understanding, operates according to its own laws, and applies these laws to whatever it conceives. This argument is based on *analogies*[265] taken from sensations. In short, the principle on which he based his system was: 'What is offered to the senses must be determined by our

---

[264] In the chronological order of our acts of knowledge, we observe, or better, *advert* first to the matter and then the form. The chronological order of our *advertence* is the opposite of that of our *direct knowledge*. Locke's strongest argument against innate ideas is founded in a lack of observation: 'But, since no proposition can be innate unless the ideas about which it is be innate, this will be to suppose all our ideas of colours, sounds, tastes, figure, &c., innate, than which there cannot be anything more opposite to reason and experience.' (Bk. 1). The absurdity that Locke finds in the opinion that some statements are innate is false. Not all statements are about colours, sounds and other sensible things; some are entirely suprasensible. Furthermore (and this is our case), in the ideas of sensible things intellective perception is as much present as sensible things. Locke failed to observe the presence of intellective perception, which is the *form* of ideas. His starting point therefore was the matter of knowledge — he *did not note* the form, and gratuitously presupposed it.

[265] *Analogy* is indeed a fertile mother of errors!

sensitivity according to certain dispositions of the spirit. The same must be true of the object offered to the intelligence: it must be determined according to concepts belonging to the spirit itself.'[266]

According to Kant, therefore, things in themselves, which he calls 'noumena', remain completely unknown to us. The experience of the senses offers us only 'phenomena', that is, appearances, and the intelligence offers us only an *ideal order*, which does not present any *real* being as such.

In many places he speaks about our absolute ignorance of things in themselves and concludes his *Metaphysical Elements of Physics* with these words:

> Hence metaphysical teaching about bodies terminates in thinking a void, that is, the incomprehensible. In this sense its destiny is the same as that of all the other efforts made by reason. In its return to principles it investigates the first causes of things, but it can understand only what is determined under certain conditions,[267] because nature presents it this way. On the one hand therefore it cannot be content with that which depends on conditions,[268] and on the other it cannot understand that which lacks all conditions. The only action left to it, when stimulated by the longing to know, is to withdraw from objects and return to itself where, instead of the final limits of things, it can examine and determine the final imprisonment of its faculty when left to itself.

1385. Although Kant had clearly admitted an absolute ignorance of the *noumena*, it seems that many people did not understand him sufficiently. Others, after him, were certainly not happy in admitting an unknown area, and went on to deny that anything existed outside the confines of human

---

[266] Speaking about movement, he says: 'The representation' (that is, the intellective thought) 'of movement cannot become experience' (that is, perceived by the senses) 'unless the *object* is determined according to the representation in the subject' (*Elementa Metaphysica Physicae*, c. 4).

[267] On the contrary, I have shown that the great, essential property of the intellect consists in its conceiving what is perfectly undetermined.

[268] This surely is a clear sign that it has the notion of what is *unconditioned*.

experience. In Germany, where mysterious, obscure expressions tend to replace solid knowledge, much was said about the *great* nothingness beyond the knowable, as if this were a sublime discovery. Others apparently attempted to do the opposite: dissatisfied that humanity should be subject to limits, and declaring, or at least doubting, that there could be a completely unknown region beyond what is knowable, they laboured to penetrate this region and made everything issue from the human spirit. Kant himself drew much from the human spirit, but finally declared that nevertheless beyond all we could possibly imagine there was *perhaps* something non-deducible from our spirit (the *noumena*).

How strange that he was able to know this secret[269] and reveal it to his fellow human beings, while his own spirit never attained these regions; nor, if his theory is true, has any human being ever attained them — we could not even suspect their existence! But, as I have said, Kant does not speak like an ordinary human, but like an immortal who, far removed from the restrictions of human nature, assesses this prison, and smiles or weeps over the poverty and captivity of unhappy nature.

1386. Allow me now to explain further my reason for saying that Kant began from an intermediate point without attaining the true principle of philosophy. I showed that this was caused by his defective analysis of human knowledge, with its consequent defective ignorance of the different kinds of knowledge. But if we consider this cause carefully, we see in it the origin of the other defect in his theory, namely, his exclusion of the *noumena* from all human knowledge whatsoever, and his declaration that such knowledge is entirely unknown to us.

The French sophists, the Encyclopedists, had destroyed the levels of human knowledge, and put on a show of believing that

[269] How in fact could Kant have named the *noumena* if he had had no concept of them? How could he know that the *phenomena* did not embrace everything, if previously he had no idea of all that is, an idea essentially universal which includes within itself all possibilities? His distinction therefore between *phenomena* and *noumena* shows that our understanding is not limited solely to the phenomena, or to his forms, but embraces everything possible. A person truly limited to the *phenomena* would not know that there *could* be *noumena* beyond the phenomena; he would in no way conceive either their existence or even their possibility.

[1386]

there was no middle term between *understanding* and *not knowing*. Relative to this vain presumption, I noted that there is undoubtedly a kind of *middle knowledge* having many levels between *comprehension* (which means *knowing perfectly*) and total *not knowing*; we sometimes know with a degree of knowledge without knowing perfectly. Voltaire, and many other pedants of that period, in their hatred of Christianity abused their ignorance, whether real or affected; they wanted us to believe that because God was incomprehensible, he was so unknown that we could neither speak nor think of him. Kant, perhaps unconsciously, came under the influence of these writers, and through the same lack of observation denied to human beings the possibility of all knowledge of the *noumena*, that is, of substances.

1387. This error can be refuted by the degrees observable in human knowledge.

Substance 'is that act by which the abstract specific essence exists in an ens' (cf. vol. 2, 657).

In order to have knowledge of a substance therefore we must think 1. being and 2. the abstract specific essence of something.

But the *essence* of anything is known in different ways and to different degrees, as I have shown elsewhere (cf. vol. 2, 646–656). These ways and degrees, according to which we know the essence of anything, correspond to the ways and degrees of our knowledge.

I call 'known essence' that which we know about anything; it is only about this essence that we can speak.[270] Sometimes, all that we know about anything is simply a *relationship* with other things better known to us. This relationship certainly distinguishes the thing from all others, but only gives negative knowledge, of which I have spoken at length.

Kant therefore 1. did not understand the nature of being in all its universality, which makes us know things *objectively*, that is, in themselves, in their essences; 2. did not observe that in addition to what sensations proffer us, there are other modes with which we are able to know the *determinations* of entia and have a secure sign of their subsistence. I am speaking of the

[270] Hence, when I wished to indicate the part of bodies unknown to us, I called such essence 'corporeal principle', not 'body'.

application of reasoning to sensible things, that is, the application of the principle of cause, which is simply the very idea of being in all its universality. But because Kant saw that this principle gave us no representations or positive qualities of things, he believed the principle to be valueless outside the sphere of the phenomena. He did not notice that this principle is as *objective* as *being*, of which it is an application. When therefore we conclude by means of this principle that an unperceived ens *necessarily* subsists, our conclusion is efficacious, and the ens sufficiently determined by the negative idea or relationship to prevent its confusion with any other.

Article 4

The starting point of Fichte's philosophy

1388. Fichte, a follower of Kant, tried to draw everything from the subject ego, and would accept as subsistent only what he had drawn from it. This explains why Kant himself refused to acknowledge such teaching as his own, and declared that his learned follower had badly misunderstood him.

Kant had divided the spirit's activity into different forms or partial activities. He had also admitted some passivity in thought (I am not sure whether he himself was aware of this), from which he had excluded the *noumena*, that is, things as they are in themselves. Fichte pin-pointed the action of thought, considered it in its unity, and claimed that all thought was pure activity. In such a system the activity of the ego was the starting point, the means and the purpose of the philosophy called 'transcendental idealism'.

1389. According to Fichte, the ego posits itself, which is equivalent to saying that it creates itself. But this first act, carried out by the ego in positing itself, although unique, is composite. The ego does not posit itself without positing the non-ego in opposition to itself. This identical act which renders the ego conscious of itself, also makes it conscious of the external world, and of everything outside itself, grouped under the title non-ego; or better expressed, the act which makes the ego conscious of something different from itself, also makes it conscious of itself. Thus, in this system, being conscious of oneself is the same as being; Fichte's ego is essentially conscious of itself. Before being conscious, therefore, the ego does not exist; its essence is its being conscious, and with the act of its own consciousness it posits and creates itself.[271]

However, according to Fichte, the act of its own consciousness, which constitutes the ego, is carried out only with the act by which it knows the external world or what is different from the subject ego, that is, the non-ego. By a first act (the first act by which the ego feels itself), the ego also feels or — to use Fichte's way of speaking — thinks and posits the external world.[272]

The only things human beings know are the ego and the non-ego. The non-ego exists not before, but contemporaneously with the ego. Thus the activity of thought that posits the ego, also posits the non-ego. Hence the existence of all thinkable things originates from the primitive activity of the ego.

Among thinkable things is God, who according to Fichte appertains to the non-ego. This explains Fichte's strange and extraordinary promise to his listeners that in his next lecture 'He would apply himself to creating God'. Thus, he arrived at the ultimate expression of pride on the part of an intelligent creature, and the shortest, most elegant formula of the sin of the fallen angel. Those few words contain a deep, essential struggle: a kind of necessity and impossibility of destruction, an everlasting annihilation. Hence, the human being, unable to acknowledge a God, an infinite being, infinitely superior to himself and source of everything, decides to make God originate from himself and with an essential lie declares himself the creator. I have no wish to attribute to Fichte such extreme malice, which

---

[271] Fichte's error here consists in his failure to observe that the first act by which the ego exists, and generally speaking the first act by which a thing exists, is certainly an act of the thing, but an act created by a cause prior to the thing. The thing has begun to be with its act, which simply means that it was created in act by God. This defect in Fichte's philosophy opened the way for Schelling's system.

[272] The confusion arises from the fact that there is something passive and active in the acts of our spirit, as I have shown (cf. vol. 2, 662 ss.). Fichte noted the *active element*, and reduced everything to it alone, forgetting to consider passivity, just as certain sensists have considered the *passive element* and neglected activity.

appertains solely to the principle of evil. My intention is to indicate what is contained in the way he expresses himself, which would be a perpetual and fearful monument to the century that gave it birth if posterity had not known the shallowness with which the most bizarre oddities were uttered at that time without serious reflection and deep conviction.

1390. Reinhold, who attempted to regulate Kant's philosophy, which lacked any single, apparent principle as its base, had started from the fact of consciousness. But the expression, 'the fact of consciousness', itself contains many uncertainties which give rise to interminable arguments concerning Reinhold's own principle. His argument can be stated as follows: I think that which takes place in my consciousness; I therefore think the fact of consciousness. Let us suppose that this first act of the spirit and the *fact of consciousness* is the first thing I think. Reinhold certainly does not mean that I have *begun* from the fact of consciousness with the first act of my spirit, but rather that I have *terminated* in the fact of consciousness with the first act of my thought. Fichte rightly says therefore that the act of my spirit precedes the fact of consciousness; we must move, not from the *fact of consciousness*, but from the *activity* of thought which bends back on itself, that is, on its own consciousness. Fichte had thus placed the starting point of philosophy in thought's *reflection* on itself, and in so doing believed he had located it further back than Reinhold.

1391. But equivocation is clearly present here. The *starting point of reasoning* is one thing, the *starting point of the human spirit* is another. Reasoning can start only from the fact of consciousness, because reasoning, especially philosophical reasoning, begins not from what we *know*, but from that to which we *advert* or from that which we know we know. The chronological order of *advertences* or reflections is the opposite of the order of *direct knowledge*, as I have often said. We first reflect on the *fact* of our own consciousness, and then on the *act* with which we reflect. Only later do we *advert* to this reflective act of the spirit, although the act *exists* before advertence to the act of consciousness. The first thing to which the philosopher *adverts*, therefore, when he meditates upon himself, is the fact of consciousness, which is thus the starting point of reasoning. But the philosopher asks himself: 'How was I able to observe the fact of my consciousness?', and replies: 'With an act of reflection upon it.' This act of reflection is a starting point of thought higher, therefore, than the fact of consciousness known through reflection.

1392. Note that I said 'a starting point of *thought*', not 'a starting point of the spirit', a distinction which escaped Fichte. He began from the reflection of thought upon itself as the first, radical act with which all facts of the human spirit can be explained. He thus reduced everything to *thought*, and even confused *feeling* with thought, although feeling differs greatly from thought, as I have shown. His confusion indicates how deeply sensism has left its mark in transcendental idealism. If he had avoided this confusion, he would not have used the formula 'the activity of thought which reflects upon itself' to indicate the starting point of the spirit. He would then have come face to face with another formula: 'the activity of thought occupied with feeling'. He could not possibly have made this formula the starting point of the spirit, because he would have seen immediately that *feeling* must exist before the *act of thought* that he had observed. On the other hand, the formula 'thought reflecting on itself', taken as starting point of the spirit, necessarily expresses a contradiction in terms by identifying thought which reflects, with thought on which reflection takes place. The formula concentrates and confuses in a single essence that which is passive and active, or rather makes what is passive active, and viceversa, which is a contradiction.

1393. This intrinsic contradiction in Fichte's principle is, in my opinion, largely responsible for the contradictions encountered in his system. An acute thinker, he tried to answer the contradictions by saying that 'in order to rise to the conception of the first act of thought where his philosophy began, a particular feeling is necessary, which is not given by nature to everybody. Anyone not given this feeling cannot understand his philosophy'. Such a reply indicates a kind of philosophical desperation. I grant that a supreme effort is required of us to rise to, and fix our gaze on the *first act of reflection*; indeed, I maintain that Fichte himself was unable to rise to this level or, perhaps more accurately, had indeed risen to the contemplation of that act but was unable to observe its true nature with the necessary attention. Consequently he conceived his bizarre opinion about the creative force of the act, and thus became the author of an enthusiasm which was not what it ought to be, that is, humble joy at the sight of truth. In fact, it was a kind of insolent audacity which human beings feel when some exaggerated power is imparted to their spirit by a combination of intellective imagination and a base desire for the superiority they have usurped. This is a condition permanently damaging the foundation of culpable humanity.

If Fichte had really known the act of reflection, he would have been aware that an act does not truly turn back on itself, but always on a pre-existing act which becomes its object. If we take any act of reflection as an example, we see that it turns back on another act which, if we wish, can itself become reflective. But we must come finally to the act of first reflection, which must turn back on a *direct* act of thought; if not, we continue *ad infinitum*, which is absurd. The direct act of thought is *intuition* and *perception*. Perception is an act of thought which unites two affections, 1. corporeal sensation, and 2. the intuition of being in all its universality. Prior to any *reflection*, therefore, *feeling* and *intuition*, that is, 1. an intellective intuition, and 2. a corporeal feeling, are the basis of everything. The two affections, united by the *unique activity* of the spirit, form a totally simple *perception* upon which the *reflection* of thought begins to act. Fichte however omitted this analysis and consequently, in my opinion, fell into error.

1394. When we perform an act with our thought, we thereby know the object in which our act terminates, although the act itself remains unknown. We have to perform another reflective act on the first, if the first act is to become object of the second act and thus be known; the second reflective act, however, itself remains unknown. If we then reflect on this second act, we carry out a third act which lets us know the second. This second act has now become the object of the third act, which however we cannot know. We can continue like this for as long as we wish. The following great law therefore can be determined concerning our way of thinking: 'Any act whatsoever of our understanding makes us know the object in which it terminates, but not the act itself.' Granted this, we must ask: 'Surely we are conscious of the act with which we know an object?' The question, we must note, is not the same as: 'Do we have any *feeling* of the act with which we know an object?' To be *conscious* is to know our act as our own, that is, to know our act and at the same time know that it is ourselves who do it. But we cannot have this knowledge except by means of another act of reflection. Contrariwise, *feeling*, although never absent from our actions, is blind. People in general, however, cannot be persuaded that we perform an act without being aware of it. The reason people think like this is that when we carry out an act with our spirit, we can immediately reflect on, and advert to the act, or certainly think we can, while not observing the other act with which we carry out our *reflection* and advertence. Thus, we easily think that an act of our spirit is adverted to and known through itself, not through some other act added by ourselves. But the act is unknown and unnoticed, although by reflecting on or adverting to it at any moment, we are able, or apparently able, to make it known to ourselves at will. Fichte was acutely aware of this error common to mankind, and to avoid it fell into the opposite difficulty. He was not satisfied with saying that we do not advert to or reflect upon the act of our spirit as such. He said that the act did not exist at all. He thus granted to the spirit's *reflection* a kind of activity to produce the act which, as I have said, he tried to identify with reflection itself.

1395. In my opinion, however, every act of the spirit, even before we reflect on it or know it, exists in us, but only as a *pure feeling*. In every act of the intelligent spirit therefore we find an *idea* and a *feeling*. The intuited, illumined *object* is called 'idea'; the act with which we perceive an object in our consciousness is simply a blind *feeling*. But, because nothing is known without an idea, we truly know nothing as long as we have only *feelings*. In particular, it is impossible, as I have so often said, to observe our state prior to reflection upon ourselves. It seems therefore to have no real existence, although in reality it is simply unknown to us.

Fichte confused not-knowing with not-existing, and said that the ego, through its own reflection, posits itself with the same act with which it posits the non-ego. To insist that the essence of the ego lies in knowledge, in thought, is useless: the ego is not originally a thought of oneself but a *feeling*. Fichte however had made *thought* absorb *feeling* without noticing the gap between them. This led him into extraordinary, profound errors.

It may be objected that although the intelligent ego has an intellective feeling, it does not finish within itself along with this feeling but terminates in being in all its universality. This, however, cannot be taken for Fichte's reflection: this elementary thought contains nothing reflective; it is the unmovable, permanent part of the human being.

Nevertheless, Fichte seems to have come near to the truth and caught some distant glimpse of it when he uttered these memorable words 'although thoughts are transient, there is in the human being a part which contemplates unmovingly'.

Article 5

Schelling's starting point

1396. It seems that Schelling had glimpsed Fichte's error of reducing everything to determined thought and failing to note the existence of feeling in the human being prior to thought. Consequently Fichte did not see that the ego can have its own root-existence with its direct act as an animal feeling intuiting being before any reflection upon itself. Schelling therefore placed the starting point of the spirit in the ego as a feeling, making the ego the *absolute* element, from which he drew everything more or less as Fichte had done. In doing this, he followed the same path as Fichte except that in place of *thought* he substituted *feeling*, which is always presupposed by thought. He made his ego the root and source of Fichte's ego and non-ego. Thus he denied the kind of duality introduced by Fichte, claiming that the ego and non-ego, which Fichte had made contraries, possessed a common seed which made them perfectly identical. Hence, he called his teaching the system of 'absolute identity'.

In this final root of all things he placed the mystery of life, and called this first, radical life 'dynamic', because it was a primitive force from which all limits are removed. He seems to have substituted 'ideal' for Fichte's ego, and 'real' for the non-ego. Schelling's primitive, infinite ego harmonises and, within itself, creates of itself the *ideal* and the *real*; from the ego, according to Schelling, a sublime, wonderful trinity in unity emerges [*App.*, no. 18].

[1396]

1397. I must explain why Schelling imagined a limitless ego. Fichte had made the non-ego the opposite of the ego and defined the former as the term of the latter. In a word, in his system, it was the ego that limited itself, and the limitation was the non-ego. This was the basic fact of Fichte's philosophy, which he neither demonstrated nor could demonstrate. But Shelling rightly noted that neglect to demonstrate the fact was a defect, not because everything had to be demonstrated, but because everything that was not *evident*, that is, undemonstrable, had to be demonstrated. Schelling denied that Fichte had fulfilled his declared intention of finding for philosophy an *evident* principle which would remove all contradictions.[273]

Schelling's objection was certainly reasonable, because there is something contradictory in the kind of ego which limits itself necessarily. If the ego necessarily limits its own nature, a law or a necessity is imposed on it. In this case, the ego has the nature to receive, but not impose the law of limitation. An unbreakable law of nature, something stronger than the ego is present, which the ego obeys, not by limiting itself but by being limited.

To understand the force of this objection, we have to concentrate our observation interiorly upon ourselves. As we do so, we realise that whatever we do, we do willingly, and that what takes place in us through a necessary limitation of nature is not done by us but happens in us, that is, is done in us without us. If in fact the imposition or non-imposition of limits depended on us, we would certainly not impose them; every limit restricts our power and diminishes our strength, and we could never want that. Perhaps the only reason for willingly setting limits to our power and strength would be to avoid some greater limitation, which would be imposed on us against our will if we did not impose it upon ourselves, as we do in the free, moral order. Limitation as such can never come from ourselves; it is imposed on us by something superior to us. This superior, limiting element, whatever it may be, cannot itself be limited; the absolute

---

[273] In his well-known *Wissenschaftslehre* and other writings Fichte assures us that his philosophy was intended to destroy scepticism! This is the intention of all modern philosophy, but the effect is the ever greater confirmation of scepticism. Modern philosophy, which claims to be moving towards the light, is in fact going the other way.

necessity of nature is such that nothing can be superior to it. Even if we thought that the thing limiting us had its own limits, we could apply to it the same argument that we apply to ourselves. Hence the necessity of coming finally to an *absolute*, limited by nothing. Once Schelling had come to this, he believed he had found the ultimate principle of philosophy, beyond which it was impossible to go.

1398. Schelling's absolute is therefore the product of Fichte's non-ego. But to show more clearly the link between the philosophies of these two men, I must say a word about the practical part of Fichte's philosophy, where the germ of Schelling's philosophy is more clearly seen.

Fichte's non-ego includes a sensible world, a first, intelligible world, and a suprasensible *order* proper to the same. The activity of the ego which has produced the non-ego outside itself (that is, all these worlds) gives us faith in these worlds. This *faith* makes the world subjectively real, that is to say, the ego firmly believes in the world and considers it real. According to Fichte, the possibility of human *freedom* lies in this faith; the supreme activity by which the ego believes in the reality of the non-ego causes an *efficacious persuasion* of capacity for action for a *purpose* in keeping with the suprasensible order. And in conforming itself to this order, the ego sees its happiness. This *faith* or persuasion is the free power itself of human beings; the suprasensible order of the world is the moral limit, the obligation, the absolute duty of human beings. It is the nature of the ego, constituted in this way, to have this order, obligation and duty among the things it opposes to itself and with which it limits itself. Moreover, by virtue of its intimate activity, the ego believes it is free relative to this moral limitation; this belief, as I have said, actuates human freedom. But free activity actuated and created in this way by means of *f*aith is only satisfied with itself when it has adapted itself fully to the suprasensible order called 'obligation' and 'absolute duty'. Free activity, in order to be completely satisfied and therefore happy, must believe in the reality of this order. Hence the soul applies itself energetically to realising the order through the activity it manifests under the form of faith and belief.

The soul, therefore, by putting its faith in the moral order of the universe, makes this order real for itself. But in making this effort, the soul finds the concept of God, which is necessary for the perfect realisation of the moral order, generated for it. This is Fichte's God, who takes his origin from the practical reason in the way I have explained.

Such a way of deducing a concept of God led to accusations of atheism against Fichte, which caused him much anguish, although his justifications do not seem to have fully satisfied public opinion. In various writings he tried to reconcile other opinions with his. One of his last works was 'on the last state of the world deduced from the first', where, as idealist and realist in his own way, he begins at one point from the activity of the ego as the only reality, and at another from the *divine absolute* as the only reality which, manifested in the image or idea, becomes consciousness.

In Germany, this explanation was taken as a modification he had made to his system to make it more conformable to common thinking. To me, however, it seems simply a new explanation of the same system; and for anyone who has gone to the root of the matter, the apparent contradiction disappears. Fichte admitted that the activity by which the ego posits the non-ego manifests itself in two ways: through the *representation* of the non-ego, and through *faith* in the non-ego. The faculty for positing and representing the non-ego is *theoretic reason*. The faculty for having faith in the non-ego is *practical reason*, the source of obligation, morality and rights. In *theoretic reason* the only *thing real* is the activity of the ego; everything comes from this activity. In *practical reason* the only *thing real* is *divine being*; everything comes from this being — the very origin and dependence of everything on this being is the moral order and source of obligation.

In such a system *reality* is clearly given two different meanings. The genuine reality, that which is *understood* and causes everything, is the activity of the ego, but the *believed* reality, that is, real for our faith, is the divine Being alone.[274]

Anyone wishing to present this system in the most favourable way would, I think, have to express it like this: 'The intrinsic exigency of human nature requires absolutely (that is,

---

[274] Fichte's God becomes real in his own way through the reality of the *faith* that produces God. But isn't this reality always relative?

independently of demonstrations) faith in the supreme reality of the divine Being.' In this way, belief in the reality of such a Being is truly necessary because belief arises from the supreme exigency of human nature. However, human beings believe themselves to be free in this. Hence, their first duty is to accept God. This thought is similar to Seneca's: 'The first duty towards God is to believe in his existence,'[275] and it contains some truth, if we suppose that God's existence *can* at least be proved by reason. But it becomes valueless when we suppose that a single, blind necessity of nature, a single, fatal illusion and self-interest (even if a noble interest) leads us *only* and inevitably to such a belief.

1399. We can see that the germ of Schelling's system was already contained in the moral part of Fichte's philosophy. Schelling based his system on the absolute order of the non-ego, the only reality available for the necessary *faith* of human nature. However, he posited the absolute as real in itself. According to him, this absolute was not made real solely by the faith of human nature, and therefore did not come from the activity of Fichte's ego. Rather everything came from the other absolute ego which is the source of all activities and power. Schelling thus hoped to have brought philosophy to the point of *evidence*. In his opinion, the *absolute* needed no proof. Everything else, in order to be, needs the absolute, which itself needs nothing, and *is intuited* directly; without the absolute, things would be inconceivable. The certainty of everything is therefore conditioned by the certainty of the absolute, in which things are possible and whose certainty they share. This reasoning is solid enough, but Schelling did not stop here; the activity impelling him to know everything, even the unknown, led him into error. Whenever a human being obstinately seeks to know what he cannot know, he must necessarily fabricate with his imagination the forbidden region where no mortal can truly penetrate. Let us see how this happened to Schelling.

1400. Three great entia are represented to human thought: the *material universe*, the *subject ego*, and *God*. Kant said (wrongly, as I have shown in volume 2) that these *representations* of objects have power to make known only themselves, not the things in themselves, their objects. To have *faith* in the representations is a free act constituting what Kant was the first to call 'practical reason'. Nevertheless, in his system, they can exist, provided they emanate from the spirit in regard to their *formal* part. How they lack subjective forms remains unknown, but some kind of *matter* in general can be admitted relative to the universe, and an ultimate *root* of things relative to God.

The *representations* are called phenomena; the things in themselves, *noumena*. We are conscious of the *phenomena*, but completely in the dark regarding the *noumena*. The darkness irritates, and both Fichte and Schelling tried to dissipate it. Fichte said that only what emanated from the ego existed; this emanation was the universe, God and generally speaking the representation of the noumena indicated by the word 'non-ego'. The ego puts faith in this representation, and thus makes its representations real. For Kant, therefore, a phenomenal ego is the source of all that is knowable and, as knowable, consists of appearances and phenomena. Whether there is anything beyond appearances and phenomena, he neither affirms nor denies — for him, these are the limits of the human mind. According to Fichte, however, the ego is *real*, and therefore presupposed as a *noumenon* or kind of *postulate* which of itself produces what exists. There were no more unknown regions, no more *noumena* other than those which the *practical reason* creates for itself with faith in the representations proffered by the ego. Schelling, on the other hand, claims to rise to a *noumenon* which could produce the ego and a phenomenal world. His firm ground is his *noumenon*, known through *intuition*, not by demonstration. He posits it as the necessary base of all phenomena; it is therefore more certain than the phenomena and *per se* evident — it is his God.

This is the only noumenon; it alone is endowed with its own proper activity; outside of it there is no other real activity. Consequently, its activity is the activity of all the things in nature, as well as of the subject ego. The only thing that these things have as proper to them is what is phenomenal; only the infinite essence subsists, and the being of all phenomena is in this essence. The subject, the object, the ideal, the real, the representations, the parts, etc., all are identified in this one essence, because their being is precisely the being of the absolute which transforms itself *phenomenally* into them all. The differences present in them are only *quantitative*, not *qualitative*, because the same being is in them all. In this way the soul and material nature have the same state, equally phenomenal in their individual existence and, relative to their real existence, grounded in the great all, the absolute. The individual is thus absorbed and perishes in the immense nature of God, more or less as human beings are after death, according to the Stoics. The reasoning underlying the whole of this system, which is difficult to defend from the accusation of pantheism, is the following: 'The arguments of critical philosophy lead us to doubt the reality of all things (the noumena). But the reality of an absolute cannot be doubted, because it is the condition on which the possibility of all the phenomena is acknowledged by critical philosophy itself. This reality therefore is more certain than any other, and from it must issue all things recognised as parts, emanations and transfigurations of the absolute.'

1401. But many observations can be used to refute this reasoning:

1. Critical philosophy itself used reasoning to deny knowledge of the *noumena*. By so doing it has acknowledged the validity of reasoning. But if reasoning correctly used leads to undoubted consequences, why is it accepted only in part? Why is it used to deny, but not to admit knowledge of the *noumena*. Critical philosophy contradicts itself and cannot be accepted.

2. If critical philosophy did not contain this intrinsic contradiction, or make it so blatant, it could defend itself in the following way against Schelling's objection, from which he deduced his system: 'You say that the phenomena or representations suppose a real absolute. You must undoubtedly deduce this by reasoning. But critical philosophy admits, among the phenomena and representations, the laws of thought, which according to this philosophy are subjective or, as it were, phenomenal. Thus these laws have no other force than to conclude subjectively and phenomenally. Hence the laws of thought certainly demand the *absolute*, and Kant himself found the absolute to be the supreme effect of thought when he spoke about *reason*. The absolute therefore, although admitted as real

[1401]

and certain by human need for it (this is practical reason), can be only a phenomenal or uncertain absolute.

3. Even if we suppose that Schelling's real absolute is reliably verified and evident of itself, and that with the use of reasoning nothing else can be acknowledged as real, it does not follow that nothing else can be real; the most we can suppose is that we cannot *know* anything else real. In this case there will indeed be an unknown region, as Kant supposed, a region more limited than his, however, because from it Schelling draws and makes real the *absolute*. But it is not sound logic to conclude: 'Because I know nothing else real, nothing else real exists or can exist.' If, however, Schelling had supported his reasoning with the pantheistic argument that 'what is infinite must include everything, nor can anything exist outside the infinite', he would have lost his case; this kind of pantheistic argument has been refuted throughout history.

1402. Examining Schelling's ideas, we see a desire to reduce everything to a systematic unity, the same desire which had previously guided Fichte. These thinkers did not try to conform their philosophy to the nature of things, but to conform things to their philosophy, to a form preconceived in the spirit and cherished as the most elegant of all forms. It was a science with a single principle where everything had a place, as if nothing could be hidden from us. It was intended as an effort to allow us to broaden our gaze, as it were, and make ourselves more like God. It was in fact an imitation and continuation of that initial, tragic deed by which our first parent was seduced to attempt to possess divine intelligence by following his own desire and tasting the forbidden fruit. But do we not recognise easily enough and experience that unassailable limits have been placed on us, on our power and knowledge? At these limits our pride has to be broken; it avails nothing to rant and rage. One of these limits is precisely the line dividing the finite from the infinite, the creature from the creator. Schelling vainly exerts himself to combine these two objects into one, in the way a drunk mixes two drinks in a glass. But they are separated by an abyss; Schelling cannot isolate or imagine or know such a single object.

I firmly believe that Schelling would never have attempted to mix everything together and define God more or less in the words of Bruno Giordano: *Est animal sanctum, sacrum et venerabile, mundus* [He is a holy animal, sacred and venerable; he is the world],[276] if, instead of plunging immediately into such extreme speculation, he had tried to understand and solve the most elementary problems of human knowledge.[277]

If his patience first of all had been sufficient to analyse all human knowledge, investigate its sources and distinguish its various species, he would undoubtedly have discovered that it has unpassable limits. He would have known that, although we have a positive notion of ourselves and of sensible things, our notion of God can be only negative, that is, we can know the supreme being only as some *essence*, determined by relationships (cf. 1237 ss.). He would have discovered that the notion of nature and of God can never be confused or reduced to a single notion. Furthermore, the *positive notion of nature* is endowed with essential characteristics that contradict the notion of God. Thus it would be absurd to attribute these characteristics to the divine essence.

1403. The first difference between the notion of nature and that of God (that is, the former is *positive*; the latter, *negative*) shows that the attempt to reduce God and nature to a single principle or substance is rash and reckless. In attempting to do so, we are simply uniting something known with something unknown, arbitrarily making them a single whole. We thus pronounce on, and dispose of what is beyond our knowledge.

The second difference between our knowledge of nature and our knowledge of God (that is, the former has characteristics essentially opposed to and contradicting the latter) renders absurd and void of meaning any attempt to unite them, because such a union can no more be thought than nothing.

1404. But in order not to pursue the argument endlessly, I will confine myself to stating and answering the various points made by Schelling apropos the first of the two reasons.

---

[276] *De immenso*, bk. 5. Cf. also, among Schelling's many works, *Von der Weltseele, eine Hypothese der Höhern Physik zur Erläuterung des allgemeinen Organismus,* Hamburg, 1798.

[277] It seems to me that in the case of method, the general weakness of German philosophy is to examine the most abstruse and difficult problems without first investigating the most obvious, the solution of which would open the way for a serious understanding and discussion of the most difficult.

He claims that an absolute is necessary, because without it nothing can exist or be known. Moreover, we know the absolute from the moment we are aware of its existence; as our means of knowing other things, it must itself be even more known to us than they are. However, Schelling grants the difference between knowing the existence of an object and knowing the object itself only in the sense that the existence of the object cannot be known without some knowledge of the object. But he does not understand that knowledge of the existence of an object may be *negative* knowledge.

Negative knowledge depends upon a natural or artificial sign which prevents confusion between the thing signified and all other things. This sign is called the *nominal essence*, or essence of relationship, of a thing. For example, if someone in authority tells me that an object exists to which a particular *name* has been given, the name would make me understand only two things about the object: 1. its existence, and 2. the name by which it was called. This would be a negative idea; I would know nothing about the object itself. *Existence*, which is common to all subsistent things, does not make me know things themselves; they are what they are in so far as they have distinct essences, not in so far as they have being in common. According to Schelling this teaching cannot be applied to the absolute, which he says is not known through an authority that reveals its name, but deduced by means of the necessary conclusions of reasoning.

This objection can be answered by clarifying further the meaning of negative knowledge, that is, knowledge of the *nominal* essence. I spoke, for example, of an *arbitrary name,* that is, of an artificial sign of an object. It is true that properly speaking this example does not conform to Schelling's absolute which is known by a *natural*, not an arbitrary *sign* or name. However, it makes no difference whether the name or sign determining the object is *arbitrary* or *natural*; what is in our mind concerning the object is simply the *essence* of its relationship to something else we know. The knowledge, therefore, remains negative, and the real, positive essence of the object is entirely unknown to us. This is the only kind of knowledge that Schelling's reasoning on the absolute can bring us.

Schelling himself, however, is unaware of this, and we need to show why this is so.

First, he would admit that we attain our knowledge of the absolute because we cannot think of any existing finite thing without an infinite absolute: if something exists, the absolute must exist. He would also admit that it is the senses and consciousness of self that tell us something exists. But he maintains that consciousness of self and the senses are not enough to provide us with the perception of the absolute; we must also have the *intuition* of the absolute.

He accepts that all individual human experience and consciousness is a *sure sign*, even a manifestation, of the existence of something absolute, something infinite, in the same way that anything showing traces of intelligence — a geometric figure or a statue, for example — is immediately recognised as a *sure sign* of the intelligent being who caused it. It is also a *natural sign*, the natural name of the thing, as it were; as the effect of the thing it shows us something that must be present in the thing.

It is this sign or natural name which provides Schelling with his knowledge of the absolute. In fact, according to him, we know the absolute as a result of some *effect* which designates the absolute as a cause distinct from all other things, without however telling us anything of the cause's mode of action or mode of being.

All we know, therefore, is the *nominal essence* of the absolute, nothing more, although the sign revealing it to us is not only conventional, but *natural* (if we can refer to it in this way) and hence helpful in allowing us to know some *real relationships* of the absolute, but nothing more. There is no other *intuition* (if we wish to call it that) than of this necessity and relationship.

The conclusion must therefore be that the proper nature of the absolute is unknown, that Schelling cannot base any system of emanations on this nature, and that he cannot declare the things of the universe to be forms or parts (or anything else we may choose to call them) of the absolute.

Schelling's teaching strikes us as odd because we know that the two ideas of *absolute* and *non-absolute* are as contrary as 'yes' and 'no'. For him, however, they are not contradictory, but different. Evidently he can think of something as simultaneously having and not having limits; in this case, the same thing as limited is non-absolute, and as unlimited is absolute. But in reality the absolute is void of limits; the non-absolute has limits.

Schelling's teaching supposes that limited things can become unlimited. In such a case, the absolute would begin to be, although previously it was not; and for this very reason it would no longer be absolute. Moreover, what moves limited things, which formerly were not absolute, to become absolute? There is an essential contradiction between their essence in their first state and in their second; duality admitted in this sense is inevitable. Any reasoning which confuses all things together, making them into transformations and modifications of a single being, must be rash and absurd — the same being cannot be conceived as subject to limitation and partiality, and then as subject of entirely contrary characteristics, that is, as subject to internal opposition and repugnancy.

I cannot see how Schelling can answer these objections in any meaningful way.

1405. We can reasonably say therefore that Schelling was led into error by his failure to premiss his other speculations with an accurate analysis of the forces present in reasoning. He was unaware that regions almost entirely unknown to human understanding existed, for example, all those entia not perceived with feeling or its modifications. This explains, as I have said, why he fell into the contrary error to Kant. Kant denied knowledge of the *existence* of suprasensible, *per se* existing entia (*noumena*); Schelling claimed to reason as if we could intuit the real *essence* itself of these entia. It is worth noting the direction taken by these philosophical ideas in Germany.

1406. The starting point was *material nature*. Then by degrees German philosophy rose to concentrate on the human *spirit*. Kant himself left the existence of material nature in doubt, or in a state of perfect concealment from human understanding; Fichte absorbed it into the spirit itself.

But the human spirit in which the universe was said to be concentrated, was much too small for the human being; the human spirit was insufficient for itself. It seemed natural therefore that if one thinker had arrived at the spirit from matter, others could arrive at God, the absolute and infinite, from the human spirit. This was the intention, but their powers were unsuited to the task.

The effort and the will to reach the infinite was present, but if the aim had really been achieved, thought would have found itself in an unknown and inaccessible region; the philosopher, prostrate before such incomprehensible nature, would have adored. But he did not want adoration and profound self-effacement before God; all he wanted was systems! The human being wanted to explain the forces present in his understanding, not gather and offer them in sacrifice to the Incomprehensible. In his philosophical journey he was guided by the desire to cast light outside himself on all the regions he could reach. So, he had to reconcile the following two intentions: 1. to attain the infinite; and 2. to attain it as something known. But the infinite is incomprehensible, and the only thing left was to bring his imagination to the aid of uncertain, defective thought! With his imagination he formed an infinite, an absolute, a God, composed of everything his imagination could design, mould and know. But the only thing known by human beings and their imagination is the world and themselves. Hence, the philosophers' absolute was, and could only be nothing more than a composition and re-shaping of the world and of human beings. This was the God or rather the idol of philosophy, the work of human hands, which *os habet et non loquetur* [has a mouth but shall not speak].

1407. It is however more important for us to show how the absolute, the starting point of Schelling's philosophy, cannot be the true starting point of human philosophy. I say human, because we must not forget that we are human; if we were God, we could undoubtedly start from another point, but as human we must begin with the examination of the human mind, and from that principle which has been given to us as light. Even at the time of Kant, thinkers acknowledged that the examination of reasoning must precede all ontology. Kant himself produced the *Critique of Pure Reason* for this reason. Fichte was the first to leave this path in order to start from the activity of thought. He should have asked himself how he could justify reasoning about the activity of thought before demonstrating that his reasoning had some authority. This would have been enough to make him turn back and realise that his reasoning was totally gratuitous without the presumption that reasoning (which he himself used to convince others of his system) was valid.

After Fichte, the need to resolve this problem of thought before undertaking the philosophy of real things was lost sight of even more. Instead of beginning from the great problem of the validity of reasoning, and placing *cognitions* in their correct order, a bold attempt was made to order the *subsistent objects* of cognitions. In such a case the *absolute* would certainly be the first in order of all the *subsistent objects* of cognitions; all other objects depend on it, and are, and can only be, through it. But how do we know that the complete, absolute being subsists; how do we know that the first, supreme ens, the source of all others subsists? What leads us to it? To say 'intuition' (as Schelling does) is to begin from a gratuitous affirmation, an arbitrary statement. This was his greatest fault, condemned by the whole of Germany, and particularly by Hegel.

It must be reasoning alone, our sole guide, that leads us to the *absolute*. If such a guide were essentially powerless, and even erroneous (as Kant claimed), nothing at all would be gained by following it; we would only be deceiving ourselves with the belief that by following it we had found the absolute. It is true that both we and our reasoning depend in a sense on the absolute, but this dependence is in the *order of real entia*, not in the *order of human cognitions*. The absolute must indeed be, if we are to be, or to have the ability to reason. But it is by no means true that we can as a consequence know all this, including the absolute, without using the faculty of knowledge, that is, of reason, with which we are endowed. We must distinguish therefore between the *order of cognitions* and the *order of real things*. Real objects are not in our mind without knowledge of them. Hence the *order of cognitions* and ideas precedes the *order of real* objects. We must therefore begin from the question of the validity of cognitions before reasoning about any real object whatsoever, even the absolute itself.

Article 6

Bouterweck's starting point

1408. Friedrich Bouterweck realised that Schelling, instead of ascending to a higher starting point of philosophy, had descended from the order of *cognitions* to *feelings*, and ultimately to the order of *real entia* which, relative to our understanding, belong to a later order. Bouterweck's objection to Schelling was: 'You begin from a real (that is, subsistent) thing, the absolute. But how do you demonstrate that there is something real? Such a demonstration requires that you first of all prove there is a faculty of knowledge designed to perceive the reality of things. This demonstration is particularly necessary after everything Kant said in order to demonstrate the impossibility of such a faculty.' And indeed it is true that Schelling's argument, which makes the *absolute evident of itself* and the necessary condition for anything to be thought or be, is valid only if we presuppose that our reason judges correctly and extends its judgments validly to real things.

When Bouterweck made this objection to Schelling, he also refuted the pure idealists: 'It is impossible to reduce *real ens* to ideas. The analysis of ideas tells us that real entia precede ideas as cause of our cognitions, and that because a *real end* is more than its *idea*, real entia are more than ideas; we cannot therefore reduce everything to futile ideas. We have to distinguish *ideas* from *real entia* and explain both, as well as their relationship and union.' Substantially, both Fichte and Schelling had tried to do this, but only by identifying entia and thoughts, or better, by making all entia issue from thought.[278]

1409. Bouterweck also noted that there can be no *knowledge* without an object or ens, and that *being* is indefinable; no philosopher can ask the meaning of being in all its universality. He concluded that being is essential to thought, and although different from thought, is given with it. Hence we must begin from an *absolute faculty of knowledge* as from a first, evident and fundamental fact; such a faculty consists precisely in the perception of *absolute existence*. The following proposition therefore can be considered fundamental to his system: 'Every feeling and thought has for its true and, therefore, absolute foundation an ens which has no other foundation, but is itself the foundation.'

1410. Bouterweck glimpsed a part of the truth, but confused *absolute existence* with *existence considered in all its universality*,

---

[278] Schelling did not sufficiently distinguish *feeling* and *thought*. He imagined a first thought *indifferent* to anything objective and subjective. This is essentially contrary to the nature of thought, as I have already observed.

or (which is the same) with most common being. If he had said that intelligence was essentially bound and formed with being in all its universality which in its application is called *most common*, he would have entered our system. But because he took *absolute being* in place of the simple *notion of being*, he lapsed unwillingly with the others into pantheism. He made a mixture, a kind of unique substance, of real, actual being and thought, as he himself said. However, in order to save the existence of the individual in this singular system, he imagined a special force that constituted the individual, a special act in the substance, which he called *virtuality*. But initially we have only a *practical knowledge* of this force, a knowledge of feeling and experienced fact, which constitutes the individual, and is known only by conceiving the difference between the subject which acts and its resistant objects. We do not have theoretic knowledge of the force, we do not immediately see its intrinsic necessity.

The *absolute faculty* of knowledge is applied to *virtuality*, which it changes into an *absolute reality*. My understanding of what Bouterweck is saying is therefore the following: the absolute faculty of knowledge sees *absolute being* and sees this being in everything — it raises everything to the level of this being. Bouterweck thus considers the individual force itself, or virtuality (as it is called), in its absolute being. This gives rise to the concept of an infinite existence and an infinite action.

1411. The error in his system therefore is the following:

1. He begins from the *act* of our spirit, when he should have begun from an accurate analysis of the *object* thought. He neglected to verify and determine the nature of the essential object of thought. He was uncertain, and confused *possible being* with *subsistent being*; he did not see that the former alone, not the latter, is the object of thought. Nor did he see that subsistent being with all it embraces is even less the object of thought than subsistent being as such. By making the object of thought the absolute subsisting being, he posited a full comprehension of God. But anyone who comprehends God *is* God. We are now in pantheism.

2. This error was facilitated by the fact that Bouterweck did not give enough attention to determining the distinction between *feeling* and *thought*. If he had carried out these elementary investigations before plunging into the sea of the

most abstruse questions, he would have seen that only thought, not feeling, needs *being* as its object and foundation. Thus he would have been aware that with the abolition of every object of thought, thought itself and the faculty of thought would have been abolished. But the subject would not be completely annihilated, because our animal part would remain and we would simply be degraded to a brute state. This observation would have been sufficient to convince him of the essential limitation of human beings whose foundation, as it were, is animal nature. Animal nature, in order to subsist, does not need the vision of subsistent entia, much less the vision of the absolute ens; it becomes rational simply with the vision of ideal being.

1412. Thus two reasons prevented Bouterweck from finding the first, simple starting point of human cognitions: 1. he began from an absolute faculty of knowledge, and therefore supposed the *idea* and *subsistent being* as previously given and as the matter of the faculty; but all this needed to be demonstrated because it depended on the principle of demonstration, prior to the faculty; 2. *absolute, subsistent being* is not known positively by us; therefore the concept of Bouterweck's absolute faculty includes what in fact it does not contain.

Article 7

Bardilli's starting point

1413. Bardilli, like Bouterweck, knew that the only starting point of philosophy was *thought*. He therefore posited the *use of thought* as a postulate, although in my opinion it is not only a postulate but a *fact*. On this basis, he then attempted a new analysis of thought to discover the *very first* thought *per se*,[279] in other words, the starting point of philosophy.

1414. Like Schelling, he took as the first thought that which in reality is the last, in other words, the absolute.[280] It is useless to

---

[279] The same investigation was undertaken by the Italian, Pini, in his *Protologia*, a work which, if printed in Germany rather than Italy, would probably have caused a furore.

[280] Bardilli fell into the same error as Schelling through supposing that the human spirit can by nature have a *positive* idea of God. This error led to false

say that the absolute is the *condition* on which all certainty and existence depends. Even if this were true, I would not need a positive idea of the absolute to make me certain of things. Prior to this idea I can have something which gives me certainty about finite, conditioned things. Hence, the absolute is *implicitly* understood and supposed in my certainty. Moreover, by reasoning about the absolute, I can discover *explicitly* its necessity. Human reasoning itself has in fact truly progressed in this way. In order to be certain of things, we need know only the *necessity* of the truth of what we see mentally. As I have shown, we conceive this necessity by means of *possible being* without need of recourse to the concept of the *subsistent*, *absolute being*. We come to this concept afterwards as the absolute condition of all certainty and of all the entia of which we are certain. This necessary progress made by our developing reasoning is due to the nature of possible being, and I have called it the *integrative faculty of the understanding* (cf. vol. 2, 624 and fn. 95).

The following observation will strengthen the argument. We come to possess knowledge of a first necessary, primal absolute in this way alone: such an absolute is the condition of all my *certainty* and of all that I *know* to exist. But if this is the case, can it be said that it is 1. only through knowledge of the absolute I can be sure of and provide a foundation for all my previous cognitions or 2. that philosophy has to start from the absolute? This is certainly not the case because the necessary existence of the absolute is a condition of the certainty of my cognitions. If this certainty did not exist, the absolute would no longer be necessary: if we remove what is conditioned, we remove the condition. The certainty and necessity of my cognitions renders the absolute certain and necessary, not vice versa. I induce the necessity of the absolute from the necessity of my cognitions; if my cognitions about what exists is doubtful, the absolute is doubtful. Hence the certainty and necessity of my knowledge

---

enthusiasm and bestowed on the human being a grandeur of intellective power which he does not have. Seeing this power as something sublime, human imagination rejoices arrogantly, and runs away with itself, the essence of enthusiasm. The subsequent suggestion that the human perception of God matches God results in irredeemable pantheism, as I have often mentioned. This is a rock on which confident and great minds easily founder, and Italy is not lacking in modern examples of such intellectual shipwreck.

is, relative to the human mind, prior to and presupposed by the certainty and necessity of the absolute, subsistent being. Philosophy therefore cannot begin from the absolute; it must terminate in it. Prior to the knowledge of the absolute, subsistent being (God), I must have some means, a principle, which makes me know or produces the certainty of my knowledge. This means or principle is the idea of undetermined being in all its universality, continually present to my spirit.

1415. Bardilli was so far from seeing the step that had caused the downfall of many contemporary philosophers in his own country that he systematised their error and sealed it. The result of my previous observations shows that those who came after Kant erred by supposing 'that the human being could have *positive* ideas about unperceived realities, and that consequently there was nothing of which he could not have positive ideas; this identified the sphere of human knowledge with the whole complex of subsistent things'. Such a supposition is implicit in all these systems, and surreptitiously directs them. Thus, on the basis of this supposition, an ens can present itself of which we can have only a negative (I would say, an empty) concept, not an adequate or positive concept (of God, for example); our imagination would then come to our aid and do its best to fill the emptiness by making the concept positive and real. But to do this, our imagination can use only the materials it possesses, that is, it can make the concept positive only by substituting it with that which it perceives. To make the concept of God positive, the imagination has to fill it and, as it were, pour into it, everything known positively, that is, nature and human beings. This error was precisely the error of all idolaters: unable to find satisfaction in a negative concept of God, they artificially formed a positive concept of him for themselves; they replaced God, whose real essence they did not know, with what they had perceived.

This intemperate desire to know everything, this repugnance to accepting and admitting one's own ignorance, in short, this basic pride which prevents us from acknowledging that we do not know what we do not know is the source of pantheism, which in the last analysis is simply idolatry perfected and clothed as it were in philosophical forms. In recent times worldly philosophy rushed headlong into universal pantheism, expounded in many different forms. This clearly demonstrates how much human beings, when abandoned to themselves, have a perpetual tendency to sink into paganism. Even in the clear light of the Gospel they have seen themselves move towards paganism where they would certainly be ruined and irredeemably lost, if it were possible to annihilate Christianity by insane, human action and by diabolical wickedness.

1416. The principle maintaining the distinction between God and nature, between creator and creature, is that which establishes two kinds of human knowledge, negative and positive. In negative knowledge we think what I have called a 'nominal essence';[281] in positive knowledge we think a *real essence*. With negative knowledge we think an *x*, whose positive, generic or specific, real essence is unknown to us. Any knowledge of this kind can in a way be called an *empty idea* or *empty knowledge*. Positive knowledge gives us either the specific, or at least the generic, real essence of things. Any knowledge of this kind is called an *apprehending idea*. A person who confuses these two distinct series of ideas and claims that all our ideas are *apprehending*, must fall into pantheism and innumerable other errors. Such a person is forced to compose imaginary and false imitations of entia of which he has only empty ideas; he is forced to create his own fabrications, and amongst them a God composed of the characteristics and properties of our limited spirit and of matter; he creates a God made of foreign elements put together in a thousand different ways, and does so without following any law because the ceaseless wandering of a disordered phantasy has no law. Here we have an inexhaustible source of the most weird, ingenious and complex systems which, although they awe and bewitch us for the moment, are as short-lived as falsehood and illusion.[282]

---

[281] For me, nominal essence is always a *generic essence*, as I have said (cf. vol. 2, 620 ss.). Nominal, generic essence contains two elements, 1. *universal essence* (that is, being in all its universality, which forms part of all ideas), and 2. the *relationship* to us of something known positively, which determines the unknown thing, and determines and individualises the *universal essence*.

[282] In antiquity many kinds of Platonism, such as that of the Valentinians, fell into a kind of idolatry precisely because they claimed to make the idea of God positive. Their idea was so homogeneous with human, positive ideas of finite creatures that they could without contradiction imagine creatures as

1417. Bouterweck had made the following proposition the start of his philosophy: 'An ens is the foundation of every feeling and every idea'. In doing this, he had upset the two established orders, and rejected the order of empty ideas. His two predecessors, Schelling and Fichte, had fallen more seriously into the same error; they had made being so dependent on thought that thought was the only source of being. *Empty ideas* could no longer exist, because thought contained all being in its very source. Although Bouterweck found something more in being than in *empty thought*, he considered the foundation of real, absolute being essential to every thought, and so excluded the existence of *negative ideas*.

1418. Bardilli, pursuing the same path, openly pronounced the abolition of the distinction between *empty ideas* and *apprehending ideas*. After this confusion, he claimed to have found the source of the errors of ancient philosophies. The basic

an emanation of the divine substance. The Manichaeans fell into the same error; St. Augustine accused Faustus of idolatry: *Ita convinceris innumerabiles deos colere* [Thus you are convicted of worshipping innumerable gods] (*Contra Faustum*, 15, 6). For this reason we can refute the errors of the German school with the same principles used by the Fathers to refute the different heresies derived from Platonism and the Cabala of the Hebrews. Finally, I would like to confirm factually what I have said above: 'Any system in which human beings imagine and persuade themselves that they can form, and have formed a positive concept of God, must produce a false enthusiasm, that is, an extraordinary exaltation of spirit'. Ancient thinkers observed this effect in all the philosophical schools which claimed to have gained entry into the divine nature and to possess the secrets which that nature contains. The Gnostics or 'Those who know', as they were called, were such: the tone of the Valentinians was unutterably superior and proud. St. Irenaeus says of them: *Perfectos semetipsos vocantes, quasi nemo possit exaequari magnitudini agnitionis ipsorum, nec si Paulum aut Petrum dicas, vel alterum quendam Apostolorum sed plus omnibus se cognovisse, et magnitudinem agnitionis illius, quae est inenarrabilis virtutis, solos ebibisse* [They call themselves perfect as if no one, Peter or Paul, or any of the Apostles, can encompass the extent of their knowledge. They know more than all others, and they alone have imbibed to the full that knowledge which is of unspeakable virtue] (Bk. 1, c. 9). And what kind of life did these perfect people lead? No vice of course could stain their holiness; infinite wisdom was sufficient for them. But if we wish to see what monstrous and repulsive things they did, we need only read St. Irenaeus himself (*loc. cit.*) and Epiphanius (*Haer.*, 31) to learn about the nature of the perfection of these philosophers to whom the whole divine nature was manifest!

[1417–1418]

difficulty, he said, was logic, and consisted in the false restriction given to the value of logical principles:

> Logic was considered as the simple law of the forms of thought, an investigation restricted solely within the limits of the thinking subject, and isolated from metaphysics and the knowledge of beings. It was possible to draw up a code of rules, but in the end it was a frame without its picture.

This is clearly the source on which Hegel drew.

Bardilli's attempt to reduce metaphysics to logic is itself nothing more than the development and clearest expression of preceding systems. And in France some thinkers, influenced by the same error and the same spirit, now say 'that all philosophy is method'. Thus, on the one hand, everything is reduced to abstract ideas, which only establish method; on the other, because *empty ideas* are not permitted, imagination has to be brought in to make what is abstract concrete, and to fill up what is empty.[283] This is muddle-headed philosophy at its worse and the source of total confusion. Great creative activity is employed in interchanging and counterfeiting ideas, but such activity is false and evil.[284]

1419. It is even more extraordinary to see Bardilli, who reduces all thought to a first source identical with the source of being, designate *being in itself* with the quaint formula B-B, meaning simply *nothing*.[285] With the substitution of *nothing* for

[283] I have already indicated the Platonists' error; they change God into an abstract idea of the human mind, or change an abstract idea into God. Thus, the human mind is divinised; an idea becomes a real being, the first amongst beings. Such confusions and distortions indicate the philosophical chaos veiling the *great nothingness of the Buddhists*.

[284] The holy Fathers recognised a great activity of spirit in the Valentinians and in other astute heretics. St. Jerome says that a person cannot invent such errors, *nisi qui ardentis ingenii est, et habet dona naturae quae a Deo artifice sunt creata* [unless he is extremely astute and has gifts of nature created by God, the maker of all things]. He adds: *Talis fuit Valentinus, talis Marcion, quos doctissimos legimus* [Valentinus was such a man, and Marcion too, and according to what we read, they were very learned men] (*In Os.*, c. 10).

[285] The letter *B*, in Bardilli's system, indicates *reality*, that is, the *characteristic* which results from thought applied to its matter. The sign -*B* indicates thought present in its application. But how can thought present in its application to matter ever be a simple negation of matter?

being, we have come to the very opposite term of what was sought. The intention was to realise and complete all thought, but instead, *nothing* has been revealed as the foundation of *all thought*. Once again we see the source of Hegelianism.

1420. Moreover, Bardilli began from the *application of thought*; without this he knew we could not know *pure thought*. But *pure thought* was the term he sought. He therefore asked: 'How can thought as thought, in its application as application, be referred to thought itself as thought?' In other words, 'How can applied thought be referred to pure thought prior to any application?'[286]

Bardilli's thought as thought is void of subject, object, and relationship between subject and object; it is expressed with an infinitive, 'to think', which is determining and determined. But this kind of thought can only be an abstract, never experienced or known to exist in reality. Truly, thought can only be an act, and no act can exist unless someone performs it, and it has a term where it ends and comes to rest. Bardilli acknowledges that such thinking cannot be known in itself, but only in its application. However, like Schelling, he presents it without any proof, as if it were something subsistent and totally active.

1421. Here we should note how much philosophers of the German school abuse abstraction. It seems to be a principle of common sense that 'if a part of something is removed, the thing becomes smaller', and generally speaking, 'if a perfection is removed from a thing, the thing is more imperfect'. The object of thought is certainly a perfection of thought. And the extent and perfection of thought is in direct proportion to the number

---

[286] In Bardilli's system it seems that this absolute, *pure thought* is last, rather than first, because he starts from the *application of thought* and then refers everything to *pure thought*. It would seem therefore that our criticism of Bardilli at the beginning of this Article applies rather to Schelling. But if we examine Bardilli's system carefully, we will see that it deserves the same comment. He placed the foundation of all *reasonable knowledge* in the referral of everything to the absolute (thought as thought). Hence there is no knowledge, no certainty, before the referral of knowledge to the absolute. In such a system knowledge and human certainty begin only from the absolute. Bardilli's arguments for discovering this absolute are all gratuitous and hypothetical. Hence his system lacks a solid base on which to rest; it starts from a necessary *supposition*, as indeed Hegel claims.

of its objects: if I diminish the objects of thought, I restrict the knowledge available to thought by reducing it and rendering it less active. If I reduce the objects of thought to a very small number and to insignificant things, I greatly impoverish it. If finally I remove all its objects, real thought no longer exists; all that exists is an abstract concept of *thinking*, of the possibility of thought. Good sense, and common sense, will certainly agree that once thought has been reduced to this, we have brought it to its most imperfect state and made it a mere potency without act. This kind of abstract *thinking*, *empty* of every object, is an extremely tenuous abstraction. But not according to Bardilli! Following the steps of Schelling, he remains totally unaware of all this, and claims to have attained maximum activity of thought with this kind of abstraction. He denies that this thought is *empty*; instead, we must call it *pure thought*. This is all very strange; we must see what led these philosophers to such a novel error.

1422. We should first note that when thinking is stripped of all its *modes*, only *essential thought* remains, in other words, that which forms the *essence* of thinking activity. But at this point it is easy to suppose that this essence exists of itself, instead of recognising it as a simple mental *abstraction*. To fall into this equivocation and transform a *mental and abstract activity* into a real activity, it is sufficient to ignore the nature of our abstract conception (which is not a conception of anything, but a beginning of conception). The confused *essential thinking*, therefore, as we conceive it abstractly and initially (where it has no real, proper existence), with complete, subsistent thinking, and supposed that human thought, separated by the power of the mind from its objects and contemplated in itself, provides a concept of some activity of *essential*, and hence infinite thought.

They were not sufficiently conversant with the nature of our conception, which (in the order of nature) does not see the essences of subsistent things in themselves, but only in so far as sense submits them to it. The only thing our conception knows that is not submitted to it by sense is most common being, which does not constitute any real essence, that is, the essence of any subsistent thing. Our philosophers confused two meanings of the Latin word *infinitum*, which can be understood to denote either: 1. that a thing is not finished and lacks its necessary end and determinations — in a word, it is *most imperfect*; or 2. that it lacks any limits and restrictions, that is, it is *most perfect*. They took as most complete and most perfect that which is *undetermined*, and hence so imperfect that it cannot exist. With their phantasy they saw in this undetermination the infinite, but in the opposite sense to that in which they should have seen it. There is indeed a *negative infinite*, an infinite in potency, which is a proper object of our intelligence, and which, because our intelligence is not determined to anything, can receive all forms and determinations; but it is not a *positive* infinite. Hence, instead of seeing in the negative infinite a great void to be filled, they were content to see an infinite activity created by their phantasy. But even so, they could only acknowledge *nothing*, that is, the absence of everything in the *negative* infinite. Schelling says: 'The ego' (he means the primitive ego) 'is in no way a being or some thing; this negative property is its only attribute. The first problem of philosophy is to discover that which can be known absolutely as a being.'[287] They admit therefore that everything is created from nothing; they turn to nothing to discover our activity! If this is not an obvious contradiction, I don't know what is! God, it seems to me, has done justice to them by confusing their language in this way. They say: 'To philosophise about nature is the same as creating nature.'[288] God allowed them to attempt to create nature, and let them confess that they looked for and discovered in nothing all the creative activity in their power! As new creators, these philosophers had thus pronounced sentence on themselves. Their speculations were magnificent and laborious. But in the end the human being is discovered to be the creating activity. From him they removed everything not attributable to this creating activity. The only thing that remained after this removal was the activity they were looking for. And what was this activity? In their own words, it was nothing, perfect nothing.

1423. From this came the erroneous belief that the simple concept of thought, stripped of its objects, contained something infinite, an infinite activity. The real, positive objects of our thought are limited, and were taken as limitations of thought.

---

[287] *System des transcendentales Idealismus*, 1800, vol. 3, pp. 48, 49.
[288] *Naturwissenschaft*, p. 3.

Consequently, our philosophers believed that if all the limitations were removed, there would be an infinite thought. But to think that the limitations would be removed from thought if the finite objects were removed is an error. This would be true if thought had *per se* an infinite, complete object limited by finite objects. But thought has *per se* an infinite object, *being in all its universality*, which is only initially, not completely infinite — we should call it undetermined rather than infinite taken in the positive sense; 'Being which we see is the act of being at its inception but lacking the terms by which the act is completed and finalised'. Furthermore, when finite, determined objects are received into the mind, being in all its universality does not cease to shine there. Such being remains immutable, and is only partially determined, completed and perfected in the limited objects presented to it. Limited objects are 'the partial perfections of the idea of being in all its universality'. This idea remains permanently in the mind, but if its partial perfections, that is, its determinations, are removed, it remains in the state of its original, maximum imperfection, as it was when it first became present to us. With the conception of particular objects the mind is drawn from potency to act. These objects of thought, that is, essences or ideas, are therefore *forms* (as the ancient thinkers clearly knew), not *matter* of the intellect which the forms perfect by drawing it to a more perfect act (cf. vol. 2, 1005 ss.).

1424. If I take a limited object and remove its limits, it becomes in some way unlimited for me. Although this reasoning can be applied to *objects* of thought, it cannot be applied to *thought* itself in the way that Bardilli and some other Germans apply it. They do not distinguish in the objects 1. what is positive, and 2. limitation, but suppose that the objects themselves are simply the limitations of thought. This is because they do not distinguish precisely enough the *act* of thought from its *object*. Instead of beginning from the object, they begin from the act, as I said above (cf. 1338 ss.); they attribute to the act of thought what is true only of its object.

1425. Moreover, we can see how the materialism of our times has penetrated such abstract speculations, which seem directed to an exaggerated spiritualism. Because materialists always direct their thoughts to what takes place in feeling, they speak of the understanding in a way applicable solely to feeling. They see *matter* in feeling, and therefore suppose that all the objects of the understanding, which according to them are similar to *matter*, restrict and limit the understanding; they do not know the being of the objects as *form*. By removing the objects from the understanding, they think they are ridding it of some material restriction.[289]

Nevertheless, they sometimes fall into the contradiction mentioned above: they put what is greatest and positive into what is negative. They are unable to see that once the understanding is despoiled of its objects, it is weakened and diminished, and finally becomes nothing.

1426. Bardilli says that thought, stripped of every object and subject, is purified, leaving only *thought as thought*, in other words, leaving essential thought. But, he says, this thought precisely as thought is the *possibility of things*. Here we find once more that ambiguity I have so often indicated: the attribution to the act of thought of what appertains only to the object of thought. As I have shown, *possibility* is merely a property of the essential object of thought, that is, of being in all its universality, but Bardilli, however, finds it in thought as thought, not in the object of thought. He has thus transferred to the act of thought that which is proper to the *object*.

1427. Moreover, Bardilli expresses this *possibility* with a negative quantity.[290] But possibility is far from being a pure negation of reality; a negative quantity is less than nothing, and cannot exist in the mind without a relationship to a positive quantity.

Nevertheless *possibility*, which for him on the one hand is a negative quantity, and on the other the foundation of *reality*, is *thought as thought*, the supreme activity, God himself!

---

[289] But St. Thomas taught that the object of thought perfected thought: *Species enim intelligibilis principium formale est intellectualis operationis, sicut forma cuiuslibet agentis principium est propriae operationis* [The intelligible species is the formal principle of intellectual action, just as the form of any agent whatsoever is the principle of its own action] (*C.G.*, I, c. 46). And in chapter 48, he says: *Intellectum est perfectio intelligentis: secundum enim hoc intellectus perfectus est quod actu intelligit* [What is understood is the perfection of the one who understands. The intellect, you see, is perfect because it understands in act].

[290] According to Bardilli, -*B* is a sign expressing *possibility*.

Possibility is therefore less than nothing, and Bardilli's God is less than nothing; not only nothing, but less than nothing is divinised! This *possibility*, however, is *thought as thought* and therefore present in the human being: human *thought*, which is declared to be less than nothing, is now declared to be God himself!

1428. According to Bardilli, *reality* is only a new determination of *possibility*; it is therefore simultaneously a determination of less than nothing and a determination of God. *Matter* brings about this determination, but matter itself exists through thought and with thought, which multiplies itself by turning back on itself. Evidently, *possibility* and *reality* are factors present in every *object*; they are the components of nature which is simply a manifestation and determination of the God who is less than nothing!

These are not simply the delerious ramblings of sick people; they are the sellf-inflicted torments of rash human beings.

CHAPTER 3

The starting point of Victor Cousin's philosophy

Article 1

The system expounded

1429. Victor Cousin, professor of philosophy in the faculty of letters at Paris, derived a great deal of his teaching from the German school. But the clarity of his language, his own mental fertility and the sounder method he used enabled him to set out the teaching more elegantly and brilliantly and, at the same time, render it more popular and more in keeping with normal, human society.

1430. He begins with a fact of consciousness which, according to him, manifests three ideas constituting the *very basis of reason*.[291] He describes this fact in the following way:

> The study of consciousness[292] is the study of humanity. In the philosophical dictionary this study is called 'psychology'. In consciousness there are as many phenomena as in the external world, but all the facts of consciousness can be reassumed, and are reassumed (as I have shown on other occasions) in a single, constant, permanent, universal fact

[291] Lesson 5, 21st March 1828, p. 15.

[292] Too much care cannot be taken about precise expression when a discussion is reduced to its final terms. When an argument is greatly developed, the *least* defect in expression is fatal and the seed of serious errors in the consequences. I do not think it useless, therefore, to note even the smallest inexactitude in what Professor Cousin states. Here, for example, I note that the statement, 'The study of consciousness is the study of humanity', although very true in one sense, nevertheless presents another, false sense. *Consciousness* is intellective, and as such leads us to things outside consciousness which are needed for the study of humanity. The word 'consciousness', therefore, either expresses a subjective affection or leads to objects outside us which differ from our consciousness in their *act* of *existence*. In the former case, it is not true that the study of humanity is bound up with this consciousness. The study of humanity is completed through the study of these objects, although they are not in our consciousness.

[1429–1430]

which remains through all possible circumstances and is present in the consciousness of a shepherd or of a Leibniz. The only condition it requires is the act of consciousness itself.[293]

He goes on to describe this principal fact:

As long as a human being does not know or perceive himself, he has no consciousness of self; he knows and perceives nothing.[294] We cannot know anything except in so far as we are for ourselves,[295] that is, in so far as we know that we are. All knowledge, therefore, implies the knowledge of oneself,[296] although not a developed knowledge. It implies that we know at least that we are.[297] As long as a human being does not exist for himself, he is as though he were not; but from the instant that he knows himself (and note that I am not speaking of a developed, scientific knowledge), he knows himself only on condition that he knows everything else in the way he knows himself.[298]

[293] The words 'constant', 'permanent,' 'universal', and so on, are not to be understood in their rigorous sense. The fact of consciousness is indeed *conditioned*. It requires that consciousness begin, that it act. But the individual consciousness of human beings is not necessary nor has it always existed. Even the fact which manifests itself in our own contingent consciousness did not always exist.

[294] *Being in all its universality* is known by us before we have the *idea* of ourselves and long before we have consciousness of ourselves. We know being in all its universality even when we have only a pure feeling of ourselves, not knowledge of ourselves (cf. vol. 2, 439 ss.). Again, we know the external world, or at least our animality, before we know ourselves as persons.

[295] This phrase, 'We are for ourselves', is completely true only in Fichte's system, in which the ego posits itself with its own proper activity. But this *new* activity totally lacks sufficient reason, as I said (cf. 1388). Hence the ego which posits, determines and freely creates itself is a chimera when applied to the human being. It is true, however, that the passage from not having consciousness of self to having it is truly marvellous. It does indeed add something to ourselves, and through it we acquire a new mode of being.

[296] I deny this. All knowledge implies the *feeling* of oneself but not the *knowledge of oneself*.

[297] We know that we are, that is, we have the idea of our existence, after we have the idea of existence in general.

[298] When we know that we are, we also know what we are. In other words, when we know our existence, we also have the idea of our specific essence, as

Everything is given in everything.[299] When human beings perceive themselves, and even as they appear to themselves, they are already mentally in touch with all that they can apprehend later.

Let us see how Cousin explains his opinion that in any knowledge of ourselves all the rest is to be found. I hope I will not burden my readers if I quote the entire passage from this rather flamboyant philosopher. He says:

> When I perceive myself, I discern myself from all that I am not.[300] In perceiving myself from all that I am not, I do two things: 1. I affirm myself as existing; 2. I also affirm as existing that from which I distinguish myself.[301] I am not myself, I am not this self which remains separate from all that is foreign to me unless I distinguish myself from all the rest;[302] and distinguishing oneself from something is to

St. Augustine maintained in other words (cf. fn. 128, and 1201). This is not the case with many other things whose existence we can know without knowing what they are positively. What we know of them is simply a *relationship* with something that we know positively.

[299] This is one of those striking phrases that say nothing in particular. It seems obvious to me that what is necessary does not embrace what is contingent (real), nor does anything contingent embrace any other contingent thing not depending on it. Therefore, everything is not given in everything.

[300] This is equivocal. If I perceived only myself, I would still not know the rest in any way. If the sentence means that I would not confuse myself with anything else, which I do not know, its meaning is only too obvious; but if it means that I distinguish myself from other things with a positive act, as Cousin intends, this can never be an indispensable condition of the immediate perception of myself.

[301] I deny this consequence. The reason for my denial is found in the previous footnote. Because I do not think in any way of all that I am not, there is no possibility of confusing myself with what I am not thinking, that is, with what I do not know. Not thinking of something is a non-affirmation of its existence.

[302] I repeat that it is enough for me to distinguish myself *negatively*, that is, it is enough for me *not* to know all other things, and to know myself alone in order for me to be distinguished from everything else. Cousin's reasoning supposes as true the very thing under examination and hence begs the question. Let us imagine that it were true that in our first knowledge of ourselves we perceived all other things. Only in this case would it be true that

suppose as existent[303] that from which one distinguishes oneself. We do not find ourselves except by finding something that surrounds us and consequently limits us.[304] Try to turn back on yourselves a little and you will see that the ego which you are is the ego limited on all sides by exterior objects.[305] The ego is, therefore, finite, and in so far as it is limited and finite, it is the ego.[306] But if the exterior world limits the ego and becomes an impediment to all my senses, the ego also acts on the exterior world, modifies it, opposes its action and to some degree imposes its own action upon it. This degree of action, although weak, is a boundary or limit of the external world.[307] So the world or the non-ego which, in its opposition to the ego is the limit

we could not perceive ourselves except by affirming at the same time the existence of the other things — existence distinct from ourselves.

[303] I grant this if we are speaking of distinguishing ourselves with a positive act, but I do not need to posit any act to ascertain that a thing perceived by me may not be confused with something else which I do not know. Let us imagine that I perceive the cupola of St. Peter's basilica. Do I have to perceive the leaning tower of Pisa as well in order not to confuse one with the other? Or affirm the existence of the Sixtine obelisk in order to say that I have perceived distinctly the Vatican Apollo? One perception is distinct from another of its nature, not through a positive act by which I separate it from other things by affirming its existence. I do not deny, however, that I form a more distinct notion of each thing when I find and note greater differences between them, especially if they are alike.

[304] We are limited by other things only in so far as they are part of our constitution; it is our nature itself that is limited. We perceive our limits therefore when we perceive our nature, which in itself is essentially distinct from other natures.

[305] External things not constituting human nature can put limits to the *exercise* of our faculties and to the *effects* that these faculties can produce outside themselves. This, however, is only a consequence, an effect; it is not an essential limitation of human nature. It is not the world which limits us essentially; if the external world did not exist, we would still be limited.

[306] Not in so far as it is limited by exterior things, but in so far as it has an internal limitation, intrinsic to its nature.

[307] The exterior world does not receive its limitation from the ego, but has it in itself, in its own nature. We cannot even say, properly speaking, that the ego limits the *action* of the forces of the exterior world. It simply modifies its effects; the quantity of action of these forces remains the same. When the ego and the forces in the world are reciprocally opposed to one another, they sometimes impede one another in their *movements* and effects, and sometimes they help and stimulate one another.

of the ego, is in its turn contradicted, modified and limited by the ego. At the same time, therefore, as the ego is constrained to acknowledge itself as limited, terminated and finite, it marks out in its turn the external world (the non-ego, from which it distinguishes itself) as terminated, limited and finite.[308] This is the mutual opposition in which we find ourselves, and it is as permanent in our consciousness as our consciousness is permanent.[309]

Up to this point we have been listening to the language of Fichte. Cousin now goes forward unhesitatingly, taking Schelling, as he thinks, for companion. He says:

Careful consideration shows us that this opposition is summed up in a single, identical notion, that is, the notion of what is finite. This ego that we are is finite; the non-ego which limits the ego is equally finite and limited by the ego.[310] Although limited in different degrees, they are both limited; we are therefore still in the sphere of the finite. Is there nothing more in consciousness?

At the moment that consciousness perceives the ego as finite in its opposition to the non-ego, which is equally finite, it refers this limited, relative and contingent ego and non-ego to a higher, absolute and necessary unity which contains them in itself and unfolds them. All the characteristics of this unity are opposite to those which the ego finds in itself and in the non-ego, which is analogous to it.[311] This unity is absolute, just as the ego and the

---

[308] All this is false, as we said in the preceding footnotes. The world would still be limited, even if human beings did not exist.

[309] We feel ourselves by means of a fundamental feeling. This feeling of ourselves accompanies the *sensations* which we receive from the exterior world. These sensations partly limit us, and partly remove our natural limitation which results from total absence of external sensible perceptions and the ignorance present in us prior to our acquisition of sensations.

[310] See the preceding footnotes.

[311] The analysis of *intellective perception* does not provide all this. But it does tell us that human beings, in perceiving something finite, such as themselves, or some real external thing (all external things are so independent in their concept that one can be perceived without the other), refer what is finite, perceived with feeling, to the *idea of being in all its universality*, and through this relationship understand the finite thing. In this first operation *being* is an absolute, necessary unity, but only in the *logical order*, where it is

non-ego are relative; and it is a substance,[312] just as the ego and the non-ego, although substantial through their relationship with substance, are in themselves simple phenomena and, like phenomena, limited and subject to appearance and disappearance.[313] Moreover, this higher unity is a cause as well as a substance. Indeed, the ego feels itself only in its acts, that is, as a cause that acts on the exterior world.[314] The exterior world enters the knowledge of the ego only through the impressions it makes upon the ego, that is, through the sensations experienced but not produced by the ego which, because it cannot destroy the sensations or refer them to itself, refers them to a cause, to something foreign to itself. This cause outside the ego is

not apprehended as a real being having *subsistence* in itself. In this respect, it would be recognised as substance and real cause. In the first perception, therefore, something absolute is present, that is, being as the *beginning of knowledge*, but not being as *subsistent*, that is, substance and supreme cause.

[312] The *idea of being* contained in perception is not yet a *subsistence* for us, and cannot therefore be called a substance or efficient cause; it is simply a formal cause. It is, of course, true that by reflection on being itself, one can arrive at knowledge of the necessary existence of a first, subsistent Being, the complement of ideal Being. This does not mean, however, that we have perceived it in the first intellective act; it does mean that we have some indication, some likeness of it, and a condition and rule enabling us to acknowledge it. In a word, we have a kind of incipient introduction to first, subsistent Being. A person may ask for directions to some place, and be told: 'This is the way'. He sees and perceives the right road, but he has not yet perceived his destination. He simply knows the way to go. Another person may be taught how to measure height, but this does not mean that he has calculated the altitude of any particular position. Knowing the *way* or *rule* for discovering things, or knowledge, is not at all the same as having the thing or the knowledge. Consequently if, in the analysis of perception or indeed in the very first act of our intelligence, we find a datum, a way or a rule according to which we can reason to the knowledge of the existence of a first, absolute Being, an essential subsistence and cause of everything, it does not follow from this that the existence of such a Being is given to us in our first intellection. Still less must we conclude that we perceive the same Being in the first of our perceptions.

[313] The intellective *myself*, having appeared once, does not disappear; it is immortal. The elements of matter do not disappear; only the various ways in which they come together.

[314] It also feels itself interiorly, and because it feels itself it feels the exterior world. However, it *adverts* to feeling itself only after it has felt the exterior world.

the world and, like the ego, is finite.[315] The unity, in other words, the substance-cause containing the ego and the non-ego, must in consequence of its nature be an infinite cause.[316]

Article 2

It is impossible to begin from Cousin's threefold perception

§1. *It is not necessary that the absolute, infinite cause be perceived in the first perception*

1431. We must not confuse the *order of real things* with the *order of ideas*, which are present only to the mind. In the order of real things it is clear that no contingent, limited ens can subsist unless an absolute, necessary ens exists to give the contingent ens existence. But granted the subsistence of limited, contingent entia, *can* they *be perceived* without need of the perception of the absolute, necessary being which has given them existence? This question appertains to the order of knowledge and to the way in which we perceive. It is not to be confused with the previous question.

1432. The direct method to follow in resolving this second question is certainly not that of examining the relationship of contingent with necessary ens. This would mean having recourse to the *order of real things*, although our present question deals with the search for the *order* and *nature of ideas* and perceptions. The true, natural method can only consist in taking

[315] Here Cousin presupposes that the human spirit 1. feels itself modified by the exterior world; 2. unable to refer these modifications to itself, refers them to an exterior agent, that is, to the world; 3. resorts finally to an unlimited cause because the world is limited. But are these not three essentially successive steps? Our spirit cannot refer its sensations to the exterior world before having first experienced the sensations themselves. Nor can it resort to the final cause without first having experienced sensations, referred them to the world, and found that the limited world requires some unlimited being. If these three steps are successive, they cannot all be found in the first act of consciousness. First, the sensations have to enter this act; then the thought of the exterior world, that is, the perception of bodies; and thirdly reflection, by which we finally raise ourselves to God.

[316] Lesson, 21st March 1829.

intellective perception as it is in fact, *observing it*, and submitting it to analysis. We must not examine it *a priori* as it *should* be, but be content with acknowledging it as it *is*.

All Cousin's arguments are reduced to establishing how perception should be. This is an abuse of *a priori* reasoning. Substantially he is saying: 'The finite cannot *stand* without the infinite; therefore the finite cannot *be perceived* without the infinite.' The principle is true, the consequence is false. The principle pertains to the *order of real things*; the consequences pertain to the *order of ideas*. The two orders have been confused. What is true in the first order need not necessarily be believed as true in the second order, unless it has been proved.

We must not begin, therefore, by imposing laws on the nature of our knowledge. Our ability does not extend that far. We must rather begin from experience, take the fact of knowledge as it is, not as we think it ought to be, analyse it and see what it contains. Then we can see what laws it follows.

But *perception* is limited and terminated in the objects perceived (cf. vol. 2, 514–517). It does not go a step beyond them. If the object is single and limited, the term of perception is equally single and limited. But doesn't the perceived object exist in dependence upon other objects? That is true, but the perception of that object exists independently of the perception of the objects on which the prior object depends. I can perceive and know a child in its own, proper existence without knowing its parents; I can know a brook without knowing its source; I can know a fruit without having seen the plant on which it has grown. Nevertheless, the child does not exist without the parents, the brook without the source, the fruit without the plant. Equally, I can perceive what is limited without positively perceiving what is unlimited, although what is limited cannot be without the unlimited. And if we wish to analyse carefully the intellective perception of limited entia, we shall find that, although intellective perception includes an incipient concept of what is unlimited (the idea of being), it has no *positive* knowledge, no *perception* of an unlimited, subsistent ens. This distinction between the *positive part* and the *empty* or *incipient part* of our ideas is sufficient to dissolve all apparent reasons serving as a basis for Cousin's opinion, which I regret I cannot share.

[1432]

§2. It is not necessary for us to perceive ourselves intellectually when we perceive the world

1433. I shall prove this proposition in the way I have proved the preceding proposition. I shall first ask the reader to follow a careful analysis of the act of perception, and then further illuminate the proof by making use of a quality common to the act of perception and any action of a finite ens. For still greater clarification again, I shall set out the whole argument in a series of propositions.

First proposition: Experience shows that every action of a limited ens has a term, either outside the agent or at least distinct from the beginning of the action. Indeed, the action of a limited ens, which begins, proceeds and finishes, is a kind of movement through which the activity of the ens passes from its state of virtuality or potency, and produces its effect. This effect, the term of the activity which unfolds and moves outwardly, is always different from the principle and root of the act. If it were in no way different, it would not be possible to conceive that any change had taken place. The concept of change contains essentially diversity and distinction.

If the action terminates outside the acting ens, this must come about through a kind of touch or extremely close, continuous *union* with the externally produced effect at the moment of its production. When the effect has been produced, it is detached, or seems to have been detached, from the action of the cause which produces the effect. Sometimes the cause ceases altogether, and the effect remains alone, perfectly distinct and exterior. The law governing the activity of every ens, therefore, is that it should move from inside itself outwards. In other words, the root of the activity is in the intimate nature of the agent, while the term is either at the extremity of, or altogether outside the agent. It follows as a corollary that the first term of the action of a finite ens is never its own root-entity.

1434. *Second proposition:* If every new action of entia proceeds from within to without entia, this must also occur relative to the human understanding when it acts in perception. This, too, is confirmed by experience. The agent who understands, therefore, can never have himself as the first object of his intellective faculty.

1435. *Third proposition:* The term of perception is its object: the object of perception is that which human beings perceive and know through perception. This proposition is obvious. Its corollary states that what is perceived with the act of perception is simply the object of the perception and nothing more. If human beings were to perceive something different from the object of perception, this perceived thing would be the *object* by definition.

1436. *Conclusion.* Therefore the human being, an intellective ens, cannot perceive himself but only something else presented to him as object. Experience confirms this: human beings do not perceive themselves except by means of a *reflective* movement through which they return upon themselves. The exterior world, on the contrary, is perceived with a direct perception by means of which human beings abandon and forget themselves, as it were, in order to go out to know the world where their perception terminates and where they arrive as a result of the limitation of their limited object.

The exterior world is not the ego who perceives; in the same way, the perception of the exterior world and that of the ego are two essentially distinct perceptions. It is impossible for human beings to perceive these two objects (the first time) with an identical perception, not only because they are essentially distinct, but also because they are presented to us by two essentially different feelings, that is, by an interior feeling and by external sensations. As a result, the act of perception in these two perceptions takes a contrary direction: the act of perceiving the world goes from inside out, while the act of perceiving oneself has as it were a circular direction[317] from within to within. But the same act cannot have two contrary directions, and it is absurd to say that a single, first perception perceives the ego and the world as one.

This false belief could have originated from confusion between *feeling* and *intellective perception*. In perceiving the

---

[317] I realise that this language is metaphorical. It does, however, express clearly the essential difference between the act with which the world is perceived and the act with which one perceives oneself.

world, or any other object, we are always accompanied by the feeling of ourselves. The conclusion, therefore, is that we also perceive ourselves intellectually. The consequence is not valid, however: feeling is essentially different from intellective perception.

§3. *The first, essential intellection from which every reasoning moves forward is that of being in all its universality*

1437. The threefold perception described by Professor Cousin as the beginning of the operations of the human spirit is, therefore, non-existent. The human spirit, when it first moves to perceive something, can perceive only what feeling administers to it. Just as feeling is twofold, that is, feeling of ourselves and of exterior things, so the spirit has only two kinds of essentially different perceptions, perception of itself and of the external world.

The perception of *what is infinite* is not experienced in this life because the infinite being does not manifest itself to our spirit as subsistent. We have, therefore, only a negative or incipient idea of the infinite being drawn from *reflection* which reasons about *perceptions* of self and the world, and through which we acknowledge that these finite entia could not be, unless there were something through which they were.

The human spirit, therefore, must take as its first step one of the two intellective perceptions mentioned above, either 1. that of the world, or 2. that of itself. Because these perceptions are mutually exclusive, the human spirit must start from one or the other; it cannot start from both.[318]

[318] St. Thomas makes the development of the human understanding begin with the perception of the sensible world. Only after this has been perceived, he thinks, does the intellect turn back on itself. And this is true. There is nothing that can move our reason to look at itself for the sake of seeing and knowing itself (an almost unnatural movement, one might say) unless it has been drawn from its natural calm by stimulation from external things, which first attract the attention of the understanding. In this respect, the understanding can be likened to the eye which never sees itself first, but turns its gaze on the exterior bodies which make up the scene it first perceives. In fact, the eye would never see itself without a mirror in which it beholds not itself but its image, as it sees the exterior body of the amalgam-coated glass.

[1437]

The analysis of both these perceptions shows that the human spirit, whether it begins its activity with one or the other, could not begin with either unless it first had an essential, interior intuition. This intuition is not of a being subsisting in itself, but of being in all its universality, *initial* being, as we have called it, which makes itself most common to all things. This *conception*, prior to all that is acquired in the mind, has to be taken as the true principle of philosophy, just as it is from this *first conception* that every human being begins his acts of reasoning. The peasant talking about his flocks and furrows, as well as the intellectual meditating on the movement of the stars and on the divine nature, depends upon this conception.

However, this second part of the similarity does not, properly speaking, harmonise with the understanding which in contradistinction to sense possesses a *reflective* power enabling it, as Dante says, 'upon itself, itself to turn'. Nevertheless before reflection, the understanding must be put into motion and drawn towards its direct act (cf. *S. T.*, I, q. 87, art. 1).

[1437]

CHAPTER 4

Pure *a priori* reasoning does not lead us to know anything in the order of subsistent, finite entia

1438. Our previous arguments have established the possibility of *a priori* reasoning. They prove the presence in our mind of a luminous point, anterior to all sensible experience and posited in us as an element, as it were, of our nature. This luminous point is *being*, always intimately present to us.

Having illustrated the possibility of *a priori* reasoning, we can use the following principle to establish its limits: 'Everything included in the idea of being, or capable of being drawn by reason from this idea alone, without help from any other datum of experience, appertains to pure *a priori* reasoning'; and everything that needs, apart from the idea of being, some other datum of external or internal experience in order to be known by us, does not appertain to pure *a priori* reasoning.

1439. With this as our basis, the analysis of the idea of *being in all its universality* will show the forces present in *a priori* reasoning by enabling us to reply to the following questions: 1. What does this idea contain in itself? 2. What does it presuppose as its condition? 3. What does it not contain? 4. What cannot be deduced by reasoning from its content? Let us begin with the last two questions so that through exclusion we may restrict the field of our enquiry.

I. What does *being* itself as present to the mind not contain?

We saw that being, as it stands essentially before the spirit, is incomplete. This lack of completion consists in lack of its terms, and explains why it is called *initial* being, and consequently *common* being. Lacking terms, it is naturally capable of being terminated and completed in infinitely different ways. A consequence of such a limitation is that this being manifests existence only in the mind — as object and nothing more.

1440. Very careful attention has to be paid here to avoid confusion between two totally different things. It is one thing to say 'a being present to the mind' and another to say 'a modification of the mind' as though the being that we see is nothing more than ourselves as modified. If this were the case, this being would be a subjective entity.

Such a distinction is almost unknown in our days, but it is nonetheless true and very relevant. I repeat what I have said so many times: philosophers must not flee before facts, but admit them *all*, and gratefully accept the results obtained from their analysis. I can indeed say on occasion 'I don't understand', and I may marvel at what stands before me, but I must accept facts, and not presume that something is only what I have imagined it to be. If I do make this presumption, I shall never attain true knowledge, but grasp today at what will elude me tomorrow; today's knowledge will be tomorrow's mistake. But, as I have said, careful analysis of the first fact concerning our mind, that is, the analysis of the intuition of being, provides us with these two truths: 1. that the being present to our mind is objective and not subsistent in itself; 2. that it is not a simple modification of our mind.

1441. 1. It is truly present to our mind, but it is still not a subsistent being in itself outside the mind. What is meant by 'a being present to the mind?' It means a being that has its existence in the mind in such a way that if we were to suppose that *no mind* existed to which it were present, this being would not be. In other words, its mode of being is intelligibility itself, outside the mind, but in the mind. Through it we know not the act of existing in itself, but the act of existing in the mind.

When this definition has been well understood, it is obvious of itself that initial, most common being presents to our spirit a simple possibility, not subsistence of any kind. It presents what I would call a project of being, but no being truly complete and actuated in itself.

To know, therefore, that innate being is a simple, logical principle, a governing rule of our spirit, an idea and still not a real ens, it is sufficient to examine and analyse impartially this being that we see naturally. Precisely because it renders itself most common to all subsistent entia, it is not any of them, nor can it be. It is simply the foundation and knowability of them all.

This truth is enough to confute philosophers, ancient and modern, who confuse the order of ideas with the order of real things, and either make a God of *ideal being* or fabricate separate intelligences for *essences* or *ideas* of things. They do not understand the nature of ideal being which, although present to the mind, is not a modification of the limited, finite subject which sees it.[319]

1442. 2. In the second place, I maintain that it is neither a simple modification of the mind, nor of the subject which intuits it.

This truth is also shown through a careful consideration of *being* itself in all its universality. As we think of being, we see that being thought by us is the *object* of our mind, or rather is the *objectivity* of all the terms of our mind, as we have said on so many occasions.

It is, therefore, of its essence distinct from the subject and from all that appertains to the subject; its light is superior to the subject; the subject, relative to being in all its universality is that which receives, while being is of its essence received in a way altogether proper to itself: the subject must see it, even more than the open eye is forced to sense the bright rays of the sun shining upon it and impressing themselves on its retina: being is immutable, it is what it is; the subject is mutable: being imposes the law, and actuates the subject by rendering it intelligent. We must note, however, that the subject cannot be said, properly speaking, to *experience* the object, because the presence of the object simply provides a mode for the subject and obliges it to arouse in itself a new activity. We must say, therefore, that an *increase of act*, rather than an *experience*, is effected in the subject.

All these observations are valuable for refuting the contrary error of the philosophers previously mentioned, and of all those who, finding the idea of being void of any real ens subsisting outside the mind, go on to deny that it has any real objectivity and maintain that it is purely subjective, that is, a pure modification of the subject.[320]

Careful observation, focused on this being which naturally shines before our minds, brings us therefore to establish that

---

[319] Hardouin's *Athei detecti*, contains an underlying, dominant and true concept, that is, to divinise *logical truth* is a kind of atheism. Read from this point of view, the book is not without interest.

[320] Even Galluppi did not avoid this slip.

'although it is an object essentially different from the subject that intuits it, nevertheless being is not thought by us as furnished with any other existence than that which shines before our mind. Consequently, if *every* mind were removed, being would no longer be conceived. In this sense one speaks of this being as an ideal ens'.

1443. Those dedicated to systematisation will now stand up and object: 'If such *being* does not subsist in itself, independently of the mind, it cannot be other than a modification of the subject. There is no middle way here.' This kind of statement, which is a continual imposition of laws on nature, and an endeavour to reduce nature to one's own point of view, leads us along a very slippery path. Is a middle way impossible? I am not investigating, I am not even interested in knowing whether a middle way is *possible*. It is enough to have pointed out that being, seen by the human mind, is neither *real and subsistent* (in so far as it is seen by us) nor a modification of our mind. If fact tells me that neither the one nor the other of these extremes is actual, I conclude without hesitation that there is a middle term. Every wise and intelligent person must be content with fact: it follows that if a thing is, it must be possible.

Having come to know the nature of *being* that shines in our minds, we can say with confidence that it neither contains in itself nor shows us any real ens subsisting outside the mind. Intuiting being, therefore, cannot provide us with any knowledge whatsoever of things which subsist in a contingent mode.

1444. II. What cannot be deduced from *being* in all its universality?

The *subsistence* of any limited being cannot be deduced. In fact, being in all its universality does not require any limited ens. Consequently every limited ens is only contingent, not necessary. We say that an ens is *necessary* when it is the condition without which the *being* in our minds would not be; in other words, the possible being shining in our minds would have to be conditional on this necessary ens.

The solution of these two questions, therefore, proves the truth of what I indicated in the title of this chapter, that is, 'the forces present in pure *a priori* reasoning are not powerful enough to enable us to attain through them to knowledge of the subsistence of a limited ens'.

1445. We can, therefore, state the rule for correct philosophical method in the following way: 'To attain to knowledge of subsistent, finite entia we must always travel without deviation the road of experience on pain of losing ourselves in vague, abstract reasoning which in the face of facts is valueless.'

CHAPTER 5

A *priori* reasoning leads us to logical principles that appertain to the order of ideal beings

Article 1

Definitions

1446. I call *a priori knowledge* that which descends from the *idea* of being, the form and supreme rule of reason.

1447. I call *pure a priori knowledge* that which not only descends from the idea of being, but also descends from it without need of any datum of internal or external experience. It is, therefore, *knowledge* which can be found on analysis in *being* itself, or can be deduced from it in the way that a condition can be deduced from that on which it is conditional.

Article 2

The extent of pure *a priori* knowledge

1448. The analysis of pure being is conducted without the intervention of any datum of experience. It does not allow us, therefore, to distinguish within this being anything except the characteristics of *unity* and perfect *simplicity*. In this way we find as given in the primal idea 1. its *first activity*, which is that of being; and 2. the essential characteristic of this *first activity*, which is that of *absolute unity*.[321] All our pure *a priori know-ledge* is reduced to these two notions, and to a few others which

---

[321] *Absolute* unity does not exist separate from the *idea of being*. We would not have imposed on it another word, *unity*, different from that which we give to *being*, if the exclusion of multiplicity from being had not been necessary. In so far as *unity* is considered separately from being, it indicates only a *negation*, the negation of *multiplicity*. This explains the futility of so much speculation on *unity*, which lacks foundation because it considers *unity* as something in itself, divided from being.

we have indicated elsewhere. Such knowledge shows us how *unity* stands at the spring of intellective knowledge, enabling us to understand how all true unity comes from the intellect, and how human cognitions share in that marvellous unity.

1449. *Multiplicity* is an *a posteriori* cognition, that is, one given by experience. Not only is it not contained in *ideal being*, but it cannot even be deduced from it by reasoning alone. Although the acts with which the spirit reflects on being can be repeated, they all end in the same, identical being, which cannot be seen to be multiplied unless it is considered in relationship with the various acts of the spirit constituting the beginning of experience.

In addition to analysis, pure *a priori* reasoning can also be employed on being. But we will speak about this in the next chapter.

Article 3

The extension of *a priori* knowledge

1450. Being that we see comes to completion and terminates in various limited ways when it is applied to the data provided by experience. Human knowledge is constituted in this way.

We know three kinds of things: 1. entia which subsist in themselves, without reference to the mind, such as bodies; 2. feelings; 3. ideal entia, essences. The first two constitute the *matter* of our knowledge; the third, the *form*. Everything formal in knowledge is *a priori* knowledge (cf. vol. 1, 304–309, 325–327). Let us now examine the extent of this knowledge.

1451. *Being* takes other names as soon as it is considered in its different relationships. These names express the relationships in which it is beheld. If *being* is seen as the fount of intellective knowledge, it is called *truth*; if it is considered as the first activity, capable of being completed with subsistence and essentially lovable, it is called *good* or *perfection*.

The ideas of *what is true* and of *what is good* arise, therefore, from the very first application of being, and constitute the two most general aspects in which the idea of being is presented in its applications. These ideas correspond to the two modes of essences, that is, in the mind and outside the mind. Being in its application in the mind as the fount of knowledge is *truth*; being in its application outside the mind as the fount of lovable subsistence is *good*.

1452. *Truth*, therefore, is the general relationship of being with other cognitions, all of which call being into play as their support and criterion. Let us consider the partial modes taken by being in its partial applications.

First, we have seen that pure *a priori* knowledge, given by the analysis of being, contained two elementary ideas, the basis of all knowledge: 1. the idea of the activity which is ideal being; and 2. the idea of absolute unity. Consequently there are two series of principles in the application of being, according to the two elements which compose it.[322]

Considered positively as activity, being takes the form of the four principles of cognition, contradiction, substance and cause that we have already expounded (cf. vol. 2, 559–569).

Considered as *absolute unity*, being is the first element and foundation of the idea of quantity, and is then transformed into the principles that govern quantity such as 'the whole is greater than its parts', and other principles of this kind, on which mathematical sciences rest.

1453. Briefly, in its application, being is changed and ends in all the *essences of things*. These essences are the principles of all the branches of knowledge, as antiquity had already affirmed.[323] The idea of being, therefore, is the fount and firm foundation of all human learning.

However, all these principles are in the order of ideas. Can we pass, therefore, from the idea of being to the sphere of reality? Does this idea possess any interior force enabling us to push

[322] This is not true composition. Unity is nothing of itself except the deletion of *multiplicity*, and does not therefore offend the simplicity of being. On the contrary, it is the very simplicity of being. But language of its nature leads to equivocal expressions. It indicates with a word not only that which is, but also the negation of that which is. Indicated in this way, even nothing appears to be something.

[323] 'The principle of all knowledge that human reason can have of anything,' says St. Thomas, 'is the concept of the thing's substance' (the *essence*), 'because the principle of demonstration is simply the essence itself of the thing' (*C. G.*, I, q. 3).

beyond it? These are the questions which we must examine in the following chapters. But first we shall confirm, with a new proof, the truth that what is deduced from being is deduced *a priori* because being itself is not produced by any abstraction, but given by nature.

CHAPTER 6

The underlying principle of the whole of this work is confirmed by a new argument: the idea of being is of such a nature that human beings cannot form it for themselves by abstraction

1454. The idea of being would not be in us prior to all experience if we could form it for ourselves through abstraction. If we could form it in this way, there would be no *a priori* reasoning, the forces proper to which I am describing in this Section. It will be useful, therefore, to reinforce the truth demonstrated in the Second and subsequent Sections, that is, that the idea of being cannot come to us through abstraction. The analysis just carried out on this idea offers us a new opportunity of doing this.

Let us examine the nature of abstraction to see what its capacities are. 'To abstract' means simply to separate a part or element of a thing and consider it as though the part from which it is separated did not exist. When I analyse an idea, therefore, I discover only what that idea contains. I do not impose any law on the idea; I simply adapt myself to it. I do not say first: 'Such and such *must* be found in this idea; such and such *must* not be found there.' I cannot establish any rule of this kind with pure abstraction, but only acknowledge that which is, without defining that which should be.

Nevertheless, the formation of abstracts is subject to certain unchangeable laws. For example, by power of abstraction I can consider extension in a straight line separately from a surface or solid extension. But the *abstract* that I have formed of the straight line is subject to the following law: 'It cannot reasonably be considered by me as a true ens, subsisting of itself and divided from the other two dimensions.' On the other hand, if I consider the upper half of a column and abstract from the lower half, I find that this kind of abstraction is subject to a different law: 'The upper half can be considered by me as an ens that really subsists, divided and detached from the lower half of the column.'

Again, I abstract the *weight* from a body. I can consider the body abstractly without weight for as long as I please, but subject to this law: 'If I consider it deprived of weight, I cannot at the same time consider it as heavy.' Either of these contraries is thinkable by me, but not the two together.

Abstraction has its limits and laws, therefore, which must be maintained. All of them can be reduced to three: abstraction cannot 1. make two contradictory things non-contradictory; 2. make it conceivable that an accident subsist without a substance; 3. make an effect conceivable without a cause. These three primary laws of abstraction are not produced by abstraction, but by the efficacy of the three principles of contradiction, substance and cause. The efficacy of these three principles cannot arise from abstraction, therefore. Abstraction is a faculty subject to these principles which it follows and obeys; it does not produce them.

But these principles, which impose limits and laws on abstraction itself, and on the other operations of human understanding,[324] are simply the *idea of being* considered in its applications.

The idea of being directs abstraction through its own intimate force, therefore, and imposes laws upon it. Consequently it cannot be produced and originated by abstraction (cf. vol. 1, 243).

1455. When in the course of this work I call the idea of being in all its universality *most abstract*, I do not mean, therefore, that it has been produced by the operation called abstraction,

---

[324] Some thinkers reduce all the operations of human understanding to *analysis* and *synthesis*. Let me simply observe that two kinds of synthesis have to be very carefully distinguished. They are very different from one another, and in one of them the understanding exercises a special efficacy which is not so marked in the other. The usual general definition of synthesis is 'a conjunction of ideas', but this cannot be considered valid because it indicates only one kind of synthesis. What it does not indicate requires greater attention because by it the spirit not only joins ideas already possessed, but produces new ideas for itself. It does this in two ways, the first of which is that of *primal synthesis*. Here the spirit, by joining a feeling to the idea of being, produces perceptions and ideas of things (cf. vol. 1, 118–132). The second appertains to the *integrating faculty* of the understanding through which we rise immediately from the idea of an effect to form that of a cause, or carry out some similar movement (cf. vol. 2, 623 ss.). *Negative* ideas are produced with the second kind of synthesis, *positive* ideas with the first.

but simply that of its own nature it is set apart and separate from all subsistent beings. It is true that in the order of formed abstractions it could be said that there is something more abstract than even the idea of being; the idea of *unity*, of *possibility*, and so on, are ideas that suppose an abstraction carried out on being itself, although they cannot be thought by the mind unless it continues to have *being* present to itself, and refers these ideas to being.

CHAPTER 7

Pure *a priori* reasoning leads to knowledge of the existence of something infinite, God

Article 1

How to reason without the use of any datum outside the idea of being

1456. Reasoning which uses no other datum than that of the idea of being in all its universality would at first seem impossible. We cannot, in fact reason without judgments and arguments, which are operations of the mind requiring several terms. The idea of being is, however, a most simple idea, and hence a single term. With being alone, therefore, every judgment and argument would seem impossible.

The difficulty vanishes, however, if we note that one and the same idea is multiplied in the mind according to the different ways in which it is used, and by the different *reflections* the mind makes on it. Every insight enabling us to see a new relationship in an idea which we possess provides us with a new idea. Let us apply this observation to the idea of being.

I have the idea of being in all its universality present to my mind. But, furnished with this idea, I can turn back on it and look at it again. As I look, I can observe, analyse and judge the idea. This is a truly extraordinary fact, but a fact nevertheless.

When I reason, for example, about the idea of being, and I say that it is universal, necessary, and so on, I am using the idea itself of being as a rule enabling me to know and judge all this. The idea of being is applied to itself, and acknowledges itself. It acts as predicate and subject, as the rule for *judging* and as the *thing judged*. The mind has this wonderful property of turning back on itself. Being, without losing its simplicity, has as it were a virginal capacity for multiplying and generating reasoning within itself.[325]

---

[325] Anyone having the idea of being, but devoid of sensation and stimuli, would never produce any reasoning. This is clear, and does not require any

Article 2

Hints about an *a priori* demonstration of the existence of God

1457. Some kind of reasoning can therefore be carried out with the idea of being as our sole datum. This reasoning is truly *a priori* and *pure* because it needs only a datum manifest *per se* to us, and not acquired by experience.

But I would go further and say that with the idea of being as our sole datum, we can elaborate a rigorous and extremely solid demonstration of the existence of God, which would therefore be an *a priori* demonstration in the sense in which we have defined it. However, I do not want to spend too long on this question and will therefore offer only some hints on the matter.

1458. *Being* in all its universality, thought naturally by the human mind, is of such a nature, we said, that on the one hand, it shows no subsistence outside the mind and can therefore be called *logical being*. On the other hand, it cannot be a modification of our spirit. In fact, its authority is such that our spirit is entirely subject to it. We are conscious to ourselves that we can do nothing against being, and cannot change it in any way whatsoever.[326] Moreover, it is absolutely unchangeable; it is the knowable act of all things, the fount of all cognitions. It has nothing contingent, and in this sense it is not like us. It is a light that we perceive naturally, but which rules, conquers and ennobles us by submitting us entirely to itself.

comment from me; the whole of my theory on the origin of ideas points to this. Such a realisation, however, does not damage our immediate question about the force present in *pure a priori* reasoning. We are not concerned with the material conditions and the *motive* which would impel us, while possessing only the idea of being, to carry out some effective reasoning. We are asking whether the idea of being itself includes all the *data* needed for this reasoning in such a way that, if the *motive* were present, the reasoning could be carried out. In a word, we are not asking stupidly and childishly if the baby in the mother's womb reasons *a priori*, but if a mature adult, and probably a philosopher can carry out *pure a priori* reasoning.

[326] *Intelligere pati est, scire autem facere* [To understand is to experience, to know is to act], says Aristotle (*De Anima*, bk 3, l. 7). By *to understand*, he meant what I call *to intuit*, that is, the intuition of essences which for this philosopher was not equivalent to *to know*. For him, *to know* meant having a reflective cognition which provides the *specific difference* between essences.

[1457–1458]

Again, although we can, if we wish, think that we might not be, it would be impossible to think that being in all its universality, that is, possibility, truth, might not be. Prior to me, what is true was true, nor is it possible for there to be a time when it could be otherwise. Yet truth is certainly not nothing. Nothing does not bind me; it does not oblige me to pronounce anything. But the nature of truth which shines within me, obliges me to say: 'This is', and even if I did not wish to make this statement, I would know that the thing would be in spite of me.

Truth, being, possibility presents itself to me as an eternal, necessary nature, and such that against it no power whatsoever can prevail. We cannot even conceive a power that can abolish truth. Nevertheless, we do not see how this truth subsists in itself, although we do feel its unconquerable force and the energy that it demonstrates within us as it subjects our own and all other minds to its gentle dominion, a fact without possibility of opposition.

This fact of truth, which stands before me and constitutes my intellectual light, tells me: 1. that there is an effect in me that cannot be produced either by myself or by a finite cause; 2. that this effect is the intuition of an object present to me as intrinsically necessary, immutable, and independent of my own mind and of every finite mind.

1459. These two elements lead me by two ways to the knowledge of the existence of God. If I apply to the first element the *principle of cause*, I must conclude: 'A cause exists that manifests an infinite power; this cause must, therefore, be infinite.' Considering the second, I see that if the cause which manifests an infinite power were to reveal itself, it would still be that same object of my mind which now presents itself as having existence in my mind alone. And so I conclude: 'The nature of this infinite cause is *to subsist* in a mind, that is, to be essentially intelligible. But if it must subsist in a mind, this mind must be eternally intelligent.'

When I compare this infinite cause with the definition of 'accident', I find that it cannot be just an accident, or generally speaking, a simple appurtenance of a substance, as it would appear if it were a purely mental object, and I conclude: 'An eternal mind exists which has the property of being *per se* intelligible, and of communicating intelligibility to other subjects, and as such is the *cause* of the infinite power manifested to our minds and of all our cognitions.'

An objection to this argument would be that it introduces us into the communication of being, and hence is not altogether pure. We reply that because we are dealing simply with a manifestation, we ourselves do not enter the argument except as the subject that intuits being. In this respect, we are somehow not separated from, although not confused with, that which is intuited.

1460. But if some purer reasoning is required, it will not be difficult to present.

Being has two aspects under which it can be regarded: relative to itself, or relative to us. Leaving aside completely the second aspect, and considering being purely as it is in itself, we found it to be simply incipient. Consequently, it is on the one hand a likeness of real, finite beings, and on the other the likeness of real, infinite being.[327] It can therefore be predicated univocally,[328] as they said in the Schools, of God and of creatures. With its terms hidden from us, it can actuate and terminate itself both in God and in creatures, but not of course in the same way.

It is also true that we do not have the necessary, internal efficacy to make being terminate without perceiving and experiencing its terms. With ideal being alone, therefore, we cannot have the perception of any subsistent ens whatsoever.

Nevertheless, contemplating initial being, we are able to know that as such it could not subsist without having its proper terms. It does not, in fact, present itself as having an absolute subsistence.[329] However, although we do not see any absolute

---

[327] *Cum ipsa intellectiva virtus creaturae non sit Dei essentia, relinquitur quod sit aliqua participata similitudo ipsius, qui est primus intellectus* [Because the intellective power of the creature is not the essence of God,' says St. Thomas, 'it has to be a kind of shared likeness of him who is the first intellect] (*S. T.*, I, q. 12, art. 2). Human beings, therefore. were created to the image and likeness of God.

[328] This question has been dealt with in the treatise of Carlo Francesco da San Floriano (Milan, 1771, tom. 2, p. 103) on the philosophy of Scotus where the work of the Doctor Subtilis is compared with that of modern philosophers.

[329] It is not necessary to prove here that initial being is not an accident or a modification of our spirit because 1. our spirit is supposed as unknown in

subsistence in it, the *principle of absolute subsistence* (which states: 'that which exists relatively supposes that which exists absolutely' and originates from being as the principle of substance does) enables us to judge that it must be reduced to and terminate in an absolute subsistence of which initial being is a mental appurtenance.

Having discovered this, we are also able to know that it is altogether impossible for this subsistent ens to be finite. If it were, it would not be a suitable term of initial being. On the contrary, it would be outside initial being; instead of forming with it an essence that is its proper term and complement, it would be something extraneous to it and its contingent effect.

Ideal being, therefore, requires an infinite, substantial actuation through which it has not only a *logical* existence before the mind but also an absolute existence — a *metaphysical* existence, as it is called. This is existence in itself: full, essential existence. And such a being is the divine essence.

In this way, subsistent, or metaphysical, *necessary being* is identified with *necessary, logical being* to which is added its natural term. We conclude, therefore, that two *per se* necessities,[330]

---

this argument, and therefore entirely excluded from it; 2. *being is per se* so distinct and separate from the spirit that it is impossible to confuse it with the spirit when both are considered *directly*. The first intuition of *being* excludes the perception of *ourselves* which, as we have said so many times, is reflective.

[330] Truly, when I say *necessity*, I can only express a pure relationship of the thing with the mind in the same way that *likeness* is only a relationship with the mind, as we have seen. When I say: 'This is a necessary ens', I am affirming that it cannot not be, that is, that its non-existence would imply a contradiction. We say it is necessary, therefore, because we see that the *principle of contradiction* forces us to admit that ens as existent. The *necessity* of an ens depends, therefore, on the principle of contradiction; and the principle of contradiction, although in the mind, is not the mind; it is logical necessity.

In fact, any ens, when considered in itself, and without relationship with its logical principles, offers us subsistence and nothing more. It does not provide us with the necessity of subsistence. Nevertheless, when human beings, furnished as they are with intelligence, perceive the subsistence of such an ens, they ask themselves: 'Could that ens not be?' If it is a necessary ens, they reply: 'No, that would be impossible. Its non-existence is repugnant.' In this way, we have compared it (its subsistence) with the possibility of its non-existence, and found a contradictory relationship. This

one logical and the other metaphysical, do not properly speaking exist. Only one exists, and this is simultaneously in the mind and in itself.

relationship is necessity. From this observation we can draw the following corollaries:

1. Logical and metaphysical necessity are a single necessity which consists in the relationship of contradiction that an ens has with its non-existence. When this relationship is considered as *possible*, we have what we call *logical necessity*, which forms the principle of contradiction; when considered as something real, it is called *metaphysical necessity*. The principle of contradiction, or logical necessity, is therefore the fount of metaphysical necessity.

2. *Necessary being* has a very close relationship with logical being. This relationship consists in the fact that *necessary being* must have an essentially intelligible nature. Otherwise, it would not be absolutely necessary, because in order to be such it would depend on something else, that is, a mind and a first idea essentially different from itself.

SECTION EIGHT

THE FIRST DIVISION OF THE BRANCHES

OF KNOWLEDGE

CHAPTER 1

The nature of the first division
of the branches of knowledge

1461. Anyone undertaking to form a genealogical tree of all the branches of knowledge has to begin by considering that whatever can be known by human beings forms a single body of knowledge. All previous divisions must be forgotten.

In our essay on the origin of ideas and the criterion of certainty, we have been led to consider all knowledge in this great unity; we ascended from the principle whence all knowledge is derived, and through which it is ascertained and justified. The first division which we met in the application of this principle was that by which all knowledge is divided into *formal* or pure knowledge and *materiated* knowledge.

1462. All materiated knowledge supposes some *form*; form on the other hand has no need of any matter in order to be conceived by the mind. But the rule for good method in dealing with all the branches of knowledge is obviously as follows: 'The things which have to be said should be distributed in such an order that what is said first has no need of what is said later in order to be understood and justified. On the contrary, what comes first should throw light on what comes later.'

1463. The *form* of knowledge is the cause and light of all other cognitions, which exist only as a result of an *application* of the form to real things. Knowledge about the form must therefore precede all other cognitions, and can be called *the first, pure branch of knowledge* (ideology). All the others are *applied branches of knowledge*. This is the first division of the branches of knowledge.

1464. The first, pure branch of knowledge deals solely with *ideal being*, the form of all the other cognitions, but does not yet offer this *being*, the supreme rule of the mind, in its application to subsistent things. *Logic*,[331] therefore, another branch of pure knowledge, which deals with the principles or rules of application of the form of reason, will be a kind of mediator between the first and the applied branches of knowledge.

1465. Let me add here a single observation on the first division of the branches of knowledge according to Bacon. He begins by dividing these branches into three according to the principal powers of *reason, memory* and *imagination*. Such a notion enables us to see clearly how backward the teaching on human knowledge was in Bacon's time. People had still not understood completely, or rather had forgotten, that *reason* alone generates the branches of knowledge. *Memory* is simply the deposit of reason; *imagination* simply provides reason with materials, or clothes the individual branch of knowledge in elegant, external signs. If all this were known, Bacon took no notice of it and found it of no benefit for the division of the branches of knowledge which could not therefore receive from him, and still less from the Encyclopedists, the unity of order that embellishes them and provides them with their striking usefulness [*App*., no. 19].

---

[331] Logic is *universal* if it contains the *principles* of application of being to all that is knowable: *particular*, if it contains the rules of application of these principles to the individual branches of applied knowledge.

[1464–1465]

CHAPTER 2

On the two ways: observation and reasoning

1466. The principle of method that we have previously considered as a way of ordering all human knowledge may be stated as follows: 'State first that which, in order to be understood or demonstrated, has no need of subsequent teaching.' This does, however, offer some difficulty to thought. It is easy to say that the final proposition must be demonstrated by means of the penultimate, the penultimate by means of its predecessor, and so on back to the first proposition. But how do I then demonstrate the *first proposition*? And if I do not demonstrate it, do I not take for granted, and consequently find useless, the demonstrations dependent upon this first proposition?

This kind of reasoning supposes something which is not the case, that is, that every proposition must be demonstrated by its preceding proposition. But we need to consider, on the contrary, that the nature of the first proposition is such that it includes proof of itself within itself. In other words, it is evident and unassailable, it is what is true *per se* because it is truth itself.

1467. But where do we discover this principle, and how do we discern it from all the others? We find it in ourselves because it is always present to us; we have no need to look for it by means of reasoning, but to *observe* it as something that we intuit naturally. The sceptic himself will see it, and conceive it reflectively, provided interiorly he turns his thought to himself. Turning the gaze of his mind on his cognitions, he will see the *idea of being* in them. If he concentrates his attention ever more carefully upon it, contemplating and analysing it while noting its essential characteristics, he will find himself unable not to perceive its light, necessity, evidence and immutability. All learned human knowledge begins with this *observation*, not with any other means. For the sceptic, too, observation is the first step on the return to the right path.

The first branch of knowledge therefore is knowledge from *observation*, not *reasoning*. This enables us to avoid the vicious circle so easy to enter when setting out the divisions of the branches of knowledge. In other words, *demonstration* terminates in *observation* which, as the intellection of truth known *per se*, is the fount of all demonstrations.

CHAPTER 3

The starting point of the system of human knowledge

1468. The system of human knowledge must therefore start from a *reflective observation* that we make on our own natural cognition. By means of this observation we recognise and discern in ourselves the *idea of being.* Having found this, and using it as a universal means, we discover and note all our other cognitions. But here we come face to face with an objection. Because we possess the direct *intuition* of the idea of being before *reflective observation* on it, would it not be more in keeping with nature if the system of human knowledge started from the intuition of being rather than from reflection on and recognition of the intuition?

The total lack of force behind this objection will be seen if we distinguish four questions which are normally confused because one is solved with an answer appropriate to another — and the answer comes easily to mind. This seems to me the principal reason why learned people have never yet agreed on the method to be followed in scientific treatises. The four questions of which I am speaking are as follows.

1469. *First question.* What is the starting point in initial human development?

External sensation is the starting point. Exterior sensations are certainly the first steps with which we develop our powers. Those who have observed this truth, but without distinguishing the beginning of real development in human beings from the beginning of philosophy, conclude that philosophy must begin from the *treatise on sensations.* They imagine that in the field of systematic knowledge they can take the same steps that they took at the beginning of their development. They do not see that if they were faithful to this principle of method, they would have to be children again and renounce any advance towards philosophy. It would be absolutely impossible to keep to this method.

1470. *Second question.* What is the starting point for the human spirit?

The *idea of being* is the starting point. Any intellective step whatsoever of the spirit always supposes and requires the prior intellection of being. However, this cannot be the starting point of philosophy. The spirit of a person wishing to philosophise is not in the same state as that of the spirit of someone taking the first step along the way of understanding. The would-be philosopher must have already developed intellectually and come to the point in which he thinks and desires to turn back and ask himself the reason for his own development. He must therefore reflect, or turn his attention back on his first steps, and what his first steps already supposed in him, to seek their justification and certainty at source.

1471. *Third question.* What is the starting point of those who begin to philosophise?

As we said, those who begin to philosophise are already in the process of development. But they can only start from the point in which they find themselves. It is impossible to do otherwise. Condillac and Bonnet speak imaginatively about returning to the first source of knowledge, and fabricate a statue endowed with a single sense. But for good or ill they take an enormous jump in doing this. They leap an abyss, totally forgetting the intellectual state in which they find themselves, and presenting themselves as spectators, with another nature, in order to observe the effect of the first sensations experienced by a human being, although this period has passed them by forever.

1472. *Fourth question.* What is the starting point of philosophy as a branch of knowledge, that is, of the system of human knowledge?

We must not confuse the starting point of the person who begins to philosophise with the starting point of philosophy that is already formed. Philosophy, when formed, is not the first, but the final step of those who dedicate themselves to philosophy; this is philosophy at its best. The order in philosophy, therefore, can be only the absolute order between truths. Those who begin to philosophise have not yet found this order; they are as it were groping for it, and can start only from the state in which they find themselves. Then they must retrace all the previous steps of their development, submit them to rigorous examination and thus throw a clearer light of certainty upon them.

[1471–1472]

Philosophy, on the other hand, must begin by first establishing that luminous point from which is derived the splendour of certainty and truth which serves all other cognitions, and by means of which these cognitions are ascertained and justified.

Let us take a horse-race as an example. When the race begins, the jockeys line up on their mounts at the start. But to get to the starting-post, they must come from somewhere. This accidental point from which they first set out to reach the start is an image of the starting point for those who begin to philosophise; the starting-post of the race is an image of the starting point of philosophy.

But what draws us to philosophise? The stimulus is *reflective observation* on ourselves, which alone is capable of enabling us to see clearly and advert to the luminous point which serves as the starting point of the whole system of knowledge. This luminous point is the idea of being, the form of reason, and the formal cause of human knowledge.

CHAPTER 4

Must our starting point be a particular or a universal?

1473. By placing the *idea of being* at the beginning of all scientific knowledge, we are inevitably confronted by those who think that the infallible rule of correct method is to go from particulars to universals. I have to note first, however, that such criticism is based on a very serious error with which we are only too familiar nowadays: universals are taken as an aggregate of particulars. I have already refuted this error (cf. vol. 1, 138–155) Moreover, an investigation of the nature of particulars and universals will show that the method directing us to move from particulars to universals cannot be upheld in any way. It is intrinsically impossible and absurd; we cannot think a single particular without using a universal.[332]

1474. Another observation escaping the attention of those who make this criticism is that in affirming the idea of being as the obligatory starting point of philosophy, we are in the happy position of being able to defend two apparently contrary propositions, that is, 'We begin from a universal', and 'We begin from a particular'.

Anyone who understands the nature of the idea of being must realise that mental being is *particular* and *universal* at the same time, and that it is much more particular or individual than universal. In fact we have shown that a universal means nothing more than the relationship of likeness that one thing has with many. But before considering a thing in its relationship of likeness with many things, we must have considered or perceived it in itself, and hence in its singularity. The unity of the thing which, as we have said elsewhere, is identified with its existence, precedes the consideration of its universality. We can rightly affirm therefore that in beginning from being we start from a singular because it is singular in itself,

---

[332] Cousin, in an excellent passage of his *Lessons*, shows with utter clarity that it is impossible for a historian of philosophy, and the same may be said for any historian of the human spirit such as a philosopher, to be faithful to the empirical method (cf. Lesson of May 8th 1829, pp. 10–17).

although it is also a light diffused universally over all knowable things.

This reflection has special force applied to the idea of being. Ideal being is extremely simple, essentially one, the principle of unity in all things, and consequently not only singular of itself, but the fount of all true unity and singularity (cf. 1450 ss.).

CHAPTER 5

Must the starting point be a fact, and in particular a fact of consciousness?

1475. By 'fact' we mean 'that which is'. Being, from which we affirm that we have to start, is not only a fact, but the principle of all facts. We are not saying therefore that we have to begin from any fact whatsoever, nor from a contingent fact. We must begin from the *first fact*, the *necessary, per se intelligible fact* which makes all other facts possible, that is, intelligible.

1476. But the question: 'Must we start from the fact of consciousness' is not without ambiguity, and can therefore be answered both negatively and positively. If by 'fact of consciousness' I mean *ideal being* conceived together with the subjective feeling that accompanies such an intuition, then in this case we have a fact of consciousness composed of two elements, feeling and idea (cf. vol. 2, 543 ss.). But intellective knowledge cannot have two starting points, nor can it start from other than what is purely intellective. Moreover, subjective feeling is not yet intellectual knowledge; it is only the matter of knowledge, which is rendered knowledge when we perceive ourselves as intelligent by giving it our attention.

If by 'fact of consciousness', we do not mean both the elements composing the fact, but only the intellective element, (the pure light of being, which is simply the term of our interior vision), we can affirm that philosophy starts from the primal fact of consciousness, that is, not from the *act* of consciousness itself, but from that which consciousness conceives along with that act and, in doing so, testifies to itself that what it conceives is its *object*.[333]

---

[333] All the objections, especially those of the author of Aenesidemus, made against Reinhold, who started from this fact of consciousness, fall with this distinction. It remains true, nevertheless, that the proposition 'systematic knowledge starts from the fact of consciousness' is neither clear nor exact.

CHAPTER 6
Doubt and methodical intelligence

1477. Descartes founded the philosophical edifice on the basis of the state of doubt with which, according to him, he viewed all his knowledge. This he called 'methodical doubt'; it was not intended as true doubt, but as an aid to the method and order in which philosophy had to be undertaken. Although Descartes was not the first to begin systematic learning with this supposed doubt, which had been admitted by the Scholastics,[334] methodical doubt did lead to serious criticism of Descartes, possibly through its abuse by some who misunderstood it.

1478. We must note two things here. First, at the beginning of philosophy, the supposed state of the philosopher is one of *methodical ignorance* rather than *methodical doubt*. If philosophy begins by indicating the origin of human cognitions, and develops by gradually deducing them from their first source, the nature of the philosophical treatise presupposes that prior to their origin these cognitions were not. But the absence of cognitions in human beings is called 'ignorance', and in this respect there is a clear difference between the character of Descartes' philosophy and ours: his philosophy has a *demonstrative* nature, and intends from the start to search for *certainty*; our philosophy goes a step further back, and begins not from *demonstration*, but from *observation* of the first facts which are the basis of demonstration itself and constitute its possibility.

The first aim of our philosophy, therefore, is *cognitions* themselves, not their *certainty*. We enquire about the existence and origin of cognitions and, as corollary to this, about the principle

[334] In accordance with the custom amongst the Schoolmen of his time, St. Thomas entitled all his treatises 'Questions', and began from the objections that could be made against the truth. For example, *Videtur quod Deus non sit* [It would seem that there is no God] and similar phrases open the questions. St. Thomas worked in this way, as he says, because *illi qui volunt inquirere veritatem, non considerando prius dubitationem, assimilantur illis qui nesciunt quo vadant* [those who want to seek the truth without first considering doubts against it, are like people who do not know where they are going].

of certainty. Nevertheless, the origin and certainty of cognitions are very much alike. Consequently, the states of methodical ignorance and methodical doubt are alike. But first, in order to remove any ambiguity and reasonable cause for criticism on this point, I must show clearly the place held among human beings by such ignorance and doubt; this is the second of the observations which I had in mind.

1479. We have already distinguished *popular* from *philosophical* knowledge, and defined the latter as the effect of deeper reflection which by analysing, demonstrating and ordering popular knowledge forms philosophical knowledge (cf. 1264 ss.). Popular knowledge is sufficient, normally speaking, for the ordinary needs of human life, although philosophical knowledge could be very useful even here. But I want to note that popular knowledge, together with its certainty, must always be preserved in us, never cancelled, and never changed into true universal doubt. On the other hand, the first steps in philosophical investigation, when deeper reflection begins, necessarily presuppose the non-existence of all parts of the philosophy that we hope to produce. This makes up the state of *methodical ignorance* from which I start. It does not consist in the perfect absence of all knowledge, but the absence of philosophical knowledge or, as I said, of deeper reflection. And I think that some passages of Descartes[335] allow us to believe that he restricted his methodical doubt more or less within these limits. However, the idea he formed of it was not sufficiently clear and precise to enable him to communicate it to others with the clarity of the distinction made above.

---

[335] In his discourse *On Method*, Descartes, who first proposes his doubt as the principle of philosophy, goes on to restrict it with several practical maxims. 'The first of which,' he says, 'would be to obey the laws and customs of my country by upholding constantly the religion in which God gave me the grace to be instructed from my infancy, and by directing myself in all things according to the most moderate and least excessive opinions which in practice would be accepted by the best of the people amongst whom I had to live.' Here we can see that Descartes deferred quite considerably to common sense. Nevertheless, some of his expressions show clearly that he had not noted the importance and the certainty of *direct* and *popular* knowledge.

Appendix

1. (1049)

[Self-deception about means for an end]

We know very little about ourselves, and are often deceived when passing judgment on things that concern ourselves. Those who think themselves the most free are often the most enslaved. Moments of enthusiasm must first pass before others can look back and examine the state of those who have preceded them. We often say we want to reach an end, but we should not believe that the means we choose must therefore lead to that end. We would frequently deceive ourselves if we believed that a good choice of means depended upon the end in view.

Philosophers are a fair example. If we read Berkeley, we find that he invented idealism for the sole purpose of refuting the many sceptics generated by the philosophy of Locke. But Locke himself had the same intention. The effect of *idealism* was simply to accelerate the progress towards scepticism. Reid, with the best of intentions, tried to halt this movement, and countered it with a system which generated critical philosophy, the most extreme scepticism that ever existed, the ultimate development and perfection of scepticism. Finally, Kant's intention in his teaching, according to his own words, was that of all his predecessors; to put paid to the sceptics, whom he calls 'a tribe of nomads who abhor all husbandry, and consistently destroy civil society' (Pref.). He then adds that there is no room for opinions in his teaching: 'I have already formed as a rule for myself that in this kind of investigation opinion is not legitimate; *hypothesis* must be avoided like the plague and denounced as soon as known' (*ibid.*). Nevertheless, after these promises and assertions, he wants to settle the matter with a massive equivocation: he admits some *necessary knowledge* but declares that the *necessity* is *apparent* and *subjective*. By this aside he destroys all knowledge and every possibility of knowledge.

This last statement is certainly typical of a sophist, although I would not dare to scrutinise his intention. However, in the other philosophers mentioned above, whose upright intention is evident, I think we find a clear example of the truth we have mentioned: when we judge ourselves we often err, and only with difficulty do we know both where we stand and the real, final effect of our way of thinking.

2. (fn. 23)

[Sextus' refutation of scepticism]

Sceptics do not deny appearances. Hence they do not deny *knowledge* but say it lacks certainty. They attack the *truth* of knowledge at its base, the ultimate principle of certainty. We should consider carefully the following passage of Sextus where he claims to oppose the dogmatists:

> If *something* (which the dogmatists say is the *most general* conception of all (καὶ μὴντὸ τὶ, ὅπερ φασὶν εἶναι πάντων γενικότατον) is false, they must accept that all other things are false. For example, if we grant the general proposition, 'That which is animal has a soul', we must also grant the other proposition: 'This (particular) thing that is animal has a soul'; in the same way, if the most universal conception of all *(something)* is false, every particular conception will be false, and there will be no truth.

Scepticism is totally bent on demonstrating that *something* (the most universal notion and principle on which all other conceptions depend) cannot be shown to be true, and that consequently all knowledge lacks certainty.

This extract from Sextus *(Hypotyp.*, bk. 2, c. 9) illustrates many important points: 1. the ancient *dogmatists* had recognised that all human knowledge can be reduced to a single principle, that is, to a *most universal conception,* which the sceptics accepted without opposition but of which they contested the certainty; 2. this most universal conception was of SOMETHING, that is, of *most common being*; 3. *knowledge* and *certainty* of knowledge were made to depend simultaneously on this

conception of most general being; 4. the sophistry of the sceptics throughout history consists in demanding a demonstration
of the *ultimate* principle, that is, a *reason* for the *final reason,*
which is a contradiction in terms.

The easy way of refuting the sceptics is to avoid aiding them
in their intellectual excess, as they try to demonstrate what is
essentially undemonstrable and indeed so evident that from it
we can draw the demonstration of every lower truth. We need
to show that their system rests on the false supposition that
truth is something beyond the ultimate reason or most universal conception. Human beings, when they say they know the
truth of a proposition, simply mean that they see the connection
between the proposition and the *final reason,* that is, the most
universal conception, totally evident in itself.

3. (1087)

[Deduction of absolute certainty]

It is possible to attempt to deduce absolute certainty from
three facts:

1. the matter of knowledge; 2. the knowing subject; and 3. the
formal object, that is, the form of knowledge.

1. Some philosophers imagined they could draw
certainty from the *matter of knowledge*, that is, from the
senses. Their efforts gave rise to the sceptics of antiquity, the
first to realise that the senses could not provide sources of
apodictic certainty. Degerando. after describing the ten *tropes*
or *divisions* used by the Pyrrhonists to encapsulate their
exceptions to certainty, makes this acute observation: 'Note
that the whole of this (sceptical) commentary is essentially an
attack on the witness of the senses, and accepts as an agreed
supposition that knowledge originates in exterior, sensible
experience *(Histoire comparée* etc., 2nd edition, t. 2, pp. 477,
478). This is the Pyhrronism generated by *sensists.*

2. Other philosophers, who saw that knowledge could
not have its source in the senses, imagined they could draw it
from the depth of our spirit, and hence from ourselves and
the laws of our intelligent nature. In a word, they deduced

certainty from the *subject*. This was the origin of *modern scepticism*, which gave rise to the critical or transcendental philosophers. This is the Pyhrronism generated by *Scottish philosphy*, which gave rise to the absurdity of *subjective truth*, or truth that is not truth.

3. The third system finds the foundation and very *essence* of knowledge in the object, that is, in the first, undetermined *idea* of being, which is 1. not *matter*, and hence cannot be altered or changed from its essential simplicity (cf. vol. 2, 426); 2. not a limited *subject* (hence not imposing partial forms on knowledge (cf. vol. 2, 417)), but an unlimited and undetermined *object* which itself receives the forms and is, according to us, the unique, unchallengeable truth standing as the firm foundation on which certainty, entirely safe from human temerity, stands unshaken.

Early Christianity had already rejected and reproved the first two systems as causes of the two kinds of scepticism that have confused and disturbed recent generations. But early Christianity has in its turn been reproved by recent generations which, acting together like the blind leading the blind, fall into a tangled abyss of uncertainty and unrest where the end is indeed intellectual exhaustion and moral debility, but from which human nature will, we hope, hasten to emerge as it rebels against the annihilation and perdition awaiting it there.

Six centuries ago, one of the brightest stars in the Italian firmament rejected these two false systems, and taught that certainty could rest on neither the *matter* of knowledge (sensations) nor on the perceiving *subject*, but only on the unchangeable and eternal nature of the *formal object*, in other words, on IDEAS, all of which, as I have shown, are finally reduced to a single idea. His words need to be considered very carefully and I quote them in their original language: *Illationis* NECESSITAS (that is, *certainty*, which implies the concept of absolute necessity) *non venit ab* EXISTENTIA REI IN MATERIA, *quia est contingens* (matter of knowledge); *nec ab existentia rei* IN ANIMA (in the perceiving subject), *quia tunc esset* fictio, *si non esset in re* (the subjective or imagined truth of the transcendentalists). *Venit igitur ab* EXEMPLARITATE *in arte aeterna* (the idea, the exemplar, the form of our knowledge), *secundum quam res habent aptitudinem et habitudinem ad invicem, ad illius aeternae artis repraesentationem* ['The NECESSITY of deduction' (that is, *certainty,* which implies the concept of absolute necessity) 'does not arise from the EXISTENCE OF SOMETHING IN MATTER, because this is contingent' (matter of knowledge), 'nor from the existence of something in the soul' (in the perceiving subject) 'because it would then be false, as not in the thing' (the subjective or imagined truth of the transcendentalists). 'It comes, therefore, from EXEMPLARINESS in eternal "praxis"' (the idea, the exemplar, the form of our knowledge) 'according to which things possess an habitual aptitude towards one another in their likeness to that eternal praxis'].

Those who date human wisdom from 1789, and hold in invincible repugnance knowledge which can be acquired from writers of previous centuries, should ask themselves what they make of the above words, which I am not inventing. They can read them in *Itinerarium mentis in Deum,* c. 3, and, provided they understand them, use them to push back by a few centuries the date of true knowledge.

4. (1127)

[Protagoras and modern philosophy]

The subjective truth of modern critical philosophy reproposes the system proposed by Protagoras in antiquity. Sextus Empiricus describes Protagoras' teaching as follows:

> The human being is the measure of all things. Protagoras makes the human being (the subject) the criterion of the value to be given to the reality of *entia* in so far as they exist, and to nothing in so far as it does not exist. Thus, Protagoras admits only what is visible to individual eyes. In his opinion, this is the general principle of acts of knowledge.
>
> (Pyrrho, *Hypotyp.,* c. 32)

Can we believe that Protagoras admitted a subjective truth in good faith or, as Sextus calls it, a *relative* truth *(Advers. Logic.,* 7)? Can we believe that he truly did not know that relative truth is no truth? Or can we reasonably suspect that he used the phrase 'relative truth' to avoid a clash wlth common sense by leading others to believe he had safeguarded truth at the very moment he intended to deny and destroy it?

This lack of honesty characterises sophists throughout history. This shiftiness, equivocation, and desire to insinuate teachings which fear the light (while having us believe otherwise) is the usual behaviour of those who disturb and destroy intelligence.

We are not being temerarious in thinking this of Protagoras; his bad faith is attested by all antiquity. It is sufficient to turn to Socrates as a witness, who indicates Protagoras' bad faith in Plato's *Theaetetus*. After presenting Protagoras' teaching on *relative truth*, which conforms exactly to the passage quoted above, he adds that this was the way Protagoras presented his philosophy to the people, while speaking more openly to his followers and plainly denying the existence of truth:

> *Socrates:* Is not Protagoras indeed a very wise man? He has indicated this truth obscurely to us, simple members of the common people, but revealed it clearly to his followers.
> *Theaetetus:* What do you think, Socrates?
> *Socrates:* I'll tell you, because the matter is important. He really meant that there is nothing true, nothing real. What a person says is large could be small, what is foul could be pretty, and so on. There is nothing that is one, nothing that is something with a determined quality. What we, using a false way of speaking, say exists, is only a kind of mixture coming together, a continual changing. Nothing exists; everything happens and changes ceaselessly.

Here we see that: 1. Protagoras' real and obvious intention was to remove all truth; 2. he did not dare reveal his intention to the public but spoke frankly to his followers; 3. he made the public understand that he safeguarded truth, declaring it relative or subjective for human beings (not everybody understood that these words contained the absolute proscription of truth); and finally 4. Protagoras had fallen into this error because he had observed only sense-knowledge which contains nuch that is subjective, that is, dependent on the nature and state of the subject, as I have shown (cf. vol. 2, 887 ss.). He had not observed nor risen to formal knowledge, nor had he penetrated its objective, absolute nature. Without grasping this nature of knowledge, he included it in the proscription of knowledge about sensible things. Thus, Protagoras' sophistry is reduced to 'applying to the whole of human knowledge that which applies to only a part'. And this is the formula to which I have reduced the error of scepticism (cf. 1066 ss.).

5. (1133)

[Subjective truth and critical philosophy]

The same argument applies to the subjective truth of Protagoras and Kant, because in the system of subjective truth doubt is essential. The sceptic says that the human being can know nothing about things as they are in themselves; only subjective appearances are known. But this teaching, if not true in itself, must be subjective, granted that scepticism is to be coherent with itself. I no longer know whether the teaching of subjective truth is real; I can only say that it seems so to me subjectively. It is not sufficient to say that the teaching of subjective truth is itself subjective. I would have to say that I pronounce the teaching of subjective truth to be subjective only by means of a judgment which itself is subjective. But if no other truth exists for me, I know only with subjective, not absolute truth.

We can easily see that such a system keeps us always *da capo* listening to an endless refrain.

Let us apply this general reasoning to some particular proposition of critical philosophy. Critical philosophy admits subjective forms, which makes all human knowledge subjective. But its sole argument for proving the existence of these forms must be the *principle of cause*. It sees that human knowledge lies within a few supreme classes, and concludes that to produce this effect there must be in our spirit an equal number of causes which determine our knowledge in this way. I call these causes 'forms'. However, the only meaning that 'principle of cause' has in critical philosophy is subjective; it is itself a form of the intellect. Kant concluded that in the human spirit there are *forms* which make knowledge subjective, and built his whole theory upon them. Consequently, by presupposing them, he entered a vicious circle. He deduced the sources of subjectivity of acts of knowledge (forms) from one of the sources of subjectivity itself, that is, from a form: he proves the form by means of pre-supposed forms. A similar objection was levelled at Kant in Germany by the fine author of Aenesidemus.

6. (1143)

[Idea and essence; potency and act]

I have already said that *the spiritual vision that we possess of being* is the primitive fact from which we have to start. We do not need therefore, to he over-subtle about the extraordinary mystery associated with this marvellous, unique fact. The normal argument, 'I cannot explain the nature of this fact, therefore the fact does not exist', is inadmissible. Rather, we should be prepared to affirm more modestly and reasonably, 'I cannot deny the existence of this fact which, however, is a mystery to me. I see nothing like it in nature; it is such that I cannot apply to it the laws which govern all other facts present in sensible nature. Nevertheless I cannot deny it'. All we can do is analyse the fact and then, after analysing it, wonder at it.

The result of our analysis, carried out thoroughly and without prejudice, will show that the root of things is in ideas, in intelligence. The *essence* that we think in the idea is the essence which subsists, except that in the idea it is *possible,* and in the subsistence is *in act.* This is the great, sublime teaching of antiquity which taught: 1. that 'essence' is what is thought by means of the idea (cf vol. 2, 646); 2. that the subsistence of any thing is the act of the essence. *Oportet... quod ipsum* esse *comparetur ad essentiam,... sicut actus ad potentiam* [It is necessary... for *being* itself to be related to *essence...* as act is related to potency] (St. Thomas, *S.T.,* 1, q. 3, art. 4). According to this teaching, therefore, the same essence is that which is thought in the idea and that which subsists, except that the former is the *potency* of the latter, the latter the *act* of the former. Hence St. Thomas teaches, 'It can rightly be said that even ens' (not only what is true, the idea of ens) 'is both in things and in the intellect', because *ens* itself is comprehended in the idea, although only in potency.

If we go on to consider *ens in potency,* which is in the idea, we can say that the essence is in things and in the intellect; but if we consider the whole *idea of ens,* we say more correctly that *truth,* rather than *ens,* is in the intellect. St. Thomas says: *Ipsa natura cui advenit intentio universalitatis, puta natura hominis, habet* DUPLEX ESSE, *unum quidem materiale secundum quod est in materia naturale, aliud autem immateriale secundum quod est in intellectu* [Nature itself — for example, the nature of the human being — when joined with the comprehension of universality has a TWOFOLD BEING. It possesses a material being in so far as it is in material nature, and an immaterial being in so far as it is in the intellect] (*De An.,* bk 2, less. 12). Elsewhere, after having said that truth properly speaking is in the intellect, he adds: *Quamvis posset dici, quod etiam ens est in rebus et in intellectu, sicut et verum licet verum principaliter in intellectu, ens vero principaliter in rebus* [Although it could be said that ens, too, is both in things and in the intellect just as that which is true is in both. That which is true is, however, principally in the intellect just as ens is principally in things] (*S. T.,* I, q. 16, art. 3).

Every thing, every (finite) essence has therefore two modes, two states, according to this ancient teaching. The first state is *in potency,* the second *in act.* In so far as it is in potency, it constitutes the *idea;* it is in the intellect, and the relationship which it has with itself in act is called *truth.* In so far as it is in act, it is the thing as subsisting; it has its own existence outside the mind, and is properly called *ens.* The distinction between *potency* and *act,* one of the most simple and necessary of all distinctions, has its first origin here, with its roots in the incipient nature itself of knowledge. It can be explained only because it is directly linked with the primary fact of human knowledge which itself bears no antecedent explanation. And here I must draw attention to a wise thought of Aristotle and St. Thomas.

Investigating the origin of materialism as it appeared in the first Greek philosophers, they found its source in the philosophers' ignorance of the distinction between *potency* and act. Who could have imagined that the lack of such a distinction would have been the cause of materialism?

But there are many superficial modern thinkers, I think, who are disposed to consider the distinction between *potency* and *act* as a useless, scholastic distinction, or at least as a distinction of little importance. It is characteristic of profound genius, on the other hand, to grasp the relationships between widely separated things, to assign the most distant causes to what takes place in human events and minds, and to foresee in the principle proper to any doctrine the ultimate consequences that will inevitably develop from it. Ordinary people will become aware of these consequences when they actually occur, and only then will people see how to judge the principle with an argument *ab absurdo,* the most common and effective argument that mankind pos- sesses.

Both Aristotle and St. Thomas made use of the wisdom which sees consequences and the most practical effects in extremely abstract principles when they ascribed the cause of materialism to the lack of the distinction between *potency* and *act*. In fact, if we reflect solely on the *actual existence* of things, and not on their *potential existence,* we are never able to form for ourselves a correct concept of the manner in which things exist in our human intelligence, but only of the way in which things exist in their matter. The *act* by which things exist is identical with their existence in their matter; *potency,* on the contrary, is synonymous with their existence in the mind. If we know only the actual existence of these things, the nature of the mind remains unknown. All that is left are things in their matter — materialism is the inevitable result. St. Thomas wrote wisely: *Quia antiqui naturales nesciebant distinguere inter* actum *et* potentiam, *ponebant animam esse corpus* [Because the natural philosophers of old were ignorant of the distinction between *act* and *potency,* they posited the soul as body] *(S. T.,* I, q. 75, art. 1, ad 2). The expressions, 'An essence is in potency', and 'An essence is in the mind', are identical. I have shown elsewhere that *essence in potency, essence in the mind, idea* and *truth* are identical phrases, and themselves identical with *representations,* that is, *likenesses* of subsistent *things* (cf. vol. 1, 106 ss. and vol. 2, 1020 ss.). We shall develop this observation later.

Our possession of *essence in potency, representation, likeness,* and so on, is what forms *knowledge,* the *intellectual light.* All these things thus receive a clear and obvious definition.

[*app.,* 6]

7. (1200)

[Truth and our own existence]

Galluppi and other subjectivists thought that St. Augustine had made Descartes' 'I exist' the first truth on which all other truths depend. But, as I have shown (cf. vol. 2, 970 ss.), Descartes' first proposition lacks conviction unless we presuppose its major. St. Augustine began from 'I exist', not as the first truth but as a truth accepted as self-evident by the Academicians whom he was refuting. When he spoke of the first truth, his mind had already abandoned the *subject* and attained the *object*, that is, to the very essence of truth, stripped of time, place, restrictions and limits. He saw its light as more certain and unshakeable than his own existence, and wrote these memorable words: FACILIUSQUE DUBITAREM VIVERE ME, QUAM NON ESSE VERITATEM QUAE PER EA QUAE FACTA SUNT INTELLECTA CONSPICITUR [I WOULD MORE EASILY DOUBT THAT I AM ALIVE THAN THAT THERE WERE NO TRUTH SEEN AND UNDERSTOOD THROUGH THE THINGS THAT HAVE BEEN MADE] (*Confess.*, 7, 10).

If we note and distinguish the persuasion we have of the first truths and the persuasion of the existence of ourselves, we are, in my opinion, totally persuaded of both, but with this notable difference. Relative to the first truths, it is impossible to simply think they do not exist; relative to myself, it is not impossible to think of my non-existence, but it is impossible for me to assent with direct knowledge to any proposition which says I do not exist.

This difference between the first *necessary truths* and the *factual truth of my contingent existence* is excellently stated by St. Thomas, and shows that it is absolutely impossible for a human being to be a sceptic and refuse assent to the first truths. He says:

> Thinking that something does not exist can be understood in two ways. The first is the simple apprehension that something may possibly not exist. In this case nothing prevents us from thinking we may not exist, just as we can think there was a time when we were not. But this is not true when we *apprehend* that the whole is simultaneously less than its part (which is one of the first truths), because

one term excludes the other. Relative to this second way we can understand how *assent* is added to apprehension. In this sense, there is no one who thinks he could not exist by assenting to his non-existence. In everything we perceive, we always (habitually) perceive ourselves.

(*De Verit.*, q. 10, art. 12)

8. (1230)

[Individuality and multiplicity]

Although antiquity maintained that knowledge is concerned only with universals, it was also known that the *individual* being of a thing is not foreign to the understanding. What cannot be assimilated by the understanding, however, is the particular condition of all contingent, finite things. This condition entails that they are not knowable *per se,* but only by means of their participation in *being.* As a result it often happens that each contingent thing does not have such a relationship with being as to exclude the possibility of an infinite number of other, equal things. The notion of a contingent thing includes the *possibility of infinite others* equal or similar to this thing, or (and this is the same) a universal notion.

In the limited things of this world, only their proper subsistence is present which, in sensible things, is the matter of which each is composed. But the very definition of matter precludes the possibility of its being *per se* the object of the human intellect.

Matter is such in so far as the particular sense terminates in it, and every intellective principle is absent from it. In fact, if we were to think of matter, it would cease to be particular, and through our intellective act would no longer be matter, but the idea of matter (possible matter). Matter of its nature cannot reach out and present itself *per se* to our intellect. Hence St. Thomas' affirmation: *Singulare non repugnat intelligenti in quantum est singulare, sed in quantum est materiale: quia nihil intelligitur nisi immaterialiter* [The particular as particular is not repugnant to the one who understands, but it is repugnant as material, because things are understood only immaterially], that is, by means of an *idea* or light (*S.T.*, I, q. 86, art. 1).

[*app.*, 8]

Even the subsistence of spiritual *entia* is not perceived by the intellect, nor is our own subsistence and individuality perceived by means of particular perception. We too are a feeling, although a simple feeling, and in order to perceive such a feeling we have to apply to it the predicate of being which remains universal in the application because it is not exhausted in the individual *SELF*.

In the sensible perception of ourselves we perceive purely and simply our reality with feeling. In the intellective perception of *OURSELVES*, however, this substantial feeling holds the place of the matter of knowledge while the form remains universal in such a way that the *essence* of human being is included in the intellective perception of ourselves. The essence, however, is repeated and renewed in all human beings, and could he repeated and renewed in many more. That which is knowable in its subsistence, of itself, is *being* alone which relative to itself is particular and individual, but relative to the things it makes known to us is universal and common. Of all the particular things we know through being, there is nothing which in itself exhausts it. That being which makes us know the individual thing makes us know at the same time and presents to us the possibility of infinite other things either equal to or different from that individual.

This accords, as far as I can see, with the mind of St. Thomas, provided he is correctly interpreted, although there are several passages which at first sight seem to mean the opposite. For instance, in some places he teaches that the *intellect* is knowable to itself *(S.T., I, q. 86, art. 1)*. But I believe that to understand St. Thomas' mind in these passages we have to be conversant with his ways of speaking. He often uses the word 'intellect' to indicate the form of the human being as, for example, in this sentence: *Intellectivum principium est forma hominis* [The intellective principle is the form of the human being]. Here the intellective principle is the intellect itself: *Intellectus est intellectualis operationis principium* [The intellect is the principle of intellectual activity] *(S.T., I, q. 86, art. 1)*. This way of speaking is partially justified by the etymology of the word 'intellect' which indicates *something understood.*

We could say the same about human common sense, which imposes names upon things. In calling the faculty of understanding 'intellect', common sense recognises the need for something already understood *per se* if the faculty of understanding is to exist. Moreover, St. Thomas sometimes applies the word *intellect* to being, the intellective form itself, because being and the one who understands together make a single thing by means of their very close and perfect union in which it can truly be said that they touch one another: *Intellectus enim in actu quodammodo est intellectum in actu* [The intellect in act is in some way what is understood in act] *(S.T.,* I, q. 76, art.4). When St. Thomas' way of speaking has been well understood, my own words, it would seem, are simply an explanation of his: *being* alone is what can be understood in its individuality. But because being, in so far as it shines in our minds and is received in them, is only *initial being,* that is, being without its terms and limitations, it can (in so far as it is conceived by each human being) rightly be called each one's *individual intellect,* and more appropriately the *intellectual principle.*

For greater confirmation of this, and so that my opinion may he seen to have the support of the authority of the ancient sages, I would ask the reader to reflect rather deeply on the whole course of philosophy from Plato, the master of Aristotle, to Descartes. He will see that this entire philosophy took as its foundation the truth of which I am speaking. Aristotle, for example, asks: 'How does knowledge come about except through the *one* seen in the *many?' (Metaph.,* 3). This explains his opinion that knowledge essentially possesses in itself something universal. Duns Scotus explains this passage of Aristotle in the following words: *Omnis scientia est de universali, quod est unum in multis, quia de singularibus non est scientia* [All knowledge is concerned with what is universal, that is, with one in many, because there is no knowledge of particular things] *(Comm., in hoc loco).* If this was the *universal knowledge* of antiquity, it certainly supposed the apprehension of what is *one,* and therefore of the *individual.* What is this *one,* this *individual,* perceived in the many? We can answer this question very clearly if we take the teaching of antiquity on the *one* in conjunction with the opinions of which we have spoken. This teaching affirmed that by *one* was understood only *undivided ens. Being* was that which constituted unity and consequently *one* was sometimes taken for *ens* and vice versa. 'One simply means undivided ENS. From this it is clear that one is interchangeable with ens' (*S.T.*,I, q. 11, art. 1). Ens, therefore, is that which is known of its nature individually because it is the same as one; ens, seen in things, *one in many*, is that which makes us know things. This relationship of one ens with many things (with its many terms) is what makes the knowledge of things necessarily universal. Universal knowledge supposes prior to itself some particular knowledge in which it is founded, that is, the knowledge of ens.

9. (1238)

[Philosophy and God]

The idea of God is made up of 1. a *negative* and 2. a *symbolic* part. Generally speaking, the symbolic part is composed of likenesses which take the place of the positive part and in some way make up for its absence. Both parts are present in religion, but the negative is the principal, fundamental part. If we remove the *symbolic* part, the negative part remains, although we have nothing to substitute for the part we have taken away. We can, however, meditate on the first part which is entirely made up of certain relationships between God and creatures.

Such meditations, although they provide us with ever more complete and wonderful knowledge of God, are never more than a development and analysis of the negative part. Nevertheless this whole development also enters of its nature into religion and the worship of God because it helps human beings to worship him with greater understanding and love.

Professor Cousin failed to indicate adequately the characteristics of *religion and philosophy* when he reduced the former to symbols and the latter to *pure conceptions* (Lesson, 17 April 1828). All *pure conceptions* about God obtained by meditation and reflection, however many they may be, form part of religion, and help worship, which is not restricted solely to symbols. On the other hand, if philosophy does away with *symbols*, it has nothing to put in their place. All that reflection can discover about God consists not in reducing *symbols* to *conceptions,* but in developing the negative part of the idea of God. Here symbols are discarded altogether. The negative part, in fact, consists in the *relationships* between God and ourselves.

It is true that this development is in part the work of time and results from the application of reflective thought on the first concepts of our direct thought. In this sense, the development we are speaking of does indeed pertain to philosophy in so far as it is carried out with the simple light of natural reason. This does not lessen its role in religion, however. There can be no opposition between reason and religion.

Surely there is no difficulty in granting that reason, or philosophy if we want to call it that, should be concerned with religious argument about God, the object of religion? This object does not cease to be religious, and become merely philosophical, as soon as reflection is turned upon it. Philosophy has no power to denature things by occupying itself with them; the God of philosophers is not less God, and the object of the intelligent soul's worship is not less the object of worship, when the soul applies its most noble part, its own intellective activity, to such an object.

The systematic division between *philosophy* and *religion* is false. Religion embraces the whole of God, and philosophy that part which is worked out with reasoning. The whole and the part are not in opposition, nor are they mutually exclusive. Religion existed before philosophy; the conclusions of philosophy, or rather natural reason, about religion were simply a greater development of religion itself. St. Thomas' sublime treatise on God did not cease to be religious despite the wonder of its depth of thought and the acumen of its reflection, nor was it ever considered other than *theology*.

We ought not to separate what is inseparable; we ought not to separate religion from what the human reason knows when it is applied to religion. Instead we should distinguish the successive states of religion itself, which has developed and been perfected across the centuries. At first, it was more symbolic; later, it contained more *pure knowledge*.

The continual increase of light coming from revelation until the coming of Jesus Christ himself was of course, of great assistance, but great help was found nevertheless in the use of reason

[*app.,* 9]

strengthened by that light. Reason was not given to human beings by God to stagnate and remain useless.

Its object is the most noble truths — and God is the most noble truth of all. For the rest, *natural reason* was never alone in the world; human reflection has always had as its matter not only what is provided by natural direct thought, but whatever God has revealed of himself to us.

10. (1242)

[St Thomas Aquinas' distinction of essences]

The distinction between the various essences of things enables us to reconcile opinions of St. Thomas Aquinas which otherwise might seem opposed to one another.

On more than one occasion he says that the substance and quiddity of a thing is the proper object of the intellect, provided however that *intellectus penetrat ad intimam naturam speciei, quae est in ipsis individuis* [the intellect penetrates the intimate nature of the species which is in the individuals themselves] (*De Verit.*, q. 10, art 5). This takes place especially in the perception of ourselves. When we perceive ourselves, we perceive the term of the very act by which we exist, and hence our essence, to which that act extends.

Elsewhere he says that 'in a mind' such as the human mind 'which receives knowledge from things, the forms' (the ideas) 'exist through a certain action of things in the soul'; *in mente enim accipiente scientiam a rebus, formae existunt per quamdam actionem rerum in animam.*

Again: 'That which is known through intellectual vision are *things themselves*, not the images of things. This takes place in the corporeal or sense-vision, not in the spiritual or imaginative vision. The objects of the imagination and sense are accidents from which are constituted certain figures or images of the things; but the object of the intellect is the very *essence* of the thing, although the intellect knows the essence of the thing through some likeness of it. This likeness is the means by which the intellect knows; it is not as though it were the object towards which it has first turned its gaze' (*De Verit.*, 10, 4).

In this passage St. Thomas is speaking of a certain *likeness* by which the intellect knows essences, and of certain *images* of things, images which the intellect does not perceive because it reaches out to see things themselves. As far as I can see, the distinction between likeness and the images is that *feeling* as such has *sensation* (properly speaking) and *corporeal sense perception*. This *corporeal sense perception* is the *term of the action* of external things on us, and renders sensation *extrasubjective*. But this *term* of the action (which we need not describe here) corresponds to St. Thomas' sensible *image*, the phenomenon of sense. The soul, however, is conscious of experiencing the *term* of action from external bodies and (in so far as the soul is intellective) sees in the term an *ens* operating on it. This ens is thought by means of the *idea* of being in all its universality which is applied and added to the *term* of action experienced in feeling. This idea is St. Thomas' *likeness* by which the intellect knows things. But things are known by the intellect because *being* is its object. Being in all its universality is determined by the *term* of action in feeling. The quality of our knowledge of things, therefore, and their *essence* as known to us, corresponds to the nature of the action carried out in us. In bodies, as we have shown, the *action* upon us is substantial. When we speak of *corporeal essence*, we mean to name the kind of power which modifies us in the way we have shown (cf. vol. 2, 692 ss.).

Even in bodies, therefore, we do not perceive the *first act* by which they are entia, but only their action, the essence known by us which we then express with the word 'body'.

Bodies, however, have different *potencies* over us which specify them from one another, or their various states. This explains why the distinction of the ideas we have of these bodies is determined solely by their *accidental* actions on us, and why such ideas enable us to know only *generic essences*, which properly speaking are not complete essences; the *potencies operating* in us take the place of *essences*. St. Thomas is speaking of these essences in passages where he maintains that the essences of things are unknown to us.

For example, in *De Verit.*, q. 10, art. 1, he says: *Quia vero rerum essentiae sunt nobis ignotae, virtutes autem earum innotescunt nobis per actus, utimur* FREQUENTER (not always, therefore) *nominibus virtutum, vel potentiarum ad essentias significandas* ['The essences of things are unknown to us, but their *power* is manifested to us through their acts, and we FRE-QUENTLY' (not always, therefore) 'use the words indicating their powers or potencies to mean their essences']. Shortly after-wards he goes on: 'The substantial differences of things are unknown to us. As a result, those who define these things sometimes (*INTERDUM*) use accidental instead of substantial dif-ferences in so far as the accidental differences indicate or notify the essence, just as effects proper to a thing notify the cause. Consequently, that which is sensible, taken as the constitutive difference of the animal, is not drawn from feeling understood as potency, but as signifying the very essence of the soul from which the potency flows.'

Our knowledge of God remains negative because we know only the *effects* of God, and effects which, as finite, are inade-quate relative to their cause. St. Thomas says: 'Our intellect, even in our state as sojourners, can in some way know the divine essence, but only what it is not, not what it is.' He answers the objection about the direction of our affection for God in the following way:

> We can love God directly without need to love anything prior to him, even though we are sometimes swept up from visible to invisible things. Nevertheless we cannot in our state as sojourners know God directly without need-ing knowledge of something prior to him. Desire follows understanding; the action of desire begins where under-standing, which proceeds from effects to causes, ends by coming finally to some kind of knowledge of God by knowing of him what he is not. Then desire reaches out to that which the intellect offers it, without its needing to take all the steps the understanding has taken.
>
> (*De Verit.*, q. 10, art. 11)

11. (1245)

[St. Augustine's philosophical development]

St. Augustine's mind passed through those stages of develop-ment which, as I have observed, are necessary to philosophy if it is to progress from its beginning as popular philosophy to become more erudite and perfect (cf. vol. 2, 29–34). Popular philosophy does not see the difficulties present in philosophical questions; it presses ahead confidently and boldly. But when it comes up against something too difficult for it, it falls into the opposite defect. In its totally bewildered state, no solution offers it any satisfaction; in the words of a modern writer, scepticism seems to be 'common sense's first form and manifestation on the philosophical stage'.

Thus St. Augustine began as an academic philosopher. Hs doubts settled, he moved naturally as it were, into Platonic philosophy. Platonic teaching on ideas appertains to *learned* philosophy, but to a philosophy still in its first period and therefore imperfect. Unable to find the simplest solutions to the difficulty it sees, it has recourse to ingenious hypotheses which sin more by *excess* than by *defect*. St. Augustine's mind, however, could not stop here. He saw that the Platonic theory postulated too much concerning the origin of ideas. He removed its excess, and so arrived at truth. Truth consisted in realising that human nature is *essentially reasonable* and hence recognises truth when it looks for and finds it. For the same reason, a child can accurately reply to questions asked methodically, even about things not previously taught it. Thus, in his *Retractions* (bk. 1, c. 8) Augustine reproaches himself for having once said that the soul seems to have brought all its skills along with it. He says that 'it is possible... for a child to answer a question because a child is an intelligent nature': *fieri enim potest...ut hoc ideo possit (interrogata respondere), quia NATURA INTELLIGIBILIS EST*. In the same place he explains what constitutes an intelligent nature, namely, an innate *light*: 'I have said that those who are learned in the liberal arts discover these disciplines within themselves but hidden from them by forgetfulness, until they disinter them. But I reject this. The more likely reason why even the unskilled, when correctly asked, can say something about any discipline is that the light of eternal reason is present to them as far as they can understand it. They see the immutable truths in this light not because they once knew them and then forgot them, as Plato and others opined': *propterea...quia praesens est eis, quantum id capere possunt, LUMEN RATIONIS AETERNAE, ubi haec immutabilia vera conspiciunt, non quia ea noverant aliquando et obliti sunt, quod Platoni vel talibus visum est (ibid., c.* 4). This is precisely the development that Plato's teaching needed, as we have observed. All ideas, instead of being considered innate, must be subordinated to one single innate idea, the light of reason. From this idea all other ideas have their origin. It is an idea in which, on the occasion of sensations and of questions, all things are seen and intellectually grasped (cf. vol. 1, 229-233). Like St. Thomas, I call this light the 'principle of knowledge' (*PRINCIPIUM COGNITIONIS*). It tells us that all we know, is known *in rationibus aeternis sicut* IN COGNITIONIS PRINCIPIO [in the eternal reasons, the principle as it were of knowledge] *(S. T.,* I, q. 84, art. 5). In order that no doubt remain concerning the understanding of *this principle of knowledge,* we should note that St. Augustine (and St. Thomas after him) calls it truth: *Nec ego utique in te (VIDEMUS VERUM), nec tu in me, sed ambo in ipsa, quae supra mentes nostras est, incommutabili VERITATE* [Neither I in you, nor you in me (SEE WHAT IS TRUE), but both see it in the immutable TRUTH itself, which is above our minds] *(Confess.,* bk. 11, c. 25). We observed that, according to St. Thomas, *truth,* in which we see all things in this present life, is the *idea of being in all its universality* (cf 1123 ss.). Thus, all that these two great men teach is harmonious and complete. Our teaching starts and continues from theirs.

12. (1246)

[St. Thomas on the senses]

In volume 2 (cf. 749 ss.), I discussed some criteria concerning the veracity of the senses. Aquinas teaches the same. Here, it will be helpful to discuss one way St. Thomas has of expressing himself, which originates from Aristotle and could be the cause of confusion in the minds of those who have no real understanding of certain expressions now forgotten. He writes: *Proprium obiectum intellectus est quod quid est: unde circa hoc non decipitur intellectus nisi per accidens. Circa compositionem autem et divisionem decipitur; sicut et sensus,* QUI EST PROPRIORUM, EST SEMPER VERUS, *in aliis autem fallitur* [The proper object of the intellect is that which something is. Hence the intellect is not deceived in this except *per accidens*. It is however deceived about composition and division, just as sense IN SO FAR AS IT IS CONCERNED WITH ITS OWN FEELING IS ALWAYS TRUE, but fails when dealing with the feeling of others] (*C.G.*, 1, q. 58). Here, St. Thomas distinguishes two objects both of the intellect and of sense: the *proper object* (about which there can be no error) and the *accidental object,* about which both the understanding and the sense can be led into error. I want to clarify St. Thomas' meaning by explaining the nature of the accidental object of the intellect and sense. I begin with sense.

In his commentary on Aristotle's work on the soul, St. Thomas explains the phrase, 'accidental object': 'Sense does not deceive us when we see something white, but it can deceive us, especially from a distance, about the particular thing which is white — for example, snow or flour or something similar' (bk. 3, less. 6). Note: our sense sees white; the understanding judges whether the white seen by our eye is snow. The judgment is made by the understanding on the basis of what sense presents (whiteness). But because this judgment follows so rapidly the sensation of whiteness, the judgment seems to be intimately united with the sensation. Hence people generally and erroneously believe the judgment to be an object of sense. Thus, if we ask someone: 'Who told you that there is snow on the mountain?', he immediately replies: 'I saw it'. He does not stop to separate two things which, although closely united, are different, that is, 1. the sensation of whiteness, and 2. the judgment made by the understanding, arguing from the whiteness to the existence of the snow on the mountain, that is, from a sign to what is signified.

Even Aristotle did not wish to distance himself from this common but false way of speaking. He had such respect for ordinary language that at times he seemed superstitious about it, ready to accept its errors. He was satisfied to say that the *judgment* was an accidental object of sense in so far as sense supplied the matter and the judgment immediately followed she sensation. It would be better, however, to avoid this way of speaking and state clearly that the judgment is in no way an object of sense but simply an object of the understanding. This allows us to understand what the *object* of the *intellect* must be.

[*app.*, 12]

Just as the *object* (properly speaking the term) *of sense* is the matter of our acts of knowledge, and the form is said to be *its accidental object*, so the *real object of the intellect* is the *form* of the acts of knowledge, and their matter is the *accidental object*. Hence the understanding, if it judges about sensible things without following sensible experience, falls into error. Finally, I observe that, according to Aristotle, sense sometimes, although rarely, deceives us even about its proper object, that is, in the case of defect in our sense. But I have excluded this exception by separating every foreign element from what is posited by sense.

13. (1258)

[Understanding and perception]

Two questions can be asked: 'How is the understanding moved to perception?' and: 'Does the understanding perceive as soon as it has a sensation or does some time pass between the sensation and the intellection, in the first stage of human development?' It will he helpful if I discuss the first of the two questions (which have much in common) and indicate how I conceive that the understanding can he moved to perceive on the occasion of sensations.

There is no difficulty in the fact that sensitivity is drawn and moved by what is sensible; sensitivity is a passive faculty, and that which is sensible is a stimulus appropriate to the nature of sensitivity. But there is neither similarity nor communication of nature between sensation and understanding. We cannot therefore imagine that sensation moves the understanding with a real action as an efficient cause.

In my opinion, sensation *occasions* the movement of the understanding and rouses it to perception without any real communication between sensation and the understanding. Such communication comes about through the UNITY of the subject. We must remember that the sensitive *myself* is the same as the intellective *myself*, and that *feeling* produces *instinct* — for example, the stimulus of hunger felt in the stomach produces the *instinct* to look for food or seize it if it is at hand. So far we are in the order of feeling. I do not think it necessary to explain how *feeling* produces *instinct;* I simply indicate the fact that when an animal has certain sensations, it feels a need which sets in motion its motor forces and all the activity within the animal. This faculty of searching to satisfy a need is called *instinct.*

Beginning with this fact, I reason as follows. *Myself* (feeling and intelligent) experiences within itself a *need* arising from its sensitive nature. In this situation *myself* stimulates itself to put all its forces into operation in order to satisfy the need and be rid of it. But the forces which *myself* possesses include intellective forces. *Myself* therefore makes use not only of its feeling activity but also of its intellective attention because in the subject the feeling activity forms one, single force and radical activity with the intellective activity. In this way feeling, without acting directly in the intelligence, occasions intellectual movement; sense stimulates *myself* (which possesses understanding) to put the understanding into action. The UNITY OF *MYSELF*, therefore, in which sense and understanding converge, is the mediator and means of communication between these two entirely different potencies.

14. (1273)

[Victor Cousin and inspiration]

The history of inspired human beings tells us that inspiration is usually accompanied by a kind of sacred enthusiasm. This arises from the extraordinary action exercised by God in souls when he communicates his secrets to them, and from the wonderful mysteries he reveals to them. Moreover this kind of *enthusiasm* is an effect which frequently accompanies *divine inspiration* or *revelation*; it is not *inspiration* or *revelation* itself. In fact God seems to have revealed things to holy people without arousing any extraordinary excitation in their souls, as for example, when he spoke to them in dreams and gave them ordinary commands (like the journey into Egypt) without revealing new, fundamental mysteries.

The general mass of people however have sometimes confused the effect of inspiration with inspiration or revelation itself. They are unaware that a kind of enthusiasm or

wonderful, sublime, intellectual excitation can spring from
natural causes, as they do from *first reflections*, with which
human beings discover great truths. It is unfortunate that
Cousin has accepted this popular equivocation, and confused
natural, poetic inspiration with divine and truly *supernatural*
inspiration. Because both are marked by a kind of enthusiasm,
he has confused what comes from human nature with what
comes from God; he has confused false religions with true religion, as if all came from the same source simply because they
produce a similar effect in nature. But would false religions have
been pale imitations if they did not in some way resemble the
truth? It is the duty of philosophy to distinguish things which
although similar are different; it must not allow itself to be
duped by similarity as the mass of people are. Professor Cousin
says:

> Such is the fact of the first affirmation prior to any reflect-
> ion and devoid of any negation. This is the fact which the
> human race has called *inspiration*. In all languages, inspira-
> tion is different from reflection. It is an apperception of
> truths, that is, of essential fundamental truths, without the
> intervention of the will or personality. Inspiration does
> not belong to us; relative to it, we are simple spectators,
> not agents. Our whole action consists in *being aware* of
> what happens. There is certainly activity here, but not a re-
> flective, willed, personal activity. The characteristic of in-
> spiration is enthusiasm. Enthusiasm is accompanied by a
> powerful. Emotion which snatches the soul from its or-
> dinary, subordinate state and releases the sublime, divine
> part of the soul's nature: *Est Deus in nobis, agitante
> calescimus illo* [It is God in us, whose action fills us with
> enthusiasm]. — This explains why at the beginning of
> civilisation anyone who possessed the wonderful gift of
> inspiration to a greater degree than others was taken to be
> God's confidant and interpreter. — Here we have the sac-
> red origin of prophecy, priesthood and worship.

Many different elements are mingled and confused in this
passage. It seems that the author's imagination, after rapidly
amassing many things, has clouded the calm insight with which
he often analyses difficult subjects. In my opinion, therefore,
the defects in the passage are the following:

1. Genuine, divine inspiration and revelation of God should have been distinguished from simple, natural knowledge which, although it may attain the sublimity of poetical inspiration, does not exceed natural limits. There is no doubt that natural knowledge can be called a participation in eternal, absolute reason, but this truth must not be abused by being confused with supernatural revelation, which philosophy can accept without finding it contradictory and impossible.

2. A distinction should have been made between inspiration resulting in enthusiasm, and the enthusiasm popularly called inspiration simply because the human being feels himself wonderfully and nobly passive in its regard.

3. Professor Cousin should have kept in mind that *imposture* causes false religions and simulates true religions. He should not have referred to a single origin falsehood and truth, pretence and sincerity, religion and superstition, or (to use the words of our author) *prophecy, priesthood* and *worship* in general.

4. He should not have said that spontaneous knowledge, which easily generates enthusiasm, is void of *all reflection* — spontaneous knowledge comes from a first, general reflection. He thus confused *direct knowledge* with *popular knowledge.*

5. He should not have excluded *personality,* that is, the personal activity proper to popular knowledge, and left only activity similar to that of a spectator at a play.

We must note that *being aware* is precisely the fact under discussion; anyone aware of something has already acted by apprehending the thing. He may be passive but he is the *subject,* the person who intervenes. The objects of his thoughts are the play, the only play there is. He is the actor in these thoughts just as the person on stage is the actor in the play. He does not create ideas but moves from one to the other, uniting and dividing them. It is not as though another is thinking for him and he sees what the other is thinking, nor do the thoughts move and act on their own account as though a subject had only to contemplate their movement. This is not accurate observation of nature. Thoughts, whether spontaneous or reflective, cannot be divided from the subject in the way that a stage is divided from the spectator. Passive or active, the *person subsists;* experiencing or operating, the person is identical, except that in experience

[*app.*, 14]

something is supposed outside the person. It is false therefore to say that the Prosfessor's 'spontaneous affirmation' is what the human race has called 'inspiration'.

15. (1294)
[Dr. Araldi and instinct]

Araldi, a doctor and philosopher from Modena, used the word 'will' with the general meaning of an internal force that determines us to act. But he said nothing about a known end, and thus erred in his use of the word as modern physiologists do. But if his use of language was mistaken, he made no mistake about the subject under discussion. His writings, which are characterised by strict logic, show his undoubted intellectual brilliance and capacity for withstanding the prejudices of his time. He defended the existence of *instinct* even in human beings in a monograph entitled *Del sonno e della sua ordinaria immediata cagione* (vol. 1, *Memorie della società medica di Bologna*, 1807). The defence consists in an excellent definition of instinct, and in several facts. However, prejudice still prevents some from accepting the existence of instinct, and it will not be out of place, I think, to offer a few examples of the action of *instinct* even in human beings. These examples are taken from Araldi.

Note first that, if we hold the definition of instinct given above [cf. 1294], it is clear that there can be only one cause of all the first actions done by human beings before the use of reflection, that is, before the human mind has received knowledge of the good brought about by those actions. This cause, which cannot depend for its action on the knowledge of an end, is indeed instinct. With this in mind, we can now examine examples of instinctive behaviour.

> Instinctive actions are those by which the foetus, finding itself in an awkward position in the womb, twists and turns to overcome its discomfort. It is clear that instinct also causes the very complicated action by which the baby, shortly after birth, sucks its first food from its mother's

breast. Darwin's suggestion, after Haller, that the baby exercises at this instant the function it had learned when sucking and swallowing liquid in the amnion, is untenable. Leaving aside any argument about the nutrition of the foetus, Darwin's assertion simply offers another example of a function due to instinct, that is, according to the concept he proposed, of a function tied by nature to certain sensations which determine the foetus to act in this way.

Breathing is another instinctive action, and its commencement is described by Araldi in the following terms:

> The foetus, in the act of emerging into light and surrounded by air, begins voluntarily (he means *instinctively*) to breathe. At that moment, it loses the characteristics and name of 'foetus' to take on those of 'baby'. The baby immediately notices its new circumstances and obeys the voice of instinct speaking to it in the language of certain sensations. One of these, a kind of discomfort experienced at the centre of the chest, is particularly noticeable. Probably the discomfort has not begun either at that moment or in the act of being born, but has already made itself felt in the womb. I am led to this fairly definite conclusion by the obvious changes which, long before birth, take place in the foetus in the special channels open to the blood, and also in the outlets through which the blood, when it reaches the heart, by-passes the lungs in great part and passes from the network of veins into the arterial aorta without going through the lungs. Without any doubt these changes can he seen in the oval aperture which becomes more restricted as birth draws near. This leads us to notice that those passages tend to become restricted, and that nature has pre-ordained total closure a long time beforehand. The restriction of these passages must cause some blockage in the circulation and with it some internal sense of discomfort, especially when pregnancy is reaching its term. This makes the foetus impatient in its prison: on the one hand, its more lively and frequent movements co-operate with other causes to arouse in the womb the contractions and exertions that herald birth; on the other hand, as it comes into the light, new sensations make it aware of the air which it draws into its chest avidly as it begins to breathe.

Sleep, according to Araldi, is also caused by instinct. This is

[*app.*, 15]

the whole thrust of the monograph that we quote, with its appendix. Araldi's capacity for acute and subtle observation of nature is shown by his clear realisation of the reason why we do not *advert* to what happens within us, nor distinguish the cause from which our own actions spring.

On my part, I am sure that the whole outcome of this work of mine depends upon a single event: 'My success in making people more diffident about their observations on themselves, and persuaded that some actions (even felt, willed and known actions) take place in them without their advertence and memory. Such actions cannot, therefore, be accounted for by the persons experiencing them, either to themselves or to others.' This is why I think it necessary to show that this truth had come to the notice of great men, and was well known to them as the natural explanation of innumerable mistakes and errors. Araldi was one of these fine people, and he gives the following explanation of the confusion between instinctive actions, and either mechanical or intellective actions:

> I have noticed that the willed determinations proper to instinct are normally preceded by very slight sensations which tend to disperse. As a result, the actions flowing from them are not surprisingly mistaken for necessary, mechanical reactions. This conclusion is reinforced by the supreme force of habit which sooner or later adds its influence to that of instinct, broadening and levelling, as it were, the path of reciprocal communication between the sense-organs and the organs of movement. The latter are rendered susceptible to even the slightest stimulus reaching them from the spirit. Relative to human beings we notice that actions preceded by reflection and examination or by a more or less obvious exercise of the faculty of reason, are so frequent in the course of their lives, and so powerful and dominant over their other actions, that we are easily led to think that all human actions are of this kind and that instinct should he left to the beasts.

16. (1318)

[Interior facts and Descartes' philosophy]

Here [at this point in the quotation from St. Augustine] we have an indication that the *observation of interior facts* is the source of the most sublime truths. This kind of observation has been abandoned by modern philosophy, which has retained only *external observation* and posits the whole of human nature in the external senses. This accounts for the materialism and degradation of this philosophy.

If we compare Descartes' philosophy with that of Locke, we find that they spring from two different sources: the former depends upon some form of *interior* observation, and the latter on purely *exterior observation*. These two philosophies were destined to have their moment, and then succumb (which they did). After them, it seems natural that the world should await a philosophy which, without excluding either of the two sources, would he derived from *interior and exterior observation* together. Only such a true, complete philosophy, free from ideology and partiality, can satisfy present needs and the expectation of humanity. Please God I have contributed at least something, as I truly desire, to such an undertaking!

For the rest, it is worth noticing how the debility of our century contributes to draw people away from the path of *interior observation* on which Descartes had set them. They forget themselves so completely that eventually the phrase 'interior observation' strikes them as something new, and as a novel ray of light rousing many of them from a deep sleep.

Descartes had spoken with the greatest clarity about *interior observation*. He noted that we could form correct ideas about the soul only by its means; without it, nothing would remain except material, confused ideas (cf. vol. 2, 983 ss.). But it is best to hear Descartes himself warn mankind about this in his famous work on *Method*:

> For many, the great difficulty in forming the notion of God, and even of their own soul, is that they never raise their spirit above sensible things (away from external observation) and are accustomed to consider everything with their imagination, which is a particular way of thinking

valid only for material things. As a result, anything which cannot be imagined is considered by them as unintelligible. — As far as I am concerned, those who want to use their imagination in order to know such things (the soul and God), act exactly as if they wanted to use their eyes to hear sounds or scent odours.

17. (1330)

[The sensists' error]

An example of the kind of error that arises from exaggerated suspension of judgment and unwillingness to give assent would be the whole series of errors to which sensists are prone as a result of their inability to rest satisfied with their research into abstract problems. Sensists find great difficulty in admitting that their mind possesses *universal concepts* through which an entire *species* of possible things can be perceived with a single glance. The difficulty has become general in our day as a consequence of the general diffusion of sensism although it undoubtedly arises from the lack of *internal observation* proper to sensists who immerse themselves in *external observation* alone. Their difficulty originates when they try to fix their attention on a *universal concept.* They find it impossible to remain in this state for a long time without setting their imagination in motion. This potency, which is very active in everyone, is brought into action by sensists as if it were our only potency. It then arouses in them images derived from the bodily senses, which are the sole source of their philosophy. Moreover, the imagination presents and impresses images or phantasms of particular things. From that moment on, therefore, the universal which sensists have undertaken to contemplate is entirely lost to them.

Having experienced their incapacity for lengthy concentration on what is purely universal sensists go on to conclude that the universal does not exist. This occurs only because they insist on such lengthy attention to the universal, and demand the formation of an *image* which it cannot provide. They should have granted and admitted the universal as soon as they thought it, without wanting to apply to it the mode of conception proper only to corporeal particular things.

Moreover fixing our attention on the pure universal is more difficult in so far as the universal is more abstract. The concept of being in all its universality, that is, the concept of *truth*, which requires the greatest abstraction, also demands the greatest isolation from images and the most immediate assent to its light. I recognise, of course, that this is the greatest obstacle to the acceptance of my theory on the part of *sensists* and those who think like them. I would point out, however, that their observation about the difficulty of paying attention to *abstracts* was not unknown to philosophers who nevertheless admitted the presence of abstracts and universals in the mind. Men of this calibre, however, did not believe they had to reject the fact of universals simply because of the difficulty of concentrating on them, a difficulty which has its source in the mixed constitution of human beings.

St. Augustine was certainly one of these philosophers, and he speaks in the following terms of the immediate assent that should be given to truth without more ado:

> When you hear it said, 'God is Truth', do not go asking what truth is. If you do, the darkness of corporeal images will rise up before you, and clouds of fantasies will appear to disturb the calm light that shone over you when I first mentioned Truth: *quae primo ictu diluxit tibi cum dicerem Veritas'.*
>
> (*De Trinit.,* bk. 8, c. 2)

St. Augustine noted, therefore, that we cannot concentrate for long on an abstract concept, that we naturally try to envelop this concept in corporeal forms, and that we have either to be satisfied with the most universal, final concept of truth as soon as we reach it or decide to fall once more from that height of thought to the level of the bodies we have already abandoned. But this observation was shared by all the best authors. I shall mention one only, the famous Scot, John Duns Scotus, who offered the following comment on our passage from St. Augustine:

> When a universal is abstracted from a particular concept, the intellect's difficulty in concentrating on the concept is

in proportion to its universality. This is the effect of our *natural inclination* to imagine something particular every time we grasp a universal. For the same reason, we can keep our attention fixed longer and more easily on a universal concept in so far as such a concept is similar to something particular and striking in the image. But the most universal concepts are those furthest from what is particular, and hence the most difficult of all from the point of view of prolonged, intellectual attention. Granted this, we ought not to ask what is truth (says St. Augustine) relative to the conception of God under the most universal concept of truth. In other words, we ought not to want to descend to some particular concept. If we do, we become embroiled in the light issuing from the fantasy of the imagination; we lose the tranquillity proper to truth, that is, the genuine truth in which God was perceived. As soon as we descend in this way, we come to perceive restricted truth, which is not fitting to God, to whom appertains truth conceived in all its generality, not restricted truth.

(In I Sent., d. 3, q. 4)

18. (1396)

[Schelling's error about feeling]

Fichte had said that the ego posited, created itself with the identical act with which it posited, created the world, the non-ego. Schelling noted that it was possible to conceive of an act of the ego devoid of *objects,* and that we must begin from this first act. But this act is a *feeling* not a *thought;* feeling differs from thought precisely because it has no *objects,* and is simple and one, as I have said (cf. vol. 2, 488 ss.). Schelling's error consists in allowing this first act of feeling greater activity than it has. He thus erred as Fichte had, except that the latter exaggerated the activity of *reflection,* while Schelling exaggerated the activity of *feeling.*

He says: 'The only way that the spirit can be conscious of itself as such is by *raising itself* above all that is *objective.* But if the spirit isolates itself from everything, it no longer finds itself.' This first proposition, which he states as if it were clear and evident, contains in germ and supposes his whole system. It supposes that when our spirit separates itself from all its objects and is left only as a *subject,* it is *raised* higher than its previous state. But, in my opinion, this is exactly what needs to be demonstrated, not supposed. If the *subject* is nobler than all its *objects,* we can in some way say that its concentration on itself is a kind of *elevation,* but if the *objects* in its thought are nobler and higher than itself, abandoning them to isolate itself leads only to self-abasement. I would go further and say that what is really clear is the very opposite of what Schelling is saying, namely, that the *intellectual object* is *always* essentially more noble than the *subject* perceiving it. To take away every object of our understanding is to reduce us to a state of perfect ignorance, a state of pure feeling, where our activity is much less than it was previously. To argue from this pure subject, present in us through abstraction, to a first, absolute subject is to set ourselves on the false path of *analogy;* we would be attempting a fatal jump from the *psychological* order into the ocean of *ontology.*

Schelling continues: 'This action, through which the spirit separates itself from every object, can only be explained through the spirit's *determining* itself. The spirit determines itself to act, and in so doing acts.' This, statement, confidently proclaimed as obvious by our author, has no foundation whatsoever. Why couldn't our spirit, instead of determining itself, be determined? Why couldn't it be passive (or receptive) rather than active in its first movement? It is absurd to say that the spirit, which is first supposed as perfectly inactive and even nothing, determines itself without a sufficient reason, and thus, as is said, posits, creates itself. A negative cannot produce a positive; nothing cannot produce something.

'The spirit gives impetus in order to raise itself above the finite. It annihilates through itself all that is finite, and then contemplates itself in the *positive absolute* which remains.' But it must be shown that the infinite presents itself to our spirit when the latter divests itself of all finite objects. Facts show the opposite: our spirit has positive ideas of finite objects alone; do away with these and our spirit is stripped of every act of knowledge. Schelling's reasoning is similar to that of a person who tries to prove that the sun would shine if at night-time we extinguished our candles.

[*app.*, 18]

'The spirit's self-determination is called "willing": the spirit *wills*, and is *free*. No foundation can be given to its willing because its action is precisely *to will* and to will absolutely.' People *will freely*, but because they have no *objects* to be willed, they do not know what they will! Here again the same fanciful hypothesis applies: human beings, without sufficient reason, determine themselves to their first act in such a way that they are *absolutely and uniquely active* without any passivity. But the opposite can he demonstrated: human beings, on the occasion of the first act of feeling, are moved and determined passively and necessarily.

However, relative to what Schelling says here, it is sufficient to reply: *Quod gratis asseritur, gratis negatur* [What is freely stated, is freely denied]. From this first act Schelling then extracts simultaneously practical reason, intelligence, law and truth. But it would be possible to extract anything from a supposed action fashioned solely to the liking of an extremely active imagination (cf. the philosophical journal published by Schelling in collaboration with Hegel, vol. 6, number 2).

19. (1465)

[Metaphysics and the branches of knowledge]

The metaphysics of antiquity, called *the first branch of knowledge and the originator of all other branches*, was in substance an 'ideology'. But heterogeneous matters were then introduced and confusion arose about teaching which dealt with ideal, mental and real beings. Metaphysics was no longer the *first branch of knowledge* in the sense which we are using here. But there was another deficiency in scholastic metaphysics considered as the first of the branches of knowledge and the source of other branches. Although recognising metaphysics as the root of the genealogical tree was a beautiful and useful truth, considerable ignorance remained about the way in which to deduce other branches of knowledge from it. As a result, metaphysics was thought to be more fruitful than it actually is, and observation of nature, which alone enables us to know the specific essences of things, was neglected. Things were then defined through abstractions and formalities, and *being in all its universality*, which of itself is not the essence of anything, took the place of all essences. This important comment comes from Fr. Malebranche who notes: 'The intimate presence of the vague idea of generic being' (he meant *being in all its universality*) 'is the cause of all inordinate abstractions of the mind' (Bk, 3, c. 8). He went on to apply his comment:

> Read as attentively as possible all the definitions and explanations that are normally given of substantial forms, and examine carefully the essence of all those infinite entities which philosophers imagine as they please, and which they then have to divide and subdivide. I am quite certain, and I dare to affirm, that these divisions can do nothing more than stimulate the mind to think the idea of being and cause in general.
>
> (*Ibid.*)

This should have been enough to enable Malebranche, good man as he was, to realise that the idea of being to which he referred was deficient; it was not the idea of God, that is, of the supreme reality, as Malebranche thought. If he had noticed this, he would not have been included by that terrible Hardouin in what we may call his catalogue of *Consequential Atheists*.

Index of Biblical References

Numbers in roman indicate paragraphs or, where stated, the appendix (app.); numbers in italic indicate footnotes. Bible references are from RSV (Common Bible) unless marked †. In these cases, where the author's use of Scripture is dependent solely upon the Vulgate, the Douai version is used.

Index of Persons

Numbers in romans indicate paragraphs or, where stated, the appendix (app.);
numbers in italics indicate footnotes.

Plato, *17, 49*; *app.* nos. 4, 8, 11
Platonists, *283*
Protagoras, *app.* nos. 4–5
Pyrrho, 1131; *25, 27*; *app.* no. 4
Pyrrhonists, *app.* no. 3

Reid, 1048; *96*; *app.* no. 1
Reinhold, 1390; *333*
Rousseau, 1255

San Floriano, C. F. da, *328*
Schelling, 1164, 1396–1408, 1414, 1417, 1420–1422, 1430; *271, 286*; *app.* no. 18
Seneca, 1398
Sextus, *19, 25, 27*; *app.* nos. 2, 4
Sichard, *184*
Socrates, *89*; *app.* no. 4

Stoics, 1401

Tertullian, 1261–1262, 1269

Thomas Aquinas (St.), 1098–1099, 1102–1103, 1109, 1123–1124, 1184–1185, 1189, 1214, 1243, 1260, 1262, 1281, 1348; *1, 22, 38, 48–49, 59, 65, 69, 90, 92, 98, 100, 106, 108, 110, 112, 128, 141, 148, 154–156, 158–159, 162–165, 167, 203, 233, 237, 239, 241, 289, 323, 327, 334*; *app.* nos. 6–12

Valentinians, *282, 284, 318*

Voltaire, 1386

General Index

Numbers in roman indicate paragraphs or, where stated, the appendix (app.); numbers in italic indicate footnotes.

idea of being as, 1071, 1078, 1091,
1189; *app.* no. 6
knowledge and certainty of, 1162,
1166
meaning, 1475
reason and, 1169
role of (in philosophy), 1090, 1098,
1475; *37*

Faculty
intellective, 1382
nature of, 1382
of ideas, *228*
of word, 1355; *228*

Faith, *see* **Belief**

Falsehood
mental entities and, 1356–1358
scepticism and, 1067
truth and, 1318, 1337, 1355; *158–159,
164*

Feeling
being and, 1178–1182; *129*
idea and, 1395
instinct and, *app.* no. 13
intellective, 1395
intellective perception and, 1202,
1436
knowledge and, 1164, 1225, 1228,
1394–1395, 1411; *296; app.* no. 18
passivity of, 1182
see also **Fundamental Feeling,
Sublime Feeling**

First Principles of Reasoning
assent to, 1153, 1338, 1353
authority and, 1353
certainty and, 1136, 1140–1141
common conceptions, 1145
common sense and, 1146, 1351–1352
idea of being and, 1339
light of, 1353
named, 1136
persuasion of, 1143–1153, 1341,
1351–1353
reflective knowledge and, 1154–1157
scepticism and, 1144

Foetus
instinct in, *app.* no. 15

Freedom
understanding and, *193*

Fundamental Feeling
knowledge and, 1167
myself as, 1196; *309*
nature of, *2*
sensation and, *2, 309*
see also **Feeling**

God
enthusiasm and, *app.* no. 14
existence of, 1212, 1308, 1457–1460
Fichte's concept of, 1389, 1398
heavenly beings' knowledge of, *106*
his knowledge, *55, 143*
human error and, 1308
idea of, 1237–1241, 1415–1416, 1437;
282; app. nos. 9, 10
intellective perception of, *312*
intuition of being and vision of, 1178
our knowledge of, 1178, 1209–1212,
1230, 1269, 1402–1403; *106, 315*
propositions concerning, *239*
real things, feelings, ideas and, 1239
reason and, 1308
religion and, *app.* no. 9

Gospel
belief in, *4*

Hegelianism
source of, 1419

Human Beings
elements of, 1042
error and, 1302–1306, 1376
forces of, 1294
knowledge and essence of, 1109
paganism and, 1415
truth and, 1245–1246, 1377

Idea(s)
analysis of, 1454
apprehending, 1416
being and, 1074–1077
certainty and clear, *187*
conception of, 1215
direct knowledge and first, *255*
essence and, *app.* no. 6
exemplar and, 1117–1120; *86*
faculty of, *228*
feeling and, 1181, 1395
generic, *70, 146*
intellect and, 1040
intellective perceptions and, 1042
language expressing, 1242
names and, 1242